Contributions to Econometric Theory and Application

R.A.L. Carter J. Dutta A. Ullah
Editors

Contributions to Econometric Theory and Application

Essays in Honour of A.L. Nagar

Springer-Verlag
New York Heidelberg Berlin
London Paris Tokyo Hong Kong

R.A.L. Carter, Department of Economics, The University of Western Ontario, London, Ontario N6A 5C2, Canada

J. Dutta, Barnard College, Columbia University, New York, NY 10027, USA

A. Ullah, Department of Economics, The University of Western Ontario, London, Ontario N6A 5C2, Canada

Library of Congress Cataloging-in-Publication Data
Contributions to econometric theory and application — Essays in honour of A.L. Nagar / R.A.L. Carter, J. Dutta, A. Ullah, editors.
p. cm.
Includes bibliographical references.
1. Econometric models. 2. Econometrics. 3. Nagar, A. L.
I. Carter, R. A. L. II. Dutta, Jaysari. III. Ullah, Aman.
HB141.C6595 1990
330'.01'5191—dc20 90-9707

Printed on acid-free paper

Camera ready copy provided by the editors.
Printed and bound by Edwards Brothers, Ann Arbor, Michigan.
Printed in the United States of America.

9 8 7 6 5 4 3 2 1

ISBN 0-387-97285-4 Springer-Verlag New York Berlin Heidelberg
ISBN 3-540-97285-4 Springer-Verlag Berlin Heidelberg New York

Preface

The purpose of this volume is to honour a pioneer in the field of econometrics, A.L. Nagar, on the occasion of his sixtieth birthday. Fourteen econometricians from six countries on four continents have contributed to this project. One of us was his teacher, some of us were his students, many of us were his colleagues, all of us are his friends.

Our volume opens with a paper by L.R. Klein which discusses the meaning and role of exogenous variables in structural and vector-autoregressive econometric models. Several examples from recent macroeconomic history are presented and the notion of Granger-causality is discussed. This is followed by two papers dealing with an issue of considerable relevance to developing countries, such as India; the measurement of the inequality in the distribution of income. The paper by C.T.West and H.Theil deals with the problem of measuring inequality of all components of total income within a region, rather than just labour income. It applies its results to the regions of the United States. The second paper in this group, by N. Kakwani, derives the large-sample distributions of several popular inequality measures, thus providing a method for drawing large-sample inferences about the differences in inequality between regions. The techniques are applied to the regions of Côte d'Ivoire.

The next group of papers is devoted to econometric theory in the context of the dynamic, simultaneous, linear equations model. The first, by P.J. Dhrymes, is concerned with forecasting using the final form of this model. Large-sample properties are developed for estimators of the parameters of both the structural and the final forms and for forecasts. The paper by R.L. Basmann and H.-S. Hwang uses Monte Carlo simulations to study the exact distributions of estimators of structural parameters when the estimation has been preceded by a test for identification. A question of interest here is whether the parameter estimators and the identifiability test statistic are independent. Monte Carlo methods are also used in the third paper, by R.A.L. Carter, to obtain nonparametric estimates of the probability density functions of the t-ratios produced by the instrumental-variables estimator. The focus of the paper is the effect on these density functions of alternative choices of instruments.

The third group of papers deal with issues of econometric theory in the context of static, simultaneous, linear equations. In the first paper J.L. Knight investigates the exact distribution of the partially restricted reduced form estimator using a combination of Monte Carlo integration, as distinct from simulation, and nonparametric density estimation. He is thus able to provide results on the shape of the distribution and its reaction to changes in the model parameters. The second paper in this group, by V.K. Srivastava, surveys the literature on the properties of Nagar's double k-class, as distinct from k-class, estimators of structural parameters. Finite sample results for the k-class estimators are extended to the double k-class. The final paper in this group, by A. Ullah, presents a straight forward technique for obtaining the exact moments and distributions of many estimators and test statistics. The method is remarkable for its simplicity and for the brevity of its derivations.

The final group of papers is more heterogeneous than the preceding groups. Its first paper, by J. Dutta, begins by discussing the general technique of resampling, whose special cases like the jacknife and the bootstrap are already familiar. The method is then applied to improve estimation and inference in the context of the linear-regression and errors-in-variables models. Next is a paper by M.D. McCarthy which discusses exact and asymptotic procedures for inference about the coefficients of factor demand equations in the context of Cobb-Douglas production functions. The techniques are then extended to multivariate regression models with certain cross-equation restrictions. The closing paper in the volume, by J.H. Drèze and M. Mouchart, is, in contrast to the other papers, written from a Bayesian perspective. But its link with the frequentist perspective of the other papers lies in its view of classical test statistics as valuable tools for Bayesian econometricians.

It is with warm wishes for many more birthdays that we dedicate this volume to our student, teacher, colleague and friend, A.L. Nagar.

Contents

Preface v

Contributors xi

Exogeniety in Economics 1
L.R. Klein

Regional Inequality by Components of Income 23
C.T. West and H. Theil

Large Sample Distribution of Several Inequality Measures: With Application to Coté d'Ivoire 50
N. Kakwani

Restricted Reduced Forms, Forecasting and the GSLEM 82
P.J. Dhrymes

A Monte Carlo Study of Structural Estimator Distributions After Performance of Likelihood Ratio Pre-Tests 132
R.L. Basmann and H.-S. Hwang

Nonparametric-Monte-Carlo Estimates of t-Ratio Distributions in Dynamic Simultaneous Linear Equations Models 160
R.A.L. Carter

The Exact Distribution of the PRRF Estimator - A Monte Carlo Integration Approach 196
J.L. Knight

Developments in Double k-Class Estimators of Parameters in Structural Equations 221
V.K. Srivastava

Finite Sample Econometrics: A Unified Approach 242
A. Ullah

On Resampling Inference in Econometric Models 293
J. Dutta

Estimation and Testing of Regression Coefficients in Cobb-Douglas and Other Models 321
M.D. McCarthy

Tales of Testing Bayesians 345
J.H. Drèze and M. Mouchart

Contributors

R.L. Basmann
Department of Economics
State University of New York
Binghampton, New York
U.S.A.

R.A.L. Carter
Department of Economics
University of Western Ontario
London, Ontario
Canada

P.J. Dhrymes
Department of Economics
Columbia University
New York, New York
U.S.A.

J. Drêze
Centre for Operations Research and Econometrics
Université Catholique de Louvain
Louvain-la-Neuve
Belgium

J. Dutta
Barnard College
Columbia University
New York, New York
U.S.A.

H.-S. Hwang
Department of Economics
Texas A. & M. University
College Station, Texas
U.S.A.

N.C. Kakwani
School of Economics
University of New South Wales
Sydney, New South Wales
Australia

L.R. Klein
Department of Economics
University of Pennsylvania
Philadelphia, Pennsylvania
U.S.A.

J.L. Knight
Department of Economics
University of Western Ontario
London, Ontario
Canada

M.D. McCarthy
Department of Economics
Temple University
Philadelphia, Pennsylvania
U.S.A.

M. Mouchart
Centre for Operations Research and Econometrics
Université Catholique de Louvain
Louvain-la-Neuve
Belgium

V.K. Srivastava
Department of Statistics
Lucknow University
Lucknow
India

H. Theil
Graduate School of Business
University of Florida
Gainsville, Florida
U.S.A.

A. Ullah
Department of Economics
University of Western Ontario
London, Ontario
Canada

The Concept of Exogeneity in Econometrics

L.R. Klein

University of Pennsylvania

Abstract

This paper is concerned with the concept of exogeneity of variables in structural econometric models. Examples from recent economic history are presented which illustrate their generation and their importance for prediction. The relationship of exogenous variables to vector autoregressive models and the notion of Granger–causality is also discussed.

1. Variable Classification and Meaning

The standard approach to econometric model specification begins with the classification of variables. There are, to begin with, three kinds of variables used in model construction: (1) endogenous, (2) exogenous, (3) random error.

The intuitive meaning of these three types is:

Endogenous—These variables have an influence on the economic model and are affected by the economic model; i.e., there is feedback between the model and endogenous variables. In other words, the endogenous variables are generated by the economic system being investigated. They are internal variables.

Exogenous—These variables have an influence on the economic model but are not affected by the economic model. They are not in feedback relationship with the model, and they are not generated by the economic system being investigated. They are external variables.

Random error—These are variables that are generated by "nature" and have an effect on the functioning of the economic model. The errors, e, are correlated with endogenous variables, y, but the joint probability distribution of e is not affected by the economic system being investigated. They are external, not directly observable, and follow a well defined probability distribution. They are governed by the laws of chance.

In a linear static system, the variables appear as in equations (1) and (2)

$$Ay + Bx = e \tag{1}$$

$$\Gamma x = u \tag{2}$$

y is an n–element column vector of endogenous variables

x is an m–element column vector of exogenous variables

e is an n–element column vector of random errors

A is a nonsingular n×n matrix of coefficients

B is a rectangular n×m matrix of coefficients

Γ is a nonsingular m×m matrix of coefficients

u is an m–element column vector of random errors

The econometric model is (1), in which all three variable types appear. Equation system (2) exists and is responsible for explaining or generating x, but does not have economic content. If we write (2) as

$$0y + \Gamma x = u$$

the concept of no–feedback from y to x via the economic system is more obvious,

$$x = \Gamma^{-1}(0y + u).$$

If y were not multiplied by a null matrix, there could be a direct feedback from y to x. In this formulation, x is stochastic because it depends on u, but the economic model with x classified as exogenous would be perfectly acceptable if x were simply a vector of fixed variables (known numbers) and not stochastic, but according to the concepts of economic models, y must be stochastic.

The enlarged system consisting of (1) and (2) together is block recursive because the matrix

$$\begin{bmatrix} A & B \\ 0 & \Gamma \end{bmatrix}$$

has a block triangular structure. It is said to be <u>fully</u> recursive if e and u are statistically independent so that the $(n+m) \times (n+m)$ covariance matrix

$$\begin{bmatrix} Eee' & Eeu' \\ Eue' & Euu' \end{bmatrix}$$

is block diagonal, i.e., if Eue' and Eeu' are both zero. The block diagonality of the covariance matrix usually simplifies the statistical inference problem for estimating the coefficient matrices because the joint probability density functions of e and u can be factored into a product of the probability densities of e and of u

$$p(e_1,\dots,e_n,u_1,\dots,u_m) = f(e_1,\dots,e_n)g(u_1,\dots,u_m)$$

If the parameter set of f and g are non overlapping, the maximum likelihood estimation of the system factors into separate maximization of f and of g (after transformation of variables) from e_t to y_t and x_t and from u_t to x_t.

In the linear case, regardless of whether e and u are jointly normal, the least squares estimate of the reduced form of (1)

$$y_t = -A^{-1}Bx_t + A^{-1}e_t$$

$$= \Pi x_t + v_t$$

provides consistent estimates of Π

$$\hat{\Pi} = \|\sum_t y_t x'_t\| \, \|\sum_t x_t x'_t\|^{-1}$$

$$\text{if } \|E\, v_t x'_t\| = 0$$

which would hold in the block diagonal covariance case.

If x_t is non stochastic, then the above condition on the covariance of v_t and x'_t automatically holds.

This formulation generalizes to nonlinear systems of the form

$$F(y',x',\theta') = e \tag{1'}$$

$$G(x',\phi') = u \tag{2'}$$

F and G are vector functions. The variables y, x, e, and u are as previously defined. The parameters of the system θ and ϕ replace A, B, Γ.

Inference in (1′) and (2′) is more complicated than in (1) and (2), but the ideas that x is generated by (2′) and that y has no effect on x still prevail.

The concepts and definitions that have been introduced are well known, and the exposition appears to be pedantic. This is familiar textbook material. It is, however, being restated in connection with a re–examination of the concept of exogeneity because some quite different concepts are being put forward in econometrics, either changing the nature of exogeneity or doing away with it entirely; so it is useful to restate basic premises in arguing for the usefulness of the standard concepts.

T.C. Koopmans made these points clear for the general model—the triangularity of the Jacobian matrix, the diagonality of the covariance matrix, the factorization of the likelihood function. In the oral discussions at the Cowles Commission, these ideas were used to show how variables could be treated as though they were exogenous in partial systems or in single equations provided they were not correlated with the disturbance terms of the equation(s) in question, even though such variables are not strictly exogenous from the point of view of an entire model of the economic system.[1]

There are two important extensions of the model (1)–(2) that should be mentioned. The stated model is static, but in both the linear and nonlinear forms, dynamics may be entered. The linear dynamic form is

$$A(L)y_t + B(L)x_t = \Delta(L)e_t \tag{3}$$

$$\Gamma(L)x_t = E(L)u_t \tag{4}$$

All the matrix expressions are written as matrix polynomials in the operator L

$$L^s y_{it} = y_{i,t-s}$$

[1]T.C. Koopmans [1950].

and similarly when operating on x_t, e_t, or u_t.

The stochastic terms e_t and u_t need not be the only conduit for probability to enter the system. The variables, whether endogenous or exogenous, could be written as

$$y_t = y_t^* + v_t$$

$$x_t = y_t^* + z_t$$

where y_t^* and x_t^* are "true" unobserved values of the measured magnitudes y_t and x_t. The random variables v_t and z_t are errors of measurement or observation. Unless there are strong assumptions made about the probability structure of v_t and z_t, we are confronted with a basic lack of identification in the system that combines the two sources of error, and the most conventional model does not use error of measurement in the stochastic specification, even though the idea is quite realistic. There are, indeed, well known measurement errors in economic statistics; but the complications that arise by recognizing them explicitly do not play a crucial role in the debates about exogeneity, although they are not wholly irrelevant.

2. Examples of Exogenous Variables

In the preceding section we have introduced some concepts, and in this section, we shall attempt to give substance to the basic ideas by citing some realistic examples. The best examples of exogenous variables are associated with the general phenomenon of weather. Crop yield in agriculture, production and sales of seasonal goods, electric power use and many other economic activities are significantly related to weather. There are many dimensions to this variable. We must consider rainfall, temperature, wind, hours of sunshine, and monthly (or shorter period) distributions of these magnitudes. In a strongly agricultural economy, weather can be enormously important. In more advanced societies with less strategic reliance on agriculture and many means of compensating for weather variables (irrigation, refrigeration, air conditioning, flood control, etc.) it may be possible to soften the extreme effects of weather variation, but such softening has only partial effect.

In general, the economy does not affect the weather (or climate). Over long periods of time, the functioning of the economy may affect the atmosphere and thereby change natural conditions, but this is not yet clear for purposes of economic modeling. In the short run there can be cloud seeding, but, here again, there are debates about its effect and its effectiveness.

The measurable characteristics of weather serve as excellent examples of exogenous variables, but weather effects are so diverse and unknown that it is difficult to obtain precise measurement. For example, we may have excellent statistics on inches of rainfall, but what rainfall should be measured for estimating crop yield—when and where? Weather indexes are approximations that are subject to error. This is a case of measurement or observation error. The index values may be accurate, but they are probably inaccurate in measuring the "true" weather effect that is needed for a particular problem. Also, extreme weather in the form of storms has great economic impact, but it occurs almost randomly.

If an exogenous variable is under control, it can be measured accurately, say temperature in a controlled experiment. But if weather is generated by the laws of meteorology according to equation system (2) it may have a large error, since we know that meteorology does not provide highly accurate information for time periods of one month or longer. The "noise–to–signal" ratio is large in meteorology, just as it is in economics.

Indian economists in 1985, 1986, and early 1987 were generally optimistic and confident about their country's economic progress. They were basing their judgment on econometric model performance, recent experience and an (exogenous) assumption that weather would continue to be normal. By mid year 1987 it became obvious that a severe drought was at hand, and that their model inputs were wrong, leading to incorrect model outputs. Just one year later, we experienced the same thing in the United States. A severe drought caused a food and grain crop shortfall of more than 25%. This changed farm income, government support, food price inflation, and world market prices very much. These are cases of stochastic exogenous variables that contain no system feedback from the economy.

It is interesting to note that the overall GNP statistics for an economy as large and as industrial as the United States show clearly the adverse effects of the drought in the summer quarter's reports because of the large drawing down of farm inventories. It is also noteworthy that end–of–year (1988) projections for 1989 generally assumed normal conditions for the next crop and harvest, because there was very little information available on weather conditions as much as six months in advance. Moreover, some of the most sophisticated projections anticipated that the official body responsible for the government's GNP statistics would allocate a seasonally adjusted increase in farm production for the first quarter of 1989 in advance of knowing whether or not weather conditions were going to be normal in the 1989 crop year. The early 1989 reports on the behavior of the economy would, it was assumed, contain an allocation of activity that had not yet occurred, and this decision was wholly unrelated to the performance of the economy in any sector. That surely describes a variable that has no feedback effect from the economy.

In general, major noneconomic events are candidates for classification as exogenous variables. The most pervasive is war, but embargoes, interdictions of transport, strikes, or perhaps the stock market crash of October 19, 1987, are major events that impact the economy yet are not explicable by systematic econometric analysis.

In some systems of thought, Marxist and other, a total interpretation of history must include economics, politics, social forces, and other phenomena all together. According to this view of the world, everything except natural events should be endogenous. At one extreme, by the economic interpretation of history, an economic model should treat war, strikes, and other major events as endogenous variables explained by the model. There is, however, an econometric argument against this view. Econometrics, as opposed to theoretical economics, has a statistical base, and for variables to be explained by the model there must be a statistical sample. Many of the major events are one–time occurrences. There are not enough wartime observations or other unusual events to establish a good sample for estimating or testing theory building related to such events. A usual procedure in econometrics is either exclude sample points with such events from the data base to be used, to use some direct exogenous measurement of the event, or to introduce a surrogate ("dummy") variable to try to estimate an effect of the event, regarding it as an exogenous variable. Data are usually not contaminated in every possible dimension by such events; therefore it is rare to throw away observations for such circumstances. World War II was so pervasive and disruptive nearly everywhere, that the affected period is usually deleted from statistical samples and no theory specification is attempted for this event. The Korean, Vietnam, or Iran–Iraq Wars, horrible though they may be, do not necessarily justify deletion from sample information for many kinds of investigations. But they are exogenous events.

The oil embargo and changes in terms of trade for energy products are usually not modeled explicitly. There have been some recent attempts to build a model of the energy markets and "explain" oil prices, but they are not very successful, and certainly not as successful as are modeling exercises for other primary product markets. During the period of great OPEC influence it would have been virtually impossible to predict oil prices from an econometric model, yet oil prices played important exogenous roles in econometric models. The situation is changing, now that OPEC is losing control to market forces, but until recently, the recommended procedure was to regard oil prices as exogenous variables.

The stock market crash of October 19, 1987, is a very very interesting case. First, is it possible to explain the crash, or what is the same, build a model that did or could project the path of equity prices during 1986, 1987, 1988? Secondly, can the effect of equity price movements, during this period, on economic behavior be explained?

The run–up of stock prices during 1986 and the first 9 months of 1987, like the run–up of the US dollar until 1985, was probably a great speculative spree fostered by new trading instruments, new hardware, new software, permissive attitudes of regulators, some breaking of rules. It was very much an economic event, but should it be endogenous? The random error, e_t, in econometric models, is made up of that myriad of factors that are not explicitly measured and put into the model; they are omitted variables, and it seems that the underlying factors shaping the crash fall into this category.

It has been extremely difficult to assess the effect of the crash. There is no discernible effect on macro behavior as far as consumer spending or producer investing are concerned. Real demand, except for some kinds of consumer spending and residential investment in the United States, has not responded. There are, however, economic effects. Investment portfolios have definitely shifted proportions away from equity holdings. Markets remain very sensitive to "news". Economic activity in the finance, insurance, and real estate sector fell and had not recovered within one year. With the help of monetary authorities, interest rates were held down for the greater part of one year after the crash, but public policy was complemented by investor preferences for safer investments in high quality debt instruments and official monetary intervention to keep markets calm during an election year.

The Crash was a one–time event; its full effect on the economy has not yet been realized; and it does not fit into the category of variables that we usually call endogenous. It was a one–time exogenous event and can be measured through many surrogate indicators, but we are not yet very sure about its effect. It is interesting to remark that Jan Tinbergen, in one of the first macroeconometric models ever built, provided an endogenous explanation of equity prices in his model of the US and found great significance for the Crash of 1929 in bringing consumer and investment spending to the low levels of the Great Depression.[2]

Together with weather, one of the most important groupings of exogenous variables in macroeconometric models is public policy, covering use of both fiscal and monetary instruments. Tax collections and transfer payments are endogenous, but the setting of tax rates and formulas for transfers are in the hands of public authorities—a minister, an executive in government, or a legislature. Decision making of individual people and even legislative bodies is too personal and too much dependent on choices by a small group of people whose actions are not statistically predictable to be based on a statistical sample. If thousands or millions make decisions, which we econometricians analyze, in market behavior, that constitutes a proper statistical sample whose regularity we study through interrelationships connecting endogenous and exogenous variables. In a sense, economics and econometrics are not "clinical" subjects; they are "field" subjects.

What has been said for tax and transfer payment policy can also be said for expenditure policy for public services, military, and other functions of government. Behavior of central

---

[2] J. Tinbergen [1939].

bank governing boards that determine official participation in financial markets does not have statistical regularity. It reflects the decisions of a few people. And these decisions frequently vary a great deal between regimes.

It is my opinion that fiscal and monetary policies (also trade or commercial policies) of governments are exogenous decisions of just a few people, but it is popular now in model building to include reaction functions. These are designed to show how official bodies will react to the economy. In particular, they would attempt to show how the Federal Reserve Open Market Committee would "lean against the wind" or follow some other strategy that the model builder thinks is appropriate for their behavior. It is perfectly legitimate to explore various assumptions about official behavior, each being portrayed by separate reaction functions, but I regard this kind of exploratory analysis only as interesting examination of assumed alternatives. It does not justify the classification of official policy variables as endogenous. Together with weather and other natural phenomena, official policy variables should also be exogenous.

Demographic variables are frequently classified as exogenous in econometric model investigation. Like political decisions, demographic decisions could be assumed to be generated by a model that is apart from the economic model being investigated. If x_t represent population size, births, deaths, migration, participation in the work force, and many other demographic magnitudes, we might be tempted to assume that they satisfy the structure of equation (2)

$$0y_t + \Gamma x_t = u_t \qquad (2)$$

This assumes that demographic variables are stochastic but generated by their own model, without feedback from y_t. This is probably a poor assumption. It is quite apparent that many economic decisions are affected by demographic variables; x_t does affect y_t, but it is probably not true that demographics can neglect the feedback effects of economic variables y_t on x_t.

Demographic variables often move slowly. In short run cyclical models, demographic variables may be approximately classified as exogenous. All the people who are to be in the next decade's work force are already born and available, although an estimated number may die during the coming period. A more volatile component of the work force comes from immigration, and all the potential immigrants are not at hand. There is less and less justification for putting demographic variables in the exogenous category. There is much feedback from economic variables to demographic variables, and econometricians must undertake the research task of shifting demographics to the endogenous category.

One demographic variable is age. If we deal with age cohorts, life cycle decisions, and interaction with medical care, we find that age is a complicated variable or group of variables. Frequently it is measured as chronological age, which advances by one unit each year. In this narrow sense it is an exogenous variable, but that does not give a satisfactory treatment of age in economics. Similarly, chronological time is often used as a trend variable standing for technical change, growth, aging, or a variety of processes. Technically, chronological time is regarded as an exogenous variable, but that is only because it is an unspecified proxy for our ignorance. Some investigators use chronological time as an exogenous instrument for estimation by the method of instrumental variables or some closely related methods such as two–stage–least squares. This is hardly a recommended choice for an instrument, particularly if it is to be a major instrument.

3. Alternative Approaches

The issue of the concept of exogeneity is only partly a matter of taking up long standing debates that have been referred to already and re–examining them. Our capabilities are now greater. We have better information, more information, more powerful computer facilities, and more experience with econometric models. One form of improvement is to reduce the scope of exogeneity (in practice) because it frequently has been used to avoid work or to seek a seemingly easy way out when analyzing specific problems. If a variable is classified as exogenous, the investigator does not have to face up to the effort of explaining it.

But the concept is now at issue because there are challenges from other approaches. Let us consider first the approach of time series analysis, in that form that minimizes the use of economic theory in econometric model specifications.

Christopher Sims has suggested and promoted use of the following model, known as the vector–autoregressive–model (VAR)

$$y_t = A(L)y_{t-1} + e_t \qquad (5)$$

y_t and e_t are n–element column vectors

Each variable y_{it} is expressed as a linear function of previous own values and previous other values with additive error. The system could be generalized. Simultaneity could be allowed; exogenous variables could be used; and the error terms could be generated by moving average or autoregressive processes. For our purposes, in the present discussion, the most interesting and relevant idea is that no exogenous variables are used. This is Sims' own choice.

This is a general system, but it has been mainly applied to macro models. In these formulations, monetary and fiscal variables are in the y_t–vector and therefore differ in concept from the point of view put forward earlier that variables decided upon by a small number of people lack statistical regularity.

Since the VAR system has little (or no?) economic theory, there is unusually heavy reliance on empirical information for the structure of the system. In many respects, this approach could be called "Measurement without Theory," which is a well–known criticism by Tjalling Koopmans of time series analysis of the National Bureau of Economic Research.[3] Since few economic theoretical restrictions are used and since y_t includes both conventional endogenous and exogenous variables, the number of economic processes that can be investigated is rather small. A mainstream macroeconometric model would have hundreds or even thousands of elements in y_t, while Sims has about 10 or, at most, 20. Other VAR systems of fewer than 10 variables have also been suggested for some macroeconometric applications.

Given an econometric model, either (1) in the linear mode or (1′) in the nonlinear mode, there are two driving forces in a

[3]T.C. Koopmans [1947].

structural model. One set of forces are the random errors, which also provides the probability base for statistical inference in the system, and the other set of forces are the exogenous variables. Key sensitivities in the model are the multipliers, i.e., the partial derivatives

$$\frac{\partial y_{it}}{\partial x_{jt}}, \text{ given } x_{kt*},\ k \neq j,$$

which show how y_{it} varies when x_{jt} changes, with all other x_{kt} held to unchanged values. In the VAR system, the only driving forces are in the error terms, unless one or more of the system's relationships undergoes shift.

The VAR system is dynamic; so an imposed change on any $y_{it'}$, $t' < t$ at an earlier time point can induce a change in y_{it} at the later time period. Earlier change becomes a force for later change. This property holds in the mainstream model (3), too. For many statistical purposes we treat historical values of y_{it} as though they were exogenous. The broader term, <u>predetermined</u> variable, includes both previous values of endogenous variables and values, contemporary or previous, of exogenous variables.

Exogenous variables and prior values of endogenous variables acting as forces in a model make up the causal structure, apart from random errors. In the context of dynamic systems, Clive Granger has defined causality as indicating that prior values of one variable (in this case y_{t-j}) are significantly correlated with x_t, as in

$$x_t = \sum_{j=1}^{m} a_j x_{t-j} + \sum_{j=1}^{m} b_j y_{t-j} + e_t \qquad (6)$$

This means that the history of y_t provides information about x_t that is not provided by x_t's own history.[4] Similarly, he would conclude that x causes y if some prior values of x_t are significantly related to y_t in

$$y_t = \sum_{j=1}^{m} c_j x_{t-j} + \sum_{j=1}^{m} d_j y_{t-j} + u_t \qquad (7)$$

In a general model such as (3), the associated reduced form would be

$$y_t = -A_0^{-1} A_1(L) y_t - A_0^{-1} B(L) x_t + A_0^{-1} \Delta(L) e_t$$

If both some b_j in (6) and some c_j in (7) are not zero, as could happen in practice, then x_t and y_t are said to be in feedback relation with each other. A_0 is the matrix of coefficients of L_0 (=I) in A(L); A_1 (L) is the polynomial matrix of coefficients of $L, L^2, \ldots$, etc. The reduced form implies that y_{it} depends linearly on $y_{i',t-j}$ (all i,j), on $x_{k',t-p}$ (all k,p) and on moving sums of errors. Empirically, it is quite possible that lagged values of some particular x_{kt} are significantly correlated with y_{it} even though the correct relationship is the reduced form equation, in which y_{it} has significant correlations with other variables too. These other variables may be predominant, and would crowd out the correlation with lags of x_{kt} if they were included in the model and in empirical tests, using the model as a guide. Also, in moderate or large models there are usually not enough degrees of freedom to estimate unrestricted reduced form types of equations,

---

[4]C.W.J. Granger [1969].

although there are, if restrictions are imposed. These restrictions are closely associated with the classification of variables in the exogenous or endogenous category. They come, to a large extent, by bringing economic theory to bear on system specification, something that is missing in the empirical time series approach to testing for causality. Causality should be studied within the context of a total system and not by pairwise lead–lag correlations, unless there happens to be some particular recursive structure in (3) that implies a bivariate relationship between y_{it} with its own lags and those of x_{kt}. This is a very special case in which the two approaches (time series analysis and structural model analysis) converge, but does not provide a general concept. The economic system is basically complicated and highly multivariate, whether being represented in microeconometric or macroeconometric models. It is highly unlikely that simple bivariate relationships will provide adequate representation of economic complexity. Particular samples may show some impressive (or impressionistic) correlations, but they always break down when repeatedly applied in an outside–sample context.

Granger causality has some empirical interest, but it is not a general concept, and it is not the same thing as causality or exogeneity as the concept has traditionally been used in econometrics. Exogeneity deals with decomposition of the joint probability distribution of the sample or, in linear systems, with the correlation between measured variables of the model and the error terms of the individual equations, whether the measured variable being considered is present in a particular equation or not.

In an interesting exploration of the concept of exogeneity, Robert Engle, David Hendry, and Jean–Francois Richard introduce the concepts of weak, strong, and super exogeneity.[5] Their concept of weak exogeneity is essentially the same as that of Koopmans, in which the likelihood function can be factored appropriately for estimation purposes.

They define strong exogeneity as weak exogeneity plus Granger noncausality. This is surely unfortunate, because Granger causality or noncausality is not related to a model of the economy; it is purely an empirical aspect of a sample of data.

In the linear case, exogeneity in the usual, time–honored definition is based on the correlation between the variables classified as exogenous and the unobserved random errors of the system. The significance of these correlations can be tested, and a statistic can be constructed that shows the strength or weakness of the concept. This would seem to provide a more appropriate way to define strong exogeneity. Since the authors remark that Granger noncausality is neither necessary nor sufficient for weak exogeneity, it is hard to see why the two unrelated concepts are put together to extend the standard concept.

Super exogeneity, on the other hand, does extend the standard concept, for it deals with the case in which the parameters of the model being considered undergo structural change. The treatment of variable parameter models is interesting. Super exogeneity defines variables whose changes do alter the parametric structure of the first factor of the likelihood

---

[5]R. Engle A., D. Hendry, and J–F Richard [1983].

function

$$f(e_1, e_2, \ldots, e_n),$$

which they call the conditional model. This extension of the concept is intended to deal with what is called the Lucas critique, by which it is asserted that the response parameters of the macro model are functions of the exogenous policy variables.[6]

[6]R.E. Lucas [1976].

References

Engle, Robert, David Hendry and Jean–Francois Richard [1983], Exogeneity, Econometrica, 51, 277–304.

Granger, C.W.J. [1969], Investigating Causal Relations by Econometric Models and Cross–Spectral Methods, Econometrica, 37, 424–38.

Koopmans, T.C. [1947], Measurement without Theory, The Review of Economic Statistics, 29, 161–72.

______________________, [1950], When Is an Equation System Complete for Statistical Purposes?, Statistical Inference in Dynamic Economic Models ed. by T.C. Koopmans (New York: John Wiley), 393–409.

Lucas, R.E. [1976], Econometric Policy Evaluation: A Critique, Carnegie–Rochester Conferences on Public Policy, ed. by K. Brunner and A. Meltzer (Amsterdam: North–Holland), 19–46.

Tinbergen, J. [1939], Business Cycles in the United States of America, 1919–1932, (Geneva: League of Nations).

Regional Inequality by Components of Income: United States, 1969-1986*

Carol Taylor West
and
Henri Theil
University of Florida

Abstract

A decomposition by income component of the Theil informational measure of inequality is derived and applied to U.S. regional income data. Besides potentially alleviating some current problems of directly estimating total inequality, the application suggests that such decomposition can additionally provide insight into asymmetries of intertemporal change, differences in inequality at a point in time compared with changes in that inequality over time, and identification of regional contribution to inequality.

1. Introduction

Income dispersion in U.S. regional analysis has been analyzed in terms of differing intraregional family income inequality [Al-Samarrie and Miller, 1967; Smith and Jennings, 1976; Long, Rasmussen and Haworth, 1977; Garofalo and Fogarty, 1979; Nelson, 1984] and differing per capita incomes among counties, states or broader geographical aggregations of states [Easterlin, 1960; Perloff, et al., 1960; Williamson, 1965, 1980; Coelen, 1978; Browne, 1980a, 1980b]. Logically, these analyses are formally linked by population group decompositions of income inequality

---

*Research supported in part by the McKethan-Matherly Eminent Scholar Chair, University of Florida.

[Cowell, 1977; Bourguignon, 1979; Shorrocks, 1980] and such linkage has been used to explain apparent paradoxes of regional income distribution [Tam and Persky, 1982; Persky and Tam, 1985].

Alternatively, inequality may be decomposed by income components [Rao, 1969; Fei, Ranis and Kuo, 1978; Fields, 1979]. This extension is less common in regional work, although the general potential of decomposition for providing explanatory insight is clearly indicated by Williamson's [1980] decomposition of regional income per worker variance. Besides yielding explanation, decomposition by component can potentially mitigate some current problems of empirical analysis. In particular, studies focusing on cross-section estimation of aggregate regional income inequality measures have recognized theoretically differential impacts by income source, but typically in specification they emphasize the labor earnings component or are hampered by multicollinearity in empirically separating effects of diverse income components. Disaggregation may alleviate this problem. In addition, there is little *a priori* reason to suppose that regional income inequality is an exception to the general empirical economics phenomenon that factors explaining cross-sectional observations at a point in time are not identical with factors explaining change over time and decomposition of aggregates is generally necessary to identify these differences.

The current research focuses on investigating regional inequality by income component and proposes a decomposition derived from considering desirable theoretical attributes of inequality measures and desirable attributes of the decomposition for empirical application. Annual time series data on U.S. regional incomes from the Bureau of Economic Analysis (BEA) are used in examination of broadly defined regional inequality and the application addresses questions: Is the traditional implicit focus on labor earnings inequality a reasonable one? Are there distinctions between inequality at a point in time and changes in that inequality over time?

Section 2 of the paper defines inequality, derives decompositions and discusses interpretation of the measures. Empirical results are presented in section 3, followed by some concluding remarks in section 4.

2. Measurement of inequality by components of income

Shorrocks [1982] has elegantly derived a measure of component contribution to inequality based on six assumptions of mathematical attractiveness. However, not included among the assumptions is that the proposed component contributions be readily interpretable and as noted by Lerman and Yitzhaki [1985], this particular feature is critical in empirical studies and policy research. The current analysis focuses on an alternative decomposition of Theil's [1967] informational measure of income inequality, an alternative which permits straightforward meaning to be attached to the components. Among the set of widely used inequality measures, Theil's is both readily decomposed [Cowell, 1977; Bourguignon, 1979] and properties of its implicit social welfare function are intuitively more desirable than those of some other common measures such as the Gini coefficient and coefficient of variation [Blackorby and Donaldson, 1978]. In addition, as shown below, a Taylor series approximation of Theil's measure permits derivation of additional information on regional concentration of component inequality, again broadening inequality analysis from a single measure to a set of measures which constitute a more informative data set for time series and cross-sectional analysis.

In the present application, the nine census divisions of the U.S. are the basic units of analysis and Theil's [1979b] proposed decomposition of inequality by income may be modified to reflect the variable populations of these units. More generally, let there be G regions and R components or sources of income. Let s_{gr} be the income received by persons in region g from source r as measured as a fraction of total income received by all regions from all sources and let n_g denote population of region g measured as a share of total population. Letting $s_{g.} = \sum_{r=1}^{R} s_{gr}$, Theil's first aggregate income inequality measure may be expressed as

$$J = \sum_{g=1}^{G} s_{g.} \log \left(\frac{s_{g.}}{n_g}\right) \tag{1}$$

where log denotes natural logarithm. The formulation in (1) is the direct regional analog of the well-known entropy measure based on individual units. Straightforwardly applying the measure in (1) to an individual component, r, inequality of that component may be measured by

$$J_r = \sum_{g=1}^{G} \frac{s_{gr}}{s_{.r}} \log \left(\frac{s_{gr}/s_{.r}}{n_g}\right) \tag{2}$$

where $s_{.r} = \sum_{g=1}^{G} s_{gr}$.

The distinction should be noted between J_r and the "pseudo-Theil" defined by Shorrocks [1982] in his discussion of "natural decompositions" of inequality measures. In the current notation, the "pseudo-Theil" corresponding to component r is $J_r^* = \sum_{g=1}^{G} s_{gr} \log \left(\frac{s_{g.}}{n_g}\right)$, a formulation impossible to interpret either intuitively or more formally from the information theory basis of the Theil measure. The correspondence between J_r^* and J is purely mathematical, identity of the summation weights $\log\left(\frac{s_{g.}}{n_g}\right)$ applied to $s_{g.}$ in J and s_{gr} in J_r^*. In contrast, J_r directly measures the income inequality of component r on the same basis as inequality of total income in (1) and hence it is possible to apply the same intuitive and information theoretic interpretations of J_r as are possible for J. These latter interpretations are extensively discussed in Theil [1967].[1]

Returning to (1) and (2), J may be expressed in terms of component inequality as:

$$J = \bar{J} - D \text{ where} \tag{3}$$

$$\bar{J} = \sum_{r=1}^{R} s_{.r} J_r \text{ and} \tag{4}$$

$$D = \sum_{g=1}^{G} \sum_{r=1}^{R} s_{gr} \log\left(\frac{s_{gr}}{s_{g.} s_{.r}}\right). \tag{5}$$

$\bar{J}$ is readily interpreted as the average inequality of the R components (weighted according to their shares in total income) and D is the expected mutual information of the regions and the income shares, a measure of dependence between income sources and regions. D vanishes only under stochastic independence, $s_{gr} = s_{g.}s_{.r}$ for all (g, r); i.e., a region always receives the same share of any total income source $\left(\frac{s_{gr}}{s_{.r}} = s_{g.}\right)$, a situation clearly not permitting relatively low

[1]It should be noted that use of the "pseudo-Theil" is not advocated by Shorrocks [1982]. It is mentioned in that article and in the present text because of its correspondence to the more familiar "pseudo-Gini" used by Fei, Ranis and Kuo [1978] and Fields [1979].

shares of one income component to be counterbalanced by relatively high shares of another. Since $\sum_{r=1}^{R} s_{gr} = \sum_{r=1}^{R} s_{g.}s_{.r}$, if there is not stochastic independence, then regional share varies across income source with at least one share exceeding $s_{g.}$ and one less than $s_{g.}$, yielding intuitive offset. At a maximum, $D = \bar{J}$, completely eliminating the aggregate inequality implied by the weighted average inequality of the R components.[2]

Since J and J_r are regional summations, it is natural to consider the relative contributions of each region to aggregate and component inequality. For example, consider a simple four region situation in which all regions have equal population. Suppose the incomes (Y_g) in the regions are $Y_1 = 95$, $Y_2 = 97$, $Y_3 = 100$, $Y_4 = 20$. Clearly the income distribution is unequal and intuitively, the major reason for that inequality is the low income in region 4 relative to the other areas. In analyzing that inequality, it would be natural to focus on that phenomenon. Alternatively, suppose $Y_1 = 97$, $Y_2 = 100$, $Y_3 = 18$, $Y_4 = 22$. In this situation, no single region stands out as primarily contributing to the aggregate inequality. Analysis of the latter would concentrate on the characteristics of regions 1 and 2 as a group compared with regions 3 and 4 as a group.

In the formulation of J and each J_r in (1) and (2), it is not possible to directly compare the relative regional contributions

---

[2]Under stochastic independence, $D = 0$, $J_r^* = s_{.r}J_r$. In general, $J_r^* + D_r = s_{.r}J_r$ where $D_r = \sum_{g=1}^{G} s_{gr} \log(\frac{s_{gr}}{s_{g.}s_{.r}})$. Since $D_r \geq 0$, J_r^* tends to be less numerically than $s_{.r}J_r$ with the difference in the measures depending upon the extent to which the income component r is distributed regionally in a pattern at variance with that of aggregate income.

because they differ in sign, $s_{g.} \log\left(\frac{s_{g.}}{n_g}\right)$ is not consistently positive or negative across all g. However, an approximation procedure permits presentation of J as the sum of positive regional contributions whose relative magnitudes can be compared. In particular, Consider a Taylor series expansion of $s_{g.} \log\left(\frac{s_{g.}}{n_g}\right)$ about the point $n_g = s_{g.}$:

$$s_{g.} \log\left(\frac{s_{g.}}{n_g}\right) \approx 0 - (n_g - s_{g.}) + \frac{(n_g - s_{g.})^2}{2s_{g.}}. \tag{6}$$

Summing over g in (6):

$$\text{(7)} \qquad J \approx \sum_{g=1}^{G} \frac{(n_g - s_{g.})^2}{2(s_{g.})} \tag{7}$$

Analogously,

$$\text{(8)} \qquad J_r \approx \sum_{g=1}^{G} \frac{(n_g - s_{gr}/s_{.r})^2}{2(s_{gr}/s_{.r})}. \tag{8}$$

Individual regional contributions to the approximations in (7) and (8) all have the same sign, permitting relative comparisons which are meaningful to the extent the approximations themselves are close to the exact values of J and J_r.

Theil's entropy measure as presented in (1) is the form typically used in the literature. That typical usage derives not from economic logic, but from historical order of presentation; the form in (1) was proposed first. That information theory based measure evaluates how well population shares as prior probabilities "predict" posterior income shares. It is equally logical [Theil, 1979b] to ask how well income shares as prior probabilities predict posterior population shares:

$$J' = \sum_{g=1}^{G} n_g \log\left(\frac{n_g}{s_{g.}}\right) \tag{1'}$$

The alternative measure, J′, may be decomposed analogously to J, yielding:

$$J_r' = \sum_{g=1}^{G} n_g \log \left(\frac{n_g}{s_{gr}/s_{.r}}\right) \quad (2')$$

$$J' = \bar{J}' - \bar{D}' \text{ where} \quad (3')$$

$$\bar{J}' = \sum_{r=1}^{R} s_{.r} J_r' \text{ and} \quad (4')$$

$$\bar{D}' = \sum_{g=1}^{G} n_g \bar{D}_g' \text{ with } \bar{D}_g' = \sum_{r=1}^{R} s_{.r} \log \left(\frac{s_{.r}}{s_{gr}/s_{g.}}\right) \quad (5')$$

$$J' \approx \sum_{g=1}^{G} \frac{(s_{g.} - n_g)^2}{2n_g} \quad (7')$$

$$J_r' \approx \sum_{g=1}^{G} \frac{(s_{gr}/s_{.r} - n_g)^2}{2n_g}. \quad (8')$$

$\bar{D}_g'$ is the expected information of the message that transforms income proportions of region g ($s_{g1}/s_{g.}$, $s_{g2}/s_{g.}$, . . ., $s_{gr}/s_{g.}$), the prior probabilities, into the corresponding aggregate proportions ($s_{.1}$, $s_{.2}$, . . ., $s_{.r}$), the posterior probabilities. Similar to D, $\bar{D}_g'$ is positive except under stochastic independence, $s_{gr} = s_{g.}s_{.r}$ for all (g, r). Without *a priori* reason for preferring one formulation over the other, it is reasonable to compute both sets of measures to determine if they are empirically consistent with respect to aggregate inequality, component inequality and regional contributions to these inequalities.[3]

---

[3]There is *a priori* mathematical reason for preferring (1) to (1′) if zero values for $s_{g.}$ occur in a data set. J′ cannot be defined in this case, but the gth element contribution to J for $s_{g.} = 0$ may be specified as $0 = \lim_{s_{g.} \to 0} s_{g.} \log \left(\frac{s_{g.}}{n_g}\right)$. Such zero shares do not occur in the present case.

3. Empirical results

Application of the decompositions was made to census division annual incomes, 1969 through 1986, with BEA incomes subdivided into three mutually exclusive and exhaustive components: net labor earnings (r=1), property income (r=2) and transfer payments (r=3).[4] The period of analysis was determined by availability of consistently defined component and aggregate income. Both entropy measures, J and J′, and their corresponding decompositions were calculated. They were uniformly very similar. Only calculations corresponding to J are provided and discussed in the text and those corresponding to J′ are presented in an appendix so the reader may verify the similarity of results.

---

[4]Net labor earnings refers to the BEA category "net earnings by place of residence," property income is BEA major component "dividends, interest and rent," and transfer payments correspond to the same-named BEA category. To avoid confusion, it should be noted that the nine census division designations do not correspond to BEA's regional grouping of the states. The census division groupings are analyzed in the current study because of their more common usage. Specifically the divisions are:

New England (NE): Maine, New Hampshire, Vermont, Massachusetts, Rhode Island, Connecticut

Middle Atlantic (MA): New York, New Jersey, Pennsylvania

East North Central (ENC): Ohio, Indiana, Illinois, Michigan, Wisconsin

West North Central (WNC): Minnesota, Iowa, Missouri, North Dakota, South Dakota, Nebraska, Kansas

South Atlantic (SA): Delaware, Maryland, District of Columbia, Virginia, West Virginia, North Carolina, South Carolina, Georgia, Florida

East South Central (ESC): Kentucky, Tennessee, Alabama, Mississippi

West South Central (WSC): Arkansas, Louisiana, Oklahoma, Texas

Mountain (MT): Montana, Idaho, Wyoming, Colorado, New Mexico, Arizona, Utah, Nevada

Pacific (PA): Washington, Oregon, California, Alaska, Hawaii.

Table 1 reports measures corresponding to those in equations (1) through (5). Reflective of longer-run trend [Browne, 1980a], aggregate regional inequality declined from 1969 through 1981. However, it rose in the ensuing five years, returning to a level characteristic of the early 1970s by 1986. As anticipated, inequality of distribution differs substantially among income components, being consistently highest for property income, lowest for labor earnings and of intermediary magnitude for transfer payments. Recall that a given component inequality enters J and $\bar{J}$ weighted by its share in income and the relatively low share of property income in the total reduces the impact of the high J_2 values on $\bar{J}$. Nonetheless, the weighted property income inequality, $s_{.2}J_2$, averages 30 percent of $\bar{J}$ over the eighteen year period, a role approximately twice its share in determination of aggregate income level. In contrast, labor earnings average 72 percent of total income 1969 through 1986, but $s_{.1}J_1$ averages only 52 percent of $\bar{J}$. The indisputable dominance of labor income in total income has focused attention in empirical cross-section estimation of regional aggregate income inequality on variables specifying labor earnings inequality. While the present findings do not contradict that emphasis, they clearly suggest significant omissions are made if other components are ignored.

The expected mutual information term, D, was relatively constant in magnitude over the eighteen year period. Consequently, the percent reduction in $\bar{J}$ from the offsetting of components rose during the decade 1969 to 1979, from 12 percent to 25 percent, but as $\bar{J}$ increased in the 1980s, the percentage offset declined to only 9 percent in 1986.

For the period investigated, Table 1 indicates an asymmetry in factors historically yielding decline in aggregate inequality and those yielding increase. Decline in inequality characterized all individual income components over the period in which aggregate inequality was diminishing. However, the rise in that aggregate since 1981 was almost exclusively a labor earnings phenomenon. In 1981, J_1 (weighted by labor income's share of 69 percent), accounted for 49 percent of $\bar{J}$. Ninety-two percent of the increase in $\bar{J}$ from 1981 to 1986 is a consequence of the rise in J_1. In a time series analysis of the present decade, there is a clear focus of attention--why did that earnings inequality rise?

The approximations derived in (7) and (8) and presented in Table 2 provide insight into that question which accords with regional industrial job growth relative to population change in the present decade. The regional approximations indicate that rise in labor earnings inequality, 1981 to 1986, is primarily attributable to three regions, New England, Middle Atlantic and West South Central, the first two being areas encompassing the northeast growth revival in the present decade and the latter embodying the adverse earnings impact of oil industry decline. In all three regions, s_{g1}/n_g was near unity, but slightly over one, at the start of the decade. It diverged further from unity in each of the regions, increasing in New England and the Middle Atlantic and decreasing in the West South Central area.

Note that Tables 2A and 2B again emphasize the distinction between inequality at a point in time and changes in that inequality. The low per capita income and labor earnings of the four-state East South Central division consistently accounts for one third to one half the aggregate total income and earnings component inequalities approximated in 2A and 2B, but little of the change in the present decade is attributable to that area. The region's trend of substantial relative improvement in the previous decade stabilized in the more recent period.

In comparing Tables 2C and 2D with 2A, the regional contribution to inequality is seen to vary across income components. The relatively low shares of the East South Central area, dominant in the labor earnings inequality, is also dominant in property income inequality, but in the latter case two other regions--West South Central also with a relatively low share and Middle Atlantic with a relatively high share--account for substantial proportions of the aggregate component inequality.[5] In contrast, the East South Central division contributes relatively little to the transfer payment inequality and regional dominance of the latter has shifted over the time period of analysis. Relatively high transfer payment shares in the Middle Atlantic and Pacific account for over half the component inequality in the earlier years and while the former is a consistent intertemporal phenomenon, the relatively high share of the Pacific region has diminished markedly, being replaced in significance by the increasingly relatively low share of the West South Central region.

4. Concluding remarks

The existence of regional income inequality presents a three-fold challenge for regional analysis. The first two are positive issues--measuring that inequality and empirically explaining it. Depending upon the outcomes of that analysis, we may wish to normatively devise policy which alters that distribution. The present research has been concerned with the first two challenges and more

---

[5]In assessing these observations on regional contribution to property income inequality, it should be noted that the approximation procedure for this component is somewhat poorer than that of either total income or the other two components.

specifically on developing decompositions of income inequality by component which may potentially aid empirical analysis. A decomposition was derived which balanced considerations of theoretically desirable attributes of income inequality measures and the need to provide interpretable decompositions. By splitting up the estimation problem, theoretically such decompositions can help resolve multicollinearity problems of direct estimation of the aggregate. In addition, the present empirical application suggested that such decomposition can provide insight into asymmetries of intertemporal change, differences in inequality at a point in time compared with changes in that inequality over time, and identification of regional contribution to inequality.

However, the preliminary effort nature of this research must be stressed. Considerably further examination is called for in: (1) empirical specification and estimation of factors determining individual component inequality; (2) potential derivation of similar decompositions for other inequality measures and comparison with the present results; (3) more extensive theoretical and empirical linkage of population group decomposition and component distribution.

Table 1. Component Decomposition of Regional Income Inequality

Year	Total Income Inequality (J)	Net Labor Earnings Inequality (J_1)	Property Income Inequality (J_2)	Transfer Payment Inequality (J_3)	Weighted Average Component Inequality ($\bar{J}$)	Component Dependency (D)	Component Shares of National Income: Net Labor Earnings	Property Income	Transfer Payments
1969	86.2	72.2	235.7	114.0	97.8	11.6	0.774	0.133	0.093
1970	75.5	61.3	199.3	115.5	85.3	9.8	0.763	0.133	0.104
1971	68.9	54.4	183.1	124.6	79.2	10.3	0.755	0.130	0.114
1972	61.8	47.6	175.1	122.5	72.4	10.5	0.758	0.126	0.116
1973	51.3	41.3	156.6	95.0	62.2	10.9	0.756	0.126	0.119
1974	50.3	40.3	143.5	89.0	60.0	9.6	0.742	0.130	0.127
1975	49.8	41.5	128.9	92.3	60.0	10.2	0.726	0.126	0.148
1976	47.7	40.8	130.2	93.8	59.6	11.9	0.730	0.124	0.146
1977	46.5	41.8	131.0	92.9	60.3	13.8	0.733	0.126	0.142
1978	43.3	39.3	127.7	85.6	57.0	13.8	0.734	0.130	0.136
1979	42.9	40.4	129.3	73.5	56.9	14.0	0.729	0.136	0.135
1980	43.7	41.9	113.6	63.0	55.5	11.8	0.708	0.147	0.145
1981	40.3	38.0	106.0	67.1	53.4	13.1	0.690	0.163	0.147
1982	42.9	42.0	100.2	69.1	55.9	13.1	0.678	0.168	0.155
1983	47.8	46.6	105.0	64.7	59.2	11.4	0.676	0.168	0.156
1984	48.9	43.5	114.7	68.6	59.4	10.4	0.682	0.171	0.147
1985	52.2	48.4	105.5	66.0	60.6	8.5	0.683	0.169	0.148
1986	62.4	59.1	111.6	64.8	68.8	6.4	0.684	0.169	0.147

Notes: J, J_1, J_2, J_3, $\bar{J}$ and D are all multiplied by 10^4. Definitions of income components are given in Footnote 4.

Table 2. Approximations of Regional Contribution to Inequality

2A. Aggregate Income Inequality (J)

Region	Year																	
	1969	1970	1971	1972	1973	1974	1975	1976	1977	1978	1979	1980	1981	1982	1983	1984	1985	1986
New England	2.6	2.5	2.0	1.5	0.8	0.7	0.5	0.4	0.4	0.3	0.4	1.0	1.2	2.2	3.4	4.4	4.9	6.7
Middle Atlantic	14.0	14.2	13.7	11.7	7.8	7.9	7.6	5.7	4.5	3.0	2.5	3.8	4.2	6.4	7.9	8.1	8.9	11.2
South Atlantic	9.1	6.4	5.3	4.1	4.0	4.2	5.3	5.5	6.4	6.2	6.6	5.0	4.7	4.0	2.3	2.1	1.7	1.3
East South Central	31.8	28.8	26.5	23.9	21.9	20.7	20.7	18.4	18.1	18.0	18.0	19.8	20.1	20.9	21.9	21.4	22.4	22.1
East North Central	2.3	0.6	0.8	0.9	1.5	1.2	0.8	1.5	2.5	1.9	1.3	0.2	0.0	0.2	0.2	0.1	0.1	0.1
West North Central	2.1	1.8	1.5	1.0	0.0	0.3	0.1	0.6	0.3	0.1	0.1	0.6	0.3	0.5	1.0	0.7	0.9	0.7
West South Central	16.1	13.7	13.9	13.8	12.2	9.5	6.7	5.6	5.0	3.7	2.9	2.0	0.6	0.6	2.4	3.7	4.7	10.8
Mountain	2.6	1.4	1.1	0.9	0.9	0.8	1.1	1.2	1.3	0.7	0.7	0.6	0.7	1.0	1.3	1.9	2.2	2.9
Pacific	12.1	11.1	8.8	8.2	6.2	8.2	9.8	10.8	10.2	11.4	12.3	12.7	10.8	9.4	9.6	8.7	8.8	9.1
Sum of regional approximations	92.7	80.5	73.6	66.0	55.3	53.5	52.6	49.9	48.7	45.3	44.9	45.8	42.5	45.2	50.1	51.2	54.6	64.9
Exact J	86.2	75.5	68.9	61.8	51.3	50.3	49.8	47.7	46.5	43.3	42.9	43.7	40.3	42.9	47.8	48.9	52.2	62.4

Table 2. Approximations of Regional Contribution to Inequality (continued)

2B. Net Labor Earnings Inequality (J_1)

Region	1969	1970	1971	1972	1973	1974	1975	1976	1977	1978	1979	1980	1981	1982	1983	1984	1985	1986
New England	1.2	1.2	0.8	0.5	0.2	0.1	0.0	0.0	0.0	0.0	0.1	0.6	0.6	1.8	3.6	4.5	5.8	8.3
Middle Atlantic	9.0	10.2	9.3	7.0	3.8	3.9	3.4	1.8	0.9	0.3	0.2	0.9	1.1	2.7	4.1	3.6	4.5	6.8
East North Central	5.7	2.5	3.2	3.2	4.4	3.7	2.6	4.3	6.3	5.2	4.0	0.7	0.1	0.3	0.5	0.1	0.1	0.0
West North Central	2.2	1.7	1.3	0.8	0.2	0.2	0.0	0.7	0.4	0.1	0.0	1.0	0.6	1.5	2.8	1.6	1.7	1.3
South Atlantic	7.7	5.4	4.3	3.3	3.7	4.1	6.2	6.7	8.3	8.4	9.7	7.8	7.6	6.2	3.7	3.4	3.0	2.2
East South Central	25.7	24.0	21.6	18.8	17.6	16.9	18.3	15.5	14.8	14.4	15.0	17.8	18.1	19.6	20.9	19.5	20.9	21.0
West South Central	13.6	11.3	11.2	11.1	10.0	7.0	3.5	2.4	1.9	1.2	0.6	0.1	0.4	0.6	0.0	0.6	1.6	7.6
Mountain	2.8	1.6	1.0	0.8	0.8	0.5	0.7	0.8	0.9	0.4	0.3	0.1	0.1	0.3	0.6	1.1	1.5	2.2
Pacific	9.4	7.6	5.5	5.4	3.8	6.3	9.1	10.2	9.8	10.6	12.0	14.4	11.4	11.3	12.5	11.1	11.3	11.5
Sum of regional approximations	77.3	65.5	58.2	50.9	44.4	42.8	43.8	42.3	43.3	40.6	41.8	43.6	40.1	44.2	48.7	45.3	50.2	60.9
Exact J_1	72.2	61.3	54.4	47.6	41.3	40.3	41.5	40.8	41.8	39.3	40.4	41.9	38.0	42.0	46.6	43.5	48.4	59.1

Table 2. Approximations of Regional Contribution to Inequality (continued)

2C. Property Income Inequality (J_2)

Region	Year																	
	1969	1970	1971	1972	1973	1974	1975	1976	1977	1978	1979	1980	1981	1982	1983	1984	1985	1986
New England	18.6	15.3	13.3	12.5	9.4	8.2	6.0	5.8	5.7	4.1	3.4	4.2	4.3	5.8	5.1	7.3	6.2	7.6
Middle Atlantic	43.3	33.8	28.8	26.3	21.9	20.4	17.4	17.1	17.8	13.9	13.2	13.4	13.1	14.4	14.9	19.4	18.8	20.3
East North Central	0.2	0.7	0.8	0.8	0.6	0.3	0.1	0.1	0.0	0.3	0.6	0.8	0.9	1.1	0.5	0.8	1.5	1.6
West North Central	1.6	1.3	0.7	0.2	0.0	0.1	1.0	1.4	2.2	1.6	1.4	1.5	2.2	4.2	3.6	1.4	0.7	0.4
South Atlantic	18.8	11.6	8.5	7.2	6.0	5.4	4.8	4.1	4.2	3.4	3.2	1.8	1.6	1.7	0.8	0.6	0.1	0.0
East South Central	134.3	117.6	114.0	112.0	104.8	97.8	88.3	89.3	90.0	90.7	90.9	79.6	72.9	66.8	71.2	73.8	73.5	69.0
West South Central	40.5	33.3	30.6	29.8	25.1	22.5	21.4	23.7	24.8	20.4	19.1	15.9	14.4	12.5	17.9	19.6	14.1	19.8
Mountain	1.9	0.5	0.3	0.4	0.3	0.5	0.6	0.7	0.8	0.5	0.4	0.9	1.4	1.8	1.7	2.9	2.5	3.0
Pacific	21.7	22.1	21.8	21.2	20.5	17.4	15.2	14.9	12.9	19.3	22.9	16.9	14.1	8.5	8.4	8.7	7.4	7.7
Sum of regional approximations	281.0	236.3	218.8	210.3	188.7	172.7	154.8	156.9	158.3	154.2	155.1	135.0	124.9	116.7	124.1	134.3	124.6	129.5
Exact J_2	235.7	199.3	183.1	175.1	156.6	143.5	128.9	130.2	131.0	127.7	129.3	113.6	106.0	100.2	105.0	114.7	105.5	111.6

Table 2. Approximations of Regional Contribution to Inequality (continued)

2D. Transfer Payment Inequality (J_3)

Region	Year																	
	1969	1970	1971	1972	1973	1974	1975	1976	1977	1978	1979	1980	1981	1982	1983	1984	1985	1986
New England	3.4	3.1	4.5	3.5	2.4	2.8	4.6	2.9	2.2	1.7	1.8	1.0	1.5	1.3	1.1	1.5	1.0	0.9
Middle Atlantic	29.9	27.1	35.7	41.4	34.1	31.4	32.7	34.2	35.1	33.0	29.0	23.0	21.9	23.2	24.4	27.6	27.1	27.5
East North Central	12.4	13.1	10.4	8.6	6.1	4.9	2.9	3.5	4.1	4.1	2.8	0.0	0.1	0.1	0.2	0.1	0.0	0.0
West North Central	1.9	2.9	4.2	5.4	3.8	4.2	6.5	6.1	5.5	4.6	4.1	3.2	2.9	2.4	2.2	2.1	2.2	1.7
South Atlantic	10.3	8.8	9.3	6.5	4.2	3.5	2.2	2.1	1.4	0.8	0.2	0.3	0.2	0.4	0.4	0.4	0.3	0.6
East South Central	12.1	9.4	10.8	11.2	8.3	6.6	6.0	5.9	6.3	6.0	3.7	3.1	3.3	3.7	3.3	3.1	3.3	3.4
West South Central	12.4	14.2	18.8	20.2	16.0	15.9	21.4	21.3	20.6	18.9	18.7	22.8	26.7	29.0	25.3	25.6	23.4	21.1
Mountain	1.9	2.1	3.1	3.8	3.9	5.0	6.1	5.8	5.8	5.7	6.5	7.7	7.1	7.6	7.2	7.9	7.4	7.5
Pacific	26.6	31.1	24.8	18.8	13.8	12.7	9.1	10.6	10.3	9.3	6.0	3.2	5.4	3.8	1.9	1.3	1.9	2.1
Sum of regional approximations	110.9	111.8	121.3	119.4	92.6	87.0	91.4	92.5	91.3	84.1	72.8	64.4	69.1	71.5	66.1	69.5	66.5	64.7
Exact J_3	114.0	115.5	124.6	122.5	95.0	89.0	92.3	93.8	92.9	85.6	73.5	63.0	67.1	69.1	64.7	68.6	66.0	64.8

Notes: All numbers are multiplied by 10^4. For explanation of approximations, see text derivation of equations (6) - (8). Income components and regions are defined in Footnote 4.

Appendix

Tables 1′ and 2′ correspond to text Tables 1 and 2, but are based upon the alternative inequality measures and decompositions described in (1′) - (8′).

Table 1′. Component Decomposition of Regional Income Inequality

Year	Total Income Inequality (J')	Net Labor Earnings Inequality (J_1')	Property Income Inequality (J_2')	Transfer Payment Inequality (J_3')	Weighted Average Component Inequality $\bar{J}'$	Component Dependency $\bar{D}'$	Component Shares of National Income: Net Labor Earnings	Property Income	Transfer Payments
1969	89.1	74.5	253.7	112.2	101.8	12.7	0.774	0.133	0.093
1970	77.7	63.2	214.2	113.3	88.5	10.8	0.763	0.133	0.104
1971	71.0	56.2	197.6	122.6	82.2	11.2	0.755	0.130	0.114
1972	63.7	49.1	189.6	120.6	75.1	11.4	0.758	0.126	0.116
1973	53.2	42.8	170.0	93.6	64.8	11.6	0.756	0.126	0.119
1974	51.8	41.5	155.7	87.8	62.3	10.5	0.742	0.130	0.127
1975	51.1	42.5	140.0	91.6	62.1	11.0	0.726	0.126	0.148
1976	48.6	41.5	141.6	92.9	61.4	12.8	0.730	0.124	0.146
1977	47.5	42.5	142.7	91.9	62.1	14.6	0.733	0.126	0.142
1978	44.2	39.9	139.0	84.6	58.8	14.6	0.734	0.130	0.136
1979	43.8	41.0	140.2	73.0	58.8	15.0	0.729	0.136	0.135
1980	44.6	42.6	122.8	63.5	57.4	12.8	0.708	0.147	0.145
1981	41.3	39.0	114.1	67.9	55.5	14.2	0.690	0.163	0.147
1982	43.9	43.0	107.4	70.1	58.0	14.1	0.678	0.168	0.155
1983	48.8	47.5	113.3	65.2	61.3	12.5	0.676	0.168	0.156
1984	49.9	44.3	123.1	68.9	61.4	11.4	0.682	0.171	0.147
1985	53.2	49.2	113.7	66.1	62.6	9.4	0.683	0.169	0.148
1986	63.5	59.9	119.3	64.6	70.6	7.1	0.684	0.169	0.147

Notes: J', J'_1, J'_2, J'_3, $\bar{J}'$ and $\bar{D}'$ are all multiplied by 10^4. Definitions of income components are given in Footnote 4.

Table 2′. Approximations of Regional Contribution to Inequality

2A′. Aggregate Income Inequality (J′)

Region	Year: 1969	1970	1971	1972	1973	1974	1975	1976	1977	1978	1979	1980	1981	1982	1983	1984	1985	1986
New England	2.9	2.8	2.1	1.6	0.9	0.8	0.5	0.5	0.4	0.3	0.4	1.1	1.2	2.4	3.7	5.0	5.7	7.9
Middle Atlantic	15.8	16.1	15.5	13.2	8.5	8.6	8.3	6.2	4.9	3.2	2.7	4.1	4.5	7.0	8.7	9.0	9.9	12.6
South Atlantic	8.2	5.8	4.8	3.8	3.8	3.9	4.9	5.1	5.8	5.7	6.0	4.6	4.3	3.7	2.2	2.0	1.6	1.2
East South Central	23.2	21.3	19.9	18.1	16.8	16.0	16.1	14.5	14.3	14.2	14.3	15.5	15.7	16.2	16.9	16.5	17.2	17.0
East North Central	2.4	0.6	0.9	0.9	1.6	1.3	0.8	1.6	2.6	2.0	1.4	0.2	0.0	0.2	0.2	0.1	0.1	0.1
West North Central	2.0	1.7	1.4	0.9	0.0	0.3	0.1	0.6	0.3	0.1	0.1	0.6	0.3	0.4	0.9	0.7	0.9	0.7
West South Central	13.4	11.6	11.7	11.7	10.4	8.3	6.0	5.0	4.5	3.4	2.7	1.9	0.6	0.6	2.2	3.4	4.3	9.4
Mountain	2.3	1.3	1.0	0.9	0.9	0.8	1.0	1.1	1.2	0.7	0.7	0.6	0.6	1.0	1.2	1.8	2.0	2.6
Pacific	13.9	12.6	9.9	9.2	6.8	9.2	11.1	12.3	11.5	13.0	14.1	14.5	12.2	10.6	10.8	9.7	9.8	10.1
Sum of regional approximations	84.0	73.8	67.2	60.3	49.7	49.1	48.8	46.9	45.6	42.5	42.2	43.1	39.5	42.1	47.0	48.2	51.4	61.6
Exact J′	89.1	77.7	71.0	63.7	53.2	51.8	51.1	48.6	47.5	44.2	43.8	44.6	41.3	43.9	48.8	49.9	53.2	63.5

Table 2′. Approximations of Regional Contribution to Inequality (continued)

2B′. Net Labor Earnings Inequality (J_1')

	Year																	
Region	1969	1970	1971	1972	1973	1974	1975	1976	1977	1978	1979	1980	1981	1982	1983	1984	1985	1986
New England	1.3	1.3	0.8	0.5	0.2	0.1	0.0	0.0	0.0	0.0	0.1	0.6	0.7	1.9	4.1	5.1	6.8	9.9
Middle Atlantic	10.0	11.3	10.3	7.6	4.0	4.2	3.6	1.8	0.9	0.3	0.2	1.0	1.1	2.9	4.4	3.8	4.8	7.5
East North Central	6.1	2.7	3.4	3.4	4.7	3.9	2.7	4.6	6.9	5.6	4.3	0.7	0.1	0.2	0.5	0.1	0.1	0.0
West North Central	2.1	1.6	1.3	0.7	0.2	0.2	0.0	0.7	0.4	0.1	0.0	1.0	0.6	1.4	2.6	1.5	1.6	1.3
South Atlantic	7.0	5.0	4.0	3.1	3.5	3.8	5.7	6.1	7.5	7.6	8.7	7.1	6.9	5.7	3.4	3.2	2.8	2.1
East South Central	19.4	18.2	16.6	14.8	13.9	13.4	14.4	12.4	12.0	11.7	12.1	14.1	14.3	15.3	16.2	15.2	16.2	16.2
West South Central	11.5	9.7	9.6	9.5	8.7	6.2	3.2	2.2	1.8	1.1	0.6	0.1	0.4	0.7	0.0	0.5	1.5	6.7
Mountain	2.5	1.4	1.0	0.7	0.7	0.5	0.6	0.8	0.8	0.4	0.3	0.1	0.1	0.3	0.6	1.0	1.4	2.0
Pacific	10.6	8.5	6.0	6.0	4.0	7.0	10.3	11.5	11.0	12.0	13.7	16.7	13.0	12.8	14.3	12.5	12.8	13.0
Sum of regional approximations	70.3	59.7	52.9	46.3	40.0	39.4	40.6	40.2	41.3	38.8	39.9	41.4	37.2	41.2	46.0	43.0	47.8	58.7
Exact J_1'	74.5	63.2	56.2	49.1	42.8	41.5	42.5	41.5	42.5	39.9	41.0	42.6	39.0	43.0	47.5	44.3	49.2	59.9

Table 2′. Approximations of Regional Contribution to Inequality (continued)

2C′. Property Income Inequality (J_2')

Region	1969	1970	1971	1972	1973	1974	1975	1976	1977	1978	1979	1980	1981	1982	1983	1984	1985	1986
New England	24.0	19.3	16.4	15.3	11.3	9.8	6.9	6.7	6.6	4.7	3.9	4.7	4.9	6.7	5.8	8.6	7.3	9.0
Middle Atlantic	53.8	40.9	34.4	31.2	25.7	23.7	20.1	19.7	20.6	15.9	15.0	15.2	14.9	16.5	17.1	22.6	21.9	23.9
East North Central	0.2	0.7	0.8	0.7	0.6	0.3	0.1	0.1	0.0	0.3	0.6	0.8	0.9	1.0	0.5	0.7	1.4	1.5
West North Central	1.5	1.3	0.7	0.2	0.0	0.1	1.1	1.4	2.3	1.8	1.5	1.6	2.4	4.6	4.0	1.5	0.7	0.4
South Atlantic	16.1	10.3	7.7	6.6	5.5	5.0	4.4	3.8	3.9	3.2	3.0	1.7	1.5	1.6	0.8	0.6	0.1	0.0
East South Central	70.8	64.4	63.1	62.4	59.5	56.6	52.5	53.1	53.4	53.7	53.8	48.7	45.5	42.5	44.6	45.8	45.6	43.4
West South Central	30.3	25.5	23.8	23.2	20.0	18.2	17.4	19.1	19.9	16.7	15.8	13.4	12.2	10.7	15.0	16.2	12.0	16.4
Mountain	1.7	0.5	0.3	0.3	0.3	0.5	0.5	0.6	0.7	0.5	0.4	0.9	1.3	1.7	1.6	2.6	2.2	2.7
Pacific	26.1	26.6	26.2	25.3	24.4	20.4	17.7	17.3	14.8	22.8	27.4	19.7	16.2	9.5	9.4	9.7	8.2	8.6
Sum of regional approximations	224.4	189.5	173.3	165.3	147.3	134.7	120.8	121.8	122.2	119.4	121.4	106.8	99.8	94.8	98.7	108.4	99.3	105.9
Exact J_2'	253.7	214.2	197.6	189.6	170.0	155.7	140.0	141.6	142.7	139.0	140.2	122.8	114.1	107.4	113.3	123.1	113.7	119.3

Table 2′. Approximations of Regional Contribution to Inequality (continued)

2D′. Transfer Payment Inequality (J_3')

Region	1969	1970	1971	1972	1973	1974	1975	1976	1977	1978	1979	1980	1981	1982	1983	1984	1985	1986
New England	3.8	3.5	5.0	3.9	2.6	3.1	5.3	3.2	2.4	1.8	1.9	1.1	1.6	1.3	1.2	1.6	1.0	1.0
Middle Atlantic	35.8	32.1	43.5	51.3	41.5	38.0	39.7	41.8	43.0	40.2	34.9	27.2	25.9	27.5	29.1	33.2	32.7	33.2
East North Central	11.1	11.7	9.3	7.9	5.6	4.5	2.7	3.3	3.9	3.9	2.6	0.0	0.1	0.1	0.2	0.1	0.0	0.0
West North Central	1.7	2.7	3.8	4.8	3.4	3.7	5.7	5.4	4.9	4.1	3.7	2.9	2.7	2.2	2.0	2.0	2.0	1.6
South Atlantic	9.2	7.9	8.3	5.9	3.9	3.3	2.0	2.0	1.3	0.8	0.2	0.3	0.2	0.4	0.4	0.4	0.3	0.6
East South Central	9.9	7.9	9.0	9.3	7.1	5.7	5.2	5.2	5.4	5.2	3.4	2.8	3.0	3.4	3.0	2.8	3.0	3.0
West South Central	10.6	11.9	15.4	16.5	13.3	13.3	17.4	17.4	16.8	15.6	15.5	18.5	21.4	23.0	20.5	20.6	19.1	17.3
Mountain	1.7	1.9	2.8	3.3	3.4	4.3	5.2	5.0	5.0	4.9	5.5	6.4	6.0	6.4	6.1	6.7	6.2	6.4
Pacific	32.6	38.7	30.1	22.2	16.0	14.5	10.2	12.0	11.6	10.4	6.6	3.4	5.9	4.1	2.0	1.4	2.0	2.2
Sum of regional approximations	116.4	118.3	127.2	125.1	96.9	90.6	93.4	95.1	94.4	87.0	74.4	62.8	66.6	68.5	64.5	68.7	66.3	65.3
Exact J_3'	112.2	113.3	122.6	120.6	93.6	87.8	91.6	92.9	91.9	84.6	73.0	63.5	67.9	70.1	65.2	68.9	66.1	64.6

Notes: All numbers are multiplied by 10^4. For explanation of approximations, see text derivation of equations (6′) - (8′). Income components and regions are defined in Footnote 4.

References

Al-Samarrie, A. and H. P. Miller [1967], State Differentials in Income Concentration, *The American Economic Review,* 57, 59-72.

Blackorby, C. and D. Donaldson [1978], Measures of Relative Equality and their Meaning in Terms of Social Welfare, *Journal of Economic Theory,* 18, 59-80.

Bourguignon, F. [1979], Decomposable Income Equality Measures. *Econometrica,* 47, 901-920.

Browne, L. E. [1980a], Narrowing Regional Income Differentials. *New England Economic Review,* September/October, 35-56.

_____ [1980b], Narrowing Regional Income Differentials: II, *New England Economic Review,* November/December, 40-59.

Coelen, S. P. [1978], Regional Income Convergence/Divergence Again, *Journal of Regional Science,* 18, 447-457.

Cowell, F. A. [1977], *Measuring Inequality*, Oxford: Philip Allan Publishers, Ltd.

Easterlin, R. A. [1960], Regional Growth of Income: Long Term Tendencies, 1880-1950, in S. Kuznets, R. E. Miller, R. A. Easterlin, *Population Redistribution and Economic Growth, United States, 1870-1950*, Philadelphia: The American Philosphical Society.

Fei, J. C. H., G. Ranis and S. W. Y. Kuo [1978], Growth and the Family Distribution of Income by Factor Components, *Quarterly Journal of Economics,* 92, 17-53.

Fields, G. S. [1979], Income Inequality in Urban Colombia: A Decomposition Analysis, *Review of Income and Wealth,* 25, 327-341.

Garofalo, G. and M.S. Fogarty [1979], Urban Income Distribution and the Urban Hierarchy-Equality Hypothesis, *The Review of Economics and Statistics,* 61, 381-388.

Lerman, R. I. and S. Yitzhaki [1985], Income Inequality Effects by Income Source: A New Approach and Application to the United States, *The Review of Economics and Statistics,* 67, 151-156.

Long, J. E., D. W. Rasmussen and C. T. Haworth [1977], Income Inequality and City Size, *The Review of Economics and Statistics,* 59, 244-246.

Nelson, J. I. [1984], Income Inequality: The American States, *Social Science Quarterly,* 65, 854-860.

Perloff, H. S., E. S. Dunn, Jr., E. E. Lampard, R. F. Muth [1960], *Regions, Resources, and Economic Growth,* Baltimore: Johns Hopkins Press.

Persky, J. J. and M. S. Tam [1985], The Optimal Convergence of Regional Incomes, *Journal of Regional Science,* 25, 337-351.

Rao, V. M. [1969], Two Decompositions of Concentration Ratio, *Journal of the Royal Statistical Society,* 132, 418-425.

Shorrocks, A. F. [1980], The Class of Additively Decomposable Inequality Measures, *Econometrica,* 48, 613-625.

_____ [1982], Inequality Decomposition by Factor Components, *Econometrica,* 50, 193-211.

Smith, D. M. and E. J. Jennings [1976], The Distribution of State Incomes: Differential Growth of Sectoral Employment, *The American Economic Review,* 66, 717-721.

Tam, M. S. and J. Persky [1982], Regional Convergence and National Inequality, *The Review of Economics and Statistics,* 64, 161-164.

Theil, H. [1967], *Economics and Information Theory*, Amsterdam: North-Holland.

_____ [1979a], World Income Inequality and its Components, *Economics Letters,* 2, 99-102.

_____ [1979b], The Measurement of Inequality by Components of Income, *Economics Letters,* 2, 197-199.

Williamson, J. G. [1965], Regional Inequality and the Process of National Development: A Description of the Patterns, *Economic Development and Cultural Change,* 13, 1-84.

_____ [1980], Unbalanced Growth, Inequality, and Regional Development: Some Lessons from U.S. History, in V. L. Arnold (ed.), *Alternatives to Confrontation*, Lexington, Mass.: D. C. Heath and Co., Lexington Books.

Large Sample Distribution of Several Inequality Measures: With Application to Côte d'Ivoire

Nanak Kakwani*

Welfare and Human Resources

The World Bank and The University of New South Wales

Abstract

Several measures have been devised to analyze income or consumption distribution inequality. This paper presents the large sample distributions of several inequality measures that are used to test whether observed differences in sample estimates are statistically significant. The results presented in the paper are used to analyze income inequality in Côte d'Ivoire from the data of the Living Standards Survey, 1985.

1. Introduction

Several inquality measures have been proposed in the literature to answer a wide range of questions: how large is income inequality and which way it is moving? How income inequality in developing countries compares with that in developed countries. Is there any trade off between growth and equity? In order to answer these and other related questions, it is essential to measure income inequality and to draw valid conclusions about its magnitude.

---

*I would like to thank Paul Glewwe, Jacques van der Gaag, and J. Dutta for their comments on an earlier draft. Kalpana Mehra provided me with expert computational assistance for which I am grateful to her. I am indebted to Maria Felix and Lynda Sollazzo for typing and to Brenda Rosa for editing the manuscript.

Since inequality measures are estimated on the basis of sample observations, we need to test whether the observed differences in their values are statistically significant, i.e. whether the differences are due to sampling errors or due to some other factors affecting income inequality. This paper presents the large sample distributions of several inequality measures which would be used to provide distribution free confidence intervals and statistical inferences about income inequality. The paper derives the results in a simple manner and presents them so that they are easily applicable to empirical work. The results presented in the paper are used to analyze income inequality in Côte D'Ivoire.

2. A Brief Review of Inequality Measures

Suppose the income, x, of an individual is a random variable with the probability distribution function F(x). Let L(p) be the Lorenz function which measures the income share of the bottom 100p percent of the population. If the society is concerned only with the welfare of the bottom 100p percent of the population, L(p) will be a suitable measure of income equality. This measure has been popular with the World Bank economists who assume $p = 0.40$, i.e. the income share of the bottom 40 percent of the population (Ahluwalia [1974]).

An inequality measure based on the income share of the bottom 100p percent of population may be defined as

$$\phi(p) = p - L(p) \tag{1}$$

which takes value zero if the income share of the bottom 100p percent of population is equal to 100p percent. $\phi(p)$ will be zero for all p in the range $0 \leq p \leq 1$ if, and only if, every individual in society receives exactly the same income.

Among all the inequality measures, the Gini index is the one most widely used to analyze the size distribution of income and wealth. The measure as proposed by Gini in 1912 is defined as

$$G = \frac{\Delta}{2\mu} \tag{2}$$

where

$$\Delta = \int_0^\infty \int_0^\infty |x-y| f(x)f(y)dxdy$$

f(x) being the probability density function and μ the mean income.[1]

The relative mean deviation is another measure of inequality which is widely mentioned in the literature. It is defined as

$$R = \frac{1}{2\mu} \int_0^\infty |x-\mu| f(x)dx. \tag{3}$$

The main drawback of this measure is that it is completely insensitive to transfers of income among individuals on one side of the mean income.

The coefficient of variation as a measure of dispersion, suggested by Pearson, is defined as

$$C = \frac{\sigma}{2\mu} \tag{4}$$

where σ is the standard deviation of the distribution. This measure is equally sensitive to transfers at all levels of income.

Theil [1967] proposed two inequality measures that are based on the notion of entropy in information theory. These measures have gained popularity because of their

---

[1]For welfare implications of the Gini index see Sen [1973] and Kakwani [1980].

decomposability property. Shorrocks [1980] has derived the entire class of measures which are decomposable. These measures are given by

$$I_c = \frac{1}{c(c-1)}\left[\frac{m_c}{\mu^c} - 1\right],\ c \neq 0,1$$
$$I_0 = \log(\mu) - \log(g) \tag{5}$$
$$I_1 = \frac{v}{\mu} - \log(\mu)$$

where

$$\log(g) = E(\log x) = \int_0^\infty \log x\ f(x)dx$$
$$m_c = E(x^c) = \int_0^\infty x^c f(x)dx$$
$$v = E(x\log x) = \int_0^\infty x\ \log x\ f(x)dx,$$

g being the geometric mean of the distribution, I_0 and I_1 are the two inequality measures proposed by Theil.

Atkinson [1970] proposed a class of inequality measures which are derived from the notion of the utility function. He assumed that the social welfare function is utilitarian and that every individual has exactly the same utility function. His class of measures under the assumption that the individual utility function is homothetic is given by

$$A(\varepsilon) = 1 - \frac{1}{\mu}[m_{1-\varepsilon}]^{\frac{1}{1-\varepsilon}},\ \varepsilon \neq 1, \tag{6}$$

where ε is a measure of the degree of inequality aversion or the relative sensitivity to income transfers at different income levels. The larger the value of ε, the greater weight is attached to the individuals at the lower end of the distribution. If ε = 0, it reflects an inequality neutral attitude, in which case the society does not care about the inequality at all. When ε = 1.0,

Atkinson's measure is given by

$$A(1.0) = 1 - \frac{g}{\mu}$$

where g given by

$$\log(g) = \int_0^\infty \log x \, f(x)dx$$

is the geometric mean of the distribution.

3. The Asymptotic Confidence Interval and Hypothesis Testing

Let $x_1, x_2, \ldots, x_n$ be a random sample of n observations drawn from a population with mean income μ and variance σ^2. Suppose θ is an inequality measure defined in terms of the population distribution and $\hat{\theta}$ is its sample estimate based on n observations, then it will be demonstrated below that $\sqrt{n}(\hat{\theta}-\theta)$ is asymptotically normally distributed with zero mean and variance $\sigma^2(\hat{\theta})$. If $\hat{\sigma}^2(\hat{\theta})$ is a consistent sample estimator of $\sigma^2(\hat{\theta})$, then

$$\eta = \sqrt{n}(\hat{\theta}-\theta)/\hat{\sigma}(\hat{\theta}) \tag{7}$$

is an asymptotic normal variate with zero mean and unit variance. Thus, η can be used to form distribution free confidence intervals for inequality measures.

Further, suppose $\hat{\theta}_1$ and $\hat{\theta}_2$ are estimates of an inequality measure θ computed on the basis of two independently drawn random samples of sizes n_1 and n_2, respectively. Let $\hat{\sigma}^2_1$ and $\hat{\sigma}^2_2$ be the sample estimators of the variances of $\sqrt{n_1}\hat{\theta}_1$ and $\sqrt{n_2}\hat{\theta}_2$, respectively, then the statistic

$$\eta^* = \frac{\hat{\theta}_1 - \hat{\theta}_2}{\sqrt{\dfrac{\hat{\sigma}^2_1}{n_1} + \dfrac{\hat{\sigma}^2_2}{n_2}}} \tag{8}$$

has an asymptotic normal distribution with zero mean and unit variance. Thus, η^* can be used to test the null hypothesis that the observed inequality differences in any two samples are statistically significant.

4. Hypothesis Testing Based on the Lorenz Curve, Gini Index and Relative Mean Deviation

Lorenz curve

Let x_p be the income level corresponding to the pth percentile of the distribution and $\hat{x}_p$ be the corresponding sample estimate, then for a sample $x_1, x_2,...,x_n$, defining

$$a_i = 1, \text{ if } x_i \leq \hat{x}_p$$
$$= 0, \text{ otherwise}$$

provides a sample estimate of the Lorenz curve ordinate L(p) as

$$\hat{L}(p) = \frac{p\bar{x}_p}{\bar{x}}$$

where

$$\bar{x}_p = \frac{\sum_{i=1}^{n} a_i x_i}{\sum_{i=1}^{n} a_i}$$

and $\bar{x}$ being the sample mean (noting that $\bar{x}_p = \bar{x}$ when $p = 1.0$). Thus, $\bar{x}_p$ is a sample estimate of $\mu L(p)/p$.

Beach and Davidson [1983] have proved that $\sqrt{n}(\hat{L}(p) - L(p))$ follows an asymptotic normal distribution with zero mean and variance

$$\sigma_L^2 = \frac{p}{\mu^2}[\lambda_p^2+(1-p)(x_p - \frac{\mu L(p)}{p})^2]+(\frac{L(p)}{\mu})^2\sigma^2-2(\frac{pL(p)}{\mu^2})[\lambda_p^2 + \frac{\mu\phi(p)}{p}(x_p - \frac{\mu L(p)}{p})]$$

where σ^2 is the variance of the entire x distribution and λ_p^2 is the variance of x conditional on $x < x_p$. Note that $\lambda_p^2 = \sigma^2$ when $p = 1.0$. A sample estimate of σ_L^2 is given by

$$\hat{\sigma}_L^2 = \frac{p}{\bar{x}^2}[\hat{\lambda}_p^2+(1-p)(x_p-\bar{x}_p)^2] + \left(\frac{p\bar{x}_p}{\bar{x}^2}\right)^2\hat{\sigma}^2 - 2\left(\frac{p^2\bar{x}_p}{\bar{x}^3}\right)[\hat{\lambda}_p^2$$

$$+(\bar{x}-\bar{x}_p)(\hat{x}_p-\bar{x}_p)]$$

where

$$\hat{\sigma}^2 = \frac{1}{n}\sum_{i=1}^{n} x_i^2 - \bar{x}^2$$

$$\hat{\lambda}_p^2 = \frac{\sum_{i=1}^{n} a_i x_i^2}{\sum_{i=1}^{n} a_i} - \bar{x}_p^2$$

It can be seen that $\sigma_L^2 = 0$ when $p = 1.0$ which happens because $L(p) = 1.0$ for $p = 1.0$.

Because p is fixed, the sample estimate of the inequality measure $\phi(p)$ in (1) will have the same variance as $\hat{L}(p)$ and, therefore,

$$\eta = \frac{\hat{\phi}(p) - \phi(p)}{(\hat{\sigma}_L/\sqrt{n})}$$

will be an asymptotic normal variate with zero mean and unit variance. Thus, for instance for $p = 0.40$, η provides distribution free statistical inference for an inequality measure based on an income share of the bottom 40 percent of the population.

Gini Index

Let us define

$$\Delta_x = \int_0^\infty |x-y| f(y)dy$$

which can also be written as

$$\Delta_x = 2xF(x) - 2\mu F_1(x) - (x-\mu),$$

where F(x) is the distribution function and $F_1(x)$ is given by

$$F_1(x) = \frac{1}{\mu} \int_0^x Xf(X)dX.$$

An unbiased estimator of Δ_x is given by

$$d_i = \frac{n}{(n-1)} [2(x_i - \bar{x}_i)p_i - (x_i - \bar{x})].$$

where $p_i = \frac{i}{n}$ and $\bar{x}_i$ is the mean of the first i individuals in the sample (when individuals are ranked in ascending order).

Since $E(\Delta_x) = \Delta$,

$$d = \frac{1}{n} \sum_{i=1}^{n} d_i$$

provides an unbiased estimator of Δ. Then by Hoeffding's [1948] theorem on order statistics, $\sqrt{n}(d-\Delta)$ has a limiting normal distribution with zero mean and variance

$$\sigma_d^2 = 4[\int_0^\infty \Delta_x^2 f(x)dx - \Delta^2]$$

A sample estimator of the Gini index is

$$\hat{G} = \frac{d}{2\bar{x}}.$$

Then applying the δ method given in Rao [1965], page 321, it follows that $\sqrt{n}(\hat{G}-G)$ has a limiting normal distribution with zero mean and variance

$$\sigma_G^2 = \frac{1}{4\mu^2} [\sigma_d^2 - 4Gn\ \mathrm{cov}(d,\bar{x}) + 4G^2\sigma^2]$$

where $\sigma^2 = \text{var}(x)$, $\text{cov}(d,\bar{x})$ is given by (Fraser [1957], page 258)

$$\text{cov}(\bar{x},d) = \frac{2}{n}\left[\int_0^\infty x\Delta_x f(x)dx - \mu\Delta\right].$$

Since σ_G^2 is in terms of population parameters, it has to be estimated from sample observations, a consistent estimator of which may be obtained as

$$\hat{\sigma}_G^2 = \frac{1}{4\bar{x}^2}[\sigma_d^2 - 4\hat{G}n\,\hat{\text{cov}}(d,\bar{x}) + 4\hat{G}^2\hat{\sigma}^2]$$

where

$$\hat{\sigma}^2 = \frac{1}{n}\sum_{i=1}^{n} x_i^2 - \bar{x}^2$$

$$\hat{\text{cov}}(\bar{x},d) = \frac{2}{n}\left[\frac{1}{n}\sum_{i=1}^{n} x_i d_i - \bar{x}d\right]$$

$$\hat{\sigma}_d^2 = 4\left[\frac{1}{n}\sum_{i=1}^{n} d_i^2 - d^2\right]$$

Relative Mean Deviation

The relative mean deviation may be estimated from a sample as

$$\hat{R} = \frac{1}{2\bar{x}}\left[\frac{1}{n}\sum_{i=1}^{n} |x_i - \bar{x}|\right]$$

which, as demonstrated by Gastwirth [1974], is asymptotically normally distributed with mean R and variance $\frac{1}{n}\sigma_R^2$, where

$$\sigma_R^2 = \frac{1}{\mu^2}[\sigma^2(F(\mu)-R)^2 + 2h^2(F(\mu)-R) + h^2-\mu^2R^2],$$

where

$$h^2 = \int_0^\mu (x-\mu)^2 f(x)dx$$

and $F(\mu)$ is the proportion of individuals having income less than or equal to μ.

Suppose in a sample of n observations, n_1 individuals have income less than or equal to the sample mean income $\bar{x}$. Then the sample estimates of $F(\mu)$ and h^2 may be obtained as

$$\hat{F}(\mu) = \frac{n_1}{n} \text{ and } \hat{h}^2 = \frac{1}{n} \sum_{i=1}^{n_1} (x_i - \bar{x})^2.$$

5. Asymptotic Distribution of a General Class of Inequality Measures

Except for inequality measures related to income shares, the Gini index and the relative mean deviation, all the remaining inequality measures considered in Section 3 can be written in a general form:

$$\theta = H[E(h(x)), \mu] \tag{9}$$

where $E(h(x))$ is the expected value of a function $h(x)$:

$$E[h(x)] = \int_0^\infty h(x)f(x)dx$$

A sample estimate of θ is given by

$$\hat{\theta} = H[\hat{E}(h(x)), \bar{x}] \tag{10}$$

where

$$\hat{E}(h(x)) = \frac{1}{n} \sum_{i=1}^{n} h(x_i)$$

and $\bar{x}$ being the sample mean.

Following Cramer [1946], it can be proved under fairly general conditions that $\sqrt{n}(\hat{\theta}-\theta)$ is asymptotically normally distributed with zero mean and variance

$$\text{var}(\hat{\theta}) = \text{var}[\hat{E}(h(x))]H_1^2 + 2\text{cov}[\hat{E}(h(x)),\bar{x}]H_1H_2 + \text{var}(\bar{x})H_2^2 \tag{11}$$

where var stands for variance and cov for covariance, and H_1 and H_2 are the values of the first order partial derivatives of H at the points E(h(x)) and μ, respectively. For this result to hold, the function H must be continuous and must have continuous derivatives of the first and second order with respect to its arguments. These conditions will always hold for all the inequality measures considered in this paper.[2]

Further, it can be verified that (Cramer, 1946):

$$\operatorname{var}\hat{E}(h(x)) = \frac{1}{n}[E(h(x))^2 - [E(h(x))^2]$$

$$\operatorname{var}(\bar{x}) = \frac{\sigma^2}{n}$$

$$\operatorname{cov}[\hat{E}(h(x)),\bar{x}] = \frac{1}{n}[E(xh(x) - \mu E(h(x))] \qquad (12)$$

then substituting these results in (11) yields the variance of the asymptotic distribution of $\hat{\theta}$.

6. Specific Inequality Measures

In this section we derive the asymptotic distributions of specific inequality measures using the general results presented in Section 5.

Coefficient of variation

A sample estimate of the coefficient of variation is

$$\hat{C} = \frac{1}{2}\sqrt{\frac{\hat{m}_2 - \bar{x}^2}{\bar{x}^2}}$$

where $\hat{m}_2 = \frac{1}{n}\sum_{i=1}^{n} x_i^2$, which is obtained from (10) when $h(x) = x^2$. It follows immediately from (11) and (12) that $\sqrt{n}(\hat{C}-C)$ is asymptotically normally distributed with zero mean and variance

[2]The result in (5.3) is also known as δ method (see Rao, 1973).

$$\text{var}(\hat{C}) = \frac{\mu^2(m_4 - m_2^2) + 4m_2(m_2^2 - \mu m_3)}{16\mu^4(m_2 - \mu^2)}$$

where $m_c = E(x^c)$, c = 2, 3 and 4. A sample estimate of $\text{var}(\hat{C})$ can be obtained by substituting, $\bar{x}$ for μ and $\hat{m}_c = \frac{1}{n}\sum_{i=1}^{n} x_i^c$ for m_c in (13), which immediately provides the standard error of $\hat{C}$.

The class of decomposable measures

A sample estimate of I_c in (5) is given by

$$\hat{I}_c = \frac{1}{c(c-1)}\left[\frac{\hat{m}_c}{\bar{x}^c} - 1\right], \; c \neq 0, 1$$

which is obtained from (9) when $h(x) = x^c$. Again, it follows from (11) and (12) that $\sqrt{n}(\hat{I}_c - I_c)$ is asymptotically normally distributed with zero mean and variance

$$\frac{1}{c^2(c-1)^2\mu^{2c}}[m_{2c} - m_c^2] + \frac{m_c^2\,\sigma^2}{(c-1)^2\mu^{2c+2}} - \frac{2m_c(m_{c+1} - \mu m_c)}{c(c-1)^2\mu^{2c+1}}$$

Next, we consider Theil's two inequality measures I_0 and I_1, the sample estimates of which are

$$\hat{I}_0 = \log\bar{x} - \log(\hat{g})$$

and

$$\hat{I}_1 = \frac{\hat{v}}{\bar{x}} - \log\bar{x}$$

where $\log(\hat{g}) = \frac{1}{n}\sum_{i=1}^{n} \log x_i$ (14)

and

$$\hat{v} = \frac{1}{n}\sum_{i=1}^{n} x_i \log x_i \qquad (15)$$

Because $\hat{I}_0$ and $\hat{I}_1$ can be obtained from (10) by substituting $h(x) = \log x$ and $h(x) = x\log x$, respectively. It immediately follows from (11) and (12) that $\sqrt{n}(\hat{I}_0 - I_0)$ and $\sqrt{n}(\hat{I}_1 - I_1)$ are asymptotically distributed with zero mean and variances.[3]

$$\mathrm{var}(\hat{I}_0) = \frac{\sigma^2}{\mu^2} + E(\log x)^2 - (\log(g))^2 - \frac{2}{\mu}(v - \mu\log(g))$$

and

$$\mathrm{var}(\hat{I}_1) = \frac{1}{\mu^2}[E(x\log x)^2 - v^2] + \frac{(\mu+v)^2\sigma^2}{\mu^4} -$$

$$\frac{2(\mu+v)}{\mu^3}[E(x^2\log x) - v\mu],$$

respectively. The sample estimates of g and v are given in (14) and (15), respectively and those of $E(x\log x)^2$ and $E(x^2\log x)$ are given by

$$\hat{E}(x\log x)^2 = \frac{1}{n}\sum_{i=1}^{n} (x_i \log x_i)^2$$

and

$$\hat{E}(x^2\log x) = \frac{1}{n}\sum_{i=1}^{n} x_i^2 \log x_i,$$

respectively.

Atkinson's Inequality Measure

A sample estimator of Atkinson's estimator is

$$\hat{A}(\varepsilon) = 1 - \frac{1}{\bar{x}}(\hat{m}_{1-\varepsilon})^{\frac{1}{1-\varepsilon}}, \quad \varepsilon \neq 1$$

where

---

[3]The asymptotic distributions of Theil's measures have been derived earlier (Nygärd and Sandström, 1981) by a rather complicated method. Moreover, their results are not presented in a fashion that makes them easily applicable to practical problems.

$$\hat{m}_{1-\varepsilon} = \frac{1}{n}\sum_{i=1}^{n} x_i^{1-\varepsilon} \tag{16}$$

Because this class of inequality measures belongs to the more general class (Section 5) and can be obtained from (10) when $h(x) = x^{1-\varepsilon}$, it follows that $\sqrt{n}(\hat{A}(\varepsilon) - A(\varepsilon))$ is asymptotically normally distributed with zero mean and variance

$$\frac{1}{\mu^2(1-\varepsilon)^2}(m_{1-\varepsilon})^{\frac{2\varepsilon}{1-\varepsilon}}(m_{2-2\varepsilon} - m_{1-\varepsilon}^2)$$

$$+ \frac{1}{\mu^4}(m_{1-\varepsilon})^{\frac{2}{1-\varepsilon}}\sigma^2 - \frac{2(m_{1-\varepsilon})^{\frac{1+\varepsilon}{1-\varepsilon}}}{\mu^3(1-\varepsilon)}(m_{2-\varepsilon} - \mu m_{1-\varepsilon}).$$

the sample estimate of which is given by (16). For $\varepsilon = 1.0$, a sample estimator of Atkinson's measure is given by

$$\hat{A}(1.0) = 1 - \frac{\hat{g}}{\bar{x}},$$

where

$$\log(\hat{g}) = \frac{1}{n}\sum_{i=1}^{n}\log x_i.$$

It can be easily shown that

$$\hat{A}(1.0) = 1 - e^{-\hat{I}_0}$$

where $\hat{I}_0$ is an estimator of Theil's first inequality measure. This equation gives

$$\mathrm{var}(\hat{A}(1.0)) = e^{-2I_0}\mathrm{var}(I_0)$$

which immediately provides the standard error of Atkinson's measure for $\varepsilon = 1.0$.

5. Application of Methodology to Côte D'Ivoire

The methodology discussed in the paper is applied to the data obtained from the Côte d'Ivoire Living Standards Survey, which was conducted by the World Bank's Living Standards Unit and the Direction de la Statistique, Ministère de l'Economic et des Finances of the Republic of Côte d'Ivoire.

In order to analyze inequality, we need to measure the economic welfare of each individual in the society. Although income is widely used to measure economic welfare, it has many serious drawbacks.[4] One of the major drawback of using income as a measure of economic welfare is that it is likely to have substantial fluctuations which are averaged out in the long run. Therefore, it has been suggested that consumption is a better indicator of the actual economic position of a household than is its current income.

In this paper we used per capita adjusted consumption as a measure of economic welfare. This measure constructed by Glewwe [1987] takes into account the imputed value of owner–occupied dwellings, depreciated value of consumer durables and regional price variations. In order to take into account the differing needs of various household members, Glewwe divided the total household consumption by the number of equivalent adults. In his formulation of equivalent adults, children were given smaller weight than adults; children less than seven years old were given a weight of 0.2, children between the ages of seven and thirteen were given a weight of 0.3 and children between the ages of thirteen and seventeen were given a weight of 0.5.

---

[4]For a detailed discussion of this issue; see Kakwani [1986].

The estimated values of various inequality measures along with their standard errors (derived in the previous section) are presented in columns 1 and 2 of Table 1. The last column in the table gives the numerical value of the statistic η as defined in (7). This statistic follows an asymptotic normal distribution with zero mean and unit standard deviation. If η exceeds 1.96, it means that the hypothesis of zero inequality is rejected at the 5% level of significance. This method is valid subject to the condition that our samples are large. In practice, it is often difficult to know whether our samples are so large that these large sample approximations are valid. However, the approximation is usually good for samples larger than 30 (Cramer [1946], page 454). Since our analysis of inequality is based on sample sizes larger than 250, the statistical inference based on asymptotic distributions is appropriate.

It can be seen from the table that the values of η are considerably larger than 1.96 which leads to the obvious conclusion that a large inequality exists in the distribution of economic welfare in Côte d'Ivoire. However, an important observation to be made is that the numerical values of η differ considerably for different inequality measures. The magnitude of η indicates how large the standard error of an inequality measure is relative to its value. Thus, the larger the value of η the greater is the precision with which the inequality measure can be estimated from a given sample. It is observed that among all the inequality measures presented in the table, the Gini index gives the smallest confidence interval relative to its value. Theil's second inequality measure performs worst on the basis of this criterion. Thus, these observations tend to suggest that the η statistic provides an additional criterion for selecting an inequality measure.[5]

Table 2 presents inequality comparisons by sex of household head. In the sample 7.9 percent of households were headed by women. It is interesting to note that the mean consumption (adjusted) of female–headed households was found to be twenty five percent larger than those of male–headed households. The difference between the mean consumption of the two groups of households was found to be statistically highly significant. This is a surprising result because in many developing countries female–headed households are often poorer than those headed by males. Part of the explanation of the situation in Côte d'Ivoire has been provided by Glewwe [1987] who observed that female–headed households are disproportionately located in Abidjan and other urban areas which are considerably richer than the rural areas.

The numerical results in Table 2 tend to suggest that inequality of consumption among female–headed households is lower than that among male–headed households. For instance the Gini index among female–headed households has a value of 42.16 whereas among male–headed households its value is 42.84. The difference in inequality appears to be even larger when we compare the values of coefficient of variation. In order to test whether the observed inequality differences are statistically significant we need to compute the values of η^* given in (8).

---

[5]The problem of choice of an inequality measures among several alternatives has been extensively discussed in the literature; see for instance Atkinson [1970], Sheshinski [1972], Newbery [1970], Dasgupta, Sen and Starrett [1973], Rothschild and Stiglitz [1973], Sen [1973] and Kakwani [1980].

η^* follows asymptotic normal distribution with zero mean and unit variance. If the absolute value of η^* is less than 1.96, we cannot reject the null hypothesis of equal inequality at the 5% significance level. The numerical values of η^* presented in the last column of Table 2 lead us to conclude that inequality differences between the female and male–headed households are statistically not significant. This conclusion is valid for all the inequality measures presented in the table. Thus, the observed differences in the values of inequality measures may lead to misleading conclusions without statistical tests.

Côte d'Ivoire may be divided into five regions, viz, Abidjan, other urban, West Forest, East Forest and Savannah. Table 3 presents the mean adjusted consumption of each region along with its standard error. It can be seen that Abidjan (the colonial capital and largest city) has the highest adjusted per capita mean consumption; almost twice that of the whole population. Other urban areas are also relatively wealthy. The remaining three rural areas are relatively very poor. The lowest average consumption is in Savannah, almost half that of the whole population, followed by the densely populated East Forest region.

In order to see if the mean consumption differs significantly between the regions, the statistics given by

$$\xi_{ij} = \frac{\bar{x}_i - \bar{x}_j}{\sqrt{\frac{\sigma_i^2}{n_i} + \frac{\sigma_j^2}{n_j}}},$$

where $\bar{x}_i$ is the per capita adjusted mean consumption of the ith

region with its estimated variance $\frac{\hat{\sigma}^2_i}{n_i}$, was computed. The numerical values are presented in Table 4. Since ξ_{ij} follows an asymptotic normal distribution with zero mean and unit variance, its value greater than 1.96 will indicate a significant average consumption differences between the regions. It can be seen from the table that all the mean consumption differences are significant at the 5% level. Thus, the observed differences in mean consumption between the regions are not due to sampling errors. These are some other factors which must be analyzed to explain such wide differences.

Since welfare depends on both the size and distribution of consumption, it will be interesting to see how inequality varies between the regions. The numerical values of various inequality measures along with their standard errors are presented for each region in Tables 5a and 5b. These results suggest that inequality varies widely among the various regions. The highest inequality is observed in Abidjan, the wealthiest region in terms of per capita average consumption. The lowest inequality is observed in the West Forest region, which has relatively recent settlements and is less heavily populated than the East Forest region (Glewwe [1985]).

To test whether observed inequality differences between the regions are statistically significant, we computed the values of η^* given in (8) for all possible pairs of regions. The numerical values are presented in Table 6. The conclusions emerging from the table are summarized below.

First, the significance of inequality differences among the regions depends on which inequality measure is selected. For instance, comparing Abidjan and Other Urban cities (see column 1, Table 6) we find that inequality differences are significant at the 5 percent level on the basis of the Gini index, Theil's first inequality measure I_0 and all measures of the Atkinson family, though the remaining measures show insignificant differences. Thus, we cannot infer that the inequality differences between these two regions are statistically significant or insignificant.

The fact that some measures show significant differences in inequality between two groups while others do not, may depend on what the different measures judge inequality to be. For example, one that is very sensitive at the positive tail of the distribution may find significant differences because one of the two groups contain some rich people, although a measure that is insensitive to positive outliers may judge that the differences in inequality are insignificant. Thus, if we think a difference in inequality exists it depends on what we judge inequality to be, as reflected in the inequality measure that most matches our value judgements.

Second, on the basis of the Gini index, the inequality differences between Abidjan, Savannah and East Forest regions are statististically insignificant. Similarly, the inequality differences between Other Urban areas and West Forest are statistically not significant. The statistically significant inequality differences are observed between Abidjan and Other Urban areas; Abidjan and West Forest; and West Forest and East Forest. From these observations we cannot make a general inference that the inequality in urban areas is higher than that in rural areas. Also, there is no significant relationship between inequality and mean consumption levels of the regions. The inequality difference between the richest region of Abidjan and the poorest region of Savannah is statistically not significant.

6. Some Concluding Remarks

The main objective of this paper has been to provide distribution free statistical inference for income or consumption inequality. The paper derives the results in a simple manner and presents them so that they are easily applicable to empirical work.

The empirical application to Côte D'Ivoire suggests that observed differences in the values of inequality measures may lead to misleading conclusions without statistical tests. The standard errors of the estimated inequality measures can be so large that the observed differences in the values of inequality measures can be statistically insignificant. Further, some measures may show significant differences in inequality while others may show insignificant differences. Thus, alternative inequality measures may lead to conflicting conclusions. This is an important finding suggesting that one should select an appropriate measure before analyzing inequality differences between populations.

Since inequality measures are estimated on the basis of sample observations, the importance of using statistical tests cannot be over–emphasized. However, these tests are based on the assumption that the samples used are representative of the populations they are drawn from. In practice this assumption may be violated due to non–response errors.[6] Moreover, non–sampling errors may be so large that it makes little sense to worry about sampling errors. In the future work greater attention should be paid to the non–sampling errors.

[6]The Living Standards Survey Data for Côte d'Ivoire, 1985 used in the present paper has a 92 percent response rate, therefore, the possibility of large non–sampling errors is very small.

Table 1:

Inequality Measures and Their Standard Errors:

Cote D'Ivoire 1985

Inequality measure	Value of Inequality Measure	Standard Error	η
Income share of bottom			
10 percent	2.02	.08	25.25
20 percent	5.36	.18	29.78
30 percent	9.84	.29	33.93
40 percent	15.34	.41	37.41
Gini index	42.87	1.06	40.44
Relative Mean Deviation	30.77	1.19	25.86
Coefficient of Variation	52.93	3.08	17.19
Theil's Inequality Measures			
I_0	31.61	1.57	20.13
I_1	34.45	2.29	15.04
Atkinson's Inequality Measures			
A(1.0)	27.10	1.14	23.77
A(1.5)	36.92	1.29	28.62
A(2.0)	45.27	1.37	33.04

Table 2:
Inequality Comparison by Sex of Household Head: Côte D'Ivoire, 1985

Inequality Measures	Female–Headed Households			Male–Headed Households			
	Value of Inequality Measure	Standard Error	η	Value of Inequality Measure	Standard Error	η	η^*
Income share of bottom 40%	15.67	1.29	12.15	15.32	0.43	35.63	0.26
Gini index	42.16	2.87	14.69	42.84	1.10	38.95	–0.22
Relative Mean Deviation	30.85	4.02	7.67	30.71	1.25	24.57	0.03
Coefficient of Variation	46.80	6.04	7.75	53.34	3.32	16.07	–0.95

Table 2 continued

Inequality Measures	Female–Headed Households			Male–Headed Households			
	Value of Inequality Measure	Standard Error	η	Value of Inequality Measure	Standard Error	η	η^*
Theil's inequality measures							
I_0	30.26	4.25	7.12	31.58	1.67	18.91	–0.29
I_1	31.39	5.13	6.12	34.57	2.46	14.05	–0.56
Atkinson's measures							
A(1.0)	26.11	3.14	8.32	27.08	1.22	22.20	–0.29
A(1.5)	35.97	3.85	9.34	36.87	1.36	27.11	–0.22
A(2.0)	44.44	4.41	10.08	45.20	1.44	31.39	–0.16
Adjusted per capita mean consumption	406.96	34.21	11.90	337.64	9.47	35.65	1.95*

Table 3:

Mean Consumption and Its Standard Error by Region: Côte D'Ivoire, 1985

Region	Mean Consumption	Standard Error	$\eta = \dfrac{\text{mean income}}{\text{standard error}}$
Abidjan	614.39	32.11	19.13
Other urban	392.23	17.25	22.74
West Forest	295.96	13.00	22.77
East Forest	244.63	11.49	21.29
Savannah	175.40	8.19	21.42
All regions	341.85	9.14	37.40

Table 4:

Statistics for Testing Significance of Differences in Mean Income Between Regions: Côte D'Ivoire, 1985

Region	Abidjan	Other Urban	West	East	Savannah
Abidjan	0.0	6.09	9.19	10.84	13.25
Other urban	−6.09	0.0	4.46	7.12	11.36
West Forest	−9.19	−4.46	0.0	2.96	7.85
East Forest	−10.84	−7.12	−2.96	0.0	4.91
Savannah	−13.25	−11.36	−7.85	−4.91	0.0

Table 5a:

Inequality Within Urban Regions: Côte D'Ivoire, 1985

Inequality Measures	Abidjan			Other Urban		
	Value	Standard Error	η	Value	Standard Error	η
Income share of bottom 40%	16.94	0.86	19.70	19.06	0.79	24.13
Gini index	40.93	1.92	21.32	35.15	1.88	18.70
Relative Mean Deviation	30.06	2.67	11.26	25.52	2.55	10.01
Coefficient of Variation	47.76	3.28	14.56	40.12	6.57	6.11
Theil's Measures						
I_0	27.79	2.64	10.53	20.40	2.28	8.95
I_1	30.90	3.22	9.60	22.15	3.60	6.15
Atkinson's Measures						
A(1.0)	24.26	2.00	12.13	18.45	1.86	9.92
A(1.5)	32.66	2.39	13.67	25.67	2.18	11.78
A(2.0)	39.60	2.62	15.11	32.01	2.43	13.17

Table 5b:
Inequality Within Rural Regions: Côte d'Ivoire, 1985

Inequality Measure	West Forest			East Forest		
	Value	Standard Error	η	Value	Standard Error	η
Income share of bottom 40%	20.92	0.90	23.24	18.12	0.83	21.83
Gini index	31.71	1.88	16.87	37.32	2.03	18.38
Relative Mean Deviation	22.60	3.26	6.93	26.74	2.63	10.17
Coefficient of Variation	33.88	3.45	9.82	44.63	4.56	9.79
Theil's Measures						
I_0	17.03	2.02	8.43	23.44	2.55	9.19
I_1	17.73	2.54	6.98	26.08	3.60	7.24
Atkinson's Measures						
A(1.0)	15.66	1.70	9.21	20.89	2.02	10.34
A(1.5)	22.40	2.18	10.28	28.78	2.39	12.04
A(2.0)	28.71	2.57	11.17	35.79	2.68	13.35

Table 5b concluded

Inequality Measure	Savannah		
	Value	Standard Error	η
Income share of bottom 40%	17.33	0.78	22.22
Gini index	37.46	1.80	20.81
Relative Mean Deviation	27.21	2.60	10.47
Coefficient of Variation	40.63	4.52	8.99
Theil's Measures			
I_0	23.60	2.30	10.26
I_1	24.36	3.14	7.76
Atkinson's Measures			
A(1.0)	21.02	1.81	11.61
A(1.5)	29.48	2.18	13.52
A(2.0)	36.84	2.43	15.16

Table 6:

Testing for Significance of Inequality Differences Between Regions:
Côte d'Ivoire, 1985

Inequality Measures	Abidjan Other Urban	Abidjan West Forest	Abidjan East Forest	Abidjan Savannah	Other Urban West Forest	Other Urban East Forest	Other Urban Savannah	West Forest East Forest	West Forest Savannah	East Forest Savannah
Income share of bottom 40% population	−1.81	−3.20	−0.99	−0.34	−1.55	0.82	1.56	2.29	3.01	0.69
Gini index	2.15*	3.43*	1.29	1.32	1.29	−0.78	−0.89	−2.03*	−2.21*	−0.05
Relative Mean Deviation	1.23	1.77	0.89	0.76	0.71	−0.33	−0.46	−0.99	−1.11	−0.13
Coefficient of Variation	1.04	2.92*	0.56	1.28	0.84	−0.56	−0.06	−1.88*	−1.19	0.62
Theil's Inequality Measures										
I_0	2.12*	3.24*	1.19	1.20	1.11	−0.89	−0.99	−1.97*	−2.15	−0.05
I_1	1.81	3.21*	1.00	1.45	1.00	−0.77	−0.46	−1.90*	−1.64	0.36
Atkinson's Measures										
A(1.0)	2.13*	3.28*	1.19	1.20	1.11	−0.89	−0.99	−1.98	−2.16*	−0.05
A(1.5)	2.16*	3.17*	1.15	0.98	1.06	−0.96	−1.24	−1.97	−2.30*	−0.22
A(2.0)	2.12*	2.97	1.02	0.77	0.93	−1.04	−1.41	−1.91	−2.30*	−0.29

*Inequality difference is significant at 5% level.

References

Ahluwalia, M.S. [1974], "Income Inequality: Some Dimensions of the Problem", in *Redistribution with Growth*, Oxford University Press, New York.

Atkinson, A.B. [1970], "On the Measurement of Inequality", *Journal of Economic Theory*, Vol. 2.

Beach, C.M. and R. Davidson [1983], "Distribution–Free Statistical Inference with Lorenz Curves and Income Shares", *Review of Economic Studies*, L, pp. 723–735.

Cramer, H. [1946], *Mathematical Methods of Statistics*, Princeton: Princeton University Press.

Dasgupta, P., A.K. Sen and D. Starrett [1973], "Notes on the Measurement of Inequality", *Journal of Economic Theory*, vol. 6, pp. 180–87.

Fraser, [1957], *Non–parametric Methods in Statistics*, New York: Wiley.

Gastwirth, J.L. [1974], "Large Sample Theory of Some Measures of Inequality", *Econometrica*, Vol. 42, pp. 191–196.

Glewwe, Paul [1987], "The Distribution of Welfare in the Republic of Côte d'Ivoire in 1985", Living Standards Measurement Study Working Paper No. 29. The World Bank, Washington, D.C.

Kakwani, N. [1980], *Inequality and Poverty: Methods of Estimation and Policy Applications*, Oxford University Press, New York.

Kakwani, N. [1986], *Analyzing Redistribution Policies: A Study Using Australian Data*, Cambridge University Press, New York.

Newbery, D. [1970], "A Theorem on the Measurement of Inequality", *Journal of Economic Theory*, Vol. 2, pp. 264–66.

Nygård, F. and A. Sandström [1981], *Measuring Income Inequality*, Almqvist & Wiksell International, Stockholm, Sweden.

Rao, C.R. [1965], *Linear Statistical Inference and Its Applications*, John Wiley & Sons, New York.

Rothschild, M. and J.E. Stiglitz [1973], "Some Further Results on the Measurement of Inequality", *Journal of Economic Theory*, Vol. 6, pp. 188–204.

Sen, A.K. [1973], *On Economic Inequality*, Oxford: Clarendon Press.

Sheshinski, E. [1972], "Relations between a Social Welfare Function and the Gini Index of Inequality", *Journal of Economic Theory*, Vol. 4, pp. 98–100.

Sendler, W. [1979], "On Statistical Inference in Concentration Measurement", *Metrika*, Vol. 26, pp. 109–122.

Shorrocks, A.F. [1980], "The Class of Additively Decomposable Inequality Measures", *Econometrica*, Vol. 48.

Theil, H. [1967], *Economics and Information Theory*, Studies in Mathematical and Managerial Economics, Vol. 7, North–Holland, Amsterdam.

Restricted Reduced Forms, Forecasting and the GLSEM

Phoebus J. Dhrymes*
Department of Economics
Columbia University

Abstract

This paper examines the problem of forecasting from a dynamic simultaneous equations model through its final form representation. It derives the limiting distribution of the estimators of the structural parameters and those of the final form; thus, it obtains approximations for the distribution of actual forecasts, in a finite sample context, on the assumption that the sequence of exogenous variables, over the forecasting horizon, is correctly specified, that the model does not undergo structural change and that the basic structural errors are independent.

1 Introduction and Summary

The purpose of this paper is to revisit the subject of determining the uncertainty surrounding a forecast from the General Linear Structural Econometric Model (GLSEM). A first attempt in this direction is the

* This paper was completed during my tenure of an NSF/ASA/Census Senior Research Fellowship over the academic year 1988-89. I am deeply indebted to these organizations for their support. In addition, I would like to record my thanks to R.A.L.Carter, the coeditor of this volume, E.P. Howrey and to an anonymous referee for useful comments on an earlier version.

Needless to say, such individuals and organizations are in no way responsible for the opinions that are expressed in this paper, nor for any remaining errors.

paper by Goldberger, Nagar and Odeh [1961], (GNO), although the earlier paper by Klein [1960] is tangentially relevant. The contribution of GNO was to express the matrix of the reduced form of the GLSEM as a function of the structural matrices and then obtain the standard errors of the former using a Taylor series expansion about the true parameter(s). A subsequent paper by Hymans [1968] addressed the issue of confidence intervals in sets of (multivariate) regression models, i.e., systems of General Linear Models (GLM). The relevance of this to the topic at hand is disclosed by the observation that the **unrestricted reduced form** is simply a particular system of GLM. The matter of obtaining confidence intervals in the context of a single GLM was, by that time, a subject already well developed by statisticians. Since a system of GLM can formally be expressed as a single GLM, one could argue that, in this survey, we should have provided a much earlier reference such as, for example, Mandel [1958]. A paper by Feldstein [1971] allowed for the fact that we do not really know the values to be assumed by the predetermined (in the case of the GLSEM) or the regressor (in the case of GLM) variables. The operational implication he drew from this observation is that the confidence intervals derived ought to allow for the uncertainty (variances and covariances) of such variables and not merely for the uncertainty surrounding the structural or reduced form parameters. Since the "estimated" exogenous variables were **assumed to be independent** of the estimators of the structural parameters, the formal aspects of this problem are quite transparent. One might, also, argue that since the exogenous variables are chosen by a more informal fashion than are the values of the (unknown) parameters of the system, one would best serve the user of such information by making clear that one is making a **conditional forecast, given a certain sequence of exogenous variables**. A subsequent paper by Dhrymes [1973] has shown that the objective of the GNO paper could be easily accomplished by a simple rewriting of the relationship between the restricted reduced form (RRF) and the structural parameters. The paper showed that the RRF is, **asymptotically, a linear transformation** of the structural parameters and provided a ranking of the relative efficiencies of the various reduced form estimators, from the least squares (unrestrictred) estimator of the reduced form

(URF), to the restricted reduced forms induced by 2SLS (RRF(2SLS)), to those induced by 3SLS (RRF(3SLS)). Implicit in this development is the (asymptotic) distribution of forecasts. Schmidt [1973], using this framework, developed the limiting distribution of the various "multipliers", which are also, asymptotically, linear transformations of the structural parameters. Chow [1973] has provided means for computing multiperiod forecasts in a **Bayesian context**.

An ancillary topic which must also be addressed is that of the limiting distribution of simultaneous equations estimators, when the GLSEM is **dynamic**. This problem was first dealt with in Mann and Wald [1943], in the case where the model did not contain exogenous variables (beyond the constant term). The case where exogenous variables, beyond the constant term, are present was treated in Koopmans Rubin and Leipnik [1950]. While the basic results therein are correct, the method of proof leaves a great deal to be desired by the standards of this day. Thus, it is fair to say that a modern proof for this distribution does not exist in the literature of econometrics. A section of this paper will address this issue.

2 Formulation of the Problem and Notation

The GLSEM is well known and will not be recounted as to its basic characteristics and origins. On the other hand, we must set the notation and the framework in which we shall operate. The GLSEM may be represented as

$$y_{t.}B^* - x_{t.}C = u_{t.}, \quad t = 1, 2, \ldots, T, \tag{1}$$

where $y_{t.}$ is an m-element row vector containing the **jointly dependent variables**. Evidently, if no restrictions are placed on its parameters, the latter cannot be **identified**, i.e., they cannot be distinguished from arbitrary linear combinations thereof. Thus, we shall begin the formal discussion of the GLSEM on the assertion that we are able to impose sufficient **a priori** restrictions on B^* and C so as to make the model in (1) **identifiable**.

We further note that the vector of predetermined variables is given by

$$x_{t\cdot} = (y_{t-1\cdot},\ y_{t-2\cdot},\ \ldots,\ y_{t-k\cdot},\ p_{t\cdot}), \tag{2}$$

where $p_{t\cdot}$ is an s-element row vector of **exogenous variables.** [1]

The basic set of assumptions under which we shall operate is

(A.1) The matrix of exogenous variables

$$P = (p_{t\cdot})\ t = 1, 2, 3, \ldots T,\ T > s,$$

is of full rank and

$$(\text{p}) \lim_{T \to \infty} \frac{1}{T} P'P = M_{pp}$$

exists and is nonsingular (positive definite).

(A.2) The matrix B^* is nonsingular.

(A.3) All the equations of the system are identified by exclusion restrictions on the elements of B^* and C;

(A.4) The system is stable, i.e., the roots of the characteristic equation of the associated homogeneous vector difference equation are less than unity in absolute value.

(A.5) The structural errors, $u_{t\cdot} : t = 0,\ \pm 1,\ \pm 2,\ \pm 3, \ldots$, are a sequence of i.i.d. random vectors with $E(u'_{t\cdot}) = 0, Cov(u'_{t\cdot}) = \Sigma$, where Σ is positive definite (notation: $\Sigma > 0$). [2]

In addition we shall employ, throughout this discussion, the following conventions.

[1] Note that whether or not there are lagged values of the exogenous variables is of no consequence in this context and is not precluded by this notation. One simply renames lagged values as new variables.

[2] This implies that if the model had contained identities, they had been removed by substitution. The reader should also understand that the error process is **independent** of the **exogenous** variables since, in the literature of simultaneous equations systems, this property is an intrinsic characteristic of exogenous variables.

Convention 1. (Normalization Rule). In the ith equation it is possible to, and we do, set the coefficient of the variable y_{ti} equal to unity.

Remark 1. Convention 1 implies that

$$B^* = I - B \tag{3}$$

with

$$B = (b_{ij}), \quad b_{ii} = 0, \quad i, j = 1, 2, \ldots m.$$

Convention 2. (Enforcement of Exclusion Restrictions). Giving effect to (A-3), the ith equation contains $m_i (\leq m)$ endogenous and $G_i (\leq G)$ predetermined variables in its right hand side (i.e., as explanatory variables).

Remark 2. By Convention 2 the ith equation may be written as

$$y_{\cdot i} = Y_i \beta_{\cdot i} + X_i \gamma_{\cdot i} + u_{\cdot i}, \; i = 1, 2, \ldots, m.$$

where $Y = (y_{t\cdot})$, $X = (x_{t\cdot})$, $t = 1, 2, 3, \ldots T$, and Y_i is the submatrix of Y containing the T observations on the m_i current endogenous variables (other than y_{ti}) not excluded from it by (A-3). Similarly X_i is the submatrix of X containing the T observations on the G_i predetermined variables not excluded from the ith equation and $u_{\cdot i}$ is simply the ith column of U containing the structural errors of the ith equation. The T observations on the GLSEM can be written more compactly as

$$YB^* = XC + U, \quad Y = (y_{ti}), \quad X = (x_{tj}), \quad U = (u_{ti}). \tag{4}$$

Giving effect to Convention 1 we can write

$$B^* = I - B, \quad \text{such that} \quad b_{ii} = 0, \quad i = 1, 2, \ldots, m. \tag{5}$$

Giving effect to Convention 2, we can write the T observations relative to the ith structural equation as

$$y_{\cdot i} = Y_i \beta_{\cdot i} + X_i \gamma_{\cdot i} + u_{\cdot i} = Z_i \delta_{\cdot i} + u_{\cdot i} \tag{6}$$

where

$$Z_i = (Y_i, \; X_i), \quad \delta_{\cdot i} = (\beta'_{\cdot i}, \; \gamma'_{\cdot i})'. \tag{7}$$

We note that $\beta_{\cdot i}$, $\gamma_{\cdot i}$ are subvectors of the ith column of B and C, respectively, and moreover that the collection of vectors

$$\{\delta_{\cdot i} : i = 1, 2, \dots m,\} \tag{8}$$

represents the totality of the structural parameters that interests us. Often, however, we have to deal with the matrices B^*, B, C as such, and it would be very convenient to show, in a simple way, the relation between these matrices or their columns and the collection of structural parameters as exhibited in (7).

Definition 1. (Partial Selection and Exclusion Matrices). Let L_{1i}, L_{2i} be permutations of m_i of the columns of I_m and G_i of the columns of I_G respectively, such that

$$YL_{1i} = Y_i, \; XL_{2i} = X_i, \; i = 1, 2, \dots m. \tag{9}$$

Moreover, let L_{1i}^* be a permutation of the columns of I_m, resulting when we have eliminated from the latter its ith column as well as the columns in L_{1i} and let L_{2i}^* be a permutation of the columns of I_G, when we have eliminated from the latter the columns appearing in L_{2i}. Thus,

$$YL_{1i}^* = Y_i^*, \quad XL_{2i}^* = X_i^*, \tag{10}$$

produce the matrices of observations on the current endogenous (Y_i^*) and predetermined (X_i^*) variables, **excluded** from the ith equation. The matrices L_{1i}, L_{2i} are said to be the **partial selection matrices**, and the matrices L_{1i}^*, L_{2i}^* are said to be the **partial exclusion matrices**, relative to the ith structural equation. Finally, if by $e_{\cdot i}$ we denote a suitably dimensioned vector, all of whose elements are zero except the ith, which is unity and put $L_{1i}^0 = (e_{\cdot i}, L_{1i})$, we have that $YL_{1i}^0 = (y_{\cdot i}, Y_i)$. The matrix L_{1i}^0 is said to be the **augmented partial selection matrix** relative to the ith equation.

Other useful permutation matrices are given in

Definition 2. (Exclusion, Selection and Augmented Matrices). The $(m+G) \times (m_i^* + G_i^*)$ matrix,

$$L_i^* = \begin{bmatrix} L_{1i}^* & 0 \\ 0 & L_{2i}^* \end{bmatrix}, \; i = 1, 2, \dots m,$$

where $m_i^* = m - m_i - 1$ and $G_i^* = G - G_i$, is said to be the **exclusion matrix**, relative to the ith structural equation. The $(m+G) \times (m_i+G_i)$ matrix,

$$L_i = \begin{bmatrix} L_{1i} & 0 \\ 0 & L_{2i} \end{bmatrix}, \quad i = 1, 2, \ldots m,$$

is said to be the **selection matrix** relative to the ith structural equation. The $(m+G) \times (m_i + G_i + 1)$ matrix,

$$L_i^0 = \begin{bmatrix} L_{1i}^0 & 0 \\ 0 & L_{2i} \end{bmatrix}, \quad i = 1, 2, \ldots m,$$

is said to be the **augmented selection matrix** relative to the ith structural equation.

Proposition 1. The following statements are true

i. $rank(L_{1i}) = m_i, \quad rank(L_{2i}) = G_i, \qquad i = 1, 2, \ldots m;$

ii. $rank(L_{1i}^0) = m_i + 1, \quad rank(L_{1i}^*) = m_i^* = m - m_i - 1;$

iii. $rank(L_{2i}^*) = G_i^* = G - G_i;$

iv. $b_{\cdot i} = L_{1i}\beta_{\cdot i}, \; c_{\cdot i} = L_{2i}\gamma_{\cdot i}$ or $\beta_{\cdot i} = L_{1i}' b_{\cdot\cdot i}, \quad \gamma_{\cdot\cdot i} = L_{2i}' c_{\cdot\cdot i};$

v. $\beta_{\cdot i}^0 = L_{1i}^{0\prime} b_{\cdot i}^* = \begin{pmatrix} b_{ii}^* \\ -\beta_{\cdot i} \end{pmatrix}$

Proof: The validity of i., ii. and iii. is obvious by construction. As for iv. and v., we note that exhibiting the ith structural equation of (4) yields

$$y_{\cdot i} = Yb_{\cdot i} + Xc_{\cdot i} + u_{\cdot i}. \tag{11}$$

Invoking the restrictions imposed by (A-3) yields (6). Using the definitions in (9) we may rewrite (6) as

$$y_{\cdot i} = YL_{1i}\beta_{\cdot i} + XL_{2i}\gamma_{\cdot i} + u_{\cdot i}. \tag{12}$$

Noting that the columns of L_{1i} and L_{2i} are **orthonormal** and comparing with (11), we have the desired result for iv. Similarly, without imposing the normalization convention we may write the ith structural equation as

$$Yb_{\cdot i}^* = Xc_{\cdot i} + u_{\cdot i}. \tag{13}$$

Put $Y_{\cdot i}^{0} = (y_{\cdot i},\ Y_i)$, and rewrite equation (11), after "undoing" the normalization convention, as

$$Y_i^0 \beta_{\cdot i}^0 = Y_i^0 \begin{pmatrix} b_{ii}^* \\ -\beta_{\cdot i} \end{pmatrix} = Y L_{1i}^0 \beta_{\cdot i}^0 = X L_{2i} \gamma_{\cdot i} + u_{\cdot i}. \tag{14}$$

Noting that the columns of L_{1i}^0 are also **orthonormal** and comparing with (13) we have the desired result for v.

q.e.d.

Occasionally, we shall also have to deal with the entities

$$A = \begin{pmatrix} B^* \\ -C \end{pmatrix}, \quad a_{\cdot i} = \begin{pmatrix} b_{\cdot i}^* \\ -c_{\cdot i} \end{pmatrix}, \quad \delta_{\cdot i}^0 = \begin{pmatrix} b_{ii}^* \\ -\delta_{\cdot i} \end{pmatrix}, \tag{15}$$

as well as a number of constructs from the selection matrices noted earlier. Specifically

$$\begin{aligned}
\bar{L}_{1i} &= (L_{1i},\ 0), \quad \bar{L}_{2i} = (0,\ L_{2i}), \quad L_i = \begin{pmatrix} \bar{L}_{1i} \\ \bar{L}_{2i} \end{pmatrix} \\
\bar{L}_{1i}^0 &= (L_{1i}^0,\ 0), \quad \bar{L}_{2i}^0 = (0,\ L_{2i}), \quad L_i^0 = \begin{pmatrix} \bar{L}_{1i}^0 \\ \bar{L}_{2i}^0 \end{pmatrix} \\
\bar{L}_{1i}^* &= (L_{1i}^*,\ 0), \quad \bar{L}_{2i}^* = (0,\ L_{2i}), \quad L_i^* = \begin{pmatrix} \bar{L}_{1i}^* \\ \bar{L}_{2i}^* \end{pmatrix} \\
L &= \mathrm{diag}(L_1,\ L_2, \ldots, L_m), \quad L^0 = \mathrm{diag}(L_1^0,\ L_2^0, \ldots, L_m^0), \\
L^* &= \mathrm{diag}(L_1^*,\ L_2^*, \ldots, L_m^*), \quad \delta^0 = (\delta_{\cdot 1}^{0\prime},\ \delta_{\cdot 2}^{0\prime}, \ldots,\ \delta_{\cdot m}^{0\prime})' \\
\bar{L}_1^0 &= \mathrm{diag}(\bar{L}_{11}^0,\ \bar{L}_{12}^0, \ldots, \bar{L}_{1m}^0), \quad \bar{L}_2^0 = \mathrm{diag}(\bar{L}_{21}^0, \bar{L}_{22}^0,\ \ldots,\ \bar{L}_{2m}^0).
\end{aligned} \tag{16}$$

An immediate consequence of the preceding is

Proposition 2. Given the definitions in (16), the following statements are true:

i. $rank(L_i^*) = m_i^* + G_i^*,\ \ rank(L_i) = m_i + G_i,\ \ rank(L_i^0) = m_i + G_i + 1$;

ii. $b_{\cdot i}^* = L_{1i}^0 \beta_{\cdot i}^0 \qquad a_{\cdot i} = L_i^0 \delta_{\cdot i}^0$

iii. $vec(A) = L^0 \delta^0, \quad vec(B^*) = \bar{L}_1^0 \delta^0, \quad vec(C) = -\bar{L}_2^0 \delta^0$.

Proof: The first statement is true by construction. As for the second statement, giving effect to (A.3) and Convention 2 we may write the ith equation of (4),

$$Yb^*_{\cdot i} = Xc_{\cdot i} + u_{\cdot i}, \tag{17}$$

as

$$Y_i^0 \beta^0_{\cdot i} = X_i \gamma_{\cdot i} + u_{\cdot i}. \tag{18}$$

Using Proposition 1 and (16) we can rewrite (18) as

$$Y L^0_{1i} \beta^0_{\cdot i} = X L_{2i} \gamma_{\cdot i} + u_{\cdot i}.$$

Comparing with (17) we conclude,

$$b^*_{\cdot i} = L^0_{1i} \beta^0_{\cdot i} = L^0_{1i} \begin{pmatrix} b^*_{ii} \\ -\beta_{\cdot i} \end{pmatrix}$$

By Convention 1, $b^*_{ii} = 1$, although this is immaterial in the present context. Similarly, (17) and (18) may be rewritten, respectively, as

$$Za_{\cdot i} = u_{\cdot i}, \quad ZL^0_i \delta^0_{\cdot i} = u_{\cdot i}. \tag{19}$$

But equation (19) implies that $a_{\cdot i} = L^0_i \delta^0_{\cdot i}$, which concludes the proof of part ii.

As for the proof of part iii. we note that the ith subvector of $L^0 \delta^0$ is given by $L^0_i \delta^0_{\cdot i}$; the ith subvector of $\overline{L}^0_1 \delta^0$ is given by $\overline{L}^0_{1i} \delta^0_{\cdot i} = L^0_{1i} \beta^0_{\cdot i}$, while the ith subvector of $\overline{L}^0_2 \delta^0$ is given by $\overline{L}^0_{2i} \delta^0_{\cdot i} = -L_{2i} \gamma_{\cdot i}$. Hence the validity of iii. follows from part ii. and Proposition 1.

q.e.d.

3 Derivation of the 2SLS and 3SLS Estimators

Given the assumptions (A.1) through (A.5), it maybe shown that $X'X$ is positive definite and, also, that

$$\operatorname{p}\lim_{\to \infty} \frac{X'X}{T} = M > 0.$$

Furthermore, there exists a **nonsingular matrix,** R, such that

$$X'X = RR'. \tag{20}$$

A number of derivations are available for the 2SLS and 3SLS estimators. We shall employ here the derivation given originally in Dhrymes [1969]. Consider, now, the following transformation of the structural equations

$$R^{-1}X'y_{\cdot i} = R^{-1}X'Z_i\delta_{\cdot i} + R^{-1}X'u_{\cdot i}, \quad i = 1, 2, \ldots, m, \tag{21}$$

and note that

$$\operatorname*{p\,lim}_{T\to\infty} \frac{1}{T}(R^{-1}X'Z_i)'R^{-1}X'u_{\cdot i} = \operatorname*{p\,lim}_{T\to\infty} \frac{1}{T}Z_i'X\left(\frac{X'X}{T}\right)^{-1}\frac{X'u_{\cdot i}}{T} = 0 \tag{22}$$

Equation (22) clearly shows that the explanatory variables and the error process of the (transformed) i^{th} structural equation, as exhibited therein, are **asymptotically uncorrelated.** This encourages us to think that, perhaps, the least squares estimator (OLS) of the parameter vector $\delta_{\cdot i}$ would be consistent. Indeed, we shall show, momentarily, that the OLS estimator of $\delta_{\cdot i}$, in the context of equations (21) and (22), **is the 2SLS estimator of that parameter.** Return to (21), put

$$R^{-1}X'y_{\cdot i} = w_{\cdot i}, \quad R^{-1}X'Z_i = Q_i, \quad R^{-1}X'u_{\cdot i} = r_{\cdot i} \tag{23}$$

and, thus, write the transform of the ith structural equation as

$$w_{\cdot i} = Q_i\delta_{\cdot i} + r_{\cdot i}, \quad i = 1, 2, \ldots, m. \tag{24}$$

Before we continue with the derivation of the 2SLS estimator, we remind the reader that the usual representation thereof is

$$\tilde{\delta}_{\cdot i(2SLS)} = (\tilde{Z}_i'\tilde{Z}_i)^{-1}\tilde{Z}_i'y_{\cdot i}, \quad \text{where} \quad \tilde{Z}_i = (\tilde{Y}_i, X_i). \tag{25}$$

We also note that

$$(\tilde{Y}_i, X_i) = (\tilde{Y}L_{1i},\ XL_{2i}) = X(\tilde{\Pi}_i,\ L_{2i}) = X\tilde{S}_i, \quad \tilde{\Pi} = (X'X)^{-1}X'Y.$$

The matrix

$$S_i = (\Pi_i,\ L_{2i}), \quad i = 1, 2, \ldots, m, \tag{26}$$

plays a very important role in the theory of 2SLS and 3SLS estimation although this is not, generally, appreciated. It is implicit in the preceding discussion that $\tilde{Z}_i'\tilde{Z}_i$, **is invertible, if and only if** S_i **is of full rank.** In addition, it may be shown that S_i **is of full rank if and only if the** i^{th} **equation is identified.** With these preliminaries aside, we are now ready to prove the fundamental

Theorem 1. Consider the GLSEM under assumptions (A.1) through (A.5) and Conventions 1 and 2. Then the 2SLS estimator of the parameters of the ith structural equation, **in the context of equation (6),** is the OLS estimator of the parameter vector $\delta_{\cdot i}$ **in the context of equation (24),** and it is a consistent estimator of $\delta_{\cdot i}$.

Proof: First we note that

$$Q_i \;=\; R^{-1}X'Z_i = R^{-1}X'\tilde{Z}_i \;=\; R'\tilde{S}_i. \tag{27}$$

Thus, the OLS estimator in the context of (24) is

$$\tilde{\delta}_{\cdot i} = (Q_i'Q_i)^{-1}Q_i'w_{\cdot i} = (\tilde{S}_i'RR'\tilde{S}_i)^{-1}\tilde{S}_i'X'y_{\cdot i}. \tag{28}$$

Since

$$\tilde{Z}_i = (\tilde{Y}_i,\; X_i) = X\tilde{S}_i,\;\; RR' = X'X,$$

a comparison with (25) shows (28) to be exactly the 2SLS estimator, as claimed. Consistency is easily shown by noting

$$\mathrm{p}\lim_{T\to\infty}(\tilde{\delta}_{\cdot i} - \delta_{\cdot i})_{2SLS} = \mathrm{p}\lim_{T\to\infty}(\tilde{S}_i'\frac{X'X}{T}\tilde{S}_i)^{-1}\mathrm{p}\lim_{T\to\infty}\frac{1}{T}\tilde{S}_i'X'u_{\cdot i}.$$

The matrix

$$\mathrm{p}\lim_{T\to\infty}(\tilde{S}_i'\frac{X'X}{T}\tilde{S}_i) = S_i'MS_i$$

is nonsingular since it may be shown that $M > 0$, every equation of the system is identifiable by assumption (A.3) and, moreover,

$$\mathrm{p}\lim_{T\to\infty}\frac{1}{T}\tilde{S}_{i'}'X'u_{\cdot i} = S_i'\mathrm{p}\lim_{T\to\infty}\frac{X'u_{\cdot i}}{T} = 0.$$

Remark 3. Evidently, the procedure above is effective in extending the range of application of OLS to structural equations **because** the transformation renders the "explanatory" variables (asymptotically) uncorrelated with the structural error term, while the properties of the latter are not disturbed. But since the GLSEM contains many equations it would be convenient to deal with all of them simultaneously instead of one at a time.

Now applying the transformation in (21) to all structural equations and setting

$$\begin{aligned} w &= (w'_{\cdot 1},\ w'_{\cdot 2}, \ldots w'_{\cdot m})' \\ Q &= diag(Q_1,\ Q_2,\ \ldots Q_m)' \\ \delta &= (\delta'_{\cdot 1},\ \delta'_{\cdot 2}, \ldots \delta_{\cdot m}),\quad r = (r'_{\cdot 1},\ r'_{\cdot 2}, \ldots r'_{\cdot m})', \end{aligned} \tag{29}$$

we can write the entire system in the compact form

$$w = Q\delta + r \tag{30}$$

which displays explicitly the vector of unknown structural parameters contained in the system as a whole. As an immediate consequence of the definitions above we have

Corollary 1. Under the conditions of Theorem 1, the 2SLS estimator of the (vector of) unknown structural parameters of the GLSEM, as exhibited in (30) is given by

$$\tilde{\delta} = (Q'Q)^{-1}Q'w \tag{31}$$

and, moreover,

$$\operatorname*{p\,lim}_{T \to \infty} \tilde{\delta} = \delta.$$

Proof: The ith subvector of (31) is simply

$$\tilde{\delta}_{\cdot i} = (Q_i'Q_i)^{-1}Q_i'w_{\cdot i},$$

which is exactly the representation of the 2SLS estimator of the structural parameters contained in the ith structural equation.

q.e.d.

Remark 4. The GLSEM as transformed and exhibited in (30) is said to be in **canonical structural form** (CSF), and "looks" very much like a GLM in the sense that

$$Q = (I \otimes R)\tilde{S},\quad S = \text{diag}(S_1,\ S_2, \ldots S_m) \tag{32}$$

S (and hence Q) is of full rank and

$$\operatorname*{p\,lim}_{T\to\infty} \frac{Q'r}{T} = \operatorname*{p\,lim}_{T\to\infty} \tilde{S}'\frac{(I \otimes X')u}{T} = 0, \quad u = \operatorname{vec}(U). \tag{33}$$

Such conditions ensure, at least, the consistency of the OLS estimator of δ in the context of (30). But is this OLS estimator efficient as well? Arguing by analogy with the standard GLM, our response would be that this would depend on the covariance structure of the error, here the vector r. Since by construction

$$r = (I \otimes R^{-1}X')u \tag{34}$$

we easily see that, at least in the case where X **does not contain lagged dependent variables,**

$$\begin{aligned} E(r \mid X) &= 0, \quad E(r) = 0 \\ \operatorname{Cov}(r \mid X) &= \Sigma \otimes I_G = \Phi. \end{aligned} \tag{35}$$

This is so since if a conditional moment does not depend on a given variable, then it is the unconditional moment as well, relative to that variable. From (35) we are encouraged to think that if we applied an Aitken or a generalized least squares procedure we would obtain relatively efficient estimators. This leads immediately to the derivation of the 3SLS. In the context of the CSF, as exhibited in (30) the Aitken estimator is given, in view of equation (35), by

$$\bar{\delta} = (Q'\Phi^{-1}Q)^{-1}Q'\Phi^{-1}w. \tag{36}$$

However, rarely do we know the structural error covariance matrix Σ; hence, rarely do we know Φ and, thus, the estimator in (36) is **not feasible.**

In practice, we deal with the **feasible** Aitken estimator obtained by substituting, in (36), the consistent estimator

$$\tilde{\Phi} = \tilde{\Sigma} \otimes I_G, \tag{37}$$

in lieu of the unknown matrix Φ. Such estimators are also known in the literature by the generic term **generalized least squares.** In any event, the substitution of $\tilde{\Phi}$ in (36) yields

$$\hat{\delta} = (Q'\tilde{\Phi}^{-1}Q)^{-1}Q'\tilde{\Phi}^{-1}w, \tag{38}$$

which is defined to be the 3SLS estimator of δ. Consistency for this estimator is easily obtained by the same method utilized above, but in the interest of brevity this will be omitted.

4 Limiting Distribution of Estimators

4.1 The 2SLS and 3SLS Problems are Identical

To derive the limiting distribution of the 2SLS and 3SLS estimators, in the context of a dynamic GLSEM, requires a certain degree of formality beyond the level employed in the preceding sections. First, we need to justify the assertion that the limit of $(X'X/T)$ exists, and second, we need to introduce the necessary framework in order that we may apply the theory of martingales or martingale differences in obtaining the limiting distributions in question. Thus, after we reduce our problem to the simplest possible form we shall digress in order to treat the topics just noted.

Making the appropriate substitutions in equations (31) and (38) we find

$$\begin{aligned}\sqrt{T}(\tilde{\delta}-\delta)_{2SLS} &= \left(\frac{Q'Q}{T}\right)^{-1}\frac{Q'r}{\sqrt{T}}\\ \sqrt{T}(\tilde{\delta}-\delta)_{3SLS} &= \left(\frac{Q'\tilde{\Phi}^{-1}Q}{T}\right)^{-1}\frac{Q'\tilde{\Phi}^{-1}r}{\sqrt{T}}.\end{aligned} \tag{39}$$

Bearing in mind the definitions

$$Q=(I\otimes R')\tilde{S}, \quad r=(I\otimes R^{-1})(I\otimes X')u, \quad u=\mathrm{vec}(U),$$

we have

$$\begin{aligned}\sqrt{T}(\tilde{\delta}-\delta)_{2SLS} &= [\tilde{S}'(I\otimes\frac{X'X}{T})\tilde{S}]^{-1}\tilde{S}'[\frac{(I\otimes X')u}{\sqrt{T}}]\\ \sqrt{T}(\tilde{\delta}-\delta)_{3SLS} &= [\tilde{S}'(\tilde{\Sigma}^{-1}\otimes\frac{X'X}{T})\tilde{S}]^{-1}\tilde{S}'(\tilde{\Sigma}^{-1}\otimes I)[\frac{(I\otimes X')u}{\sqrt{T}}].\end{aligned} \tag{40}$$

Defining

$$A_3 = \operatorname*{p\,lim}_{T\to\infty}[\tilde{S}'(\tilde{\Sigma}^{-1}\otimes\frac{X'X}{T})\tilde{S}]^{-1}\tilde{S}'(\tilde{\Sigma}^{-1}\otimes I)$$

$$
\begin{aligned}
&= [S'(\Sigma^{-1} \otimes M)S]^{-1}S'\Phi^{-1} \\
A_2 &= \operatorname{p}\lim_{T\to\infty} [\tilde{S}'(I \otimes \frac{X'X}{T})\tilde{S}]^{-1}\tilde{S}' = [S'(I \otimes M)S]^{-1}S' \\
M &= \operatorname{p}\lim_{T\to\infty} \frac{X'X}{T} = \bar{R}\bar{R}'. \qquad (41)
\end{aligned}
$$

we see that, asymptotically,

$$
\begin{aligned}
\sqrt{T}(\tilde{\delta} - \delta)_{2SLS} &\sim A_2[\frac{(I \otimes X')u}{\sqrt{T}}] \\
\sqrt{T}(\tilde{\delta} - \delta)_{3SLS} &\sim A_3[\frac{(I \otimes X')u}{\sqrt{T}}, \qquad (42)
\end{aligned}
$$

which shows that the problems of determining the limiting distribution of the 2SLS and 3SLS estimators are, *mutatis mutandis*, identical, in that both involve the determination of the limit, M, and the determination of the limiting distribution of the vector $\xi_T^* = [\frac{(I \otimes X')u}{\sqrt{T}}]$.

We now digress in order to provide the requisite foundation for these two tasks.

4.2 The Final Form of the dynamic GLSEM

The **final form** of the dynamic GLSEM is simply the long run solution of the underlying vector difference equation. This was obtained in the literature, for example in Dhrymes [1970] or Theil and Boot [1962]. Using the approach in Dhrymes, we have the representation

$$
y_{t\cdot}B^* = y_{t-1\cdot}C_1 + y_{t-2\cdot}C_2 + \ldots + y_{t-k\cdot}C_k + p_{t\cdot}C_0 + u_{t\cdot}, \qquad (43)
$$

from which we obtain the reduced form

$$
y'_{t\cdot} = \Pi'_1 y'_{t-1\cdot} + \Pi'_2 y'_{t-2\cdot} + \ldots + \Pi'_k y'_{t-k\cdot} + \Pi'_0 p'_{t\cdot} + v'_{t\cdot}, \qquad (44)
$$

where $\Pi_i = C_i D$, $i = 0, 1, \ldots, k$, and $D = B^{*-1}$. In terms of the **lag operator**, L, we can write

$$
\left(I - \sum_{i=1}^{k} \Pi'_i L^i\right) y'_{t\cdot} = \Pi'_0 p'_{t\cdot} + v'_{t\cdot}.
$$

If the roots of the equation

$$| I - \sum_{i=1}^{k} \Pi_i' \lambda^i | = 0 \tag{45}$$

are less that unity in absolute value then we can write, formally,

$$\left(I - \sum_{i=1}^{k} \Pi_i' L^i \right)^{-1} = \frac{A(L)}{b(L)}, \tag{46}$$

where $A(L)$ is the **adjoint (matrix), corresponding to the matrix** $\Pi(L) = I - \sum_{i=1}^{k} \Pi_i' L^i$, and $b(L)$ is the **determinant of (the matrix)** $\Pi(L)$. It follows, immediately, that the final form of the GLEM is

$$y_{t\cdot}' = \frac{H(L)}{b(L)} p_{t\cdot}' + \frac{G(L)}{b(L)} u_{t\cdot}' = \bar{y}_{t\cdot}' + v_{t\cdot}^{*\prime}, \tag{47}$$

where $H(L) = A(L)\Pi_0$ and $G(L) = A(L)D'$.

Remark 5. We note that in the representation of equation (47) the component $\bar{y}_{t\cdot}'$ is **independent of the error process**, while the component $v_{t\cdot}^{*\prime}$ is **a rational function of the error process**. In fact, we note for future reference that

$$v_{t\cdot}^{*\prime} = \frac{G(L)}{b(L)} u_{t\cdot}' = \sum_{\tau=0}^{\infty} G_\tau u_{t-\tau\cdot}', \qquad \sum_{\tau=0}^{\infty} G_\tau = \frac{G(1)}{b(1)}. \tag{48}$$

The entity $G(1)/b(1)$ is well defined and finite, since unity is not one of the roots of the characteristic equation of the system. It is, further, simple to demonstrate that

$$\begin{aligned} \mathrm{Cov}(v_{t\cdot}^{*\prime}) &= \sum_{\tau=0}^{\infty} G_\tau \Sigma G_\tau' = H(0), \\ \mathrm{Cov}(v_{t-i\cdot}^{*\prime}, v_{t-j\cdot}^{*\prime}) &= \sum_{\tau=0}^{\infty} G_{\tau+(i-j)} \Sigma G_\tau' = H(i-j), \quad i \geq j, \end{aligned} \tag{49}$$

and, moreover, that $H(i-j) = H'(j-i)$. Thus, we may write,

$$E\left(\frac{V_*'V_*}{T}\right) = H = \begin{bmatrix} H(0) & H'(1) & \dots & H'(k-1) \\ H(1) & H(0) & \dots & H'(k-2) \\ \vdots & & & \\ H(k-2) & H(k-3) & \dots & H'(1) \\ H(k-1) & H(k-2) & \dots & H(0) \end{bmatrix}, \tag{50}$$

where $V_{-i}^{*} = (v_{t-i\cdot}^{*})$ and $V_{*} = (V_{-1}^{*}, V_{-2}^{*}, \ldots, V_{-k}^{*})$. This enables us to derive the limit of $X'X/T$, the existence of which was repeatedly asserted earlier. To do so, we note first that

$$X = \bar{X} + (V_{*},\ 0), \quad \bar{x}_{t\cdot} = (\bar{y}_{t-1\cdot}, \bar{y}_{t-2\cdot}, \ldots, \bar{y}_{t-k\cdot},\ p_{t\cdot}), \quad \bar{X} = (\bar{x}_{t\cdot})$$

and, thus, we would expect that

$$\mathrm{p}\lim_{T\to\infty} \frac{X'X}{T} = (\mathrm{p})\lim_{T\to\infty} \frac{\bar{X}'\bar{X}}{T} + H^{*},$$

where

$$H^{*} = \begin{bmatrix} H & 0 \\ 0 & 0 \end{bmatrix}. \tag{51}$$

This is so since

$$\frac{X'X}{T} = \frac{\bar{X}'\bar{X}}{T} + \frac{(V_{*},\ 0)'(V_{*},\ 0)}{T}$$

and, for every $i \geq 0$, we would expect

$$\frac{\bar{X}'V_{-i}^{*}}{T} \xrightarrow{\mathrm{P}} 0, \qquad \frac{V_{*}'V_{*}}{T} \xrightarrow{\mathrm{P}} H. \tag{52}$$

Remark 6. This is a convenient point to discuss the question of how to deal with convergence issues entailing random vectors and matrices when, in fact, most textbook discussions of such issues focus on (scalar) random variables. When dealing with relatively simple problems it is often a rather easy matter to obtain the covariance matrix of an estimator and show that it vanishes as $T \longrightarrow \infty$. This approach, in effect, is quite attractive when dealing with the standard General Linear Model. As problems become more complex, however, these ad hoc procedures do not work as well. Moreover, with this approach we overreach our objective, since, in fact, we show **convergence in quadratic mean.** We attain our objective only by using that fact that **convergence in quadratic mean implies convergence in probability.**

In most of econometrics one deals, at worst, with vectors and matrices of real numbers, or real valued random vectors. It would be very inconvenient to deal with issues of convergence on an element by element basis, even though this has the advantage of allowing us to continue operating in the realm of (scalar) random variables. Instead, it would be desirable to find a way of dealing with them as a single entity. This is afforded us by the theory of random elements. Note that an m-element random vector, say X, is a transformation,

$$X : \Omega \longrightarrow R^m$$

where $(\Omega, \mathcal{A}, \mathcal{P})$ is the usual probability space, and $(R^m, \| \cdot \|)$ is the m-dimensional normed Euclidean space. Given the usual norm, i.e., if $x \in R^m$, then $\| x \| = (x_1^2 + x_2^2 + \ldots + x_m^2)^{\frac{1}{2}}$, we can define a metric by $\rho(x, y) = \| x - y \|$. The same approach may be applied to random matrices, since if A is a matrix of dimension $m \times n$, then we may think of it as an element in the space R^{mn}, by simply dealing with $a = \text{vec}(A)$. Thus, while there may be other ways in which we can define a norm for a matrix, our discussion above suggests that **if A is any matrix,** then

$$\| A \|^2 = \text{vec}(A)'\text{vec}(A) = tr(A'A) = tr(AA') = \sum_{i,j} a_{ij}^2. \tag{53}$$

This leads us immediately to the conclusion that if we wish to show that a sequence of random elements, say $X = \{X_n : n \geq 0\}$, converges to X_0, in probability, *a.c.*, or in mean of order p, i.e., L^p convergence, it will be sufficient to show, respectively,

$$\| X_n - X_0 \| \xrightarrow{\text{P}} 0, \quad \| X_n - X_0 \| \xrightarrow{\text{a.c.}} 0, \quad E(\| X_n - X_0 \|^p) \longrightarrow 0.$$

Note that since $\| X \|$ is, for every random element, X, a random variable, the usual implications hold, i.e., convergence *a.c.* and at least L^2 convergence imply convergence in probability.

Finally, we note that the mean of a random element is said to exist whenever $E(\| X \|) < \infty$, and the variance of a random element is defined by $\text{Var}(X) = E \| X - E(X) \|^2$, provided $X - E(X)$ is a random element. This need not be so in arbitrary metric spaces, but this is always so in the context of Euclidean m-space, where a random element is a random vector, and its expectation is an m-dimensional vector of constants.

Returning now to the discussion at hand we need to show that for every $i = 1, 2, \ldots, k$, $(\bar{X}'V_{-i}^{*}/T) \xrightarrow{\text{P}} 0$. Since the expectation of this entity is zero, and we are required to show that

$$\| \frac{\bar{X}'V^*_{-i}}{T} \| \xrightarrow{\text{P}} 0,$$

it will be sufficient to show that

$$E\left(\| \frac{\bar{X}'V^*_{-i}}{T} \|^2\right) \longrightarrow 0.$$

This is so, since if we put

$$\alpha_T = \frac{\bar{X}'V_*}{T}, \quad \text{we have that} \quad \sigma_T^2 = \text{Var}(\alpha_T) = E \parallel \frac{\bar{X}'V_*}{T} \parallel^2 .$$

Hence, if $\sigma_T^2 \longrightarrow 0$ we conclude that, for any integer, r, however large,

$$\textit{Probability } (\| \alpha_T \| > \frac{1}{r}) \longrightarrow 0,$$

which shows convergence in probability. Actually, this is a rather circuitous route, since in fact we show convergence in quadratic mean, and then use the fact that the latter implies convergence in probability. We formalize this discussion in

Lemma 1. Given assumptions (A.1) through (A.5), and in the context of the discussion immediately preceding, for each $i = 0, 1, 2, \ldots, k$

$$\frac{\bar{X}'V^*_{-i}}{T} \xrightarrow{\text{P}} 0.$$

Proof: For notational ease we deal with the case $i = 0$; other cases are absolutely identical. Using the results in chapter 4, Dhrymes [1984], we can vectorize the entity above to

$$\psi_T = \frac{1}{T}\text{vec}(\bar{X}'V^*) = \frac{1}{T}\sum_{t=1}^{T}(I \otimes \bar{x}_{t\cdot}')v_{t\cdot}^{*\prime} = \frac{1}{T}\sum_{t=1}^{T}(v_{t\cdot}^{*\prime} \otimes \bar{x}_{t\cdot}').$$

Since $E(\psi_T) = 0$, then by the preceding discussion it will be sufficient to show that

$$\lim_{T\to\infty} E \parallel \psi_T \parallel^2 = 0.$$

To further simplify the notation, put $z_{.t} = (v_{t.}^{*'} \otimes \bar{x}_{t.}')$, and note that

$$
\begin{aligned}
J_T &= E \parallel \psi_T \parallel^2 = \frac{1}{T^2} \sum_{t=1}^{T} \sum_{t'=1}^{T} E(z_{.t}' z_{.t'}) \\
&= \frac{1}{T^2} \sum_{t=1}^{T} \sum_{t'=1}^{T} E(v_{t.}^{*} v_{t.'}^{*'})(\bar{x}_{t.} \bar{x}_{t.'}') = \sum_{t=1}^{T} \sum_{t'=1}^{T} tr(H(t-t'))(\bar{x}_{t.} \bar{x}_{t.'}') \\
&= \frac{1}{T} \left[tr H(0) \frac{tr \bar{X}' \bar{X}}{T} + 2 \sum_{\tau=1}^{T-1} H(\tau) \left(\sum_{t=1}^{T} \frac{1}{T} \sum_{\tau=1}^{T-\tau} \bar{x}_{t.} \bar{x}_{t+\tau.}' \right) \right] \\
&\leq \frac{1}{T} \left[K \frac{tr(\bar{X}' \bar{X})}{T} \left(\sum_{\tau=0}^{T-1} \lambda_{max}^{\tau} \right) \right] \longrightarrow 0, \quad \text{with } T. \qquad (54)
\end{aligned}
$$

The expression after the inequality, follows from (a) replacing

$$
\mid \frac{1}{T} \sum_{t=1}^{T-\tau} \bar{x}_{t.} \bar{x}_{t+\tau.}' \mid \qquad \text{by} \qquad \frac{tr(\bar{X}' \bar{X})}{T},
$$

which is perfectly accurate, neglecting large end point effects and (b) from using the bound $\mid tr H(\tau) \mid \leq K_1 \lambda_{max}^{\tau}$, which is justified as follows: first, we note that $H(\tau) = H(-\tau)'$ and, moreover that $H(\tau) = \sum_{j=0}^{\infty} G_{\tau+j} \Sigma G_j'$, where G_j is the coefficient of L^j, in the expansion of $\Pi(L)^{-1}$. If we set

$$
\lambda_{max} = \max_{i \leq n} \mid \lambda_i \mid,
$$

where the λ_i are the roots of equation (45), then since the system is assumed to be stable, we must have $\lambda_{max} < 1$. Thus,

$$
\sum_{\tau=0}^{\infty} \lambda_{max}^{\tau} = \frac{1}{1 - \lambda_{max}} < \infty.
$$

q.e.d.

Remark 7. We note, with interest, that Proposition 32, chapter 5, in Dhrymes [1989] shows that for (zero mean) covariance stationary sequences, $\{\xi_j : j \geq 1\}$, the entity $(\sum_{j=1}^{n} \xi_j / n)$, converges in mean square to zero if and only if

$$
\lim_{n \to \infty} \frac{1}{n} \sum_{j=0}^{n} R(j) = 0, \quad \text{where } R(j) = E(\xi_{t+j} \xi_t).
$$

Note, also, that in the proof of Lemma 1, convergence (to zero) of the entity $(\sum_{j=0}^{T-1} \mid tr H(j) \mid / T)$ has played a crucial role; note further that, in the vector context, $H(j)$ is, roughly, the analogue of $R(j)$. In particular, the reader should bear in mind that **in view of the stability of the system** there exists a constant K, such that $\| H(j) \|^2 \leq K\lambda^{2j}$.

Just to anticipate our discussion, we also note from Proposition 34, chapter 5, of the same reference that, for **normal** stationary sequences, the entity

$$\frac{1}{n}\sum_{j=1}^{n}\xi_j\xi_{j+\tau} \xrightarrow{L^2} R(\tau),$$

if and only if

$$\lim_{n\to\infty}\frac{1}{n}\sum_{j=0}^{n-1}(R(j))^2 = 0.$$

Finally, we should point out that, roughly speaking, in the case of random vectors $\| H(j) \|^2$ corresponds to $(R(j))^2$!

We turn our attention now to the requirement that we show that

$$\frac{V_*'V_*}{T} \xrightarrow{P} H.$$

Since the typical block element of the matrix above is given by

$$\frac{V_{-i+s}^{*\prime}V_{-i}^{*}}{T}$$

it will suffice to show that, for $0 \leq s \leq k$,

$$\frac{V_{-i+s}^{*\prime}V_{-i}^{*}}{T} \xrightarrow{P} H(s).$$

We shall follow exactly the approach of Lemma 1, and show, in fact, convergence in quadratic mean which, as noted earlier, implies convergence in probability. We formalize our discussion in

Lemma 2. Given assumptions (A.1) through (A.5), and the preceding discussion, and **explicitly assuming that the structural errors are jointly normal**[3] then

$$\frac{1}{T}V_*'V_* \xrightarrow{P} H. \tag{55}$$

---

[3] The normality assumption is invoked here so that the reader will have relatively easy access to the underlying basic result for scalar sequences, in Dhrymes [1989], chapter 5, Proposition 34, part ii. The proof of Lemma 2 is, in fact, an adaptation of the proof of that proposition.

It might appear that we are being unduly restrictive and we should, perhaps have

Proof: Since the typical block element is given by $(V^{*\prime}_{-i+s}V^{*}_{-i}/T)$, it will suffice to show that it converges in quadratic mean to $H(s) = E(V^{*\prime}_{-i+s}V^{*}_{-i}/T)$. Let $h_s = \text{vec}(H(s))$, $z_{.t} = (v^{*\prime}_{t-i.} \otimes v^{*\prime}_{t-i+s.}) - h_s$, and note that we are required to show

$$J_T \longrightarrow 0, \quad \text{where } J_T = E \parallel \frac{1}{T}\sum_{t=1}^{T} z_{.t} \parallel^2 .$$

We have

$$\begin{aligned} J_T &= \frac{1}{T^2}\sum_{t=1}^{T}\sum_{t'=1}^{T} E(z'_{.t}z_{.t'}) \\ &= \sum_{t=1}^{T}\sum_{t'=1}^{T}\left[E\left((v^{*}_{t-i.}v^{*\prime}_{t'-i.})(v^{*}_{t-i+s.}v^{*\prime}_{t'-i+s.})\right) - E\left((v^{*}_{t-i.} \otimes v^{*}_{t-i+s.})h_s\right)\right] \\ &\quad -\sum_{t=1}^{T}\sum_{t'=1}^{T}\left[E\left(h'_s(v^{*\prime}_{t'-i.}v^{*\prime}_{t'-i+s.})\right) + h'_s h_s\right] \\ &= \sum_{t=1}^{T}\sum_{t'=1}^{T}\left[E\left((v^{*}_{t-i.}v^{*\prime}_{t'-i.})(v^{*}_{t-i+s.}v^{*\prime}_{t'-i+s.})\right) - h'_s h_s\right] \\ &= \sum_{t=1}^{T}\sum_{t'=1}^{T} J_{tt'}. \end{aligned} \tag{56}$$

We now come to the laborious part of evaluating $J_{tt'}$.[4] In that evalua-

---

had recourse to Theorem 6, of Hannan [1970] p. 210. That theorem, however, merely invites us to assume whatever is necessary about fourth order moments; when this is done, the moments of the sequence behave like the moments of a normal sequence. This is so since fourth order moments are expressed as sums of products of second order moments, plus appropriate cumulants. In the normal case, the cumulant term is not present. In the case of Theorem 6, it is required that the cumulant contribution to an appropriate sum vanish. Since this is the only role played by cumulants in the proof of that Theorem our characterization is basically correct. Not wishing to discuss cumulants in this context, we are content to assume normality. The reader should note, however, that normality is not used for any other purpose in the remainder of this discussion.

[4] It is only at this stage that the normality assumption plays a role in simplifying the derivation. If the assumption had not been made then, in addition to the three terms we shall obtain in equation (57), we would have had to deal with the cumulants of the distribution in question. This means that we would have in (57) **additional terms involving the cumulants**. Incidentally, as we pointed out in footnote 3, Hannan's theorem simply assumes that the contribution of the cumulants vanishes as $T \longrightarrow \infty$, i.e., that they play no role in the final result. Thus, there is no material

tion we have to compute the expectation

$$E\left((v^*_{t-i.}v^{*'}_{t'-i.})(v^*_{t-i+s.}v^{*'}_{t'-i+s.})\right) = \sum_{j_1=1}^{m}\sum_{j_2=1}^{m} E\left(\zeta_{tj_1}\zeta_{t'j_2}\right),$$

where $\zeta_{tj_1} = \left(v^*_{t-i,j_1}v^*_{t'-i,j_1}\right)$ and $\zeta_{t'j_2} = \left(v^*_{t-i+s,j_2}v^*_{t'-i+s,j_2}\right)$. The expectation in the right member, above, yields three components

$$\begin{aligned} E(v^*_{t-i,j_1}v^*_{t'-i,j_1})\ E(v^*_{t-i+s,}v^{*'}_{t'-i+s.}) &= h^{(t-t')}_{j_1,j_1}h^{(t-t')}_{j_2,j_2} \\ E(v^*_{t-i,j_1}v^*_{t-i+s,j_2})\ E(v^*_{t'-i+s,j_1}v^*_{t'-i+s,j_2}) &= h^{(-s)}_{j_1,j_2}h^{(-s)}_{j_1,j_2} \\ E(v^*_{t-i,j_1}v^*_{t'-i+s,j_2})\ E(v^*_{t'-i,j_1}v^*_{t-i+s,j_2}) &= h^{(t-t'-s)}_{j_1,j_2}h^{(t'-t-s)}_{j_1,j_2}. \end{aligned} \tag{57}$$

Since $H(s) = H(-s)'$, $\quad H(t'-t-s) = H(t-t'+s)'$, we conclude that

$$J_{tt'} = (trH(t-t'))^2 + h_s'h_s + tr\left(H(t-t'-s)H(t-t'+s)\right);$$

moreover, since $(\mathrm{tr}H(t-t'))^2 \leq \| H(t-t') \|^2$, we obtain

$$\begin{aligned} J_T &= \frac{1}{T^2}\sum_{t=1}^{T}\sum_{t'=1}^{T}\left[(trH(t-t'))^2 + tr(H(t-t'-s)H(t-t'+s))\right] \\ &\leq \frac{1}{T^2}\sum_{t=1}^{T}\sum_{t'=1}^{T}\left(\| H(t-t') \|^2 + \| H(t-t'+s) \|^2\right) \\ &\quad + \frac{1}{T^2}\sum_{t=1}^{T}\sum_{t'=1}^{T}\left(\| H(t-t'-s) \|^2\right). \end{aligned}$$

Since the terms following the inequality above converge to zero with T, the proof is complete.

q.e.d.

Remark 8. In the proof above we have made use of a number of results which were assumed to be known or, at least, easily grasped in the context of the discussion. Should this not be the case, here is a brief demonstration.

We have asserted that for (any $m \times m$) matrix, A,

$$(\mathrm{tr}(A))^2 \leq \| A \|^2 .$$

---

difference between that and assuming normality, since no other use of the assumption is being made.

The proof of this is trivial if one notes that

$$\operatorname{tr}(A) = \operatorname{vec}(A)'\operatorname{vec}(I_m), \qquad \| A \|^2 = \operatorname{vec}(A)'\operatorname{vec}(A).$$

We have, also, made use of the fact that

$$| \operatorname{tr}(AB) | \leq \| A \|^2 + \| B \|^2 .$$

To establish the validity of this claim, let $a = \operatorname{vec}(A)$ and $b = \operatorname{vec}(B)$, and note that by the Cauchy inequality we have

$$| \operatorname{tr}(A'B) | = | a'b | \leq \| A \| \| B \| .$$

Since for nonnegative c, d we have $(c - d)^2 \geq 0$, we conclude that $c^2 + d^2 \geq 2cd \geq cd$. But this implies

$$| \operatorname{tr}(H(t-t'-s)H(t-t'+s)) | \leq \| H(t-t'-s) \|^2 + \| H(t-t'+s) \|^2,$$

which is what is required.

Finally, we have asserted that, for any[5] $0 \leq s \leq k$,

$$\frac{1}{T^2}\sum_{t=1}^{T}\sum_{t'=1}^{T} \| H(t-t'+s) \|^2 \longrightarrow 0, \quad \text{with } T.$$

Let us write the components of J_T, defined near the end of the proof of Lemma 2, as J_{T1}, J_{T2}, and J_{T3}. The second component corresponds to the term $\| H(t-t'+s) \|^2$, and it will be sufficient to show that this converges to zero with T. We have

$$\begin{aligned} J_{T2} &= \frac{1}{T^2}\sum_{t=1}^{T}\sum_{t'=1}^{T} \| H(t-t'+s) \|^2 = \frac{1}{T^2}\sum_{t=1}^{T-s}\sum_{t'=1}^{t+s} \| H(t-t'+s) \|^2 \\ &+ \frac{1}{T^2}\sum_{t=1}^{T-s-1}\sum_{t'=t+s+1}^{T} \| H(t'-t-s) \|^2 \qquad (58) \\ &= \frac{1}{T^2}\sum_{t=1}^{T-s}\sum_{j=0}^{t-1+s} \| H(j) \|^2 + \frac{1}{T^2}\sum_{t=1}^{T-s-1}\sum_{j=1}^{T-t-s} \| H(j) \|^2 \end{aligned}$$

[5] Even though, for the sake of definiteness, we require s to be nonnegative, whether it is or is not does not matter at all. This is so since the terms following the inequality, at the end of the proof, are symmetric in s, and we are trying to show that such terms converge to zero with T.

$$
\begin{aligned}
&\leq \frac{K}{T^2}\sum_{t=1}^{T-s}\sum_{j=0}^{t-1+s}\lambda_{max}^{2j}+\frac{K}{T^2}\sum_{t=1}^{T-s-1}\sum_{j=1}^{T-t-s}\lambda_{max}^{2j}\\
&= \frac{K}{T^2}\sum_{t=1}^{T-s}\left(\frac{1-\lambda_{max}^{2(t+s)}}{1-\lambda_{max}^2}\right)+\frac{K}{T^2}\sum_{t=1}^{T-s-1}\left(\frac{\lambda_{max}^2-\lambda_{max}^{2(T-s-t+1)}}{1-\lambda_{max}^2}\right)\\
&= \frac{K}{T^2(1-\lambda_{max}^2)}\left[(T-s)(1+\lambda_{max}^2)-\lambda_{max}^2-\frac{\lambda_{max}^{2(s+1)}}{1-\lambda_{max}^2}\right]\\
&\quad+\frac{K}{T^2(1-\lambda_{max}^2)}\left[-\frac{\lambda_{max}^4}{1-\lambda_{max}^2}+\frac{\lambda_{max}^{2(T+1)}}{1-\lambda_{max}^2}+\frac{\lambda_{max}^{2(T-s+1)}}{1-\lambda_{max}^2}\right],
\end{aligned}
$$

which, evidently, converges to zero with T, as claimed in the proof of Lemma 2.

4.3 The Underlying Probability Space

Unfortunately, in order to proceed with the derivation of the limiting distribution of 2SLS and 3SLS estimators in the context of the dynamic GLSEM in a responsible way and without excessive "hand waving" we need to introduce more structure into our discussion; by way of illustration we shall first apply this structure to the **static** GLSEM, and then in the next section we shall take up the dynamic model.

The basic random elements of the problem are the random vectors $\{u'_{t.} : t \geq 1\}$ and the context also includes the **exogenous** sequence $\{p'_{t.} : t \geq 1\}$ and the parameter space, which consists of the admissible values of the triplet (B^*, C, Σ). Thus, let $(\Omega, \mathcal{A}, \mathcal{P})$ be a (sufficiently large) probability space such that the sequence $\{u'_{t.} : t \geq 1\}$ may be defined on it and such that it also contains the collection of "events" corresponding to the sequence $\{\xi_T^* : T \geq 1\}$, i.e., ξ_T^* is $\mathcal{A}$-measurable. Let

$$
\mathcal{A}_t = \sigma(u'_{s.}, s \leq t), \tag{59}
$$

i.e., $\mathcal{A}_t$ is the σ-algebra **generated** by the first t random vectors. It is clear that $\mathcal{A}_{t-1} \subset \mathcal{A}_t \subset \mathcal{A}$, and that $\xi'_{t.}$ is $\mathcal{A}_t$-measurable. Moreover, if $\mathcal{A}_{tT}$ is the σ-algebra corresponding to $\frac{u'_{t.}}{\sqrt{T}}$, then $\xi'_{tT.}$ is $\mathcal{A}_{tT}$-measurable and $\mathcal{A}_{t-1,T} \subset \mathcal{A}_{tT}$. In this probabilistic framework we need to apply a

CLT on the trangular array $\xi_T^* = \sum_{t=1}^{T} \xi_{tT.}$ as $T \rightarrow \infty$. To better understand the structure of the problem confronting us, and using the results in chapter 4, section 2 Dhrymes [1984], we can write

$$\begin{aligned}
\xi_T^* &= \frac{(I \otimes X')u}{\sqrt{T}} = \frac{1}{\sqrt{T}}\text{vec}(X'U) = \frac{1}{\sqrt{T}}\sum_{t=1}^{T}\text{vec}(x_{t.}'u_{t.}) \\
&= \frac{1}{\sqrt{T}}\sum_{t=1}^{T}(I \otimes x_{t.}')u_{t.}' = \sum_{t=1}^{T}\xi_{tT.}' \qquad (60) \\
\xi_{tT.} &= \frac{1}{\sqrt{T}}\xi_{t.}, \quad \xi_{t.}' = (I \otimes x_{t.}')u_{t.}' \qquad (61)
\end{aligned}$$

and we see that, in view of assumption (A.5), we require a CLT for independent **not identically** distributed random variables, since the summands in equation (60) obey

$$E(\xi_{t.}') = 0, \qquad \Psi_t = \text{Cov}(\xi_{tT.}') = \frac{1}{T}\Sigma \otimes x_{t.}'x_{t.},$$

and, moreover,

$$\sum_{t=1}^{T}\Psi_t \longrightarrow \Sigma \otimes M. \qquad (62)$$

We further note from Dhrymes [1989], chapter 4 Proposition 32, that for a sequence of random vectors

$$X_n \xrightarrow{\text{d}} X,$$

if and only if **for any** conformable real vector λ

$$\lambda' X_n \xrightarrow{\text{d}} \lambda' X.$$

To apply this setup to our context, let

$$\zeta_T = \lambda'\xi_T^* = \sum_{t=1}^{T}\zeta_{tT}, \qquad \zeta_{tT} = \xi_{tT.}\lambda, \qquad (63)$$

and note that the random variables ζ_{tT} constitute, for each T, a sequence of independent, not identically distributed square integrable $\mathcal{A}_{tT}$-measurable random variables obeying

$$E(\zeta_{tT}) = 0, \qquad \text{Var}(\zeta_{tT}) = \lambda'(\Sigma \otimes \frac{x_{t.}'x_{t.}}{T})\lambda = \sigma_{tT}^2,$$

where

$$\sum_{t=1}^{T} \sigma_{tT}^2 = \lambda'(\Sigma \otimes \frac{X'X}{T})\lambda \longrightarrow \lambda'(\Sigma \otimes M)\lambda \geq 0. \tag{64}$$

It follows, then, from Dhrymes [1989] chapter 4 Proposition 43, that to show that ζ_T converges in distribution, it will suffice to show that the sequence above obeys a **Lindeberg** condition. We have

Lemma 3. Given the context provided in the informal discussion above, the sequence $\{\zeta_{tT} : t \leq T,\ T \geq 1\}$ obeys a **Lindeberg** condition, i.e., if we define

$$\mathcal{L}_T = \sum_{t=1}^{T} \int_{|\zeta_{tT}| > \frac{1}{r}} | \zeta_{tT} |^2 \, d\mathcal{P}, \tag{65}$$

then,

$$\lim_{T \to \infty} \mathcal{L}_T = 0. \tag{66}$$

Proof: Note that

$$| \zeta_{tT} |^2 \leq \frac{1}{T} | \lambda |^2 \| I \otimes x'_{t.} \|^2 | u'_{t.} |^2,$$

define

$$\begin{aligned} A_{tT1} &= \{\omega : | \zeta_{tT} | > \frac{1}{r}\} \\ A_{tT2} &= \{\omega : | u'_{t.} | > \frac{\sqrt{T}}{r \mid \lambda \mid \| I \otimes x'_{t.} \|}\} \end{aligned} \tag{67}$$

and observe that $A_{tT1} \subset A_{tT2}$, owing to the fact that

$$\frac{1}{r} < | \zeta_{tT} | \leq \frac{1}{\sqrt{T}} | \lambda | \| I \otimes x'_{t.} \| \, | u'_{t.} | .$$

Consequently, the integral in equation (65) may be evaluated as

$$\int_{|\zeta_{tT}| > \frac{1}{r}} | \zeta_{tT} |^2 \, d\mathcal{P} \leq | \lambda |^2 \frac{m(x_{t.}x'_{t.})}{T} \int_{|u'_{t.}| > \frac{\sqrt{T}}{r|\lambda| \, (m x_{t.} x'_{t.})^{\frac{1}{2}}}} | u'_{t.} |^2 \, d\mathcal{P}.$$

Even though we have simplified considerably the representation of the integral of the Lindeberg condition, still we are not able show that it vanishes asymptotically. Further simplifications are required. We note, however, that we have not used the assumption in (A.5), i.e., the i.i.d.

assumption regarding the basic structural errors, nor have we used assumption (A.1), viz., that the limit of $\frac{X'X}{T}$ is well behaved.[6] The fact that the structural errors are i.i.d. means that we can remove the subscript t from the integrand; the fact that $\frac{X'X}{T} \longrightarrow M$, means that for sufficiently large T there exists $\alpha \in (0,1)$ such that $x_{t.}x'_{t.} \leq T^{\alpha}$. Define, now

$$A_T = \{\omega : | u'_{t.} | > \frac{1}{r} \frac{T^{\frac{1}{2}(1-\alpha)}}{| \lambda | m^{\frac{1}{2}}}\}$$

and note that $A_{tT2} \subset A_T$. It follows, therefore, that

$$\mathcal{L}_T \leq | \lambda |^2 \text{ m tr}(\frac{X'X}{T}) \int_{A_T} | u'_{1.} |^2 d\mathcal{P}. \qquad (68)$$

The conclusion follows immediately, if we note that as $T \longrightarrow \infty$ the integral above converges to zero, owing to the fact that the structural errors have finite second moments while, for every λ, the other component of the right member of equation (68) converges to m tr$M < \infty$.

q.e.d.

Corollary 2. Under the conditions of Lemma 3,

$$\xi^*_T \xrightarrow{d} \xi^*, \quad \xi^* \sim N(0, \Sigma \otimes M).$$

Proof: By Proposition 43 of chapter 4, of Dhrymes [1989]

$$\zeta_T \xrightarrow{d} \zeta, \quad \zeta \sim N(0, \lambda'(\Sigma \otimes M)\lambda).$$

---

[6] It would appear that, in order to prove the consistency and asymptotic normality of the 2SLS and 3SLS estimators, the minimum set of conditions we can place on the exogenous variables is that $d_T^2 \longrightarrow \infty$ and

$$\lim_{T\to\infty} \sup_{t \leq T} \frac{x_{t.}x'_{t.}}{d_T^2} = 0, \quad \text{where} \quad d_T^2 = \text{tr}X'X.$$

In such a case we would not have dealt, for example, with $\sqrt{T}\left(\tilde{\delta} - \delta\right)_{2SLS}$, but rather with $d_T\left(\tilde{\delta} - \delta\right)_{2SLS}$, and ξ^*_T would not have been divided by $\sqrt{T}$, but rather by d_T. It has been traditional in this literature, however, to assume that the second moments of explanatory variables are well defined both in finite samples and in the limit and this fact accounts for the normalization by $\sqrt{T}$.

Since $\zeta_T = \lambda'\xi^*_T$, it further follows by Proposition 32, chapter 4 of Dhrymes [1989], that

$$\xi^*_T \xrightarrow{d} \xi^*, \quad \xi^* \sim N(0, \Sigma \otimes M).$$

q.e.d.

4.4 Limiting Distributions for Dynamic GLSEM

In this section we provide the details of establishing the limiting distribution when the model is dynamic. Returning to the context of equations (60) and (61), we need to find the limiting distribution of

$$\xi^*_T = \frac{1}{\sqrt{T}} \sum_{t=1}^{T} \mathrm{vec}(x'_{t \cdot} u_{t \cdot}) = \frac{1}{\sqrt{T}} \sum_{t=1}^{T} \xi'_{t \cdot}, \quad \xi'_{t \cdot} = (I \otimes x'_{t \cdot}) u'_{t \cdot}.$$

An alternative notation for $\xi'_{t \cdot}$ is

$$\xi'_{t \cdot} = (u'_{t \cdot} \otimes x'_{t \cdot}).$$

The important difference between the nature of the problem in the static and dynamic cases is that in the former, the individual summands, i.e., the vectors $\xi_{t \cdot}$ constitute a **sequence of independent**, though not identically distributed, random vectors, while in the latter (dynamic) case they form a sequence of **dependent vectors**. To see this note that from the representation implicit in equations (47) we have

$$x_{t \cdot} = \bar{x}_{t \cdot} + (v^*_{t-1 \cdot}, v^*_{t-2 \cdot}, \ldots, v^*_{t-k \cdot}, 0) = \bar{x}_{t \cdot} + w^*_{t \cdot} \tag{69}$$

so that, for example, $\xi_{t \cdot}$ and $\xi_{t+1 \cdot}$ have $v^*_{t-1 \cdot}, v^*_{t-2 \cdot}, \ldots, v^*_{t-k+1 \cdot}$ in common; thus, they cannot be independent, in fact they are not even uncorrelated! To examine the issues arising in the dynamic context we introduced the probability space and the family of nested sub σ-algebras defined in connection with equation (59) and we also stipulate that $\mathcal{A}_{-j} = (\emptyset, \Omega)$, for $j = 0, 1, \ldots, k-1$, i.e., **we take initial conditions as given and nonstochastic.** Moreover, as we had done in the earlier discussion we convert the problem to one involving the **scalar** random variables

$$\zeta_T = \lambda'\xi^*_T = \sum_{t=1}^{T} \zeta_{tT}, \quad \zeta_{tT} = \frac{1}{\sqrt{T}}(u_{t \cdot} \otimes x_{t \cdot})\lambda,$$

where λ is an arbitrary conformable real vector. We note first that ζ_{tT} is $\mathcal{A}_{tT}$-measurable and that the stochastic sequence $\{(\zeta_{tT}, \mathcal{A}_{tT}) : t \leq T\}$ is, for each $T \geq 1$ a **martingale difference**, owing to the fact that $E(\zeta_{tT}) = 0$. Moreover, it may be shown to obey a **Lindeberg** condition. Thus, we have

Lemma 4. In the context of the dynamic GLSEM subject to assumptions (A.1) through (A.5), and the preceding discussion, the martingale difference $\{(\zeta_{tT}, \mathcal{A}_{tT}) : t \leq T\}$ obeys a **Lindeberg** condition, i.e., if we put, for arbitrary integer r

$$\mathcal{L}_T = \sum_{t=1}^{T} \int_{|\zeta_{tT}| > \frac{1}{r}} | \zeta_{tT} |^2 \, d\mathcal{P}(\omega \mid \mathcal{A}_{t-1,T}), \quad \text{then} \quad \operatorname{p}\lim_{T\to\infty} \mathcal{L}_T = 0. \quad (70)$$

Proof: We note that

$$| \zeta_{tT} | \leq \frac{1}{T} | \lambda |^2 \, \| (I \otimes x_{t.}') \|^2 \, | u_{t.}' |^2,$$

and we also define, for arbitrary integer, r,

$$A_{tT1} = \{\omega : | \zeta_{tT} | > \frac{1}{r}\} \qquad A_{tT2} = \{\omega : | u_{t.}' | > \frac{\sqrt{T}}{c_0 q_t}\},$$

where

$$c_0 = r m^{\frac{1}{2}} \mid \lambda \mid, \qquad q_t = (\bar{x}_{t.}\bar{x}_{t.}')^{\frac{1}{2}} + (w_{t.}^{*} w_{t.}^{*'})^{\frac{1}{2}}.$$

Since $\bar{X}'\bar{X}/T$ converges, then for T sufficiently large there exists $\alpha \in (0,1)$ such that $\bar{x}_{t.}\bar{x}_{t.}' \leq T^{\alpha}$. Define, in addition,

$$A_{tT3} = \{\omega : | u_{t.}' | > \frac{\sqrt{T}}{c_0 \left(T^{\frac{1}{2}\alpha} + (w_{t.}^{*} w_{t.}^{*'})^{\frac{1}{2}}\right)}\}$$

and observe[7] that $A_{tT1} \subset A_{tT2} \subset A_{tT3}$. Note, further, that from equation (69) we have

$$E(w_{t.}^{*} w_{t.}^{*'}) = E\left(\sum_{j=1}^{k} v_{t-j.}^{*} v_{t-j.}^{*'}\right) = k \operatorname{tr} H(0) < \infty.$$

[7] The set inclusions, $A_{tT1} \subset A_{tT2} \subset A_{tT3}$, are seen to be valid if we note that, by the triangle inequality,

$$\| (I \otimes x_{t.}') \| \leq \| (I \otimes \bar{x}_{t.}') \| + \| (I \otimes w_{t.}^{*}) \| = q_t.$$

From the Chebyshev-Markov inequality we find

$$\mathcal{P}(\bar{B}_T) \le \frac{k\mathrm{tr}H(0)}{T^\alpha}, \quad \text{where } B_T = \{\omega : w_{t.}^* w_{t.}^{*'} \le T^\alpha\}$$

and we further note that

$$A_{tT3} = (A_{tT3} \cap B_T) \cup (A_{tT3} \cap \bar{B}_T) \subset (A_{tT3} \cap B_T) \cup \bar{B}_T. \tag{71}$$

Consequently, we may write the integral of the Lindeberg condition as

$$\begin{aligned} L_{tT} &= \int_{|\zeta_{tT}| > \frac{1}{r}} | \zeta_{tT} |^2 \, d\mathcal{P}(\omega \mid \mathcal{A}_{t-1,T}) \\ &\le \frac{1}{T} | \lambda |^2 m(x_{t.}x_{t.}^{'}) \int_{A_{tT1}} | u_{t.}^{'} |^2 \, d\mathcal{P} \\ &\le \frac{1}{T} | \lambda |^2 m(x_{t.}x_{t.}^{'}) \int_{A_{tT3}} | u^{'} |^2 \, d\mathcal{P} \\ &\le \frac{1}{T} | \lambda |^2 m(x_{t.}x_{t.}^{'}) \left(\int_{A_{tT3} \cap B_T} | u^{'} |^2 \, d\mathcal{P} + \int_{\bar{B}_T} | u^{'} |^2 \, d\mathcal{P} \right) \\ &= L_{T1} + L_{T2}. \end{aligned} \tag{72}$$

In the preceding the first inequality is the result of the application of the triangle inequality and taking outside the integrand entities which are $\mathcal{A}_{t-1,T}$-measurable; the second and third inequalities simply follow because of set inclusions, i.e., $A_{tT1} \subset A_{tT3}$ and $A_{tT3} \subset (A_{tT3} \cap B_T) \cup \bar{B}_T$, and the fact that the vectors $u_{t.}$, $t \ge 1$, are **identically** distributed. Thus, we may deduce from equation (70) and (72)

$$\mathcal{L}_T \le (m \mid \lambda \mid^2) \mathrm{tr} \left(\frac{X'X}{T} \right) [L_{T1} + L_{T2}]. \tag{73}$$

Since

$$\begin{aligned} \operatorname*{p\,lim}_{T \to \infty} \mathrm{tr} \left(\frac{X'X}{T} \right) &= \mathrm{tr}M < \infty \\ \lim_{T \to \infty} L_{T1} &= \lim_{T \to \infty} \int_{|u| > \frac{T^{\frac{1}{2}(1-\alpha)}}{c_0}} | u |^2 \, d\mathcal{P} = 0, \end{aligned}$$

we need only be concerned with the behavior of L_{T2}. Letting I_T^* be the indicator function of the set $\bar{B}_T$, we find

$$\begin{aligned}\lim_{T\to\infty} L_{T2} &= \lim_{T\to\infty} \int_{\bar{B}_T} | u |^2 \, d\mathcal{P} = \lim_{T\to\infty} \int_{\Omega} | u |^2 \, I_T^* d\mathcal{P} \\ &\leq \lim_{T\to\infty} \mathcal{P}(\bar{B}_T)(\mathrm{tr}\Sigma) = 0.\end{aligned}$$

q.e.d.

We are now in a position to prove

Lemma 5. Under the conditions of Lemma 4,

$$\xi_T^* \xrightarrow{\mathrm{d}} \xi^*, \quad \xi^* \sim N(0, \Sigma \otimes M).$$

Proof: From chapter 5 Proposition 21 in Dhrymes [1989], we may show that $\zeta_T \xrightarrow{\mathrm{d}} \zeta$ by showing that

$$\sum_{t=1}^{T} E(\zeta_{tT}^2 \mid \mathcal{A}_{t-1,T}) \xrightarrow{\mathrm{P}} \sigma^2 \geq 0. \tag{74}$$

Since

$$E(\zeta_{tT}^2 \mid \mathcal{A}_{t-1,T}) = \frac{1}{T} E\left(\lambda'(u_{t.}' u_{t.} \otimes x_{t.}' x_{t.})\lambda\right) = \lambda'(\Sigma \otimes \frac{x_{t.}' x_{t.}}{T})\lambda$$

it follows that

$$\sum_{t=1}^{T} E(\zeta_{tT}^2 \mid \mathcal{A}_{t-1,T}) = \lambda'(\Sigma \otimes \frac{X'X}{T})\lambda \xrightarrow{\mathrm{P}} \lambda'(\Sigma \otimes M)\lambda \geq 0,$$

which demonstrates that for every conformable real vector, λ,

$$\zeta_T \xrightarrow{\mathrm{d}} \zeta, \quad \text{and} \quad \zeta \sim N(0, \lambda'(\Sigma \otimes M)\lambda).$$

It follows, therefore, from chapter 4 Proposition 32 in Dhrymes [1989], that

$$\xi_T^* \xrightarrow{\mathrm{d}} \xi^*, \quad \text{and} \quad \xi^* \sim N(0, \Sigma \otimes M).$$

q.e.d.

We may therefore summarize our discussion in the important

Theorem 2. Consider the GLSEM, subject to assumptions (A.1) through (A.5). The 2SLS, 3SLS estimators are, asymptotically, of the generic form

$$\sqrt{T}\left(\tilde{\delta}-\delta\right) \sim A\,\xi_T^*,$$

with

$$\xi_T^* \xrightarrow{d} \xi^*, \quad \xi^* \sim N(0, \Sigma \otimes M),$$

and A is a fixed nonstochastic matrix, specific to the particular estimator; in particular, for the 2SLS estimator it is

$$A = A_2 = (S^{*\prime}S^*)^{-1}S, \qquad S^* = (I \otimes \bar{R}')S, \tag{75}$$

while for the 3SLS estimator is

$$A = A_3 = (S^{*\prime}\Phi^{-1}S^*)^{-1}S'\Phi^{-1}. \tag{76}$$

Proof: Lemmata 1,2,3,4 and 5.

5 Forecasting and Reduced Forms

5.1 Restricted and Unrestricted Reduced Forms

The **reduced form** of the model in (1) is simply

$$y_{t\cdot}' = \Pi' x_{t\cdot}' + v_{t\cdot}', \tag{77}$$

where

$$\Pi' = D'(C_1', C_2', \ldots, C_k', C_0') = (\Pi_1', \Pi_2', \ldots, \Pi_k', \Pi_0'). \tag{78}$$

An estimator of Π that does not take into account its dependence on the (structural matrices) C_i, $i = 0, 1, \ldots, k$ is said to be an **unrestricted reduced form (URF)** estimator, while one that does is said to be a **restricted reduced form (RRF)**.

The URF estimator is the least squares estimator $\hat{\Pi} = (X'X)^{-1}X'Y$, while the 2- or 3SLS induced RRF is given by $\tilde{\Pi} = \tilde{C}\tilde{D}$, where $\tilde{C}$ and $\tilde{D} = \tilde{B}^{*-1}$ correspond to the 2- or 3SLS estimated structural parameters.[8]

Since, given Convention 1, the RRF is derived from the relationship

$$\Pi = CD, \quad D = (I - B)^{-1},$$

we must look to the properties of the estimators of the matrices C and B for determining the properties of Π. Let their estimators be, respectively, $\hat{C}$, $\hat{D}$, $\hat{\Pi}$ and consider

$$\begin{aligned} \hat{\Pi} - \Pi &= \hat{C}\hat{D} - CD = \hat{C}\hat{D} - \hat{C}D + \hat{C}D - CD \\ &= \hat{C}\hat{D}(D^{-1} - \hat{D}^{-1})D + (\hat{C} - C)D, \end{aligned}$$

which may be rewritten more constructively as

$$\hat{C}\hat{D} - CD = \hat{\Pi} - \Pi = (\, \hat{C}\hat{D}, \quad I\,)\begin{bmatrix} \hat{B} - B \\ \hat{C} - C \end{bmatrix} D. \tag{79}$$

Using the notation of equation (16) and of Proposition 2, we note that

$$\delta^0_{\cdot i} = L^{0'}_i a_{\cdot i} = \begin{bmatrix} e'_{\cdot i} & 0 \\ L'_{1i} & 0 \\ 0 & L'_{2i} \end{bmatrix} \begin{pmatrix} b^*_{\cdot i} \\ -c_{\cdot i} \end{pmatrix}. \tag{80}$$

Defining $J_i = (0, \; -I_{m_i+G_i})$, we see, from (7) and (15), that

$$\delta_{\cdot i} = J_i\delta^0_{\cdot i} = -L'_i a_{\cdot i} = L'_i \begin{pmatrix} b_{\cdot i} \\ c_{\cdot i} \end{pmatrix}. \tag{81}$$

Thus, from chapter 4 in Dhrymes [1984], we conclude

$$\begin{aligned} \sqrt{T}\left(\mathrm{vec}(\hat{\Pi} - \Pi)\right) &= \sqrt{T}(\hat{\pi} - \pi) \\ &= -\sqrt{T}\left(D' \otimes (\hat{\Pi}, \; I)\right) \mathrm{vec}\left(\begin{bmatrix} \hat{B} - B \\ \hat{C} - C \end{bmatrix}\right) \\ &= \sqrt{T}\left(D' \otimes (\hat{\Pi}, \; I)\right) L[\sqrt{T}(\hat{\delta} - \delta)] \\ &= (D' \otimes I)\hat{S}[\sqrt{T}(\hat{\delta} - \delta)], \end{aligned} \tag{82}$$

[8] In this discussion, we shall not adhere strictly to the notation that has $\hat{\Pi}$ representing the **unrestricted reduced form** and $\tilde{\Pi}$ representing the **restricted reduced form** estimators. Rather we shall use the notation $(\hat{\pi} - \pi)_{URF}$ and $(\hat{\pi} - \pi)_{RRF}$, to differentiate betyween the two, where $\pi = \mathrm{vec}(\Pi)$.

where $S = (I \otimes (\Pi, I))\, L$ is as defined in equation (26) and (32).

Theorem 3. Consider the GLSEM under assumptions (A.1) through (A.5) and the standard normalization convention. Asymptotically, the following statements are true, whether the model is static or dynamic:

$$\text{i.} \quad \sqrt{T}(\hat{\pi} - \pi)_{URF} \sim N(0,\ G_{(1)});$$

$$\text{ii.} \quad \sqrt{T}(\hat{\pi} - \pi)_{RRF(2SLS)} \sim N(0,\ G_{(2)});$$

$$\text{iii.} \quad \sqrt{T}(\hat{\pi} - \pi)_{RRF(3SLS)} \sim N(0,\ G_{(3)}),$$

where

$$\begin{aligned} G_{(1)} &= (D \otimes \bar{R}^{-1})'\Phi(D \otimes \bar{R}^{-1}), \\ G_{(2)} &= (D \otimes \bar{R}^{-1})'A^{*}\Phi A^{*}(D \otimes \bar{R}^{-1}), \\ G_{(3)} &= (D \otimes \bar{R}^{-1})'\left(S^{*}\Phi^{-1}S^{*}\right)^{-1}(D \otimes \bar{R}^{-1}), \\ A^{*} &= S^{*}(S^{*\prime}S^{*})^{-1}S^{*}, \quad \text{and} \quad \pi \;=\; \mathrm{vec}(\Pi). \end{aligned}$$

Proof: The results follow immediately from Theorem 2, if we note that

$$\begin{aligned} \hat{\Pi} - \Pi &= (X'X)^{-1}X'UD, \quad \text{or} \\ \sqrt{T}(\hat{\pi} - \pi)_{URF} &= (D \otimes I)'(I \otimes \left(\frac{X'X}{T}\right)^{-1})\frac{1}{\sqrt{T}}(I \otimes X')\,u, \end{aligned}$$

and

$$(\hat{\pi} - \pi)_{RRF} = (D \otimes I)'\hat{S}(\hat{\delta} - \delta).$$

q.e.d.

While the discussion above has established the limiting distribution of the various reduced form estimators, the following theorem establishes their relative efficiencies.

Theorem 4. Under the conditions of Theorem 3, the following statements are true:

i. $G_{(1)} - G_{(3)} \geq 0$;

ii. $G_{(2)} - G_{(3)} \geq 0$;

iii. $G_{(1)} - G_{(2)} \geq 0$, if and only if $\Phi_{21}^{*} = 0$; otherwise it is indefinite;

iv. $\Phi_{21}^{*} = 0$, if at least one of the following three conditions holds, otherwise $\Phi_{21}^{*} \neq 0$, where Φ_{21}^{*} will be defined below;

1. $\sigma_{ij} = 0$, for all $i \neq j$;
2. all equations are just identified;
3. $\sigma_{ij} \neq 0$, for some pair say (i_0, j_0), implies that the corresponding equations are just identified.

Proof: Put

$$G_{(1)} - G_{(3)} = (D \otimes \bar{R}^{-1})'[\Phi - S^{*}(S^{*\prime}\Phi^{-1}S^{*})^{-1}S^{*\prime}](D \otimes \bar{R}^{-1});$$

the matrix in the left member is positive semidefinite if and only if[9]

$$\Phi - S^{*}(S^{*\prime}\Phi^{-1}S^{*})^{-1}S^{*\prime} \geq 0.$$

Consider the characteristic equation

$$| \lambda\Phi - S^{*}(S^{*\prime}\Phi^{-1}S^{*})^{-1}S^{*\prime} | = 0,$$

and note that it has exactly the same characteristic roots as

$$| \lambda I - S^{*}(S^{*\prime}\Phi^{-1}S^{*})^{-1}S^{*\prime}\Phi^{-1} | = 0,$$

whose nonzero characteristic roots are exactly those of

$$| \mu I - (S^{*\prime}\Phi^{-1}S^{*})^{-1}S^{*\prime}\Phi^{-1}S^{*} | = | \mu I - I_k | = 0, \quad k = \sum_{i=1}^{m}(m_i + G_i).$$

From Dhrymes [1984, ch. 2] we conclude that there exists a nonsingular matrix P such that

$$\Phi = PP', \quad S^{*}(S^{*\prime}\Phi^{-1}S^{*})^{-1}S^{*\prime} = P\begin{bmatrix} I_k & 0 \\ 0 & 0 \end{bmatrix}P,$$

[9] Note that it is a simple implication of equations (75) and (76), in the statement of Theorem 2, that $C_2 = (S^{*\prime}S^{*})^{-1}S^{*\prime}\Phi S^{*}(S^{*\prime}S^{*})^{-1}$ and $C_3 = (S^{*\prime}\Phi^{-1}S^{*})^{-1}$ are, respectively, the covariance matrices of the limiting distribution of the 2- and 3SLS estimators.

so that

$$\Phi - S^*(S^{*\prime}\Phi^{-1}S^*)^{-1}S^{*\prime} = P\begin{bmatrix} 0 & 0 \\ 0 & I_{mG-k}\end{bmatrix}P' \geq 0.$$

To prove part ii. we note that

$$G_{(2)} - G_{(3)} = (D \otimes \bar{R}^{-1})'S^*[C_2 - C_3]S^{*\prime}(D \otimes \bar{R}^{-1}),$$

which is evidently positive semidefinite due to the fact that 3SLS is efficient relative to 2SLS, i.e., that $C_2 - C_3 \geq 0$.

As for part iii. we have that

$$G_{(1)} - G_{(2)} = (D \otimes \bar{R}^{-1})'[\Phi - J\Phi J](D \otimes \bar{R}^{-1}), \quad \text{where } J = S^*(S^{*\prime}S^*)^{-1}S^{*\prime}.$$

In view of the fact that $(D \otimes \bar{R}^{-1})$ is **nonsingular**, the matrix in the left member above is positive semidefinite, negative semidefinite or indefinite according as the matrix in square brackets (in the right member above) shares these properties. Now, since J is a symmetric idempotent matrix, it obeys rank$(J) = \sum_{i=1}^{m}(m_i + G_i) \leq mG$. Thus, there exists an **orthogonal** matrix E, such that

$$J = E\begin{bmatrix} I_k & 0 \\ 0 & 0\end{bmatrix}E'.$$

Consequently, we can write

$$E'[\Phi - J\Phi J]E = \Phi^* - \begin{bmatrix} I_k & 0 \\ 0 & 0\end{bmatrix}\Phi^*\begin{bmatrix} I_k & 0 \\ 0 & 0\end{bmatrix} = \begin{bmatrix} 0 & \Phi_{12}^* \\ \Phi_{21}^* & \Phi_{22}^*\end{bmatrix},$$

where $\Phi^* = E'\Phi E$. Since, by assumption, Φ is nonsingular, it follows that Φ_{22}^* is also nonsingular. Thus, $G_{(1)} - G_{(2)} \geq 0$, if and only if $\Phi_{21}^* = 0$. The sufficiency part of this statement is obvious, so let us demonstrate its necessity. Thus, suppose $G_{(1)} - G_{(2)} \geq 0$ and $\Phi_{21}^* \neq 0$; we derive a contradiction. Since the latter holds there exists at least one vector, say $\alpha \neq 0$, such that $\Phi_{21}^*\alpha \neq 0$. Consider, then

$$\begin{aligned}\phi(\alpha,\beta) &= 2\alpha'\Phi_{12}^*\beta + \beta'\Phi_{22}^*\beta \\ &= 3\alpha'\Phi_{12}^*\Phi_{22}^{*-1}\Phi_{21}^*\alpha > 0, \quad \text{for } \beta = \Phi_{22}^{*-1}\Phi_{21}^*\alpha, \\ &= -\alpha'\Phi_{12}^*\Phi_{22}^{*-1}\Phi_{21}^*\alpha < 0, \quad \text{for } \beta = -\Phi_{22}^{*-1}\Phi_{21}^*\alpha.\end{aligned}$$

Thus, the matrix $G_{(1)} - G_{(2)}$ is **indefinite** unless special circumstances hold, which brings us to the consideration of part iv.

To prove part iv. we note that $J = diag(J_1, J_2, \ldots, J_m)$, where $J_i = S_i^*(S_i^{*\prime} S_i^*)^{-1} S_i^{*\prime}$, for $i = 1, 2, \ldots, m$ and each is symmetric idempotent of rank $m_i + G_i$. Let E_i be their respective matrices of characteristic vectors and partition $E_i = (E_{i1},\ E_{i2})$, such that E_{i1} corresponds to the unit (characteristic) roots and E_{i2} corresponds to the zero roots. Define

$$E_{(1)} = \text{diag}(E_{11}, E_{21}, \ldots, E_{m1}), \quad E_{(2)} = \text{diag}(E_{12}, E_{22}, \ldots, E_{m2})$$

and note that $E = (E_{(1)},\ E_{(2)})$. Consequently,

$$\Phi_{12}^* = (\sigma_{ij} E_{i1}' E_{j2}), \quad \Phi_{21}^* = \left(\sigma_{ji} E_{j2}' E_{i1}\right), \tag{83}$$

and we see that $\Phi_{12}^* = 0$ **if** $\sigma_{ij} = 0$, **or if** $E_{i1}' E_{j2} = 0$, **for all** i **and** j. It is interesting to note that if all equations of the system are just **identified**, then the condition $E_{i1}' E_{j2} = 0$ will obviously hold,[10] and conversely if $E_{i1}' E_{j2} = 0$, for all i and j, **then all equations in the system are just identified.** To see this let ν_s denote the **dimension of the column null space, i.e, the nullity of** E_{s1}'. By the condition above we have

$$E_{11}' E_{s2} = 0, \quad \text{for all } s.$$

Since E_{12} is a **basis** for the column null space of E_{11}', there exists a unique matrix, say C_{s2}, such that $E_{s2} = E_{12} C_{s2}$, and moreover, we must have $\nu_s \leq \nu_1$. Repeating this argument with E_{21}, E_{31}, etc., we conclude that

$$\nu_1 \geq \nu_s,\ \nu_2 \geq \nu_s,\ \ldots,\ \nu_m \geq \nu_s, \quad \text{for} \quad s = 1, 2, \ldots, m.$$

But this implies that $\nu_s = \nu_1$, for all s. Similarly, from the condition $E_{12}' E_{s1} = 0$, for all s, we conclude that $E_{s1} = E_{11} C_{s1}$ and, moreover, that the dimension of the column null space of E_{12} is equal to that of the column null space of E_{s2}, for all s. This means that the matrices,

[10] A particularly simple way of demonstrating this is to note that in the case where all equations are just identified then $J_s = I_G$, for all $s = 1, 2, \ldots m$, and thus $\Phi - J\Phi J = 0$!

C_{s1} are square and **nonsingular** and have the same dimension for all s; the same is true of the matrices C_{s2}. Using the results above we find

$$J_s E_{s1} = E_{s1}, \quad \text{or} \quad J_s E_{11} C_{s1} = E_{11} C_{s1}, \quad \text{or} \quad J_s E_{11} = E_{11}, \tag{84}$$

which implies that E_{11} is the matrix of characteristic vectors corresponding to the unit roots of J_s, for all s. By a similar argument we establish that $J_s E_{12} = 0$, for all s. We have now established that $E_s = E_1 C_s$, where $C_s = \text{diag}(C_{s1}, C_{s2})$; since we must also have $E_s' E_s = E_s E_s' = I_G$, we conclude that the block components of C_s must each be **orthogonal matrices**. Consequently, since

$$J_s = E_s \begin{bmatrix} I_{k_s} & 0 \\ 0 & 0 \end{bmatrix} E_s' = E_1 C_s \begin{bmatrix} I_{k_s} & 0 \\ 0 & 0 \end{bmatrix} C_s' E_1' = E_{11} C_{s1} C_{s1}' E_{11}' = E_{11} E_{11}',$$

we conclude that $J_s = J_1$, for all s. Moreover,

$$S_i^{*\prime} J_i = S_i^{*\prime}, \quad \text{or} \quad S_i^{*\prime} J_1 = S_i^{*\prime}, \quad i = 1, 2, \ldots m. \tag{85}$$

Since all predetermined variables of the system appear in at least one equation, the part of (85) above that reads

$$L_{2i}' \bar{R} J_1 = L_{2i} \bar{R}, \quad \text{implies} \quad \bar{R} J_1 = \bar{R}, \quad \text{or} \quad J_1 = I.$$

In turn, this result leads to the conclusion that S_i is a square invertible matrix, for every i, or that **every equation of the system is just identified**. Finally, as to part iii.3 we note that if whenever $\sigma_{ij} \neq 0$, we have that the ith and j^{th} equations are just identified, then from the discussion above $E_{i1}' E_{j2} = 0$, so that $\Phi_{21}^* = 0$.

q.e.d.

Remark 9. The results of Theorem 3 appear to be partly counterintuitive, particularly those in parts iii. and iv. One would be tempted to think that if "more information is used", as in the case of RRF(2SLS), one would gain some efficiency over the case where "less information is used", as in the case of URF. A little reflection, however, would show that the conclusions of this Theorem do not violate this intuition. The trouble is that we are not necessarily, or unambiguously, using "more information" in the case of RRF(2SLS) vis a vis the case of URF. We remind the reader that **in this context** there are two types of information; one is sample information, the other is "a priori" information. In URF we are using **all sample information** in estimating every element of the parameter matrix Π, **but none of the prior information**, i.e., we do not use the fact that $\Pi = CD$ and, thus, **we do not use any of the prior restrictions placed on the elements of these structural matrices.** By constrast, RRF(2SLS) uses **all prior information**, i.e., uses the fact that $\Pi = CD$ and respects all prior restrictions on the structural matrices, but does not necessarily use all sample information.[11] Since the two procedures leave out, or fail to use, a different subset of the information available, it is not surprising that our formal discussion finds that it is not possible to place an unambiguous ranking on the relative efficiency of URF and RRF(2SLS) estimators.

5.2 Forecasting from Static and Dynamic Models

Forecasting from a **static** GLSEM is relatively straight forward; thus, suppose that the reduced form has been somehow estimated. Upon specifying the sequence of exogenous variables over the forecasting horizon, say $1, 2, \ldots, \tau$, we have

$$\hat{y}_{T+j\cdot} = p_{T+j\cdot}\hat{\Pi}. \tag{86}$$

Obtaining the conditional mean $\bar{y}_{T+j\cdot} = E(y_{T+j\cdot} \mid p_{T+j\cdot}) = p_{T+j\cdot}\Pi$, we may write

$$\text{vec}\,(\hat{y}_{T+j\cdot} - \bar{y}_{T+j\cdot}) = (I \otimes p_{T+j\cdot})(\hat{\pi} - \pi). \tag{87}$$

Noting further that the **forecast error** is typically defined by

$$e_{T+j\cdot} = y_{T+j\cdot} - \hat{y}_{T+j\cdot} = v_{t\cdot} - p_{T+j\cdot}(\hat{\Pi} - \Pi). \tag{88}$$

Thus, the quantity in (87), **which is proposed as a measure of the uncertainty adhering to the forecast** is simply the forecast error,

[11] In this context, it is the failure of 2SLS to use all sample information that renders it inefficient relative to the 3SLS estimation procedure.

without its structural error component.[12]

In view of the preceding discussion we may state

Theorem 5. Under the conditions of Theorem 4, the following statements are (asymptotically) true **for static models:**

i. $\sqrt{T}\text{vec}\left((\hat{y}_{T+\tau\cdot} - \bar{y}_{T+\tau\cdot})_{URF}\right) \sim N\left(0,\ (I \otimes p_{T+\tau\cdot})G_{(1)}(I \otimes p_{T+\tau\cdot})'\right)$;

ii. $\sqrt{T}\text{vec}\left((\hat{y}_{T+\tau\cdot} - \bar{y}_{T+\tau\cdot})_{RRF(2SLS)}\right) \sim N\left(0,\ G^*_{(2)}\right)$,
where $G^*_{(2)} = (I \otimes p_{T+\tau\cdot})G_{(2)}(I \otimes p_{T+\tau\cdot})'$;

iii. $\sqrt{T}\text{vec}\left((\hat{y}_{T+\tau\cdot} - \bar{y}_{T+\tau\cdot})_{RRF(3SLS)}\right) \sim N\left(0,\ G^*_{(3)}\right)$,
where $G^*_{(3)} = (I \otimes p_{T+\tau\cdot})G_{(3)}(I \otimes p_{T+\tau\cdot})'$;

Proof: Implicit in the preceding discussion and Theorem 4.

In dealing with dynamic models in a previous section we had employed lag operators and we had obtained a formal solution of the underlying difference equation involved, by inverting an appropriate polynomial operator. This particular approach is not useful in the present context since in making forecasts from a dynamic model **it is very important that we take into account initial conditions.** The formal solution obtained earlier does away with initial conditions and, thus, may be interpreted as a **long run solution.** If we are to predict or forecast $y_{T+1\cdot}$ given information up to time T it would be foolhardy to ignore the information conveyed by $y_{T-i\cdot}$, for $i = 0, 1, 2, \ldots k$. Thus, an alternative approach is indicated. Given the model

$$y_{t\cdot} = y_{t-1\cdot}\Pi_1 + y_{t-2\cdot}\Pi_2 + \ldots + y_{t-k\cdot}\Pi_k + p_{t\cdot}\Pi_0 + v_{t\cdot}, \tag{89}$$

and observations for $t = 1, 2, \ldots T$, we obtain the estimators of the parameter matrices, $\hat{\Pi}_i$, $i = 0, 1, 2, \ldots k$, by some appropriate method and we forecast

$$\hat{y}_{T+\tau\cdot} = \hat{y}_{T+\tau-1\cdot}\hat{\Pi}_1 + \hat{y}_{T+\tau-2\cdot}\hat{\Pi}_2 + \ldots + \hat{y}_{T+\tau-k\cdot}\hat{\Pi}_k + p^*_{T+\tau\cdot}, \tag{90}$$

[12] It should be noted here that many practitioners find that **it is precisely the structural error component that contributes the bulk of the forecasting error.**

where, for ease of notation, we have put $p^*_{T+\tau.} = p_{T+\tau.}\hat{\Pi}_0$.[13] Write this as

$$\begin{aligned}
\hat{y}'_{T+\tau.} &= \hat{A}_1^{(\tau)}y'_{T.} + \hat{A}_2^{(\tau)}y'_{T-1.} + \ldots + \hat{A}_k^{(\tau)}y'_{T-k+1.} \\
&\quad + \hat{B}_1^{(\tau)}p^{*\prime}_{T+1.} + \hat{B}_2^{(\tau)}p^{*\prime}_{T+2.} + \ldots + \hat{B}_\tau^{(\tau)}p^{*\prime}_{T+\tau.} \\
\hat{A}_1^{(1)} &= \hat{\Pi}'_1, \; \hat{A}_2^{(1)} = \hat{\Pi}'_2, \ldots, \hat{A}_k^{(1)} = \hat{\Pi}'_k.
\end{aligned} \tag{91}$$

We shall now attempt to determine the matrices $A_i^{(j)}$, and $B_s^{(j)}$, for $i = 1, 2, \ldots, k$, $s = 1, 2, \ldots \tau$ and $j = 1, 2, \ldots \tau$, by establishing a recursive relation. Thus,

$$\begin{aligned}
\hat{y}'_{T+j.} &= \hat{A}_1^{(1)}\left[\sum_{i=1}^{k} \hat{A}_i^{(j-1)}y'_{T-i+1.}\right] + \hat{A}_2^{(1)}\left[\sum_{i=1}^{k} \hat{A}_i^{(j-2)}y'_{T-i+1.}\right] + \ldots \\
&\quad + \hat{A}_k^{(1)}\left[\sum_{i=1}^{k} \hat{A}_i^{(j-k)}y'_{T-i+1.}\right] + \hat{A}_1^{(1)}\left[\sum_{s=1}^{j-1} \hat{B}_s^{(j-1)}p^{*\prime}_{T+s.}\right] \\
&\quad + \hat{A}_2^{(1)}\left[\sum_{s=1}^{j-1} \hat{B}_s^{(j-2)}p^{*\prime}_{T+s.}\right] + \ldots \\
&\quad + \hat{A}_k^{(1)}\left[\sum_{s=1}^{j-k} \hat{B}_s^{(j-k)}p^{*\prime}_{T+s.}\right] + p^{*\prime}_{T+j.}
\end{aligned} \tag{92}$$

Collecting terms we find

$$\hat{A}_i^{(j)} = \sum_{s=1}^{k} \hat{A}_s^{(1)}\hat{A}_i^{(j-s)} \qquad \hat{B}_r^{(j)} = \sum_{s=1}^{k} \hat{A}_s^{(1)}\hat{B}_r^{(j-s)}, \tag{93}$$

where $i = 1, 2, \ldots, k$, $r = 1, 2, \ldots, j$ and $j = 1, 2, \ldots \tau$. In order to make the formal definitions of equation (93) operational we need to impose certain "initial conditions", beyond those imposed in (91). These conditions may be summarized in equation (94) below.

$$\begin{aligned}
A_i^{(-s)} &= 0, \; s \geq 0, \text{ except that} \\
A_i^{(-(i-1))} &= I, \; i = 1, 2, \ldots, k \\
B_i^{(j)} &= I, \; i = j, \\
B_i^{(j)} &= 0, \; i > j, \text{ as well as for } j \leq 0.
\end{aligned} \tag{94}$$

---

[13] The matrices A_i^j, B_s^j, below, are not related to the matrices A_i, B_j, of equations (3) and (15).

It is an immediate consequence of the definitions above that

$$\hat{B}_i^{(j)} = \hat{A}_1^{(j-i)}, \quad \text{for } j > i > 0. \tag{95}$$

Remark 10. It should be stressed again that the avoidance of the formal solution of equation (47) in generating the forecast of equation (90) or (91) is not a matter of whim. The form in (47), while analytically very useful, would be totally inappropriate for generating forecasts. First, its use, as it stands, would oblige us to generate a forecast in the form

$$\hat{y}'_{T+\tau \cdot} = \sum_{j=0}^{T+\tau} \hat{H}_j p'_{T+\tau-j \cdot}, \tag{96}$$

where the matrices H_j are defined implicitly in the expansion of the operator $H(L)/b(L)$ and by analogy to the matrices G_τ in the expansion of equation (48), i.e.,

$$\frac{H(L)}{b(L)} = \sum_{j=0}^{\infty} H_j L^j.$$

Second, even if initial conditions were to be taken into account, by considering the general solution to the homogeneous part of the vector difference equation, this approach would still be undesirable in that it would require additional computational burdens entailed by the extraction of the (characteristic) roots, and their associated characteristic vectors, of the equation

$$| I - \sum_{j=1}^{k} \Pi'_j \lambda^j |= 0. \tag{97}$$

We have now completed the solution of the problem of how to obtain forecasts from a dynamic model. [14] Next we take up the issue of how to determine the degree of uncertainty surrounding such forecasts. We note that, when dealing with dynamic models, the simple linear properties of static models vanish and nonlinearities arise which make distributional issues a great deal more complicated. In the static case of the discussion immediately preceding, it is apparent from equation (86), that the

[14] In the language of engineering such a model would be termed a vector autoregressive model with "forcing function(s)" $p_{t\cdot}$ and $v_{t\cdot}$, or perhaps more appropriately a stochastic vector autoregressive model with "forcing function", $p_{t\cdot}$.

forecast is simply a linear transformation of the estimated parameters. Hence, its distribution is easily derived; this is, decidedly, not the case in the current context. Just by way of illustrating the difficutlies encountered in dynamic models let us compute explicitly the forecast for the τth period after the sample.

Example 1. Since in the notation created by the preceding discussion we had represented the forecast in question as

$$\hat{y}'_{T+\tau\cdot} = \sum_{i=1}^{k} \hat{A}_i^{(\tau)} y'_{T-i+1\cdot} + \sum_{s=1}^{\tau} \hat{B}_s^{(\tau)} p^{*\prime}_{T+s\cdot},$$

let us obtain the coefficient matrices of the representation above for the case $k = 3$. From equation (93) we find, by direct computation, for $\tau = 4$,

$$\begin{aligned}
\hat{A}_1^{(4)} &= \hat{\Pi}_1'^4 + \hat{\Pi}_1'^2\hat{\Pi}_2' + \hat{\Pi}_1'\hat{\Pi}_2'\hat{\Pi}_1' + \hat{\Pi}_1'\hat{\Pi}_3' + \hat{\Pi}_2'\hat{\Pi}_1'^2 + \hat{\Pi}_2'^2 + \hat{\Pi}_3'\hat{\Pi}_1' \\
\hat{A}_2^{(4)} &= \hat{\Pi}_1'^3\hat{\Pi}_2' + \hat{\Pi}_1'^2\hat{\Pi}_3' + \hat{\Pi}_1'\hat{\Pi}_2'^2 + \hat{\Pi}_2'\hat{\Pi}_1'\hat{\Pi}_2' + \hat{\Pi}_2'\hat{\Pi}_3' + \hat{\Pi}_3'\hat{\Pi}_2' \\
\hat{A}_3^{(4)} &= \hat{\Pi}_1'^3\hat{\Pi}_3' + \hat{\Pi}_1'\hat{\Pi}_2'\hat{\Pi}_3' + \hat{\Pi}_2'\hat{\Pi}_1'\hat{\Pi}_3' + \hat{\Pi}_3'^2;
\end{aligned} \tag{98}$$

for $\tau = 3$, we find

$$\begin{aligned}
\hat{A}_1^{(3)} &= \hat{\Pi}_1'^3 + \hat{\Pi}_1'\hat{\Pi}_2' + \hat{\Pi}_2'\hat{\Pi}_1' + \hat{\Pi}_3' \\
\hat{A}_2^{(3)} &= \hat{\Pi}_1'^2\hat{\Pi}_2' + \hat{\Pi}_1'\hat{\Pi}_3' + \hat{\Pi}_2'^2 \\
\hat{A}_3^{(3)} &= \hat{\Pi}_1'^2\hat{\Pi}_3' + \hat{\Pi}_2'\hat{\Pi}_3';
\end{aligned} \tag{99}$$

for $\tau = 2$, we find

$$\hat{A}_1^{(2)} = \hat{\Pi}_1'^2 + \hat{\Pi}_2', \quad \hat{A}_2^{(2)} = \hat{\Pi}_1'\hat{\Pi}_2' + \hat{\Pi}_3', \quad \hat{A}_3^{(2)} = \hat{\Pi}_1'\hat{\Pi}_3'. \tag{100}$$

Since, in equation (95), we had shown that $\hat{B}_i^{(j)} = \hat{A}_1^{(j-i)}$, for $0 < i < j$, our task is completed.

The example shows that even for moderately complex models it is almost impossible to obtain in closed form, explicit, finite sample distributional results for the forecast **even if the distribution of the parameter estimators is completely known.** Hence, in the case of dynamic models, for forecasts involving **more than one period beyond the sample's end** we must have recourse to **asymptotic theory.**

5.2.1 Distributional Aspects of Forecasts from Dynamic Models

Solving the model in (89) with initial conditions as in (90), we obtain

$$\begin{aligned} y'_{T+\tau\cdot} &= A_1^{(\tau)} y'_{T\cdot} + A_2^{(\tau)} y'_{T-1\cdot} + \ldots + A_k^{(\tau)} y'_{T-k+1\cdot} \\ &\quad + B_1^{(\tau)} \Pi'_0 p'_{T+1\cdot} + B_2^{(\tau)} \Pi'_0 p'_{T+2\cdot} + \ldots + B_\tau^{(\tau)} \Pi'_0 p'_{T+\tau\cdot} \\ &\quad + B_1^{(\tau)} v'_{T+1\cdot} + B_2^{(\tau)} v'_{T+2\cdot} + \ldots + v'_{T+\tau\cdot}. \end{aligned} \tag{101}$$

Consequently,

$$\begin{aligned} \bar{y}_{T+\tau\cdot} &= E\left(y_{T+\tau\cdot} \mid y_{T\cdot}, y_{T-1\cdot}, \ldots, y_{T-k+1\cdot}, p_{T+1\cdot}, \ldots, p_{T+\tau\cdot}\right) \\ &= A_1^{(\tau)} y'_{T\cdot} + A_2^{(\tau)} y'_{T-1\cdot} + \ldots + A_k^{(\tau)} y'_{T-k+1\cdot} \qquad (102) \\ &\quad + B_1^{(\tau)} \Pi'_0 p'_{T+1\cdot} + B_2^{(\tau)} \Pi'_0 p'_{T+2\cdot} + \ldots + B_\tau^{(\tau)} \Pi'_0 p'_{T+\tau\cdot}, \end{aligned}$$

and, thus,

$$\hat{y}_{T+\tau\cdot} - \bar{y}_{T+\tau\cdot} = \sum_{s=1}^{k} y_{T-s+1\cdot} \left(\hat{A}_s^{(\tau)} - A_s^{(\tau)}\right)' + \sum_{j=1}^{\tau} p_{T+j\cdot} \left(\hat{A}_1^{(\tau-j)} \hat{\Pi}'_0 - A_1^{(\tau-j)} \Pi'_0\right)' \tag{103}$$

Although equation (103) might appear hopeless, in fact, it can serve as the basis for some asymptotic theory regarding forecasts with dynamic models. From Example 1, we see that the entities $(\hat{A}_s^{(\tau)} - A_s^{(\tau)})'$ involve terms of the form,[15] say, $\hat{\Pi}_i^m \hat{\Pi}_j^n - \Pi_i^m \Pi_j^n$, and sums of terms of this form. We see, however, that by adding and subtracting $\Pi_i^m \hat{\Pi}_j^n$

$$\hat{\Pi}_i^m \hat{\Pi}_j^n - \Pi_i^m \Pi_j^n = (\hat{\Pi}_i^m - \Pi_i^m)\hat{\Pi}_j^n + \Pi_i^m (\hat{\Pi}_j^n - \Pi_j^n).$$

Hence, the only remaining problem is a suitable representation for entities of the form $(\hat{\Pi}_j^n - \Pi_j^n)$. But it is a rather simple operation to show that

$$(\hat{\Pi}_j^n - \Pi_j^n) = \sum_{i=1}^{n} \Pi_j^{i-1} (\hat{\Pi}_j - \Pi_j) \hat{\Pi}_j^{n-i}.$$

---

[15] When a model with lags of order k is considered, i.e., when we are dealing with a kth order vector difference equation, we should have to deal with products of at most k terms. In such a case it may be shown that

$$\hat{\Pi}_1^{s_1} \hat{\Pi}_2^{s_2} \ldots \hat{\Pi}_k^{s_k} - \Pi_1^{s_1} \Pi_2^{s_2} \ldots \Pi_k^{s_k} = \sum_{r=1}^{k} \left[\left(\prod_{i=1}^{r-1} \Pi_i^{s_i} \right) (\hat{\Pi}_r^{s_r} - \Pi_r^{s_r}) \left(\prod_{i=r+1}^{k} \hat{\Pi}_i^{s_i} \right) \right].$$

Thus, the ensuing discussion is fully relevant and exhaustive.

Thus, we conclude that there exist matrices, say $(A_{ji}^{(\tau)} \otimes B_{ji}^{(\tau)})$, such that

$$\mathrm{vec}\left((\hat{A}_i^{(\tau)} - A_i^{(\tau)})'\right) = \sum_{j=1}^{k}(A_{ji}^{(\tau)} \otimes B_{ji}^{(\tau)})(\hat{\pi}_j - \pi_j),$$

where $(\hat{\pi}_j - \pi_j) = \mathrm{vec}(\hat{\Pi}_j - \Pi_j)$. The remaining term obeys

$$\hat{\Pi}_0 \hat{A}_1^{(\tau-j)'} - \Pi_0 A_1^{(\tau-j)'} = (\hat{\Pi}_0 - \Pi_0)\hat{A}_1^{(\tau-j)'} + \Pi_0 \left(\hat{A}_1^{(\tau-j)} - A_1^{(\tau-j)}\right)'.$$

Thus,

$$\begin{aligned}
\mathrm{vec}\left((\hat{A}_1^{(\tau-j)}\hat{\Pi}_0' - A_1^{(\tau-j)}\Pi_0')'\right) &= \Pi_0^* \sum_{s=1}^{k}\left((A_{s1}^{(\tau-j)} \otimes B_{s1}^{(\tau-j)})(\hat{\pi}_s - \pi_s)\right) \\
&\quad + (\hat{A}_1^{(\tau-j)} \otimes I)(\hat{\pi}_0 - \pi_0), \\
\Pi_0^* &= (I \otimes \Pi_0).
\end{aligned}$$

Substituting in equation (103) we obtain

$$\begin{aligned}
\mathrm{vec}(\hat{y}_{T+\tau\cdot} - \bar{y}_{T+\tau\cdot}) &= \sum_{j=1}^{k}(F_{j1} + F_{j2})(\hat{\pi}_j - \pi_j) \\
&\quad + \left[\sum_{i=1}^{\tau}(A_1^{(\tau-i)} \otimes p_{T+i\cdot})\right](\hat{\pi}_0 - \pi_0) \\
F_{j1} &= \sum_{s=1}^{k}\left((I \otimes y_{T-s+1\cdot})(A_{js}^{(\tau)} \otimes B_{js}^{(\tau)})\right) \\
F_{j2} &= \sum_{i=1}^{\tau}\left((I \otimes p_{T+i\cdot}\Pi_0)(A_{j1}^{(\tau-i)} \otimes B_{j1}^{(\tau-i)})\right) \qquad (104)
\end{aligned}$$

for $j = 1, 2, \ldots, k$; moreover, defining

$$\begin{aligned}
S_{(j)}^{(\tau)} &= \sum_{s=1}^{k}(I \otimes y_{T-s+1\cdot})(A_{js}^{(\tau)} \otimes B_{js}^{(\tau)}) \\
&\quad + \sum_{i=1}^{\tau}(I \otimes p_{T+i\cdot}\Pi_0)(A_{j1}^{(\tau-i)} \otimes B_{j1}^{(\tau-i)}) \\
S_{(0)}^{(\tau)} &= \sum_{i=1}^{\tau}(\hat{A}_1^{(\tau-i)} \otimes p_{T+i\cdot}) \\
S^{(\tau)} &= (S_{(1)}^{(\tau)}, S_{(2)}^{(\tau)}, \ldots, S_{(k)}^{(\tau)}, S_{(0)}^{(\tau)}) \\
\Pi &= (\Pi_1', \Pi_2', \ldots, \Pi_k', \Pi_0)', \qquad (105)
\end{aligned}$$

we can represent the vector of forecasts as

$$S^{(\tau)} \begin{bmatrix} \hat{\pi}_1 - \pi_1 \\ \hat{\pi}_2 - \pi_2 \\ \vdots \\ \hat{\pi}_k - \pi_k \\ \hat{\pi}_0 - \pi_0 \end{bmatrix} = \mathrm{vec}(\hat{y}_{T+\tau\cdot} - \bar{y}_{T+\tau\cdot}). \tag{106}$$

Comparing the vector in the left member of (106) with $\mathrm{vec}(\hat{\Pi} - \Pi)$ we note that while the two have the same number,[16] and exactly the same type, of elements their arrangement is different. But this means that there exists a permutation matrix, say $I'_{(n,n)}$, such that

$$I'_{(n,n)} \begin{bmatrix} \hat{\pi}_1 - \pi_1 \\ \hat{\pi}_2 - \pi_2 \\ \vdots \\ \hat{\pi}_k - \pi_k \\ \hat{\pi}_0 - \pi_0 \end{bmatrix} = \mathrm{vec}(\hat{\Pi} - \Pi) = (\hat{\pi} - \pi), \qquad n = m(mk+s).$$

It follows, therefore, that

$$\mathrm{vec}(\hat{y}_{T+\tau\cdot} - \bar{y}_{T+\tau\cdot}) = S^{(\tau)} I_{(n,n)}(\hat{\pi} - \pi). \tag{107}$$

Thus, if it is known that $\sqrt{T}(\hat{\pi} - \pi)$ has a limiting distribution of the form, say,

$$\sqrt{T}(\hat{\pi} - \pi) \sim N(0, \ \Psi),$$

then, if the sample is sufficiently large, we whould be able to argue that

$$T(\hat{y}_{T+\tau\cdot} - \bar{y}_{T+\tau\cdot})(S^{(\tau)} I_{(n,n)} \Psi I'_{(n,n)} S^{(\tau)\prime})_g (\hat{y}_{T+\tau\cdot} - \bar{y}_{T+\tau\cdot})' \sim \chi_r, \tag{108}$$

where,

$$r = \mathrm{rank}\left((S^{(\tau)} I_{(n,n)} \Psi I'_{(n,n)} S^{(\tau)\prime})_g \right),$$

and $(S^{(\tau)} I_{(n,n)} \Psi I'_{(n,n)} S^{(\tau)\prime})_g$ is the generalized inverse.

Upon reflection, we see that this is, indeed, the situation with URF, RRF(2SLS) and RRF(3SLS) estimators, i.e., the limiting distribution of

[16] We remind the reader that by assumption (A.1), the number of exogenous variables, i.e., the number of elements in $p_{t\cdot}$, is s; thus the vectors in question have $n = m(mk + s)$ elements.

these reduced form estimators is given in Theorem 4, above; moreover, the covariance matrix of their respective limiting distributions can easily be estimated from the sample. Hence, we may summarize the development immediately above in

Theorem 6. Under the conditions of Theorem 3, the following statements are true[17], **for dynamic models** and $\tau \geq 1$, on the assertion that the sample size, T, is sufficiently large:

i. $\sqrt{T}\text{vec}\left((\hat{y}_{T+\tau\cdot} - \bar{y}_{T+\tau\cdot})_{URF}\right) \sim N\left(0,\ S^{(\tau)}G_{(1)}S^{(\tau)\prime}\right)$;

ii. $\sqrt{T}\text{vec}\left((\hat{y}_{T+\tau\cdot} - \bar{y}_{T+\tau\cdot})_{RRF(2SLS)}\right) \sim N\left(0,\ S^{(\tau)}G_{(2)}S^{(\tau)\prime}\right)$;

iii. $\sqrt{T}\text{vec}\left((\hat{y}_{T+\tau\cdot} - \bar{y}_{T+\tau\cdot})_{RRF(3SLS)}\right) \sim N\left(0,\ S^{(\tau)}G_{(3)}S^{(\tau)\prime}\right)$.

Proof: The results follow immediately from the preceding discussion and Theorem 3.

[17] The statement of this Theorem contains certain logical incongruities, viz., when we contemplate the distribution of the normalized deviations of the left members we simultaneously want to take the "initial conditions", i.e., the $y_{T\cdot}, y_{T-1\cdot}, \ldots, y_{T-k+1\cdot}$, as **given**, but we also wish to utilize the limiting distribution of the underlying structural parameters, which, of course, depends on these very initial conditions! Thus, if one wished to be exceedingly puristic one should not have stated these results as a "Theorem". On the other hand, in this paper, we also use the statement of a theorem in order to summarize prominently the results of a certain discussion. Thus, Theorem 7 is to be viewed in this light, and should be thought of as a framework for a good working approximation in empirical applications and **not** as a rigorous derivation of the distribution of forecasts from dynamic GLSEM.

REFERENCES

Anderson, T. W. [1950] "Estimation of the Parameters of a Single Equation by the Limited Information Maximum Likelihood Method", chapter 9 in Koopmans, T.C. **Statistical Inference in Dynamic Economic Models**, Monograph No. 10, Cowles Foundation for Research in Economics, New York, J. Wiley and Sons Inc.

______ and H. Rubin [1949] "Estimation of the Parameters of a Single Equation in a Complete System of Stochastic Equations", **Annals of Mathematical Statistics**, vol. 20, pp. 46-63.

____________ [1950] "The Asymptotic Properties of Estimates of the Parameters of a Single Equation in a Complete Systems of Stochastic Equations", **Annals of Mathematical Statistics**, vol. 21, pp.570-582.

Chow, G.C. [1973] "Multiperiod Predictions from Stochastic Difference Equations by Bayesian Methods", **Econometrica**, vol. 41, pp.109-118.

Dhrymes, P.J. [1969] "Asymptotic Tests of Significance and Related Aspects of 2SLS and 3SLS Estimated Parameters", **Review of Economic Studies**, vol. , pp.

_______ [1970] **Econometrics: Statistical Foundations and Applications**, New York, Harper and Row; also revised edition, New York, Springer-Verlag, 1974.

_______ [1973] "Restricted and Unrestricted Reduced Forms: Asymptotic Distribution and Relative Efficiency", **Econometrica**, vol. 41, pp. 119-134.

_______ [1984] **Mathematics for Econometrics**, New York, Springer-Verlag.

_______ [1989] **Advanced Econometrics, vol. I, Probability and Inference Theory**, New York, Springer-Verlag (in press).

Feldstein, M.S. [1971] "The Error of Forecast in Economic Systems, when the Forecast-Period Exogenous Variables are Stochastic", **Econometrica**, vol. 39, pp.55-60

Goldberger, A.S., A.L. Nagar and H.S. Odeh [1961] "The Covariance

Matrix of Reduced Form Coefficients and of Forecasts for a Structural Econometric Model", **Econometrica** vol. 29, pp. 556-573.

Hannan, E.J. [1970] **Multiple Time Series**, New York, John Wiley and Sons Inc.

Hymans, S. [1968] "Simultaneous Confidence Intervals in Econometric Forecasting", **Econometrica**, vol. 36, pp. 18-30.

Klein, L. R. [1960] "The Efficiency of Estimation in Econometric Models", in Pfouts, R.W. (ed.) **Essays in Economics and Econometrics**, Chapel Hill, University of North Carolina Press.

Mandel, J. [1958] "A Note On Confidence Intervals in Regression Problems", **Annals of Mathematical Statistics**, vol. 29, pp. 903-907.

Mann, H. B. and A. Wald, [1943] "On the Statistical Treatment of Linear Stochastic Difference Equations", **Econometrica**, vol. 11, pp. 173-120.

Rubin, H. [1950] "Consistency of Maximum Likelihood in the Explosive Case", chapter 9 in Koopmans, T.C. (ed.) **Statistical Inference in Dynamic Economic Models**, New York, John Wiley and Sons Inc.

Schmidt, P. [1973] "The Asymptotic Distribution of Dynamic Multipliers", **Econometrica**, vol. 41, pp.161-164.

Theil, H. and J.C.G. Boot, [1962] "The Final Form of Econometric Equation Systems", **Review of International Statistical Institute**, vol. 30, pp.136-152.

A Monte Carlo Study of Structural Estimator Distributions After Performance of Likelihood Ratio Pre-Tests

R. L. Basmann
Dept. of Economics
SUNY-Binghamton

Hae-Shin Hwang
Dept. of Economics
Texas A&M University

Abstract

This study is concerned with the effect of an identifiability pretest on the locations and shapes of conditional distributions of structural coefficient estimators in a simultaneous equations model. We examine whether there are important cases in which the identifiability test statistic and (correctly) restricted structural coefficient estimators such as 2SLS and 3SLS are "approximately" statistically independent over a broad range of Type I error levels of for the test statistic. The results of the Monte Carlo experiments based on the Klein model I are not conclusive, though they tend to support approximate independence in most cases.

1. Introduction

This article is dedicated to A. L. Nagar on the occasion of his sixtieth birthday. His contributions to statistical inference in econometric equation systems, Nagar (1959, 1960, 1961, 1962, 1969, 1973), Nagar and Ullah (1972), Nagar and Carter (1974), Ullah and Nagar (1974), Carter and Nagar (1977) have done much to make the analysis of econometric estimators and test statistics a suitable base strategy for modern econometric expert systems. Sustained development of expert systems has already begun in other branches of statistics, cf. Hand (1986), Oldford and Peters (1986), Pregibon (1986), Tukey (1986). The reader who is not acquainted with expert systems should consult Gale (1986a) and the description of REX (Regression EXpert), Gale (1986b). REX is an expert statistical system built by William Gale and Daryl Pregibon; it advises users on various aspects of regression analysis, including the testing of assumptions, indicating transformations when assumptions are violated, interpreting intermediate and final results, justifying its recommendations, and providing instructions in statistical concepts, Gale (1986b, p. 173). Hand (1986) uses multivariate analysis of variance (MANOVA) to illustrate a suitable base strategy for one kind of statistical expert system, Hand (1986, pp. 358-369). Discriminant analysis affords another ideal area for application of an expert system, Hand (1986, p. 371). It is only to be expected that econometricians and econometric statisticians, already familiar with multivariate analysis, will quickly follow suit.

Knowledge acquisition is an essential part of the building of an expert system. Cf. Martin and Oxman (1988, pp. 25, 171-178), Brooking (1986), Thisted (1986, pp. 273-274). Knowledge acquisition for an econometric expert system presupposes the existence of expert knowledge, cf. Martin and Oxman (1988, p. 7), Harmon and King (1985, pp. 31-33), about the distributional behavior of econometric test statistics and estimators. Such expert knowledge would include knowledge of exact mathematical expressions of finite sample distributions where they are known. However existing knowledge of mathematical forms of exact distributions of econometric estimators and test statistics is too scanty and grows too slowly to support alone the development of useful econometric expert systems. This is not difficult to see. Even where the exact distribution function of an econometric estimator is known, the form of approximation (used to calculate numerical values) often differs considerably from one subject matter domain to another, e.g., from simultaneous macromodels to models of discrimination in employment. The construction of useful econometric expert systems calls for such expert knowledge. From the point of view of expert system design and construction knowledge of exact expressions for distributions is not essential to success.

Today's computer technology has greatly enhanced the usefulness of Monte Carlo studies to generate knowledge of distributions of econometric estimators and test statistics. Nagar (1960) is to be numbered among the earliest econometric statisticians to appreciate the potential of such Monte Carlo experiments even in the days of antique computers, cf Wagner (1958), Basmann (1958, 1960b, 1960c, 1960d), Summers (1958,1965). Basmann et al (1974a, 1974b) studied the distributions of reduced-form and structural parameter estimators in models with lagged endogenous variables. Kadane (1974) and Maddala (1974) studied the distributions of test criteria.

This article focusses on the use of likelihood ratio (LR) tests as a preliminary to estimation of structural parameters by "two-stage least squares" (2SLS) and "three-stage least squares" (3SLS). Koopmans and Hood (1953, pp. 184-185) considered it natural to abandon without further computation any set of restrictions strongly rejected by LR tests, and to forego use of parameter estimates that have been forced to satisfy a strongly rejected set of restrictions. Consider the restrictions imposed on a single structural equation. If the 2SLS identifiability test statistic strongly "rejects" those restrictions, then much of the rationale for using 3SLS to estimate the whole system is destroyed. Moreover, if the 2SLS full-system identifiability test statistic "rejects" the set of all restrictions, there is even less rationale for proceeding to estimate by 3SLS.

This study is concerned with the effect of such pretesting of structural coefficient restrictions. More precisely, this paper is concerned with the effect of such pretests on the locations and shapes of conditional distributions of structural coefficient estimators. We are concerned directly with problems of distribution as logically prior to problems of optimal estimator choice, Fisher (1922, p. 314). The proposing of risk functions for various pretest estimators based on 2SLS and 3SLS estimators of structural coefficients is beyond the scope of the present paper. Several fundamental logical problems of simultaneous equations models and difficulties with causal interpretations, for instance, Basmann (1988), make the design of such pretest estimators less straightforward than in the case of ordinary regression models. Important results by, e.g., James and Stein (1961), Toro-Vizcarrondo and Wallace (1968), Judge et al (1973), Toyoda and Wallace (1976), Aigner and Judge (1977), Judge and Bock (1978), Greenberg (1980), Ohtani and Toyoda (1980) should carry over to structural systems, but with considerable modification.

Here is a typical question for our immediate research: Suppose identifying restrictions are tested at a given level of Type I error. Suppose that the restrictions are correctly specified. Consider the conditional distribution of a structural coefficient estimator, given that the identifiability test statistic is in the prescribed acceptance region. How does that conditional distribution differ from the marginal distribution of the estimator? How does it differ from (say) the conditional distribution of the same coefficient estimator given that the identifiability test statistic falls into the rejection region? For instance, how do these conditional distributions differ in respect of location of their medians? in respect of the magnitudes of their dispersions?, in respect of skewness?, in respect of their "kurtosis"? Do these differences of distributions vary considerably with changes in the Type I error level one selects?

Consider this extreme case: Suppose the conditional distributions above are identical for all levels of Type I error. That implies that the coefficient estimator and the identifiability test statistic are statistically independent. Of course we do not expect to encounter this extreme case in practice. On the other hand, we do want to know whether there are important cases in which the identifiability test statistic and structural coefficient estimators such as 2SLS and 3SLS are "approximately" statistically independent over a broad range of Type I error levels for the test statistic.

Why is that knowledge important in the case of structural estimators and test statistics? Consider the case of a single equation linear regression model with a null hypothesis that correctly specifies restrictions, e.g., zero values, on a subset of coefficients. Under the null hypothesis the test statistic, F, and the restricted OLS estimators of the remaining coefficients are independently distributed. Committing a Type I error, i.e., incorrectly "rejecting" a subset of sample estimates, does not affect the unbiasedness, variance, etc of the restricted OLS estimators on the "accepted" subset of sample estimates.

The specification of identifying restrictions on a single structural equation is analogous to the specification of linear restrictions on ordinary regression coefficients, though not completely so. Users' interpretations of the structural identifiability test outcomes are almost universally strictly analogous to the corresponding interpretations properly made for the ordinary linear regression case. This is a convenient practice. It is readily understood by most applied users of 2SLS and 3SLS methods who do not have time to acquire expertise in econometric statistics. Probably this practice is not seriously misleading within fairly broad limits. However, it is important for econometric statisticians to search out those limits. Assessing the extent to which the identifiability test statistic and (correctly) restricted structural estimators, 2SLS or 3SLS, are "approximately" statistically independent is an important aspect of the search.

At present not much is known about this matter. Lack of independence may be either beneficial or inconvenient. For instance, in the case of structural estimation methods such as 2SLS and 3SLS it may be that the conditional distributions of structural estimators, given commission of Type I error in the test of identifiability restrictions, will turn out to be more concentrated and more symmetric about the population coefficients than the marginal distributions. Or, as Arnold Zellner has suggested, these conditional distributions might possess means and/or variances where the marginal distributions do not. That would be advantageous, since users do conceptualize more readily in terms of means and variances. Knowing under what conditions of data and model structure such effects are likely to occur, and being able to transmit that kind of information to nonexpert users of (say) 2SLS and 3SLS, is an important objective of econometric statistical research.

2. The Structural Model for Monte Carlo Experiments: Klein Model I

In a Monte Carlo experiment, the "true" structure operates repeatedly on a single matrix of exogenous observations to generate a sequence of random samples of endogenous variables. From each sample and the matrix of exogenous variables, the unconstrained reduced-form, the structural estimates by 2SLS and 3SLS, and their respective constrained reduced-forms, and all LR test criteria, are computed.

In this part of our study we use a designed "true" structure that is based on Klein's pioneer Model I, Klein (1950). We chose Klein's Model I for several reasons. One reason was that the number of independent structural relations is small, namely, three. We believe it is unlikely that the conjectured "approximate" statistical independence of indentifiability test statistics and the conditional distributions of coefficient estimators, given outcomes of significance tests, is much affected by the number of structural equations in a model.

The second reason for choosing Klein's Model I as the "true" structure was that it is very widely known to economists and econometricians. Textbooks of econometrics, such as Gujarati (1988, pp. 561-562, 610-611), Maddala (1977, pp. 241-242), have acquainted many undergraduates with Model I. Many readers will have already interpreted coefficient estimates and test statistics from Model I, cf. Gujarati (1988, p. 611, Example 19.2).

Another reason for choosing Klein's Model I is that it is a classic illustration of a simultaneous equations model yielding "reasonable" coefficient estimates, with signs predicted by economic theory, while at the same time being overwhelmingly "rejected" by LR tests. [We present the test statistics and their implicit significance levels below.] Occurrence of that kind of outcome is important in the building of any kind of expert system, especially in the knowledge acquisition phase, Martin and Oxman (1988, pp. 195-197). It can be the occasion for an illuminating and highly fruitful discussion among the ground domain expert --- the economic expert who builds the model --- the interviewer, and the knowledge engineer, who transfers the model-builder's expert knowledge to the expert system. A domain expert (economist, econometrician) who is socially competent and patient, and who takes the time to field the statistician's questions concerning his evaluation of such "rejected" parameter sets (cf. Brooking (1986, p. 327)) is essential, however.

Klein (1950) considered all of the point estimates obtained by full information maximum likelihood (FIML) to look very reasonable, seeming not to contradict the "general evidence that would be based on experience other than that contained in the data used, and all have the signs that we should expect on the basis of economic theory", Klein (1950, p. 68). The nature and existence of such "general evidence that would be based on experience other than that contained in the data" are still not well-understood. Development of expert econometric statistical systems will require considerable clarification of this oft-cited support for sets of econometric parameter estimates. [Ideally, a user of an expert econometric system would be able to query the system for an explanation.] Fortunately the importance of the Klein (1950) appraisal of structural estimates to the present study does not depend on our having a precise clarification.

However, Klein's appraisal of the coefficient estimates as "reasonable" is related to our main conjecture about conditional distributions of structural coefficient estimators. If the latter approximate the marginal distributions of the coefficient estimators, then the agreement of structural estimates and economic theory should occur often, even when the model itself is strongly "rejected" by the LR, or identifiability, test.

We mention one more reason for choosing Klein Model I. The time-series used in Klein (1950) is only moderately long. Consequently we do not have to deal with the problem of reducing specified Type I error levels for exceedingly large sample sizes. The problem is only partly one for solution by statisticians; specifying Type I error is primarily a matter for subject domain experts.

Our search for suitable parameter values for the designed "true" structure began with the FIML coefficient estimates presented by Klein (1950, p. 68). According to Klein (1950, p. 67) maximum likelihood was applied in the special case of Model I for which the structural variance matrix is diagonal, Klein (1950, p. 67). However zero covariance restrictions were not actually imposed on the structural estimates, as Klein (1950, p. 71) points out.

Statistical testing of theoretical restrictions, and getting test outcomes favorable to those restrictions are logically prior to the forcing of such theoretical restrictions on parameter estimates. So we examine LR test criteria and their associated significance probabilities, i. e., the probability of Type I error. Since Klein (1950) did not publish these test outcomes, we have evaluated likelihood ratios for the FIML and LIML estimates he did publish. For his FIML estimates the log-likelihood ratio is -103.4919, and the test criterion $-2\ln(\lambda)=206.9838$. The significance probability, based on the distribution of chi-square with 11 degrees of freedom, is essentially zero. In other words, the set of theoretical zero-order restrictions could be "accepted" only by a prespecified level of Type I error equal to zero. We emphasize that this is not an unusual situation in macro-econometrics. For instance, Barro (1981, p. 152) reports a model for which the significance probability is 0.00058 based on the chi-square test criterion (=34.4) with twelve degrees of freedom.

Klein (1950, p.71) presents LIML structural coefficient estimates. We computed the corresponding structural variance matrix estimate and evaluated the LR test criterion and significance probability. The likelihood support for the LIML estimates is marginally stronger than the likelihood support for the FIML estimates. The log-likelihood ratio is -47.4249, and the test criterion $-2\ln(\lambda)=94.8498$. The significance probability is 1.85×10^{-15}. The fact that the LIML estimates yield a greater likelihood than FIML is probably due to the particular selection of initial values for "hill-climbing" in the FIML program Klein used.

We have computed estimates of Klein Model I using 2SLS. The likelihood support for the 2SLS estimates is stronger than for the FIML estimates provided by Klein (1950, p. 68). It is also stronger than for the Klein's OLS estimates. It is less strong than that of LIML. The test criterion $-2\ln(\lambda)=134.1718$, and the significance probability is zero, i. e., too small to be computed. We have computed estimates of Klein Model I using 3SLS as well. The 3SLS estimates receive the strongest likelihood support afforded by Klein's data batch. The test criterion $-2\ln(\lambda)=78.8098$, and the significance probability is 2.5×10^{-12}.

3. Description of Monte Carlo Experiments

3.1 Design of Parent Population

Klein (1950) included time as an exogenous variable in one structural equation. However in the design of artificial parent populations for Monte Carlo experiments it is preferable to avoid the use of time as an exogenous variable. Klein model I has three endogenous variables: y_1=consumption, y_2=income net of taxes, and y_3=total wage bill, and seven predetermined variables (excluding the time trend term): x_1=lagged profits, x_2=lagged capital stock, x_3=taxes, x_4=government expenditure, x_5=government wage bill, x_6=lagged private sector income, and x_7=constant, where

$$x_{t1}=y_{t-1,2} - y_{t-1,3}, \qquad x_{t6}=y_{t-1,2} + x_{t-1,3} - x_{t-1,5}.$$

Writing the general specification of a simultaneous equations model as

$$Y_tB + X_t\Gamma + U_t = 0, \quad U_t \sim \text{i.i.N}(0, \Omega),$$

the parameter values that we used for our Monte Carlo study are specified below:

$$B = \begin{bmatrix} -1.0 & -1.0 & 0.0 \\ 0.014 & 0.076 & 0.475 \\ 0.795 & 0.924 & -1.0 \end{bmatrix}$$

$$\Gamma = \begin{bmatrix} 0.219 & 0.119 & 0.0 \\ 0.0 & -0.021 & 0.0 \\ 0.0 & 1.0 & 0.545 \\ 0.0 & -1.0 & 0.0 \\ 0.0 & 0.0 & 0.525 \\ 0.0 & 0.0 & 0.144 \\ 16.580 & 11.409 & -0.979 \end{bmatrix}$$

$$\Omega = \begin{bmatrix} 1.527 & 0.195 & -0.339 \\ 0.195 & 1.996 & -0.168 \\ -0.339 & -0.168 & 0.928 \end{bmatrix}$$

The parameter values listed above are estimated values from Klein model I by 2SLS using his original data set. Notice that, in addition to the normalization and zero restrictions, there are four linear restrictions in the model: $\beta_{22}+\beta_{32}=1$, $\tau_{32}=1$, $\tau_{42}=-1$, and $\beta_{23}+\tau_{53}=1$.
In our experiments the predetermined variables x_2, x_3, x_4 and x_5 are treated as strictly exogenous and generated by the procedure described below. Define an interval $I_{ij}=[a_{ij}, b_{ij}]$, where $a_{ij}=1+iN/j$ and $b_{ij}=(i+1)N/j$, and N is the size of the sample.

$$\begin{aligned} x_{t2} &= 216.7 \quad \text{if } t\in I_{ij} \text{ for } i=0 \text{ and } j=2 \\ &= 180.1 \quad \text{if } t\in I_{ij} \text{ for } i=1 \text{ and } j=2 \\ x_{t3} &= 11.6 \quad \text{if } t\in I_{ij} \text{ for } j=4 \text{ and } i=0,2 \\ &= 3.4 \quad \text{if } t\in I_{ij} \text{ for } j=4 \text{ and } i=1,3 \\ x_{t4} &= 13.8 \quad \text{if } t\in I_{ij} \text{ for } j=8 \text{ and } i=0,2,4,6 \\ &= 2.4 \quad \text{if } t\in I_{ij} \text{ for } j=8 \text{ and } i=1,3,5,7 \\ x_{t5} &= 8.5 \quad \text{if } t\in I_{ij} \text{ for } j=16 \text{ and } i=0,2,4,6,8,10,12,14 \\ &= 2.2 \quad \text{if } t\in I_{ij} \text{ for } j=16 \text{ and } i=1,3,5,7,9,11,13,15 \end{aligned}$$

The values specified for x_{tk}'s above are the largest and smallest values of Klein's data for each variable. The purpose of the construction of these variables is to maintain a similar range for the variables as in Klein's data set. It also minimizes the variance estimators and avoids problems of nonstationarity.

The data for the endogenous variables and their lagged values are generated by generating three-variate normal random vectors with covariance matrix Ω specified above from the IMSL subroutine GGNML. For each data set thus generated, 2SLS and 3SLS estimates of structural coefficients are computed. The total number of replication is 1000, and the size of the sample for each replication is N=32.

3.2 Pre-testing Using System and Individual Equation LR Tests

Using the 2SLS or 3SLS estimates of coefficients, four LR tests of "identifiability" are computed: Three individual equation test statistics and the system-wide test statistic. Let $\tilde{B}$ and $\tilde{\Gamma}$ be the 2SLS (or 3SLS) estimates of coefficient matrices, and

$\tilde{\Omega}=(Y\tilde{B}+X\tilde{\Gamma})'(Y\tilde{B}+X\tilde{\Gamma})/N$, $\quad \hat{\Omega}=\tilde{B}'Y'(I-X(X'X)^{-1}X')Y\tilde{B}/N$

The i-th equation identifiability test statistic is computed by

$TLR_i=\tilde{\Omega}_{ii}/\hat{\Omega}_{ii} - 1, \quad i=1,2,3,$

where $\tilde{\Omega}_{ii}$ is the i-th diagonal element of $\tilde{\Omega}$, and similarly for $\hat{\Omega}_{ii}$. The asymptotic null distribution of N TLR_i is a chi-square with the degrees of freedom equal to the number of overidentifying restrictions (see Hwang (1987)). The system-wide LR test is computed by

$TLR_o=|\tilde{\Omega}|/|\hat{\Omega}| - 1.$

For each test statistic the empirical critical values were found for the significance levels α=0.1, 0.3 and 0.5 by arranging the 1000 samples of a test statistic in ascending order. These critical values are point estimates of unknown exact critical values for the sample size 32. The sets of all 1000 samples are partitioned into the "rejected" and "nonrejected" sets of samples according to the estimated exact critical values. The rejected set thus includes the samples that yield the largest 100α percent values of the a test statistic, and the remaining samples are the nonrejected set.

Since we have four test statistics, there are four pairs of rejected and nonrejected sets of samples for a given significance level. For expositional convenience we denote the full set of samples by FS; the sets of subsamples not rejected at the significance level α by the system test and the i-th equation test by $NS_0(\alpha)$ and $NS_i(\alpha)$, respectively; and the set of subsamples rejected by the system test and the i-th equation test by $RS_0(\alpha)$ and $RS_i(\alpha)$, respectively. In each set of samples, we compute the empirical conditional distributions, the sample bias, sample variance, root mean square error (RMSE), median, skewness, kurtosis, and the lengths of 50%, 80% and 100% intervals of coefficient estimators.

4. Report of Results

4.1 Independence of Identifiability Test and Coefficient Estimators

We first examine our central question, i.e., whether a change of the level of Type I error for the identifiability test affects the conditional distributions of the coefficient estimators. For this we conduct the Kolmogorov-Smirnov tests of the equality of the conditional distributions of each coefficient estimator between $NS_i(\alpha)$ and $NS_i(\alpha')$, and between $RS_i(\alpha)$ and $RS_i(\alpha')$, where $\alpha \neq \alpha'=0.1, 0.3, 0.5$. For example, the test compares the conditional distribution of a coefficient estimator in the subsample not rejected by the identifiability test at 10% against the conditional distribution of the same coefficient in the subsample not rejected by the identifiability test at 30%, etc. The levels of significance at which the Kolmogorov-Smirnov test will reject the equality of the conditional distributions are reported in Table 1.A and 1.B for the 2SLS estimators, and in Table 2.A and 2.B for the 3SLS estimators.

A cursory inspection of Table 1.A and 1.B indicates that the equality of the conditional distributions of coefficient estimators in different subsamples is not rejected at the conventional level of significance for all coefficients estimators and for all subsamples. The smallest significance level in Table 1.A is 34% in the comparison of the distributions of $\hat{\tau}_{53}$ between $NS_3(0.1)$ and $NS_3(0.5)$. The rejected subsamples in Table 1.B tend to show in general more significant differences than the nonrejected subsamples in Table 1.A. The smallest significance level in Table 1.B is 13% in the comparison of distributions of $\hat{\beta}_{21}$ between $RS_0(0.1)$ and $RS_0(0.5)$.

The results for the 3SLS estimators in Table 2.A and 2.B are similar to the results for the 2SLS estimators except for two cases.

The test rejects at 8% significance level the equality of the conditional distributions between $RS_0(0.1)$ and $RS_0(0.5)$ for two coefficient estimators: $\hat{\beta}_{21}$ and $\hat{\tau}_{71}$. The significance levels are also relatively low in Table 2.B for $\hat{\beta}_{21}$ between $RS_0(0.1)$ and $RS_0(0.3)$, and for $\hat{\beta}_{31}$ between $RS_0(0.1)$ and $RS_0(0.5)$. Overall, however, the Kolmogorov-Smirnov tests do not reject the equality of coefficients distributions in different subsamples.

4.2 Effects of Identifiability Pre-test on the Conditional Distributions of Coefficient Estimators

We examine in this section the conditional distributions of structural coefficient estimators, given that the identifiability test statistic is in the acceptance or rejection region of size α. We compare such conditional distributions with the full sample marginal distributions of coefficient estimators first by using the Kolmogorov-Smirnov tests and then on the basis of their sample bias, sample variance, root mean square error (RMSE), median, skewness, kurtosis, and the lengths of 50% and 80% intervals of coefficient estimators.

Table 3 reports the significance levels at which the Kolmogorov-Smirnov test will reject the equality of the distributions of 2SLS coefficient estimators (i) between FS and $NS_i(\alpha)$, (ii) between FS and $RS_i(\alpha)$, and (iii) between $NS_i(\alpha)$ and $RS_i(\alpha)$, i=0,1,2,3, for α=0.1. The results for the 3SLS estimators are reported in Table 4. There are practically no differences in the distributions of each coefficient between FS and $NS_i(\alpha)$ for all i. The smallest significance level at which the test will reject the equality of distributions is 0.9 in the comparison of the 2SLS estimator $\hat{\tau}_{53}$ between FS and NS_1.

There are more noticeable differences in the distributions of coefficient estimators between the full sample (FS) and the subsamples (RS_i) rejected by the identifiability tests. Although the equality of distributions is not rejected at the conventional significance level for all coefficients in the second and third equations, the equality of the distributions is rejected in several cases for the coefficient estimates in the first equation. This result, however, should be viewed with a caution because of the severe disparity of the sample sizes between the full sample and the rejected subsample at α=0.1. In fact, we find no significant differences when the sample sizes are more comparable, i.e., between FS and $RS_i(0.5)$.

The differences in the distributions of the coefficient estimates between the nonrejected (NS_i) and the rejected (RS_i) subsamples are more profound. Significant differences are found in the estimators of the first equation coefficients when the system test or the third equation test of identifiability is used at α=0.1. The sample size disparity between subsamples NS_i and RS_i in this case does not seem to be the cause of the significant differences. On the contrary, we find more cases of significantly different distributions between subsamples NS_i and RS_i when their samples sizes are equal (α=0.5). It is interesting to notice that the third equation test of identifiability yields more cases of statistically different distributions of the coefficient estimates. The source of this difference is not clear. There is no difference in the degree of overidentifying restrictions, which is equal to 3 for all three equations.

Various sample statistics of the coefficient estimators ($\hat{\beta}_{21}$ and $\hat{\beta}_{31}$) of the endogenous regressors in the first equation are presented in 5.A and 5.B for the full sample, and the subsamples not rejected and rejected by the system test and the third equation test of identifiability restrictions. One immediately notices that the biases in the rejected subsamples are substantially higher than those in the full sample or nonrejected subsamples. These differences can not be accounted for by the Monte Carlo sampling errors alone. It is easy to calculate standard errors of the means reported in Table 5.A and 5.B. For the 2SLS estimates of β_{21}, for example, they are 0.854×10^{-3} for the full sample, 0.90×10^{-3} for the nonrejected subsamples, and 2.70×10^{-3} for the rejected subsamples. They are much larger than the biases in the full sample and the nonrejected subsamples. This suggests that most differences among their sample statistics are due to Monte Carlo sampling errors. However, for the rejected subsamples, the biases are larger than two times the standard errors of the means, and hence, large biases in the rejected subsamples can not be accounted for by the sampling errors. Notice that the biases of the nonrejected and rejected samples are in the opposite direction: When the nonrejected samples have negative biases, the rejected samples have positive biases. The rejected subsamples also have higher values of the root mean squared errors

(RMSE). The nonrejected samples have densities that are more flat around the center (i.e., larger negative coefficients of kurtosis) than the rejected samples. There is no definite relationship in the skewness of coefficient estimators, although the length of 80% interval tends to be larger in the rejected samples.

For all other coefficients we report a general tendency of the differences in sample statistics between the rejected and nonrejected subsamples. Out of total 14 coefficients, the 2SLS estimators of 12 coefficients have smaller biases in the subsample not rejected by the system test (NS_0) compared to the rejected subsample (RS_0). Overall, more coefficient estimators by the 2SLS have smaller biases, smaller RMSE's, smaller skewnesses, and smaller 80% intervals in the nonrejected subsamples when compared to the corresponding rejected subsamples. We find more coefficient estimators in the rejected subsamples that have smaller sample variances and less flat distributions around the center (kurtosis) than in the nonrejected subsamples. For the 3SLS estimators, the results are similar, except that more coefficient estimators have smaller sample variances in the nonrejected subsamples.

4.3 Comparisons of the 2SLS and 3SLS Estimators

We briefly report here the comparisons of the 2SLS and 3SLS estimators of each coefficient. For each coefficient we record which estimator yields a smaller bias, a smaller variance, etc., and then count the number of coefficients which have smaller biases (variances, etc.) with the 3SLS than with the 2SLS. In the full sample, the 2SLS estimator yields smaller biases in 9 coefficients, and smaller variances and RMSE's in 12 out of total 14 coefficients. The 2SLS estimator shows more skewness in 12 coefficients, and more flatness around the center (coefficient of kurtosis) in 8 coefficients, and wider 80% intervals in 7 coefficients. Thus, the 2SLS estimators have definite advantages in the RMSE's, while the 3SLS estimators are less skewed.

In the subsample not rejected by the system test at the significance level α=0.1, the number of coefficients for which the 3SLS estimators have smaller RMSE's is 7, while the number of coefficients for which the 3SLS estimators have smaller bias, smaller skewness, less flatness, and smaller 80% intervals has not changed much from the full sample.

Except for the bias, therefore, the 3SLS estimators dominate the 2SLS estimators in the subsample not rejected by the system test.

5. Conclusion

In the case of a single equation linear regression model with a null hypothesis that correctly specifies restrictions, the test statistic, F, and the restricted OLS estimators of the remaining coefficients are independently distributed under the null hypothesis. Committing a Type I error, i.e., incorrectly "rejecting" a subset of sample estimates, does not affect the unbiasedness, variance, etc of the restricted OLS estimators on the "accepted" subset of sample estimates. The specification of identifying restrictions on a single structural equation is analogous to the specification of linear restrictions on ordinary regression coefficients, though not completely so. The interpretations of the structural identifiability test outcomes have thus been almost universally analogous to the corresponding interpretations properly made for the ordinary linear regression case. This practice is not seriously misleading within fairly broad limits.

We examine in this paper whether there are important cases in which the identifiability test statistic and (correctly) restricted structural coefficient estimators such as 2SLS and 3SLS are "approximately" statistically independent over a broad range of Type I error levels for the test statistic. Using the Klein model I as the basis of the true structural system, we conducted Monte Carlo experiments, in which the sample is classified by the system test as well as the individual equation tests of identifiability restrictions.

The results of the experiments are not conclusive, although they tend to support approximate independence between the identifiability test statistic and restricted structural coefficient estimators in most cases. According to the Kolmogorov-Smirnov tests, the conditional marginal distributions of 2SLS and 3SLS estimators of most structural coefficients do not vary considerably with changes in the Type I error level α of the identifiability test. The equality of the marginal distributions between different levels of α is more strongly supported in the sets of subsamples not rejected by the identifiability tests. The rejection of the equality occurs only in the sets of subsamples rejected by the identifiability tests.

The Kolmogorov-Smirnov tests also strongly support the equality of the marginal distributions of coefficient estimators between the full sample and the sets of subsamples not rejected by the identifiability tests. However, the equality of the marginal distributions between the full sample and the sets of rejected subsamples and between the nonrejected and rejected subsamples are frequently rejected, particularly for the coefficients in the first equation which has more endogenous (and fewer exogenous) regressors than other equations.

The lack of clear independence between the identifiability test statistic and restricted structural coefficient estimators make it precarious to use the common diagnostic statistics like R^2 and t-test in the 2SLS or 3SLS estimation. An important issue that our Monte Carlo experiments did not examine is the effect of the degree of overidentification. This requires a further study in the future.

Table 1.A

Significance Levels of Kolmogorov-Smirnov Test of Equality of Coefficient Distributions in Nonrejected Subsamples $NS_i(\alpha)$ and $NS_i(\alpha')$: 2SLS

	α=0.1 vs α'=0.3				α=0.1 vs α'=0.5				α=0.3 vs α'=0.5			
Coef	System	Eq.1	Eq.2	Eq.3	System	Eq.1	Eq.2	Eq.3	System	Eq.1	Eq.2	Eq.3
β_{21}	1.00	1.00	1.00	0.99	1.00	1.00	1.00	0.69	1.00	1.00	1.00	0.98
β_{31}	1.00	1.00	1.00	1.00	1.00	1.00	1.00	0.77	1.00	1.00	1.00	0.98
τ_{11}	1.00	1.00	1.00	1.00	0.99	1.00	0.85	0.67	1.00	1.00	0.92	0.93
τ_{71}	1.00	1.00	1.00	1.00	0.99	1.00	0.99	0.93	1.00	1.00	0.98	1.00
β_{22}	0.99	1.00	0.99	0.99	0.76	0.99	0.85	0.61	1.00	1.00	0.99	1.00
β_{32}	0.83	1.00	0.85	0.86	0.55	0.98	0.72	0.37	0.99	1.00	0.96	0.92
τ_{12}	0.99	1.00	1.00	0.93	0.58	1.00	0.68	0.58	0.82	1.00	0.97	0.99
τ_{22}	1.00	1.00	1.00	1.00	0.91	1.00	0.78	0.67	1.00	1.00	0.96	0.84
τ_{72}	1.00	1.00	1.00	1.00	0.97	1.00	0.87	0.50	1.00	1.00	0.98	0.81
β_{23}	0.84	0.99	0.82	1.00	0.99	0.98	0.58	0.90	1.00	0.93	0.85	0.97
τ_{33}	0.99	1.00	1.00	1.00	0.91	0.99	1.00	1.00	1.00	1.00	1.00	1.00
τ_{53}	0.99	0.94	1.00	0.72	0.76	1.00	0.89	0.34	0.75	1.00	0.94	0.60
τ_{63}	1.00	0.86	1.00	0.80	1.00	0.88	0.91	0.87	1.00	0.99	1.00	1.00
τ_{73}	1.00	1.00	1.00	1.00	0.77	1.00	0.99	0.94	0.96	1.00	1.00	0.96

Table 1.B
Significance Levels of Kolmogorov-Smirnov Test of Equality of Coefficient Distributions in Rejected Subsamples $RS_i(\alpha)$ and $RS_i(\alpha')$: 2SLS

	α=0.1 vs α'=0.3				α=0.1 vs α'=0.5				α=0.3 vs α'=0.5			
Coef	System	Eq.1	Eq.2	Eq.3	System	Eq.1	Eq.2	Eq.3	System	Eq.1	Eq.2	Eq.3
β_{21}	0.49	0.95	0.72	0.77	0.13	1.00	0.75	0.48	0.87	0.98	1.00	0.99
β_{31}	0.58	0.98	0.72	0.81	0.33	0.94	0.78	0.40	0.99	0.87	0.99	1.00
τ_{11}	0.63	0.97	0.97	0.77	0.63	0.72	0.94	0.51	1.00	0.87	1.00	1.00
τ_{71}	0.72	1.00	0.53	0.63	0.38	0.69	0.66	0.45	1.00	0.92	1.00	1.00
β_{22}	0.98	0.95	0.95	0.97	0.96	0.94	0.84	0.93	1.00	1.00	0.98	1.00
β_{32}	0.99	0.92	0.92	0.99	0.93	0.86	0.78	0.94	0.99	1.00	0.86	1.00
τ_{12}	0.97	0.89	0.77	0.77	0.96	0.60	0.43	0.86	1.00	1.00	0.99	0.99
τ_{22}	0.89	0.49	0.95	0.86	0.93	0.43	0.88	0.88	1.00	1.00	1.00	1.00
τ_{72}	0.95	0.53	0.72	0.95	0.98	0.45	0.81	0.91	0.99	1.00	1.00	1.00
β_{23}	0.77	0.99	1.00	0.92	0.57	0.86	0.96	0.88	0.85	0.96	0.75	0.93
τ_{33}	0.81	0.98	1.00	0.44	0.94	0.99	1.00	0.33	1.00	0.97	0.99	1.00
τ_{53}	0.63	0.97	0.98	1.00	0.45	0.72	0.98	0.97	1.00	0.82	0.96	0.99
τ_{63}	0.72	0.81	0.89	0.99	0.75	0.45	0.94	0.99	0.98	0.72	0.96	0.87
τ_{73}	0.58	0.98	0.99	0.92	0.72	1.00	0.97	0.75	0.99	0.88	0.96	0.96

Table 2.A
Significance Levels of Kolmogorov-Smirnov Test of Equality of Coefficient Distributions in Nonrejected Subsamples $NS_i(\alpha)$ and $NS_i(\alpha')$: 3SLS

	α=0.1 vs α'=0.3				α=0.1 vs α'=0.5				α=0.3 vs α'=0.5			
Coef	System	Eq.1	Eq.2	Eq.3	System	Eq.1	Eq.2	Eq.3	System	Eq.1	Eq.2	Eq.3
β_{21}	1.00	1.00	1.00	0.99	0.99	0.91	1.00	0.94	1.00	1.00	1.00	0.99
β_{31}	1.00	1.00	0.97	1.00	0.99	0.94	0.98	0.92	1.00	1.00	1.00	0.99
τ_{11}	1.00	1.00	1.00	1.00	1.00	0.99	0.92	0.81	1.00	1.00	0.98	0.92
τ_{71}	1.00	1.00	1.00	1.00	1.00	0.99	1.00	0.94	1.00	1.00	1.00	0.98
β_{22}	1.00	1.00	0.99	1.00	0.75	0.99	0.89	0.66	0.99	1.00	0.99	1.00
β_{32}	0.96	1.00	0.92	0.97	0.56	0.93	0.79	0.55	0.93	1.00	0.96	0.97
τ_{12}	1.00	0.99	1.00	0.72	0.54	0.97	0.56	0.36	0.78	1.00	0.88	0.88
τ_{22}	1.00	1.00	1.00	1.00	0.77	0.72	0.92	0.90	0.98	0.88	0.99	0.95
τ_{72}	1.00	1.00	1.00	1.00	0.90	0.94	0.93	0.93	0.99	1.00	1.00	0.98
β_{23}	0.99	1.00	0.94	1.00	1.00	0.64	0.72	0.85	1.00	0.55	0.91	0.99
τ_{33}	1.00	1.00	1.00	1.00	0.85	1.00	1.00	0.95	0.98	1.00	1.00	0.99
τ_{53}	1.00	0.96	1.00	0.71	0.98	0.98	0.99	0.47	0.96	0.97	0.95	0.71
τ_{63}	1.00	0.60	1.00	0.86	0.99	0.74	0.94	0.93	0.96	1.00	1.00	1.00
τ_{73}	1.00	1.00	1.00	1.00	0.91	0.99	1.00	0.90	1.00	0.99	1.00	0.90

Table 2.B

Significance Levels of Kolmogorov-Smirnov Test of Equality of Coefficient Distributions in Rejected Subsamples $RS_i(\alpha)$ and $RS_i(\alpha')$: 3SLS

	$\alpha=0.1$ vs $\alpha'=0.3$				$\alpha=0.1$ vs $\alpha'=0.5$				$\alpha=0.3$ vs $\alpha'=0.5$			
Coef	System	Eq.1	Eq.2	Eq.3	System	Eq.1	Eq.2	Eq.3	System	Eq.1	Eq.2	Eq.3
β_{21}	0.12	0.89	0.72	0.53	0.08*	0.88	0.75	0.21	0.99	1.00	0.98	0.85
β_{31}	0.18	0.98	0.53	0.63	0.12	0.99	0.72	0.29	1.00	0.97	0.98	0.99
τ_{11}	0.20	0.81	0.67	0.72	0.18	0.57	0.91	0.38	1.00	0.98	0.99	0.97
τ_{71}	0.20	0.81	0.29	0.63	0.08*	0.66	0.43	0.27	0.98	0.99	0.99	0.99
β_{22}	1.00	1.00	0.92	0.92	0.93	1.00	0.81	0.94	0.96	1.00	0.97	1.00
β_{32}	0.98	0.99	0.89	0.97	0.91	0.99	0.78	0.96	0.87	1.00	0.90	0.99
τ_{12}	0.92	0.86	0.86	0.81	0.99	0.54	0.78	0.86	1.00	1.00	1.00	0.94
τ_{22}	0.95	0.40	0.63	0.58	0.88	0.27	0.54	0.54	1.00	1.00	0.87	0.98
τ_{72}	0.99	0.36	0.67	0.95	0.91	0.29	0.45	0.94	1.00	1.00	0.96	0.97
β_{23}	0.89	0.98	0.98	0.77	0.75	0.99	0.69	0.84	0.99	0.90	0.78	0.82
τ_{33}	0.99	0.53	0.99	0.53	0.99	0.72	0.88	0.29	0.99	1.00	0.99	0.97
τ_{53}	0.77	1.00	0.98	0.89	0.63	0.86	0.94	0.96	0.98	0.39	0.99	0.97
τ_{63}	0.77	0.86	0.89	1.00	0.96	0.33	0.99	1.00	1.00	0.55	1.00	0.85
τ_{73}	1.00	0.92	0.99	0.81	0.96	0.78	0.97	0.48	1.00	0.99	1.00	0.86

* Rejected at 10% level of significance

Table 3

Significance Levels of Kolmogorov-Smirnov Test of Equality of Coefficient Distributions: 2SLS

	Between Full Sample and Subsamples (α=0.1)								Between Rejected and Nonrejected Subsamples							
	Sample Not Rejected by				Sample Rejected by				Test by (α=0.1)				Test by (α=0.5)			
Coef	System	Eq.1	Eq.2	Eq.3	System	Eq.1	Eq.2	Eq.3	System	Eq.1	Eq.2	Eq.3	System	Eq.1	Eq.2	Eq.3
β_{21}	1.00	1.00	1.00	1.00	0.10*	0.98	0.78	0.11	0.05*	0.95	0.67	0.06*	0.90	0.98	0.98	0.02*
β_{31}	1.00	1.00	1.00	1.00	0.17	0.95	0.59	0.08*	0.11	0.90	0.48	0.05*	0.98	0.86	0.90	0.03*
τ_{11}	1.00	1.00	1.00	1.00	0.56	0.59	0.86	0.13	0.43	0.49	0.77	0.07*	0.72	0.98	0.17	0.07*
τ_{71}	1.00	1.00	1.00	1.00	0.25	0.45	0.54	0.16	0.16	0.34	0.41	0.09*	0.72	0.86	0.46	0.23
β_{22}	1.00	1.00	1.00	1.00	0.73	0.92	0.42	0.57	0.63	0.89	0.32	0.46	0.05*	0.41	0.03*	0.02*
β_{32}	1.00	1.00	1.00	1.00	0.78	0.96	0.47	0.67	0.67	0.91	0.34	0.54	0.08*	0.46	0.05*	0.03*
τ_{12}	1.00	1.00	1.00	1.00	1.00	0.37	0.31	0.95	0.99	0.27	0.21	0.90	0.08*	0.77	0.20	0.15
τ_{22}	1.00	1.00	1.00	1.00	0.98	0.45	0.69	0.37	0.95	0.33	0.59	0.26	0.33	0.90	0.08*	0.03*
τ_{72}	1.00	1.00	1.00	1.00	1.00	0.33	0.70	0.35	0.99	0.24	0.58	0.25	0.51	0.77	0.15	0.01*
β_{23}	1.00	1.00	0.97	1.00	0.38	0.69	1.00	0.84	0.29	0.58	0.99	0.77	0.46	0.82	0.20	0.05*
τ_{33}	1.00	1.00	1.00	1.00	0.84	0.88	0.99	0.35	0.75	0.80	0.97	0.24	0.13	0.46	0.77	0.93
τ_{53}	0.95	0.90	0.99	0.95	0.50	0.84	0.98	0.93	0.37	0.74	0.95	0.86	0.67	0.82	0.10*	0.17
τ_{63}	0.99	0.96	1.00	0.99	0.94	0.57	0.67	0.98	0.88	0.44	0.59	0.96	0.72	0.77	0.07*	0.86
τ_{73}	1.00	1.00	1.00	1.00	0.54	0.95	0.96	0.61	0.41	0.91	0.92	0.49	0.06*	0.67	0.56	0.46

* Rejected at 10% Level of Significance

Table 4
Significance Levels of Kolmogorov-Smirnov Test of Equality of Coefficient Distributions: 3SLS

	Between Full Sample and Subsamples (α=0.1)								Between Rejected and Nonrejected Subsamples							
	Sample Not Rejected by				Sample Rejected by				Test by (α=0.1)				Test by (α=0.5)			
Coef	System	Eq.1	Eq.2	Eq.3	System	Eq.1	Eq.2	Eq.3	System	Eq.1	Eq.2	Eq.3	System	Eq.1	Eq.2	Eq.3
β_{21}	0.98	1.00	1.00	0.99	0.01*	0.97	0.51	0.03*	0.00*	0.93	0.38	0.01*	0.15	0.20	0.77	0.07*
β_{31}	1.00	1.00	1.00	1.00	0.03*	0.95	0.59	0.04*	0.01*	0.89	0.48	0.02*	0.46	0.41	0.77	0.05*
τ_{11}	1.00	1.00	1.00	1.00	0.09*	0.42	0.75	0.23	0.04*	0.32	0.63	0.14	0.72	0.46	0.20	0.08*
τ_{71}	1.00	1.00	1.00	1.00	0.07*	0.48	0.25	0.16	0.03*	0.37	0.16	0.09*	0.90	0.51	0.67	0.26
β_{22}	1.00	1.00	1.00	1.00	0.67	0.94	0.37	0.57	0.56	0.89	0.27	0.46	0.05*	0.41	0.05*	0.02*
β_{32}	1.00	1.00	1.00	1.00	0.73	0.97	0.44	0.65	0.61	0.92	0.32	0.53	0.06*	0.51	0.06*	0.03*
τ_{12}	1.00	1.00	1.00	1.00	0.81	0.31	0.67	0.93	0.70	0.22	0.54	0.88	0.15	0.96	0.04*	0.07*
τ_{22}	1.00	1.00	1.00	1.00	0.76	0.17	0.36	0.20	0.65	0.10*	0.26	0.12	0.33	0.13	0.20	0.11
τ_{72}	1.00	1.00	1.00	1.00	0.62	0.18	0.31	0.36	0.51	0.11	0.21	0.26	0.23	0.23	0.33	0.08*
β_{23}	1.00	1.00	1.00	1.00	0.42	0.95	0.98	0.85	0.34	0.91	0.94	0.80	0.72	0.51	0.51	0.07*
τ_{33}	1.00	1.00	1.00	1.00	0.95	0.54	0.76	0.17	0.92	0.41	0.68	0.10*	0.15	0.67	0.37	0.56
τ_{53}	0.95	0.96	0.99	0.99	0.59	0.99	0.81	0.96	0.46	0.98	0.79	0.91	0.93	0.33	0.37	0.20
τ_{63}	0.99	0.94	1.00	0.98	0.98	0.40	0.48	1.00	0.96	0.28	0.38	1.00	0.82	0.67	0.07*	0.72
τ_{73}	1.00	1.00	1.00	1.00	0.57	0.67	0.92	0.45	0.44	0.56	0.85	0.34	0.15	0.41	0.90	0.41

* Rejected at 10% Level of Significance

Table 5.A
Sample Statistics: Coefficient $\hat{\beta}_{21}$
(α=0.1)

	Full Sample	Sample Not Rejected by System	Sample Not Rejected by Eq. 3	Sample Rejected by System	Sample Rejected by Eq. 3
		2SLS Estimator			
Mean	0.014	0.014	0.014	0.020	0.020
Bias×1000	0.399	-0.279	-0.274	6.500	6.459
SD	0.027	0.027	0.027	0.027	0.027
RMSE	0.027	0.027	0.027	0.028	0.028
Median	0.013	0.012	0.012	0.019	0.020
Skewness	0.135	0.155	0.121	-0.045	0.266
Kurtosis	-0.385	-0.387	-0.424	-0.228	-0.203
50% Range	0.039	0.039	0.039	0.036	0.036
80% Range	0.072	0.072	0.072	0.072	0.074
		3SLS Estimator			
Mean	0.014	0.014	0.014	0.022	0.021
Bias×1000	0.381	-0.448	-0.330	7.843	6.778
SD	0.028	0.027	0.027	0.028	0.027
RMSE	0.028	0.027	0.027	0.029	0.028
Median	0.014	0.012	0.013	0.024	0.023
Skewness	0.091	0.137	0.104	-0.339	-0.017
Kurtosis	-0.361	-0.332	-0.389	-0.179	-0.023
50% Range	0.040	0.039	0.040	0.038	0.034
80% Range	0.072	0.071	0.072	0.073	0.070

Table 5.B
Sample Statistics: Coefficient $\hat{\beta}_{31}$
(α=0.1)

	Full Sample	Sample Not Rejected by System	Sample Not Rejected by Eq. 3	Sample Rejected by System	Sample Rejected by Eq. 3
		2SLS Estimator			
Mean	0.795	0.797	0.797	0.783	0.781
Bias×1000	0.198	1.609	1.753	-12.399	-13.703
SD	0.062	0.062	0.062	0.062	0.065
RMSE	0.062	0.062	0.062	0.063	0.066
Median	0.798	0.801	0.801	0.788	0.785
Skewness	-0.168	-0.183	-0.141	-0.038	-0.322
Kurtosis	-0.460	-0.467	-0.550	-0.271	0.010
50% Range	0.088	0.088	0.089	0.085	0.080
80% Range	0.161	0.160	0.160	0.154	0.177
		3SLS Estimator			
Mean	0.795	0.797	0.797	0.779	0.780
Bias×1000	0.156	1.993	1.830	-16.274	-14.819
SD	0.063	0.062	0.062	0.065	0.065
RMSE	0.063	0.062	0.062	0.067	0.066
Median	0.798	0.801	0.800	0.776	0.778
Skewness	-0.138	-0.180	-0.137	0.268	-0.077
Kurtosis	-0.414	-0.379	-0.511	-0.288	0.286
50% Range	0.089	0.088	0.089	0.087	0.076
80% Range	0.162	0.159	0.160	0.173	0.169

References

Aigner, D. J., and G. G. Judge, 1977, Application of pre-test and Stein estimators to economic data, *Econometrica 45*, 1279-1280.

Barro, Robert J., 1981, *Money, expectations, and business cycles*, (Academic Press, New York, NY)

Basmann, R. L., D. H. Richardson, and R. J. Rohr, 1974, Finite sample distributions associated with stochastic difference equations - Some experimental evidence, *Econometrica, 42* (5), 825-840.

Basmann, R. L., D. H. Richardson, and R. J. Rohr, 1974b, An experimental study of structural estimators and test statistics associated with dynamical econometric models, *Econometrica 42* (4), 717-730.

Basmann, R. L., 1988, Causality tests and observationally equivalent representations of econometric models, *Journal of Econometrics 39*, 69-104.

Brooking, Annie G., 1986, The analysis phase in development of knowledge based systems, in *Artificial intelligence and statistics*, (ed) William A. Gale (Addison-Wesley Publishing Company, Reading, MASS).

Carter, R. A. L. and A. L. Nagar, 1977, Coefficients of correlation for simultaneous equation systems, *Journal of Econometrics 6*(1), 39-50.

Greenberg, E., 1980, Finite sample moments of a preliminary test estimator in the case of possible heteroscedasticity, *Econometrica 48*, 1805-1814.

Fisher, R. A., 1922, On the mathematical foundations of theoretical statistics, *Philosophical Transactions of the Royal Society of London, Series A, 222*, 309-368.

Gale, William A., 1986a, Overreview, in *Artificial intelligence and statistics*, (ed) William A. Gale (Addison-Wesley Publishing Company, Reading, MASS).

Gale, William A., 1986b, REX review, in *Artificial intelligence and statistics*, (ed) William A. Gale (Addison-Wesley Publishing Company, Reading, MASS).

Hand, David J., 1986, Patterns in statistical strategy, in *Artificial intelligence and statistics*, (ed) William A. Gale (Addison-Wesley Publishing Company, Reading, MASS).

Harmon, Paul and David King, 1985, *Expert systems* (John Wiley & Sons, Inc., New York, NY)

Hwang, Hae-shin, 1987, Tests of overidentifying restrictions, Unpublished working paper.

James, W., and C. Stein, 1961, Estimation with quadratic loss. *Proceedings of the Fourth Berkeley Symposium on Mathematical Statistics and Probability*, 1, 361-279.

Judge, G., and M. Bock, 1978, *Statistical implications of pretest and Stein-Rule estimators in Econometrics* (North-Holland Publishing Company, Amsterdam, NETH)

Judge, G., Yancey, T., and M. Bock, 1973, Properties of estimators after preliminary tests of significance when stochastic restrictions are used in regression, *Journal of Econometrics*, *1*, 29-48.

Kadane, Joseph B., 1974, Testing a subset of the overidentifying restrictions, *Econometrica 42* (5), 853-857.

Klein, Lawrence R., 1950, *Economic fluctuations in the United States* (John Wiley & Sons, Inc. New York, NY).

Maddala, G. S., 1974, Some small sample evidence on tests of significance in simultaneous equations models, *Econometrica 42* (4), 841-852.

Martin, James and Steven Oxman, 1988, *Building expert systems* (Prentice Hall Englewood Cliffs, NJ).

Nagar, A. L., 1959, The bias and moment matrix of the general k-class estimators of the parameters in structural equations, *Econometrica 27*, 575-595.

Nagar, A. L., 1960, A Monte Carlo study of alternative simultaneous equations estimators, *Econometrica 28*(3), 659-660.

Nagar, A. L., 1961, A note on the residual variance estimation in simultaneous equations, *Econometrica 29*(2), 238-243.

Nagar, A. L., 1962, Double k-class estimators of parameters in simultaneous equations and their small sample properties, *International Economic Review*, *3*(2), 168-188.

Nagar, A. L., 1969, Simultaneous equations estimation: the two- and three-stage least squares, *Indian Economics Review*, *4*(1), 1-34.

Nagar, A. L., and Aman Ullah, 1972, Exact moments of the two-stage least squares estimator and their approximations, Delhi School of Economics, Working Paper.

Nagar, A. L., 1973, Note on approximate skewness and kurtosis of the two-stage least squares estimators, *Indian Economic Review*, *8*(1), 69-80.

Nagar, A. L. and R. A. Carter, 1974, Minimum second moment estimation in simultaneous equation systems, International *Economic Review*, *15*(1), 31-38.

Ohtani, K., and T. Toyoda, 1980, Estimation of regression coefficients after a preliminary test for homoscedasticity, *Journal of Econometrics 12*, 151-160.

Oldford, R. Wayne and Stephen C. Peters, 1986, Implementation and study of statistical strategy, in *Artificial intelligence and statistics*, (ed) William A. Gale (Addison-Wesley Publishing Company, Reading, MASS).

Pregibon, Daryl, 1986, A DIY guide to statistical strategy, in *Artificial intelligence and statistics*, (ed) William A. Gale (Addison-Wesley Publishing Company, Reading, MASS).

Thisted, Ronald A., 1986, Representing Statistical Knowledge for Expert Data Analysis System, in *Artificial intelligence and statistics*, (ed) William A. Gale (Addison-Wesley Publishing Company, Reading, MASS).

Toro-Vizcarrondo, C., T.D. Wallace, 1968, A Test of Mean Square Error Criterion for Restrictions in Linear Regression, *Journal of the American Statistical Association*, *63*, 558-572.

Toyoda, T. and T.D. Wallace, 1976, Optimal critical values for pre-testing in regression, *Econometrica*, *46*, 365-375.

Tukey, John, 1986, An alphabet for statistician's expert systems, in *Artificial intelligence and statistics*, (ed) William A. Gale (Addison-Wesley Publishing Company, Reading, MASS).

Ullah, Aman and A. L. Nagar, 1974, The exact mean of the two-stage least squares estimator of the structural parameters in an equation having three endogenous variables, *Econometrica 42* (4), 749-758.

Wagner, H. M., 1958, A Monte Carlo study of estimates of simultaneous linear structural equations, *Econometrica, 26*(1), 117-133.

Zellner, Arnold, Luc Bauwens, and Herman K. van Dijk, 1988, Bayesian specification analysis and estimation of simultaneous equation models using Monte Carlo methods, *Journal of Econometrics* (forthcoming).

Nonparametric-Monte-Carlo Estimates of t-Ratio Distributions in Dynamic Simultaneous Linear Equations Models

R.A.L. Carter*
Department of Economics
University of Western Ontario

Abstract

This paper reports the results of Monte Carlo simulations of the distributions of t-ratios obtained using instumental variables to estimate the coefficients of dynamic simultaneous linear equations models. Various versions of the instrumental variables estimator were obtained by using differing amounts of prior information to choose the instrument set. The results suggest that the asymptotically correct standard normal distribution is a poor approximation when samples are very small.

---

*I am grateful to A. Bera, N.E. Savin, Aman Ullah and to participants in the Canadian Econometric Study Group meeting, September 1986, and the econometrics seminar at the University of Illinois, Urbana-Champaign, for helpful comments. Remaining errors are mine alone. This research was funded in part by a SSHRCC General Research Grant administered by the Faculty of Social Science at the University of Western Ontario. Some of the work was done while I was a visitor at the University of Iowa, which generously provided computer and word processing assistance.

1. Introduction

One of the aims of econometrics is to draw inferences about structural parameters of economic interest. Such inferences are typically based on test statistics, often referred to as "t-ratios", which are the difference between the estimated and hypothesized value of the parameter divided by the standard error. The large-sample asymptotic distributions of these t-ratios are standard normal, under the null hypothesis, for almost all popular econometric estimators which employ stationary variables. However, their exact distributions appear to be unknown in some important cases; in particular, for the t-ratios associated with the structural coefficients of dynamic, simultaneous linear equations containing random exogenous variables. The literature on this question in the context of simultaneous linear equations, which has been thoroughly surveyed by Phillips [1982], deals with static models whose exogenous variables are held fixed in repeated samples. The two papers of most relevance to the work discussed here are Richardson and Rohr [1971] and Sargan [1975]. Research in the context of dynamic models (see Basmann, Richardson and Rohr [1974], Dickey [1976], Phillips [1977], Phillips and Perron [1988], Dickey and Fuller [1979], Evans and Savin [1981], [1984] Nankervis and Savin [1985], [1987]) deals with single equations, sometimes containing exogenous variables, with stationary or non-stationary dynamic components.

More recently Phillips and Hansen [1988] and Hansen and Phillips [1988] have studied the properties of instrumental variables and least squares estimators and test statistics in linear simultaneous equations relating cointegrated variables. They find that, in contrast to the case employing stationary variables, the limiting distributions of the estimates are not normal and the usual t and χ^2 statistics are not useful for inference in either small or large samples until they have been suitably corrected.

Kiviet [1985] has conducted an extensive simulation study in the context of a dynamic, linear, simultaneous equation. He estimated exact rejection probabilities for a variety of specification and misspecification tests employing "F-ratios" based on instrumental variables (IV) estimators. He concludes that these tests are unreliable in small samples. In particular, the estimated sizes of tests of restrictions on the coefficients were usually much different to the asymptotic sizes and they varied widely with changes in the set of instruments. However, the variables he employed were cointegrated so the relevant asymptotic distributions were not χ^2, as he supposed, but were those given by Phillips and Hansen [1988].

The Monte Carlo experiments discussed here refer to the t-ratios associated with IV estimates of individual coefficients of a dynamic simultaneous equation involving stationary variables. This focus allows us to identify properties of the small-sample distribution of these ratios (e.g., bias, skewness) which account for the disparity between estimated and asymptotic test sizes. This is accomplished by employing nonparametric techniques to estimate the complete probability density functions (pdfs) of the t-ratios. These techniques have the advantage of providing informative graphical results which do not depend upon unwarranted assumptions about the existence of moments. Unfortunately, these results are so bulky that only a few representative graphs could be included here. Also this paper reports asymptotic LM tests of the hypotheses that asymptotic and exact t-test sizes are identical. These tests were conducted at several asymptotic sizes to see if any disparity carried over to other sizes than 5%.

In designing the simulations the non-experimental nature of economics was captured by allowing the exogenous variables to vary randomly between samples. In practice, models of this sort may have rather poorly defined lists of instruments because the structure of equations other than the one under study have not been specified. Therefore, a particular focus of the paper is the effect that different choices of instruments, all leading to consistent estimators, will have on the distributions of the t-ratios and, hence, the true size of t-tests in small samples.

2. The Model

The model considered here is

$$y_{1t} = \alpha_1 + \beta_{01}x_{1t} + \beta_{11}x_{1t-1} + \gamma_{02}y_{2t} + \gamma_{11}y_{1t-1} + \gamma_{12}y_{2t-1} + u_{1t} \quad (2.1)$$

$$y_{2t} = \alpha_2 + \beta_{02}x_{2t} + \beta_{03}x_{3t} + \beta_{04}x_{4t} + \gamma_{01}y_{1t} + u_{2t} \quad (2.2)$$

which can be written in matrix notation as

$$\Gamma_0 y_t = \Gamma_1 y_{t-1} + B_0 x_t + B_1 x_{t-1} + u_t \quad (2.3)$$

where:

$$\Gamma_0 = \begin{pmatrix} 1 & -\gamma_{02} \\ -\gamma_{01} & 1 \end{pmatrix} \quad , \quad \Gamma_1 = \begin{pmatrix} \gamma_{11} & \gamma_{12} \\ 0 & 0 \end{pmatrix}$$

$$B_0 = \begin{pmatrix} \beta_{01} & 0 & 0 & 0 \\ 0 & \beta_{02} & \beta_{03} & \beta_{04} \end{pmatrix} \quad , \quad B_1 = \begin{pmatrix} \beta_{11} & 0 & 0 & 0 \\ 0 & 0 & 0 & 0 \end{pmatrix}$$

$$\alpha = \begin{pmatrix} \alpha_1 \\ \alpha_2 \end{pmatrix} \quad , \quad y = \begin{pmatrix} y_{1t} \\ y_{2t} \end{pmatrix} \quad , \quad u = \begin{pmatrix} u_{1t} \\ u_{2t} \end{pmatrix}$$

$$x_t' = (\, x_{1t} \quad x_{2t} \quad x_{3t} \quad x_{4t} \,) \qquad \text{and} \quad t = 1, \ldots, T \quad .$$

The disturbance vector u_t is assumed to be a random drawing from the bivariate normal distribution with a zero mean vector and a positive-definite covariance matrix

$$\Sigma = \begin{pmatrix} \sigma_{11} & \sigma_{12} \\ \sigma_{12} & \sigma_{22} \end{pmatrix}$$

The exogenous variables x_{1t} , x_{2t} , x_{3t} and x_{4t} are assumed to be stationary, invertible ARMA (1,1) processes

$$x_{it} = \mu_i + \phi_i x_{it-1} + \epsilon_{it} - \theta_i \epsilon_{it-1} \quad , \quad i = 1, \ldots, 4$$

which satisfy the conditions for weak exogeniety as set out by Engle, Hendry and Richard [1983]. Both structural equations are over identified without further parameter restrictions. The model is dynamically stable for all values of the parameters such that the roots of the determinental equation

$$| \Gamma_0 - \Gamma_1 L |= 0$$

(where the lag operator L is treated as a variable) lie outside the unit circle; i.e. all values for which the single nonzero root

$$\frac{1 - \gamma_{01}\gamma_{02}}{\gamma_{11} + \gamma_{01}\gamma_{12}} > 1.0$$

While this model is small it incorporates many realistic features. Equation (2.1), which is the equation of interest, contains an intercept, a distributed lag in a random exogenous variable plus dynamic behavior directly, through y_{1t-1}, and indirectly, through y_{2t-1}. The presence of x_{2t}, x_{3t} and x_{4t} in equation (2.2) will allow for the selection of several different instrument sets depending upon the amount of information the researcher is assumed to have about the structure of (2.2) and the properties of (2.1). By suitable parameter restrictions (2.1) could be transformed into a variety of simpler, but still interesting models. Generalizations could be obtained by assuming stationary ARMA structures for u_{1t} and u_{2t}.

3. IV Coefficient Estimators

Because of their computational simplicity and desirable asymptotic properties, IV estimators are often used, instead of maximum likelihood estimators, in the context of models like (2.1), (2.2). Assuming the availability of T observations, we can write equation (2.1) as

$$y = Z\psi + u \tag{3.1}$$

where y is the $T \times 1$ vector of observations on y_{1t} and Z is the $T \times K$, $K = 6$, matrix of observations on the right hand variables in (2.1) whose t^{th} row is

$$Z_t' = [1.0 \quad x_{1t} \quad x_{1t-1} \quad y_{2t} \quad y_{1t-1} \quad y_{2t-1}].$$

The parameter vector is

$$\psi' = [\alpha_1 \quad \beta_{01} \quad \beta_{11} \quad \gamma_{02} \quad \gamma_{11} \quad \gamma_{12}].$$

The $T \times 1$ vector u contains T random elements u_{1t}. The general IV estimator of ψ is

$$\hat{\psi} = (Z'P_w Z)^{-1} Z'P_w y \tag{3.2}$$

where: $P_w = W(W'HW)^{-1}W'$, W is a $T \times L$ matrix of T observation on L instrumental variables and H is a known, fixed $T \times T$ matrix. A variety of IV estimators can be obtained from (3.2) by varying the values chosen for H and W: see Bowden and Turkington [1981], pages 69 and 70, and Harvey [1981], page 80. Here H is set equal to I.

In order for the matrix inverse in (3.2) to exist we need: (i) Z of full column rank K, (ii) $\hat{Z} = P_w Z$ of full column rank K. In contrast to the Classic Linear Model, W, Z and $\hat{Z}$ are random so that for some samples one or both of these conditions may(computationally) fail. If the first condition always holds (i.e., Z has rank K for every sample), then the rank of $Z'P_w Z$ depends on the properties of W. At one extreme, if $L < K$ then $Z'P_w Z$ will be singular for every sample. Alternatively, we speculate that if $L = K$ the probability of $Z'P_w Z$ being computationally singular is greater than if $L > K$.

Variations between IV estimators can be produced by varying the content of the instrument matrix W. Several alternative situations will be considered:

1. The researcher who is interested in estimating the parameters of (2.1) correctly assumes: the structure of (2.1), the exogeniety of the x's. the independent nature of the error u_{1t}, and the presence of x_{2t}, x_{3t}, and x_{4t} in the remainder of the model. Such a researcher would set the tth row of W to

$$W_t' = [1.0 \quad x_{1t} \quad x_{1t-1} \quad y_{1t-1} \quad y_{2t-1} \quad x_{2t}, \quad x_{3t} \quad x_{4t}].$$

   In what follows we refer to this as the correct W.

2. The researcher correctly assumes the structure of (2.1), the exogeniety of x_{1t}, and the independent nature of u_{1t}

but is ignorant of the presence of one or two of x_{2t}, x_{3t} and x_{4t}. This would have the effect of removing one or two of the elements from W_t' above, i.e., of removing one or two columns from W. If the research is aware of only one of the exogenous variables x_{2t}, x_{3t} or x_{4t} equation (2.1) becomes just identified to that researcher and so, based on analytic results for static models with fixed exogenous variables (see Mariano [1977]), we speculate that the coefficient estimators and, hence, the t-ratios possess no finite integer moments. Similarly, if the researcher is aware of only two of x_{2t}, x_{3t} and x_{4t} the degree of over identification would be one and so we speculate that the distributions of both the coefficient estimators and the t-ratios possess first, but not higher, moments.

3. The researcher correctly assumes the systematic structure of (2.1) and is aware of x_{2t}, x_{3t} and x_{4t} but he is unwilling to make any assumption about the properties of u_{1t} over time. Such a researcher would be reluctant to include y_{1t-1} and y_{2t-1} in the instrument set, and might, therefore, set

$$W_t' = [1.0 \quad x_{1t} \quad x_{1t-1} \quad x_{2t} \quad x_{3t} \quad x_{4t}].$$

We speculate that in this case too the distribution of t-ratios would have no finite integer moments. Also, both here and in the previous case, we speculate that samples for which $Z'P_wZ$ is very ill conditioned will be observed more frequently than in the first case.

4. The researcher from 3 above who was distressed by the prospect of no moments and the increased probability of multi-collinearity might employ as additional instruments "extra" exogenous variables; i.e., exogenous variables that played no role in the generation of the y_{1t} and y_{2t} data. We assume the existence of two such variables, x_{5t} and x_{6t}, which are also generated by stationary, invertible ARMA(1,1) processes of the form (2.4). Essentially this researcher has replaced the knowledge of the independence of u_{1t} by knowledge of the existence of x_{5t} and x_{6t}. Because x_{5t} and x_{6t} are, by assumption and construction,

asymptotically uncorrelated with y_{2t}, y_{1t-1} and y_{2t-1} they would seem to be ineligible for use as instruments. Indeed, their only role is to increase the rank of the W matrix. The consistency of IV in this case is assured by the validity of the constant, x_{1t}, x_{1t-1}, x_{t2}, x_{t3} and x_{t4} in their roles as instruments.

4. The Experiments

For each of the experiments discussed here the structural parameters were set at the following values:

$$\alpha = \begin{pmatrix} 1.0 \\ 1.0 \end{pmatrix} \quad B_0 = \begin{pmatrix} 1.0 & 0 & 0 & 0 \\ 0 & 1.0 & 1.0 & 1.0 \end{pmatrix}$$

$$B_1 = \begin{pmatrix} .5 & 0 & 0 & 0 \\ 0 & 0 & 0 & 0 \end{pmatrix}$$

$$\Gamma_0 = \begin{pmatrix} 1.0 & -.8 \\ .5 & 1.0 \end{pmatrix} \quad \Gamma_1 = \begin{pmatrix} .6 & .4 \\ 0 & 0 \end{pmatrix}$$

Note that $1 - \gamma_{01}\gamma_{02} = 1.4$ while $\gamma_{11} + \gamma_{01}\gamma_{12} = .4$, so that the model is dynamically stable. The parameters of the exogenous processes were:

i :	1	2	3	4	5	6
μ_i :	.07	.09	.02	.08	.03	.04
ϕ_i :	.60	$-.20$	0	.60	.10	$-.50$
θ_i :	0	.60	.60	.20	.50	$-.10$

The errors in these processes were all white noise normal with means zero, variances 1.0 and covariances 0.0.

With these parameter values a permanent one unit change in each x has an impact multiplier of

$$\Gamma_0^{-1} B_0 = \begin{pmatrix} .714 & .571 & .571 & .571 \\ -.357 & .714 & .714 & .714 \end{pmatrix}$$

and a total multplier of

$$(I-\Gamma_1)^{-1}(B_0+B_1)(I-\Phi)^{-1} = \begin{pmatrix} 3.750 & 1.00 & 1.20 & 3.00 \\ -1.875 & .333 & .400 & 1.00 \end{pmatrix}.$$

Half the adjustment to the new equilibrium would be completed within 2 periods for y_{1t} and within 8 periods for y_{2t}. After 12 periods more than 95% of the adjustment would be completed for both variables.

The structural errors were also white noise normal with zero means. Two values of the covariance matrix Σ were employed:

$$(i) \quad \Sigma = \begin{pmatrix} 2.0 & 1.0 \\ 1.0 & 2.0 \end{pmatrix} \text{ for "tight fit" experiments}$$

$$(ii) \quad \Sigma = \begin{pmatrix} 20.0 & 10.0 \\ 10.0 & 20.0 \end{pmatrix} \text{ for "loose fit" experiments}$$

One of the useful results of Richardson and Rohr [1971] is that the basic parameter determining the shape of the distribution of the t-ratio they studied[1] is a noncentrality parameter which is proportional to the sample size and inversely proportional to the error variance; i.e., *ceteris parabis*, decreasing the error variance has the same qualitative effect upon the behaviour of their t-ratio as increasing the sample size. This may also be true for the present problem so that tight fit experiments may show what would have happened had the loose fit been retained and the sample size increased, with some saving in computing costs. In any case T was set equal to 20 for all our experiments. This is the number of annual observations which might typically be available in third-world countries or in countries which had recently experienced structural shifts. Nonparametric techniques, like the density estimation discussed below, are known to require large samples to give good results. Therefore, the number of replications, N, was set

[1]Note that the t-ratio studied by Richardson and Rohr [1971], which was originally proposed by Dhrymes [1969], is not the "usual" t-ratio studied in this paper. Instead, their t-ratio employs an estimator of the error variance which has, asymptotically, degrees of freedom equal to the degree of over identification.

equal to 2500. Uniform pseudo-random numbers were generated by Marsaglias' SUPERDUPER random number generator as implemented by McLeod [1982]. They were transformed into normal pseudo-random deviates by use of the inverse normal probability distribution function. The observations on the exogenous variables were generated from (2.4) by imposing initial values of $x_{i0} = 0.0$, $i = 1, \ldots, 6$, generating 45 observations and discarding the first 25. Similarly, the endogenous data was generated from the reduced form

$$y_t = \Gamma_0^{-1}\alpha + \Gamma_0^{-1}\Gamma_1 y_{t-1} + \Gamma_0^{-1}B_0 x_t + \Gamma_0^{-1}B_1 x_{t-1} + \Gamma_0^{-1}u_t \quad (4.1)$$

by imposing $y_0 = 0$, generating 45 observations and discarding the first 25.

Each experiment produced values of

$$t_{ij} = \frac{\hat{\psi}_{ij} - \psi_{ij}}{as(\hat{\psi}_{ij})} \quad ; \quad i = 1, \ldots, N \quad ; \quad j = 1, \ldots, 6 \quad (4.2)$$

where:

$$as(\psi_{ij}) = \left[\hat{\sigma}_{ii}\,(Z'P_wZ)_i^{jj}\right]^{1/2}, \quad (4.3)$$

$$\hat{\sigma}_{ii} = T^{-1}(y_i - Z_i\hat{\psi}_i)'(y_i - Z_i\hat{\psi}_i) \quad (4.4)$$

and $(Z'P_wZ)_i^{jj}$ is the jth diagonal element of $(Z'P_wZ)_i^{-1}$. The subscript j ranges over the 6 coefficients of equation (2.1) while i ranges over the N=2500 samples. Thus $\hat{\psi}_{ij}$ is the estimate of the jth coefficient obtained from sample i and t_{ij} is its t-ratio.

The empirical distributions of the t_{ij} were analyzed using two complementary, nonparametric tools which required no assumptions about the existence of moments of the sampling distribution of the t_{ij}. The first was the evaluation of the empirical cumulative distribution function (cdf) at the points: -2.5758, -2.3263, - 1.96, -1.6449, -1.2816, 1.2816, 1.6449, 1.96, 2.3263, 2.5758. These points define right and left tail probabilities under the standard normal distribution of: .005, .01, .025, .05 and .10. The asymptotic, standard normal distribution is useful for conducting one or two tailed tests of hypotheses about individual coefficients, at common significance levels, only if the values of the empirical cdf differs from these tail probabilities only because of Monte Carlo sampling error; i.e. only if we are unable to reject the hypothesis that the exact sampling distribution of any t_j is N(0,1).

If we are forced to reject this hypothesis we would like to know in what way the exact sampling distribution differs from N(0,1). Do they have different locations, dispersions, skewness, kurtosis or some combination of these? An alternative to using moments for this purpose is to estimate the probability density function (pdf) for the exact distribution and visually compare the estimated pdf to that of N(0,1). At any point τ_j on the t axis the value of the pdf for t_j is estimated by the kernel estimator.

$$\hat{f}(\tau_j) = \frac{1}{Nh} \sum_{i=1}^{N} (2\pi)^{-1/2} exp\left[-.5 \left(\frac{t_{ij} - \tau_j}{h} \right)^2 \right] \qquad (4.5)$$

where $h = N^{-1/5}$ is the window width. Then an asymptotic 95% confidence interval for $f(\tau_j)$ is

$$f(\tau_j) = \hat{f}(\tau_j) \pm 1.96 \left[\frac{\hat{f}(\tau_j)}{2hN\sqrt{\pi}} \right] \qquad (4.6)$$

Values of $\hat{f}(\tau_j)$ and the asymptotic 95% confidence interval were computed for 101 evenly spaced τ_j points between -5 and +5.

Four groups of experiments were conducted with the aim of answering the following questions:

1. When all information on the structure, identifying restrictions and error properties is correctly used (i.e., under scenario 1 in section 3) does the standard normal distribution provide a good approximation to the exact distribution of the t-ratios in the sense that the tail areas of the two distributions are close to one another? Does the quality of this asymptotic approximation differ for the coefficients of current and lagged exogenous and endogenous variables? Does a ten-fold reduction in Σ produce a useful improvement in the quality of the approximation?

2. How are the distributions of t-ratios affected by ignoring some identifying restrictions, i.e., ignoring the presence of some exogenous variables as in scenario 2 of section 3? In particular, do the exact distributions appear to have tail areas close to those for N(0,1)?
3. If, as in scenario 3 of section 3, the independent nature of the error was ignored and only the exogenous variables, plus x_{1t-1}, were included in W, would the distributions of the t- ratios look the same as in case 2 above? Would exact and asymptotic tail probabilities be close to one another?
4. If, as in scenario 4 of section 3, the lagged endogenous variables in W were replaced by "extra" exogenous variables would the distributions of the t-ratios look the same as in case 1 above? Is the incidence of multicollinearity reduced as compared to cases 2 and 3 above?

5. Results of the Experiments

Tables 1 to 6 contain estimated tail probabilities for the t-ratios associated with coefficients 1 to 6: α_1, β_{01}, γ_{11}, γ_{02}, γ_{11}, γ_{12}. The numbers across the top are the tail probabilities for the standard normal distribution. We are primarily interested in whether the true tail probabilities, p, for which the numbers in the body of the tables are unbiased estimates, are equal to the numbers at the heads of the columns. That is, we want to test H_0: $p = p_0$ against H_1: $p \neq p_0$ where $p_0 = .005$ or .01 or .025 or .05 or .10. Under H_0 the test statistic

$$z = \frac{\hat{p} - p_0}{s(\hat{p})}, \tag{5.1}$$

where

$$s(\hat{p}) = \left[\frac{p_0(1-p_0)}{N}\right]^{1/2}, \tag{5.2}$$

is asymptotically N(0,1). Values of $\hat{p}$ appear in the body of Tables 1 to 6 while values of z are shown beneath them in brackets. Of course, large z values of either sign cast doubt upon H_0. However, large positive z values have a different interpretation the large negative z values. Large positive z values mean that actual test sizes are larger than the nominal sizes derived from the N(0,1) asymptotic approximation; i.e., in using N(0,1) to set the critical value a researcher is bearing a higher probability of type I error than he intended. Alternatively, large negative z values imply that using N(0,1) critical values produces smaller probability of type I error than intended. But at least in this case the asymptotic size provides an upper bound for the true size. In both cases the researcher's use of N(0,1) critical values has produced a different trade off between size and power than what was desired.

The results for the case in which all available information is correctly used (i.e., using the correct W) are shown in the top rows of each panel (Loose Fit, Tight Fit) of each table. Since there are six coefficients, ten tail probabilities and two Σ versions there are 120 z values. Ninety-four of them exceed 2.0, 49 exceed 10.0, only 11 are negative and only 7 are less than -2.0. The z values lying between -2.0 and 2.0 are concentrated in Tables 4 (especially the right tail with loose fit), 5 (the right tail especially with tight fit) and 6 (the left tail). An inspection of the estimated pdfs revealed no strong skewness. The pdfs for t_2 and t_4 were centered close to zero so the large tail probabilities for t_2 were due to its fat tails. The pdfs for t_1, t_3 and t_6 were centered right of zero while that for t_5 was centered left of zero (see[2] Graph 1). However, the fat tails for t_1 and t_3 meant that even their left tail probabilities were bigger than those for N(0,1). The shifts away from zero of the t_5 and t_6 pdfs were sufficient to counteract their fat tails and so produce probabilities in the tail away from the shift which were close to those for N(0,1).

The experiments in the second and third groups were intended to show the effect of omitting some valid instrumental variables from W. In some of these experiments this resulted in W having the same number of columns as Z: e.g. if two of x_{2t}, x_{3t}, x_{4t} are omitted or if only the constant, x_{1t}, x_{1t-1}, x_{2t}, x_{3t} and x_{4t} are used as instruments. For some samples in

[2]The values of $\hat{f}(\tau_j)$ are marked by crosses. The fitted curve is a cubic spline. The cross hatches above and below the curve show the asymptotic 95% confidence band.

some of these experiments $Z'P_wZ$ was too ill conditioned to be inverted using the IMSL double precision subroutine DLINDS on an IBM 4381, which has a double precision word length of 32 bits. However, these inversions proceeded without difficulty using the single precision IMSL subroutine LINDS on a CYBER 835 with a single precision word length of 64 bits. The details are shown below:

Instruments Used: Constant, x_{1t}, x_{1t-1}, plus:	Fit	No. of Failures out of 2500
$x_{3t}, y_{1t-1}, y_{2t-1}$	loose	2
$x_{4t}, y_{1t-1}, y_{2t-1}$	loose	2
$x_{4t}, y_{1t-1}, y_{2t-1}$	tight	1
x_{2t}, x_{3t}, x_{4t}	loose	4
x_{2t}, x_{3t}, x_{4t}	tight	4

These cases were omitted from further consideration. In two experiments, loose and tight fit, employing as instruments the constant, x_{1t}, x_{1t-1}, x_{2t}, x_{3t}, x_{4t} and the two extra instruments x_{5t} and x_{6t} no inversion failures were observed.

The use of W matrices different from the correct W had the effect, in almost every case, of reducing the tail area probabilities: i.e., within each block (Loose Fit, Tight Fit) of each table the largest number in any column is at the top, associated with the use of the constant, x_{1t}, x_{1t-1}, x_{2t}, x_{3t}, x_{4t}, y_{1t-1} and y_{1t-2} as instruments. The exceptions to this general trend occurred when x_{2t} was omitted from W under tight fit: see Tables 2, 3 and 5. Even here there was only one case in Table 2 where the smallest left tail probability was increased slightly, in the other cases it was unchanged. In many cases the altered W matrix produced a large enough reduction in tail probabilities that z values which had been positive using the correct W became negative. Also in some cases we would now be unable to reject the hypothesis that the exact and asymptotic tail probabilities were equal. This was especially noticeable in Table 4, both tails; Table 5, right tail; and Table 6, left tail. An inspection of the estimated pdfs indicated that these effects were caused more by changes in the shape of the distributions than by changes in their location: e.g. compare Graph 2 to

Graph 1 and Graph 5 to Graph 4. The effect of shrinking tail probabilities was most striking in the results of the fourth group of experiments in which y_{1t-1} and y_{2t-1} in the correct W were replaced by x_{5t} and x_{6t}. These results appear in the bottom row of each block in Tables 1 to 6. In 105 out of 120 cases the z value was negative, in 82 cases it was less than -2.0 and in 38 cases it was between -2.0 and 2.0. The estimated pdfs indicated that the reason for these results was a reduction in dispersion and a thinning of the tails of the distributions rather than a change in location: e.g. see Graphs 3 and 6.

6. Conclusions

For the population and instrument sets studied here several conclusions can be drawn:

1. When all information about the structure of the equation, the white noise character of the error and the identifying restrictions was correctly used, but the sample was very small, the asymptotic, N(0,1), distribution was not a good approximation to the exact distributions of t-ratios associated with the intercept or with the coefficients of current or lagged exogenous variables. A combination of shifts away from zero and fat tails produced tail probabilities for the exact distributions which exceeded those for N(0,1). The approximation was more successful for the t-ratios related to a current endogenous variable but it worsened when the error variance was reduced. In the case of lagged endogenous variables, the approximation seemed better for one tail but was much worse for the other. Again, reductions in the error variance did not improve the quality of the approximation, in some cases (Table 4) they made it worse. In conclusion, the asymptotic distribution is not a reliable basis for inferences about the coefficients because actual probabilities of type I error are higher than those given by the approximation.
2. Omitting relevant instruments had several effects. When two instruments were omitted multicollinearity severe enough to prevent computation of the estimates occurred for some samples. When this did not occur, or when

only one instrument was omitted, the t-ratio tail probabilities were almost always smaller than with the correct W. This reduction sometimes made the asymptotic approximation closer to the exact distribution, especially for the coefficient of a current endogenous variable, but in other cases the exact tail probabilities became much smaller than N(0,1) tail probabilities. This was most noticeable in both tails for the case of the current endogenous variable and in one tail for the lagged endogenous variables.

3. When the lagged endogenous variables were replaced in the instrument set by extraneous exogenous variables the tails of the exact distribution became much thinner than the tails of N(0,1). This effect occurred for the t-ratios associated with all types of variables; endogenous or exogenous, current or lagged. In addition, the multicollinearity which resulted from merely omitting the lagged endogenous variables from the instrument set was now absent. Inferences in this case would have smaller probability of type I error than what was suggested by the asymptotic approximation. A researcher who found these points desirable could easily generate extraneous exogenous variables with a random number generator.

While generalizations to other populations are hazardous, it does seem safe to conclude that the asymptotic distribution of the t-ratios is not a reliable basis for inference when samples are as small as those available in developing or rapidly changing economies.

Table 1
Estimated Tail Probabilities for t-Ratios
Coefficient 1: α_1

Instruments constant, x_{1t} x_{1t-1}, plus:	Left Tail N(0,1) .500E-2	.100E-1	.250E-1	.500E-1	.100	Right Tail N(0,1) .100	.500E-1	.250E-1	.100E-1	.500E-2
	Loose Fit									
	Left Tail Estimated					Right Tail Estimated				
x_{2t}, x_{3t}, x_{4t} y_{1t-1}, y_{2t-1}	.140E-1 (6.38)	.256E-1 (7.84)	.440E-1 (6.08)	.732E-1 (5.32)	.115 (2.47)	.169 (11.5)	.100 (11.6)	.656E-1 (13.0)	.389E-1 (14.5)	.264E-1 (15.2)
x_{2t}, y_{1t-1}, y_{2t-1}	.920E-2 (2.98)	.140E-1 (2.01)	.240E-1 (-.320)	.412E-1 (-2.02)	.764E-1 (-3.93)	.110 (1.60)	.616E-1 (2.66)	.388E-1 (4.42)	.184E-1 (4.22)	.136E-1 (6.10)
x_{2t}, x_{3t} y_{1t-1}, y_{2t-1}	.124E-1 (5.25)	.192E-1 (4.62)	.376E-1 (4.04)	.644E-1 (3.30)	.106 (.999)	.148 (8.05)	.840E-1 (7.80)	.536E-1 (9.16)	.300E-1 (10.1)	.200E-1 (10.6)
x_{2t}, x_{4t} y_{1t-1}, y_{2t-1}	.120E-1 (4.96)	.188E-1 (4.42)	.356E-1 (3.39)	.608E-1 (2.48)	.101 (1.99)	.146 (7.73)	.912E-1 (9.45)	.572E-1 (10.3)	.340E-1 (12.1)	.220E-1 (12.1)
x_{2t}, x_{3t}, x_{4t} x_{5t}, x_{6t}	.160E-2 (-2.41)	.600E-2 (-2.01)	.156E-1 (-3.01)	.272E-1 (-5.23)	.596E-1 (-6.73)	.804E-1 (-3.27)	.376E-1 (-2.84)	.184E-1 (-2.11)	.840E-2 (-.804)	.440E-2 (-.425)

Table 1 (continued)
Estimated Tail Probabilities for t-Ratios
Coefficient 1: α_1

Instruments constant, x_{1t} x_{1t-1}, plus:	Left Tail N(0,1)					Right Tail N(0,1)				
	.500E-2	.100E-1	.250E-1	.500E-1	.100	.100	.500E-1	.250E-1	.100E-1	.500E-2
	Tight Fit									
	Left Tail Estimated					Right Tail Estimated				
x_{2t}, x_{3t}, x_{4t}	.160E-1	.224E-1	.372E-1	.680E-1	.114	.202	.141	.892E-1	.596E-1	.436E-1
y_{1t-1}, y_{2t-1}	(7.80)	(6.23)	(3.91)	(4.13)	(2.27)	(17.0)	(20.9)	(20.6)	(24.9)	(27.4)
x_{2t}, y_{1t-1}, y_{2t-1}	.840E-2	.152E-1	.268E-1	.492E-1	.972E-1	.158	.968E-1	.604E-1	.356E-1	.220E-1
	(2.41)	(2.61)	(.576)	(-.184)	(-.467)	(9.73)	(10.7)	(11.3)	(12.9)	(12.1)
x_{3t}, y_{1t-1}, y_{2t-1}	.560E-2	.104E-1	.212E-1	.412E-1	.764E-1	.155	.916E-1	.604E-1	.332E-1	.272E-1
	(.425)	(.201)	(-1.22)	(-2.02)	(-3.93)	(9.13)	(9.54)	(11.3)	(11.7)	(15.7)
x_{2t}, x_{3t}	.132E-1	.208E-1	.340E-1	.652E-1	.108	.188	.127	.804E-1	.504E-1	.360E-1
y_{1t-1}, y_{2t-1}	(5.81)	(5.43)	(2.88)	(3.49)	(1.40)	(14.7)	(17.7)	(17.7)	(20.3)	(22.0)
x_{2t}, x_{4t}	.132E-1	.192E-2	.340E-1	.612E-1	.112	.196	.130	.864E-1	.528E-1	.344E-1
y_{1t-1}, y_{2t-1}	(5.81)	(4.62)	(2.88)	(2.57)	(1.93)	(16.0)	(18.4)	(19.7)	(21.5)	(20.8)
x_{3t}, x_{4t}	.104E-1	.176E-1	.292E-1	.576E-1	.101	.198	.129	.844E-1	.516E-1	.372E-1
y_{1t-1}, y_{2t-1}	(3.83)	(3.82)	(1.35)	(1.74)	(1.32)	(16.3)	(18.2)	(19.0)	(20.9)	(22.8)
x_{2t}, x_{3t}, x_{4t}	.000	.120E-1	.680E-2	.200E-1	.412E-1	.101	.396E-1	.184E-1	.760E-2	.400E-2
x_{5t}, x_{6t}	(-3.54)	(-4.42)	(-5.38)	(-6.88)	(-9.80)	(.132)	(-2.39)	(-2.11)	(-1.21)	(-.709)

Table 2
Estimated Tail Probabilities for t-Ratios
Coefficient 2: β_{01}

Instruments constant, x_{1t} x_{1t-1}, plus:	Left Tail N(0,1) .500E-2	.100E-1	.250E-1	.500E-1	.100	Right Tail N(0,1) .100	.500E-1	.250E-1	.100E-1	.500E-2
Loose Fit	Left Tail Estimated					Right Tail Estimated				
x_{2t}, x_{3t}, x_{4t} y_{1t-1}, y_{2t-1}	.144E-1 (6.66)	.272E-1 (8.64)	.500E-1 (8.01)	.824E-1 (7.43)	.140 (6.73)	.121 (3.47)	.720E-1 (5.05)	.388E-1 (4.42)	.200E-1 (5.03)	.148E-1 (6.95)
x_{2t}, y_{1t-1}, y_{2t-1}	.840E-2 (2.41)	.176E-1 (3.82)	.284E-1 (1.09)	.472E-1 (-.642)	.840E-1 (-2.67)	.756E-1 (-4.07)	.392E-1 (-2.48)	.288E-1 (-.705)	.116E-1 (-.804)	.680E-1 (1.28)
x_{2t}, x_{3t} y_{1t-1}, y_{2t-1}	.128E-1 (5.53)	.256E-1 (7.84)	.448E-1 (6.34)	.732E-1 (5.32)	.125 (4.13)	.112 (1.93)	.600E-1 (2.29)	.304E-1 (1.73)	.172E-1 (3.62)	.180E-1 (4.11)
x_{2t}, x_{4t} y_{1t-1}, y_{2t-1}	.124E-1 (5.25)	.216E-1 (5.83)	.392E-1 (4.55)	.672E-1 (3.95)	.121 (3.47)	.103 (.466)	.580E-1 (1.84)	.328E-1 (2.50)	.172E-1 (3.62)	.116E-1 (4.68)
x_{3t}, x_{4t} y_{1t-1}, y_{2t-1}	.124E-1 (5.25)	.204E-1 (5.23)	.412E-1 (5.19)	.692E-1 (4.40)	.122 (3.67)	.107 (1.20)	.576E-1 (1.74)	.308E-1 (1.86)	.144E-1 (2.21)	.100E-1 (3.54)
x_{2t}, x_{3t}, x_{4t} x_{5t}, x_{6t}	.280E-2 (1.56)	.560E-2 (-2.21)	.160E-1 (-2.88)	.300E-1 (-4.59)	.624E-1 (-6.27)	.656E-1 (-5.73)	.288E-1 (-4.86)	.108E-1 (-4.55)	.400E-1 (-3.02)	.240E-1 (-1.84)

Table 2 (continued)
Estimated Tail Probabilities for t-Ratios
Coefficient 2: β_{01}

Instruments constant, x_{1t} x_{1t-1}, plus:	Left Tail N(0,1)					Right Tail N(0,1)				
	.500E-2	.100E-1	.250E-1	.500E-1	.100	.100	.500E-1	.250E-1	.100E-1	.500E-2
	Tight Fit									
	Left Tail Estimated					Right Tail Estimated				
x_{2t}, x_{3t}, x_{4t} y_{1t-1}, y_{2t-1}	.220E-1 (12.1)	.356E-1 (12.9)	.604E-1 (11.3)	.980E-1 (11.0)	.159 (9.86)	.144 (7.40)	.884E-1 (8.81)	.532E-1 (9.03)	.272E-1 (8.64)	.160E-1 (7.80)
x_{2t}, y_{1t-1}, y_{2t-1}	.156E-1 (7.51)	.248E-1 (7.44)	.416E-1 (5.32)	.692E-1 (4.40)	.121 (3.53)	.112 (2.07)	.656E-1 (3.58)	.360E-1 (3.52)	.880E-1 (3.22)	.220E-1 (2.69)
x_{3t}, y_{1t-1}, y_{2t-1}	.148E-1 (6.95)	.220E-1 (6.03)	.404E-1 (4.93)	.724E-1 (5.14)	.122 (3.73)	.104 (.732)	.560E-1 (1.38)	.268E-1 (.576)	.112E-1 (.603)	.800E-1 (2.13)
x_{2t}, x_{3t} y_{1t-1}, y_{2t-1}	.224E-1 (12.3)	.344E-1 (12.3)	.556E-1 (9.80)	.916E-1 (9.54)	.151 (8.53)	.139 (6.46)	.832E-1 (7.62)	.476E-1 (7.24)	.240E-1 (7.04)	.800E-1 (6.10)
x_{2t}, x_{4t} y_{1t-1}, y_{2t-1}	.176E-1 (8.93)	.292E-2 (9.65)	.552E-1 (9.67)	.888E-1 (8.90)	.148 (8.00)	.136 (6.00)	.832E-1 (7.62)	.484E-1 (7.49)	.236E-1 (6.83)	.132E-1 (5.81)
x_{3t}, x_{4t} y_{1t-1}, y_{2t-1}	.196E-1 (10.3)	.292E-1 (9.65)	.536E-1 (9.16)	.920E-1 (9.63)	.154 (8.93)	.133 (5.47)	.752E-1 (5.78)	.464E-1 (6.85)	.220E-1 (6.03)	.136E-1 (6.10)
x_{2t}, x_{3t}, x_{4t} x_{5t}, x_{6t}	.760E-1 (1.84)	.100E-1 (0.00)	.268E-1 (-.576)	.444E-1 (-1.28)	.808E-1 (-3.20)	.768E-1 (-3.87)	.320E-1 (-4.13)	.156E-1 (-3.01)	.840E-2 (-.804)	.480E-2 (-.142)

Table 3
Estimated Tail Probabilities for t-Ratios
Coefficient 3: β_{11}

Instruments constant, x_{1t} x_{1t-1}, plus:	Left Tail N(0,1) .500E-2	.100E-1	.250E-1	.500E-1	.100	Right Tail N(0,1) .100	.500E-1	.250E-1	.100E-1	.500E-2
	Loose Fit									
	Left Tail Estimated					Right Tail Estimated				
x_{2t}, x_{3t}, x_{4t} y_{1t-1}, y_{2t-1}	.136E-1 (6.10)	.212E-1 (5.63)	.400E-1 (4.80)	.632E-1 (3.03)	.110 (1.73)	.154 (9.06)	.908E-1 (9.36)	.608E-1 (11.5)	.320E-1 (11.1)	.212E-1 (11.5)
x_{2t}, y_{1t-1}, y_{2t-1}	.600E-2 (.709)	.116E-1 (.804)	.200E-1 (-1.60)	.392E-1 (-2.48)	.728E-1 (-4.53)	.964E-1 (-.601)	.524E-1 (.551)	.304E-1 (1.73)	.164E-1 (3.22)	.100E-1 (3.54)
x_{2t}, x_{3t} y_{1t-1}, y_{2t-1}	.880E-2 (2.69)	.148E-1 (2.41)	.296E-1 (1.47)	.544E-1 (1.01)	.968E-1 (-.534)	.134 (5.73)	.772E-1 (6.24)	.524E-1 (8.78)	.280E-1 (9.05)	.180E-1 (9.22)
x_{2t}, x_{4t} y_{1t-1}, y_{2t-1}	.960E-1 (3.26)	.172E-1 (3.62)	.312E-1 (1.99)	.548E-1 (1.10)	.980E-1 (-.334)	.135 (5.80)	.776E-1 (6.33)	.476E-1 (7.24)	.284E-1 (9.25)	.172E-1 (8.65)
x_{3t}, x_{4t} y_{1t-1}, y_{2t-1}	.116E-1 (4.68)	.164E-1 (3.22)	.312E-1 (1.99)	.516E-1 (.367)	.900E-1 (-1.67)	1.37 (6.13)	.748E-1 (5.69)	.476E-1 (7.24)	.244E-1 (7.24)	.164E-1 (8.08)
x_{2t}, x_{3t}, x_{4t} x_{5t}, x_{6t}	.200E-2 (-2.13)	.400E-2 (-3.02)	.108E-1 (-4.55)	.208E-1 (-6.70)	.408E-1 (-8.67)	.840E-1 (-2.67)	.408E-1 (-2.11)	.212E-1 (-1.22)	.104E-1 (.201)	.720E-1 (-1.56)

Table 3 (continued)
Estimated Tail Probabilities for t-Ratios
Coefficient 3: β_{11}

Instruments constant, x_{1t}, x_{1t-1}, plus:	Left Tail N(0,1) .500E-2	.100E-1	.250E-1	.500E-1	.100	Right Tail N(0,1) .100	.500E-1	.250E-1	.100E-1	.500E-2
	Tight Fit: Left Tail Estimated					Right Tail Estimated				
x_{2t}, x_{3t}, x_{4t}, y_{1t-1}, y_{2t-1}	.124E-1 (5.25)	.176E-1 (3.82)	.380E-1 (4.16)	.620E-1 (2.75)	.940E-1 (-1.00)	.199 (16.5)	.129 (18.2)	.840E-1 (18.9)	.516E-1 (20.9)	.352E-1 (21.4)
x_{2t}, y_{1t-1}, y_{2t-1}	.920E-1 (2.89)	.140E-1 (2.01)	.280E-1 (.961)	.456E-1 (-1.01)	.796E-1 (-3.40)	.153 (8.86)	.980E-1 (11.0)	.576E-1 (10.4)	.328E-1 (11.5)	.220E-1 (12.1)
x_{3t}, y_{1t-1}, y_{2t-1}	.640E-2 (.922)	.920E-2 (-.402)	.232E-1 (-.576)	.420E-1 (-1.84)	.716E-1 (-4.73)	.151 (8.46)	.920E-1 (9.63)	.528E-1 (8.90)	.308E-1 (10.5)	.204E-1 (10.9)
x_{2t}, x_{3t}, y_{1t-1}, y_{2t-1}	.108E-1 (4.11)	.176E-1 (3.82)	.352E-1 (3.27)	.620E-1 (2.75)	.924E-1 (-1.27)	.190 (15.1)	.119 (15.9)	.776E-1 (16.8)	.460E-1 (18.1)	.308E-1 (18.3)
x_{2t}, x_{4t}, y_{1t-1}, y_{2t-1}	.100E-1 (3.54)	.160E-1 (3.02)	.348E-1 (3.14)	.596E-1 (2.20)	.912E-1 (-1.47)	.187 (14.5)	.118 (15.6)	.772E-1 (16.7)	.472E-1 (18.7)	.328E-1 (19.7)
x_{3t}, x_{4t}, y_{1t-1}, y_{2t-1}	.100E-1 (3.54)	.156E-1 (2.81)	.324E-1 (2.37)	.540E-1 (.918)	.880E-1 (-2.00)	.189 (14.8)	.120 (16.1)	.788E-1 (17.2)	.424E-1 (16.3)	.308E-1 (18.3)
x_{2t}, x_{3t}, x_{4t}, x_{5t}, x_{6t}	.400E-1 (-3.26)	.240E-1 (-3.82)	.760E-1 (-5.57)	.136E-1 (-8.35)	.396E-1 (-1.01)	.109 (1.53)	.572E-1 (1.65)	.300E-1 (1.60)	.132E-1 (1.61)	.680E-1 (1.28)

Table 4
Estimated Tail Probabilities for t-Ratios
Coefficient 4: γ_{02}

Instruments constant, x_{1t} x_{1t-1}, plus:	Left Tail N(0,1)					Right Tail N(0,1)				
	.500E-2	.100E-1	.250E-1	.500E-1	.100	.100	.500E-1	.250E-1	.100E-1	.500E-2
	Loose Fit									
	Left Tail Estimated					Right Tail Estimated				
x_{2t}, x_{3t}, x_{4t} y_{1t-1}, y_{2t-1}	.640E-1 (.992)	.136E-1 (1.81)	.372E-1 (3.91)	.608E-1 (2.48)	.127 (4.47)	.110 (1.67)	.576E-1 (1.74)	.304E-1 (1.73)	.128E-1 (1.41)	.600E-1 (.709)
x_{2t}, y_{1t-1}, y_{2t-1}	.120E-2 (-2.69)	.280E-1 (-3.62)	.840E-1 (-5.32)	.212E-1 (-6.61)	.564E-1 (-7.24)	.520E-1 (-8.00)	.192E-1 (-7.07)	.520E-2 (-6.34)	.160E-2 (-4.22)	.400E-3 (-3.26)
x_{2t}, x_{3t} y_{1t-1}, y_{2t-1}	.320E-2 (-1.28)	.480E-2 (-2.61)	.212E-1 (-1.22)	.464E-1 (-.826)	.928E-1 (-1.20)	.816E-1 (-3.07)	.388E-1 (-2.57)	.168E-1 (-2.63)	.400E-2 (-3.02)	.200E-2 (-2.13)
x_{2t}, x_{4t} y_{1t-1}, y_{2t-1}	.240E-2 (-1.84)	.560E-2 (-2.21)	.192E-1 (-1.86)	.480E-1 (-.459)	.103 (-.466)	.912E-1 (-1.47)	.424E-1 (-1.74)	.184E-1 (-2.11)	.720E-2 (-1.41)	.280E-2 (-1.56)
x_{3t}, x_{4t} y_{1t-1}, y_{2t-1}	.360E-2 (-.992)	.600E-2 (-2.01)	.216E-1 (-1.09)	.464E-1 (-.826)	.100 (-.001)	.820E-1 (-3.00)	.396E-1 (-2.39)	.188E-1 (-1.99)	.640E-2 (-1.81)	.480E-2 (-.142)
x_{2t}, x_{3t}, x_{4t} x_{5t}, x_{6t}	.320E-2 (-1.28)	.400E-2 (-3.02)	.116E-1 (-4.29)	.268E-1 (-5.32)	.624E-1 (-6.27)	.492E-1 (-8.47)	.160E-1 (-7.80)	.800E-2 (-5.44)	.160E-2 (-4.42)	.800E-3 (-2.98)

Table 4 (continued)
Estimated Tail Probabilities for t-Ratios
Coefficient 4: γ_{02}

Instruments constant, x_{1t} x_{1t-1}, plus:	Left Tail N(0,1)					Right Tail N(0,1)				
	.500E-2	.100E-1	.250E-1	.500E-1	.100	.100	.500E-1	.250E-1	.100E-1	.500E-2
	Tight Fit									
	Left Tail Estimated					Right Tail Estimated				
x_{2t}, x_{3t}, x_{4t} y_{1t-1}, y_{2t-1}	.236E-1 (13.2)	.344E-1 (12.3)	.604E-1 (11.3)	.104 (12.4)	.158 (9.66)	.143 (7.20)	.944E-1 (10.2)	.584E-1 (10.7)	.312E-1 (10.7)	.188E-1 (9.78)
x_{2t}, y_{1t-1}, y_{2t-1}	.560E-2 (.425)	.120E-1 (1.01)	.256E-1 (.192)	.520E-1 (.459)	.988E-1 (-.201)	.920E-1 (-1.33)	.460E-1 (-.918)	.244E-1 (-.192)	.108E-1 (.402)	.320E-2 (-1.28)
x_{3t}, y_{1t-1}, y_{2t-1}	.320E-2 (-1.28)	.760E-2 (-1.21)	.228E-1 (-.705)	.444E-1 (-1.28)	.996E-1 (-.0675)	.868E-1 (-2.20)	.304E-1 (-4.50)	.172E-1 (-2.50)	.480E-2 (-2.61)	.240E-2 (-1.84)
x_{2t}, x_{3t} y_{1t-1}, y_{2t-1}	.148E-1 (6.95)	.248E-1 (7.44)	.488E-1 (7.62)	.872E-1 (8.53)	.142E-1 (7.00)	.139 (6.46)	.752E-1 (5.78)	.412E-1 (5.19)	.192E-1 (4.62)	.116E-1 (4.68)
x_{2t}, x_{4t} y_{1t-1}, y_{2t-1}	.148E-1 (6.95)	.236E-1 (6.83)	.516E-1 (8.52)	.764E-1 (6.06)	.138 (5.93)	.132 (5.40)	.832E-1 (7.62)	.436E-1 (5.96)	.240E-1 (7.04)	.124E-1 (5.25)
x_{3t}, x_{4t} y_{1t-1}, y_{2t-1}	.132E-1 (5.81)	.224E-1 (6.23)	.476E-1 (7.24)	.848E-1 (7.98)	.149 (8.20)	.127 (4.53)	.712E-1 (4.86)	.416E-1 (5.32)	.212E-1 (5.63)	.124E-1 (5.25)
x_{2t}, x_{3t}, x_{4t} x_{5t}, x_{6t}	.520E-2 (.142)	.100E-1 (0.00)	.192E-1 (-1.86)	.424E-1 (-1.74)	.808E-1 (-3.20)	.720E-1 (-4.67)	.368E-1 (-3.03)	.180E-1 (-2.24)	.800E-2 (-1.01)	.480E-2 (-1.42)

Table 5
Estimated Tail Probabilities for t-Ratios
Coefficient 5: γ_{11}

Instruments constant, x_{1t}, x_{1t-1}, plus:	Left Tail N(0,1) .500E-2	.100E-1	.250E-1	.500E-1	.100	Right Tail N(0,1) .100	.500E-1	.250E-1	.100E-1	.500E-2
	Loose Fit: Left Tail Estimated					Right Tail Estimated				
x_{2t}, x_{3t}, x_{4t}, y_{1t-1}, y_{2t-1}	.320E-1 (19.1)	.524E-1 (21.3)	.840E-1 (18.9)	.138 (20.3)	.220 (20.1)	.616E-1 (-6.40)	.312E-1 (-4.31)	.712E-1 (-2.50)	.920E-1 (-.402)	.520E-1 (.142)
x_{2t}, y_{1t-1}, y_{2t-1}	.144E-1 (6.66)	.204E-1 (5.23)	.416E-1 (5.32)	.688E-1 (4.31)	.124 (4.07)	.308E-1 (-11.5)	.144E-1 (-8.17)	.480E-2 (-6.47)	.160E-2 (-4.23)	.800E-3 (-2.98)
x_{2t}, x_{3t}, y_{1t-1}, y_{2t-1}	.248E-1 (14.0)	.380E-1 (14.1)	.692E-1 (14.2)	.108 (13.4)	.186 (14.3)	.512E-1 (-8.13)	.244E-1 (-5.87)	.136E-1 (-3.65)	.680E-2 (-1.61)	.320E-2 (-1.28)
x_{2t}, x_{4t}, y_{1t-1}, y_{2t-1}	.228E-1 (12.6)	.376E-1 (13.9)	.672E-1 (13.5)	.113 (14.4)	.188 (14.7)	.504E-1 (-8.27)	.268E-1 (-5.32)	.112E-1 (-4.42)	.320E-2 (-3.42)	.160E-2 (-2.41)
x_{3t}, x_{4t}, y_{1t-1}, y_{2t-1}	.228E-1 (12.6)	.384E-1 (14.3)	.636E-1 (12.4)	.112 (14.2)	.186 (14.4)	.508E-1 (-8.20)	.240E-1 (-5.96)	.108E-1 (-4.55)	.680E-2 (-1.61)	.400E-2 (-.709)
x_{2t}, x_{3t}, x_{4t}, x_{5t}, x_{6t}	.440E-2 (-.425)	.720E-2 (-1.41)	.184E-1 (-2.11)	.440E-1 (-1.38)	.103 (.466)	.192E-1 (-13.5)	.720E-2 (-9.82)	.200E-2 (-7.37)	.400E-3 (-4.82)	.000 (-3.54)

Table 5 (continued)
Estimated Tail Probabilities for t-Ratios
Coefficient 5: γ_{11}

Instruments constant, x_{1t} x_{1t-1}, plus:	Left Tail N(0,1) .500E-2	.100E-1	.250E-1	.500E-1	.100	Right Tail N(0,1) .100	.500E-1	.250E-1	.100E-1	.500E-2
Tight Fit	Left Tail Estimated					Right Tail Estimated				
x_{2t}, x_{3t}, x_{4t} y_{1t-1}, y_{2t-1}	.452E-1 (28.5)	.656E-1 (27.9)	.106 (25.8)	.150 (22.9)	.226 (21.0)	.800E-1 (-3.33)	.480E-1 (-4.59)	.284E-1 (1.09)	.136E-1 (1.81)	.720E-1 (1.56)
x_{2t}, y_{1t-1}, y_{2t-1}	.268E-1 (15.5)	.352E-1 (12.7)	.684E-1 (13.9)	.105 (12.6)	.173 (12.1)	.640E-1 (-6.00)	.296E-1 (-4.68)	.172E-1 (-2.50)	.840E-2 (-8.04)	.520E-2 (.142)
x_{3t}, y_{1t-1}, y_{2t-1}	.248E-1 (14.0)	.388E-1 (14.5)	.648E-1 (12.7)	.104 (12.4)	.169E-1 (11.5)	.540E-1 (-7.67)	.264E-1 (-5.41)	.148E-1 (-3.27)	.560E-2 (-2.21)	.320E-2 (-1.28)
x_{2t}, x_{3t} y_{1t-1}, y_{2t-1}	.424E-1 (26.5)	.588E-1 (24.5)	.952E-1 (22.5)	.136 (19.8)	.210 (18.4)	.756E-1 (-4.07)	.436E-1 (-1.47)	.284E-1 (1.09)	.124E-1 (1.21)	.720E-2 (1.56)
x_{2t}, x_{4t} y_{1t-1}, y_{2t-1}	.396E-1 (24.5)	.568E-1 (23.5)	.952E-1 (22.5)	.142 (21.0)	.222 (20.3)	.788E-1 (-3.53)	.388E-1 (-2.57)	.216E-1 (-1.09)	.104E-1 (.201)	.680E-2 (1.28)
x_{3t}, x_{4t} y_{1t-1}, y_{2t-1}	.408E-1 (25.3)	.564E-1 (23.3)	.952E-1 (22.5)	.142 (21.1)	.216 (19.3)	.752E-1 (-4.13)	.376E-1 (-2.84)	.236E-1 (-.448)	.880E-2 (-.603)	.440E-2 (-.425)
x_{2t}, x_{3t}, x_{4t} x_{5t}, x_{6t}	.400E-2 (-.709)	.840E-2 (-.804)	.196E-1 (-1.73)	.452E-1 (-1.10)	.107 (1.20)	.272E-1 (-12.1)	.600E-2 (-10.1)	.120E-2 (-7.62)	.800E-3 (-4.62)	.400E-3 (-3.26)

Table 6
Estimated Tail Probabilities for t-Ratios
Coefficient 6: γ_{12}

Instruments constant, x_{1t}, x_{1t-1}, plus:	Left Tail N(0,1) .500E-2	.100E-1	.250E-1	.500E-1	.100	Right Tail N(0,1) .100	.500E-1	.250E-1	.100E-1	.500E-2
	Loose Fit									
	Left Tail Estimated					Right Tail Estimated				
x_{2t}, x_{3t}, x_{4t} y_{1t-1}, y_{2t-1}	.640E-2 (.992)	.104E-1 (.201)	.212E-1 (-1.22)	.384E-1 (-2.66)	.732E-1 (-4.47)	.174 (12.3)	.106 (12.8)	.624E-1 (12.0)	.300E-1 (10.0)	.216E-1 (11.8)
x_{2t}, y_{1t-1}, y_{2t-1}	.240E-2 (-1.84)	.480E-2 (-2.61)	.840E-2 (-5.32)	.176E-1 (-7.43)	.448E-1 (-9.20)	.106 (.999)	.616E-1 (2.66)	.332E-1 (2.63)	.164E-1 (3.22)	.108E-1 (4.11)
x_{2t}, x_{3t} y_{1t-1}, y_{2t-1}	.440E-2 (-.425)	.760E-2 (-1.21)	.164E-1 (-2.75)	.336E-1 (-3.76)	.664E-1 (-5.60)	.152 (8.73)	.908E-1 (9.36)	.496E-1 (7.88)	.272E-1 (8.64)	.180E-1 (9.22)
x_{2t}, x_{4t} y_{1t-1}, y_{2t-1}	.520E-2 (.142)	.680E-2 (-1.61)	.140E-1 (-3.52)	.312E-1 (-4.31)	.668E-1 (-5.53)	.147 (7.86)	.888E-1 (8.90)	.544E-1 (9.42)	.212E-1 (5.63)	.160E-1 (7.80)
x_{3t}, x_{4t} y_{1t-1}, y_{2t-1}	.360E-2 (-.992)	.760E-2 (-1.21)	.168E-1 (-2.63)	.288E-1 (-4.86)	.636E-1 (-6.07)	.145 (7.46)	.820E-1 (7.34)	.476E-1 (7.24)	.228E-1 (6.43)	.160E-1 (7.80)
x_{2t}, x_{3t}, x_{4t} x_{5t}, x_{6t}	.800E-3 (-2.98)	.120E-2 (-4.42)	.280E-2 (-7.11)	.880E-2 (-9.45)	.336E-1 (-11.1)	.572E-1 (-7.13)	.168E-1 (-7.62)	.520E-2 (-6.34)	.400E-3 (-4.82)	.000 (-3.54)

Table 6 (continued)
Estimated Tail Probabilities for t-Ratios
Coefficient 6: γ_{12}

Instruments constant, x_{1t} x_{1t-1}, plus:	Left Tail N(0,1) .500E-2	.100E-1	.250E-1	.500E-1	.100	Right Tail N(0,1) .100	.500E-1	.250E-1	.100E-1	.500E-2
Tight Fit	Left Tail Estimated					Right Tail Estimated				
x_{2t}, x_{3t}, x_{4t} y_{1t-1}, y_{2t-1}	.116E-1 (4.68)	.192E-1 (4.62)	.382E-1 (2.50)	.568E-1 (1.56)	.980E-1 (-.334)	.187 (14.5)	.124 (17.0)	.824E-1 (18.4)	.464E-1 (18.3)	.316E-1 (18.9)
x_{2t}, y_{1t-1}, y_{2t-1}	.600E-2 (.709)	.960E-2 (-2.01)	.224E-1 (-.833)	.412E-1 (-2.02)	.784E-1 (-3.60)	.142 (7.06)	.852E-1 (8.07)	.480E-1 (7.37)	.244E-1 (7.24)	.160E-1 (7.80)
x_{3t}, y_{1t-1}, y_{2t-1}	.480E-2 (-.142)	.880E-2 (-.603)	.180E-1 (-2.24)	.312E-1 (-4.31)	.696E-1 (-5.07)	.128 (4.60)	.728E-1 (5.23)	.384E-1 (4.29)	.188E-1 (4.42)	.124E-1 (5.25)
x_{2t}, x_{3t} y_{1t-1}, y_{2t-1}	.960E-2 (3.26)	.164E-1 (3.22)	.296E-1 (1.47)	.504E-1 (.0917)	.976E-1 (-.401)	.179 (13.1)	.111 (14.0)	.684E-1 (13.9)	.380E-1 (14.1)	.220E-1 (12.1)
x_{2t}, x_{4t} y_{1t-1}, y_{2t-1}	.960E-2 (3.26)	.164E-1 (3.22)	.312E-1 (1.99)	.528E-1 (.642)	.940E-1 (-1.00)	.181 (13.5)	.115 (15.0)	.732E-1 (15.4)	.400E-1 (15.1)	.240E-1 (13.5)
x_{3t}, x_{4t} y_{1t-1}, y_{2t-1}	.100E-1 (3.54)	.148E-1 (2.41)	.312E-1 (1.99)	.528E-1 (.642)	.928E-1 (-1.20)	.171 (11.9)	.112 (14.2)	.696E-1 (14.3)	.388E-1 (14.5)	.216E-1 (11.8)
x_{2t}, x_{3t}, x_{4t} x_{5t}, x_{6t}	.400E-3 (-3.26)	.480E-3 (-4.82)	.800E-2 (-5.44)	.192E-1 (-7.07)	.436E-1 (-9.40)	.712E-1 (-4.80)	.268E-1 (-5.32)	.112E-1 (-4.42)	.360E-2 (-3.22)	.280E-2 (-1.56)

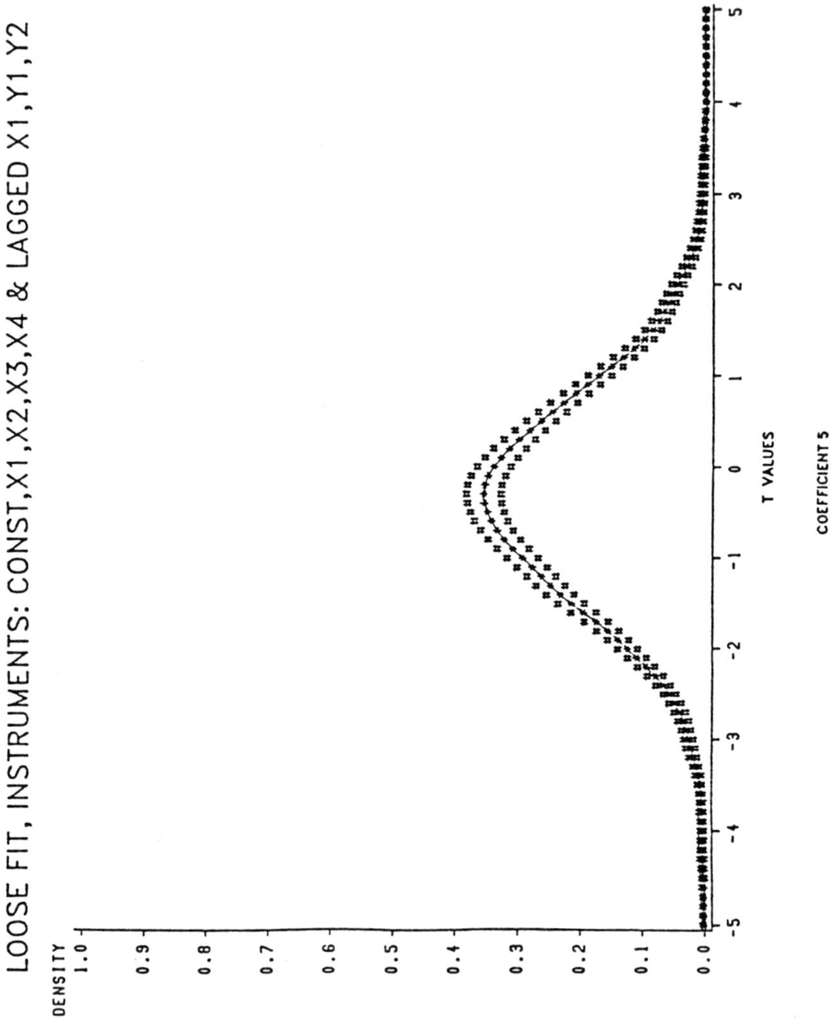
LOOSE FIT, INSTRUMENTS: CONST,X1,X2,X3,X4 & LAGGED X1,Y1,Y2
DENSITY
1.0
0.9
0.8
0.7
0.6
0.5
0.4
0.3
0.2
0.1
0.0
-5
-4
-3
-2
-1
0
1
2
3
4
5
T VALUES
COEFFICIENT 5
GRAPH 1

LOOSE FIT, INSTRUMENTS: CONST,X1,X3,X4 & LAGGED X1,Y1,Y2

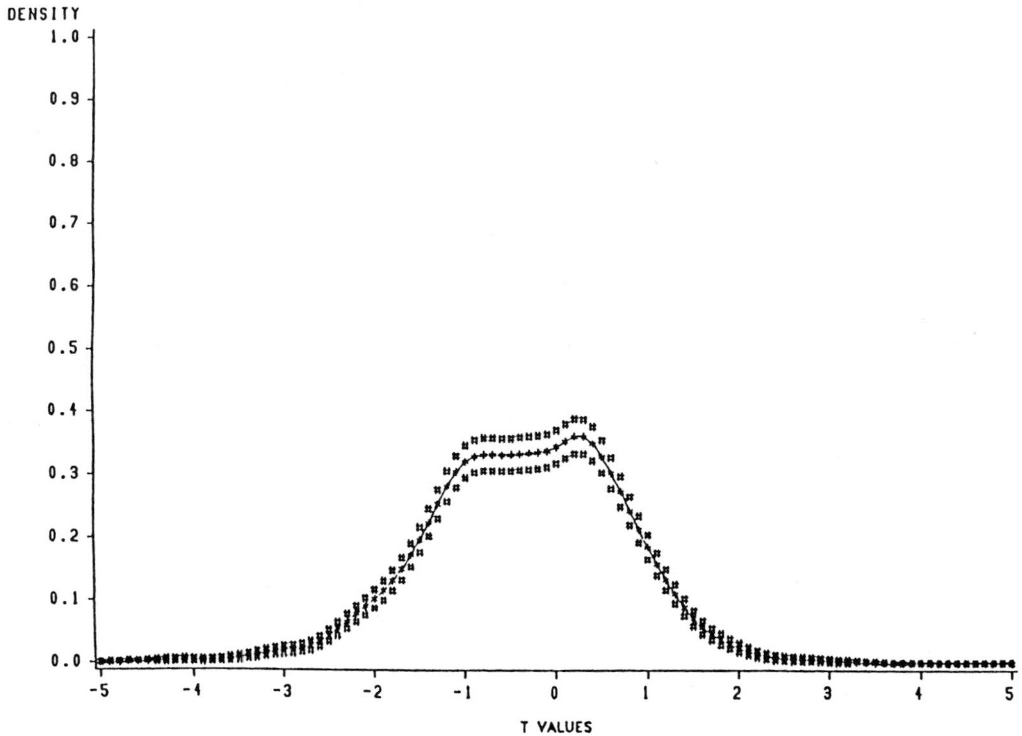

COEFFICIENT 5
GRAPH 2

LOOSE FIT, INSTRUMENTS: CONST,X1,X2,X3,X4,X5,X6 & LAGGED X1

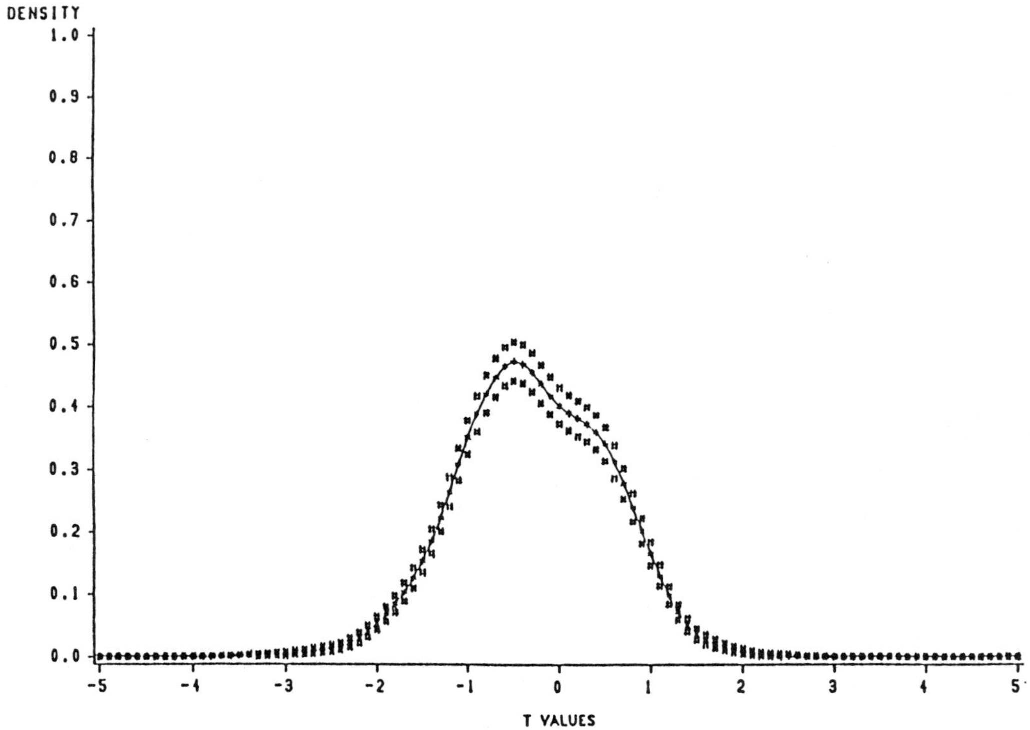

COEFFICIENT 5
GRAPH 3

TIGHT FIT, INSTRUMENTS: CONST,X1,X2,X3,X4 & LAGGED X1,Y1,Y2

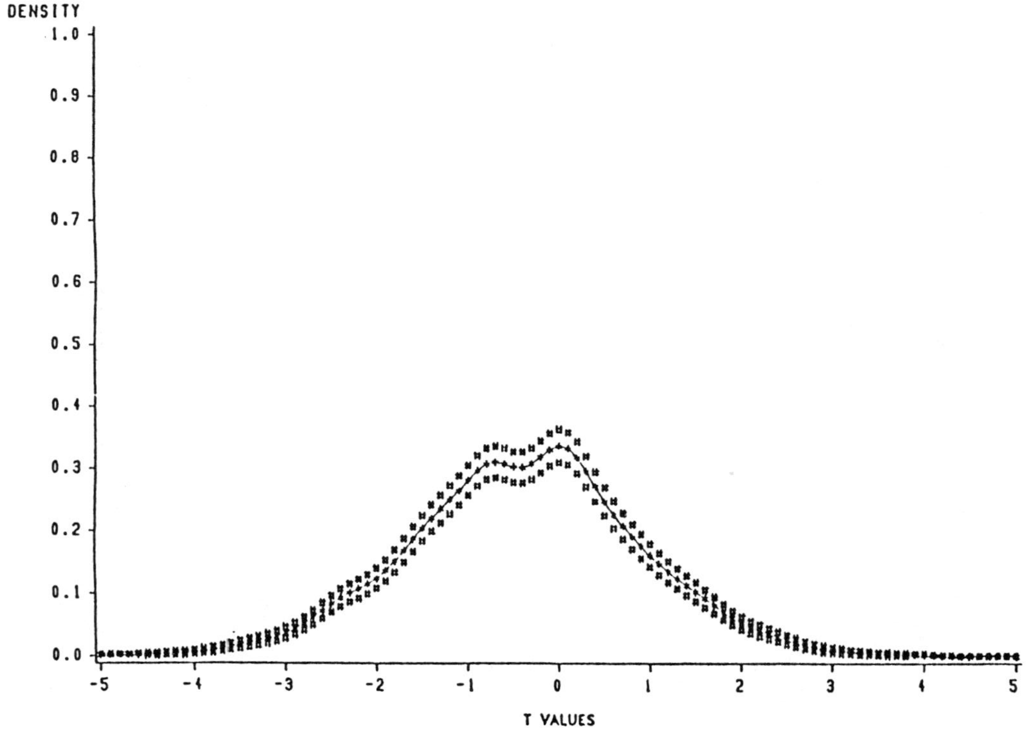

COEFFICIENT 5
GRAPH 4

TIGHT FIT, INSTRUMENTS: CONST,X1,X3,X4 & LAGGED X1,Y1,Y2

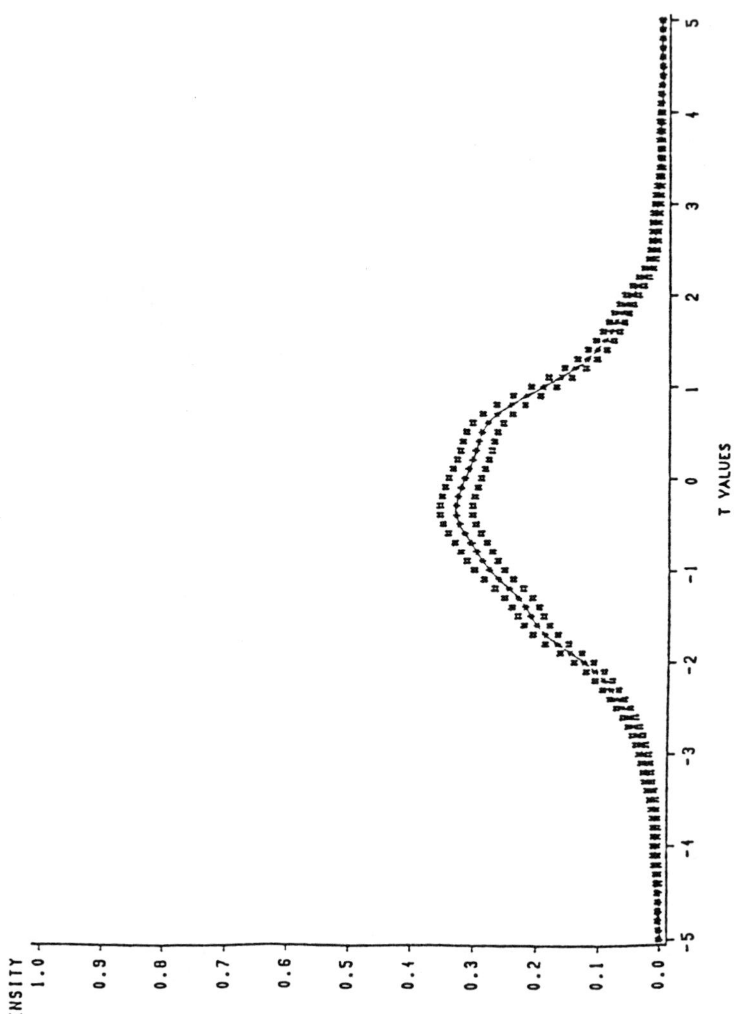

COEFFICIENT 5
GRAPH 5

TIGHT FIT, INSTRUMENTS: CONST,X1,X2,X3,X4,X5,X6 & LAGGED X1

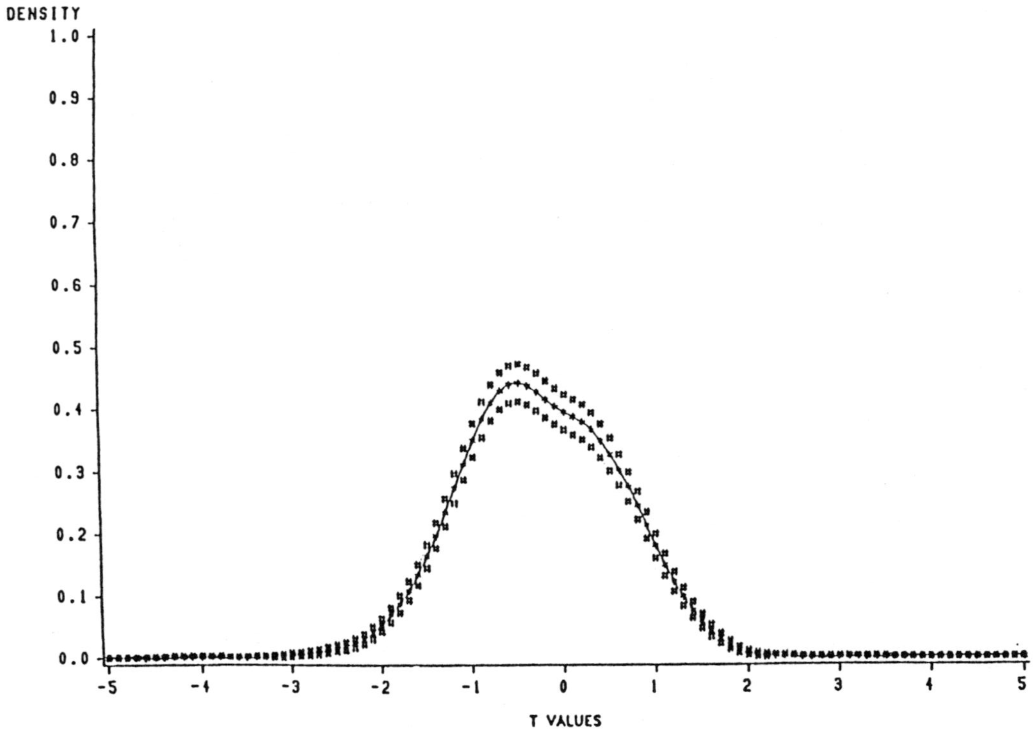

COEFFICIENT 5
GRAPH 6

References

Basmann, R.L., D.H. Richardson and R.J. Rohr [1974], An Experimental Study of Structural Estimators and Test Statistics Associated with Dynamical Econometric Models, *Econometrica*, 42, 717-730.

Bowden, R.J. and D.A. Turkington [1984], *Instrumental Variables*, Cambridge, Cambridge University Press.

Dhrymes, P.J. [1969], Alternative Asymptotic Tests of Significance and Related Aspects of 2SLS and 3SLS Estimated Parameters, *Review of Economic Studies*, 36, 213-226.

Dickey, D.A. [1976], *Estimation and Hypotheses Testing for Nonstationary Time Series*, Ph.D. Thesis, Iowa State University, Ames, Iowa.

Dickey, D.A. and W.A. Fuller [1979], Distribution of the Estimators for Autoregressive Time Series with a Unit Root, *Journal of the American Statistical Association*, 74, 428- 431.

Engle, R.F., D.F. Hendry and J.F. Richard [1983], Exogeniety, *Econometrica*, 51, 277-304.

Evans, G.B.A. and N.E. Savin [1981], Testing for Unit Roots: 1, *Econometrica*, 49, 753-779.

Evans, G.B.A. and N.E. Savin [1984], Testing for Unit Roots: 2, *Econometrica*, 52, 1241-1269.

Hansen, B.E. and P.C.B. Phillips [1988], *Estimation and Inference in Models of Cointegration: A Simulation Study*, Cowles Commission for Research in Economics, Yale University.

Harvey, A.C. [1984], *The Econometric Analysis of Time Series*, Oxford, Philip Alan.

Kiviet, J. [1985], Model Selection Test Procedures in a Single Linear Equation of a Dynamic Simultaneous System and Their Defects in Small Samples, *Journal of Econometrics*, 28, 327-362.

Mariano, R.S. [1977], Finite-Sample Properties of Instrumental Variable Estimators of Structural Coefficients, *Econometrica*, 45, 487-496.

McLeod, A.I. [1982], *Efficient FORTRAN Coding of a Random Number Generator*, Department of Statistical and Actuarial Science, The University of Western Ontario, TR-82-08.

Nankervis, J.C. and N.E. Savin [1985], Testing the Autoregressive Parameter With the t-Statistic, *Journal of Econometrics*, 27, 143-162.

Nankervis, J.C. and N.E. Savin [1987], Finite Sample Distributions of t and F Statistics in an AR(1) Model with an Exogenous Variable, *Econometric Theory*, 3, 387-408.

Phillips, P.C.B. [1977], Approximations to Some Finite Sample Distributions Associated with a First Order Stochastic Difference Equation, *Econometrica*, 45, 463-486.

Phillips, P.C.B. [1982], Exact Small Sample Theory in the Simultaneous Equations Model, M.D. Intriligator and Z. Griliches (Eds) *Handbook of Econometrics* Vol 1, Amsterdam, North-Holland.

Phillips, P.C.B. and B.E. Hansen [1986], *Statistical Inference in Instrumental Variables Regression with I(1) Processes*, Cowles Foundation for Research in Economics, Yale University.

Phillips, P.C.B. and P. Perron [1988], Testing for a Unit Root in Time Series Regression, *Biometrika*, 75, 335-346.

Richardson, D.H. and R.J. Rohr [1971], The Distribution of a Structural t-Statistic for the Case of Two Included Endogenous Variables, *Journal of the American Statistical Association*, 66, 375-382.

Sargan, J.D. [1975], Gram-Charlier Approximations Applied to t- Ratios of k-Class Estimators, *Econometrica*, 42, 169-176.

The Exact Distribution of the PRRF Estimator – A Monte Carlo Integration Approach

J. L. Knight*
Department of Economics
University of Western Ontario

Abstract

Exact expressions are now available for both the pdf and moments of the PRRF estimator associated with a general structural equation. However, due to the complexity of the pdf, involving invariant polynomials with several matrix arguments, little is known of its distributional shape or its sensitivity to parameter changes. In this paper extensive numerical computations are undertaken, using Monte Carlo integration, along with non–parametric density estimation, to bridge this gap.

1. Introduction

Although great advances have recently been made in exact distribution theory in relation to structural estimators, the same is not true of reduced form estimators. The exception to this is in relation to the partially restricted reduced form estimator (PRRF) where now quite a large amount is known about its finite sample properties. We know that all moments exist as shown by Knight [1977] with alternative derivations given by Swamy and

---

*I wish to thank Yanqin Fan and Paul Gomme for excellent research assistance with the numerical computations. Thanks also go to Robin Carter and an anonymous referee for helpful comments. Financial support from The Natural Sciences and Engineering Research Council of Canada is gratefully acknowledged.

Metha [1980] and McCarthy [1981]. Nagar and Sahay [1978] were the first to publish exact expressions for the moments in a two endogenous variable canonical model. Most recently, Knight and Kinal [1989] derived the exact pdf and moments in a general structural equation with $(n+1)$ endogenous variables.

One could thus conclude that our knowledge of this estimator is now complete. Unfortunately, this is not the case. While we have analytical expressions for the pdf and moments we have no information on the general shape characteristics of the distribution. Nor do we have any idea on the sensitivity of the pdf or moments to changes in the underlying parameters specifying the distribution.

It is thus the purpose of this article to undertake extensive numerical computations, evaluating the pdf and moments under various parameter specifications. Section 2 introduces the model and notation. Section 3 examines the distribution and moment results and discusses the approach to be followed in the numerical experiments. The design of the experiments is given in Section 4 and the results discussed in Section 5. A brief conclusion is contained in Section 6.

2. Model and Notation

Consider a single structural equation containing two endogenous variables

$$y_1 = y_2\beta + X_1\gamma + u \tag{2.1}$$

where y_1, y_2 are both $T\times 1$ vectors, X_1 a $T\times K_1$ matrix of included exogenous variables and u a $T \times 1$ vector of disturbances. β is a scalar and γ a $K_1\times 1$ vector of structural parameters.

The associated reduced form is assumed to exist and is given by

$$y_1 = X_1\pi_{11} + X_2\pi_{21} + v_1 = \bar{y}_1 + v_1 \qquad (2.2a)$$

$$y_2 = X_1\pi_{12} + X_2\pi_{22} + v_2 = \bar{y}_2 + v_2 \qquad (2.2b)$$

We assume, without loss of generality, that $X'X = T \cdot I_K$ where $X = (X_1 \colon X_2)$ with X_2 being $T \times K_2$, $K = K_1 + K_2 < T$ and $K_2 > 1$ so that (1) is apparently identified. Also, the rows of $(v_1\ v_2)$ are assumed to be independently and normally distributed, i.e. $(v_1\ v_2) \sim N(0, \Omega)$ where

$$\Omega = \begin{bmatrix} \sigma_1^2 & \rho\sigma_1\sigma_2 \\ \rho\sigma_1\sigma_2 & \sigma_2^2 \end{bmatrix}.$$

The PRRF estimator associated with (2.2a) is, under the above assumptions, given by

$$\begin{bmatrix} \tilde{\pi}_{11} \\ \tilde{\pi}_{21} \end{bmatrix} = \frac{1}{T} \begin{bmatrix} X_1'y_1 \\ X_2'y_2\tilde{\beta} \end{bmatrix} \qquad (2.3)$$

where $\tilde{\beta} = (y_2'X_2X_2'y_2)^{-1}y_2'X_2X_2'y_1$ is the 2SLS estimator of β in (2.1). Since $\tilde{\pi}_{11}$ is simply the OLS estimator of π_{11} in (2.2a), in what follows, we will confine our attention to $\tilde{\pi}_{21}$.

Due to the normality of $(v_1\ v_2)$ it is clear that

$$(y_1\ y_2) \sim N((\bar{y}_1, \bar{y}_2), \Omega)$$

and letting

$$z_1 = \frac{1}{\sqrt{T}} X_2'y_1 \text{ and } z_2 = \frac{1}{\sqrt{T}} X_2'y_2$$

we have

$$(z_1\ z_2) \sim N((\bar{z}_1\ \bar{z}_2), \Omega)$$

where

$$\bar{z}_1 = \sqrt{T}\,\pi_{21} \text{ and } \bar{z}_2 = \sqrt{T}\,\pi_{22}$$

and due to the identifiability of (2.1)

$$\pi_{21} = \pi_{22}\beta$$

implying

$$\bar{z}_1 = \bar{z}_2\beta.$$

From the definition of z_1, z_2, the 2SLS estimator $\tilde{\beta}$ is given by

$$\tilde{\beta} = (z_2' z_2)^{-1} z_2' z_1$$

and the PRRF estimator $\tilde{\pi}_{21}$ given by

$$\tilde{\pi}_{21} = \frac{1}{\sqrt{T}} z_2(z_2' z_2)^{-1} z_2' z_1 \tag{2.4}$$

and from the joint normality of $(z_1\ z_2)$ we have

$$z_1 | z_2 \sim N(\bar{z}_1 + \frac{\rho\sigma_1}{\sigma_2}(z_2 - \bar{z}_2), \sigma_1^2(1 - \rho^2) \cdot I)$$

and thus

$$\tilde{\pi}_{21} | z_2 \sim N(\mu(z_2), \Sigma(z_2)) \tag{2.5}$$

where

$$\mu(z_2) = \frac{\rho\sigma_1}{\sqrt{T}\ \sigma_2} z_2 + z_2(z_2' z_2)^{-1} z_2' \pi_{22}(\beta - \frac{\rho\sigma_1}{\sigma_2}) \tag{2.6}$$

$$\Sigma(z_2) = \frac{\sigma_1^2(1-\rho^2)}{T} \cdot z_2(z_2' z_2)^{-1} z_2' \tag{2.7}$$

For a linear combination of the elements in $\tilde{\pi}_{21}$, or indeed for the marginal distribution we have immediately that for a $K_2 \times 1$ vector of constants, say a,

$$a'\tilde{\pi}_{21} | z_2 \sim N(a'\mu(z_2), a'\Sigma(z_2)a). \tag{2.8}$$

3. The Exact Distribution and Moments

Our attention will focus on the distribution and moments of the linear combination $a'\tilde{\pi}_{21}$. We first consider the analytical results currently available and then discuss the approach to be followed in this investigation.

3.1 Distribution

Knight and Kinal [1989] in their study of the exact results for the PRRF estimator work with the conditional distribution given by (2.8). They first find the unconditional characteristic function and then invert this to get the pdf. They consider two approaches which lead to two forms for the pdf. The first involves using the techniques of multivariate analysis and results in an exact analytical expression for the pdf which involves invariant polynomials with several matrix arguments. That is, they derive the characteristic function by solving the integral

$$\phi(t) = \int_{-\infty}^{\infty} exp[ita'\mu(z_2) - \frac{1}{2}t^2a'\Sigma(z_2)a]pdf(z_2)dz_2 \quad (3.1)$$

and then find the pdf by inversion:

$$pdf(a'\tilde{\pi}_{21}) = \frac{1}{2\pi}\int_{-\infty}^{\infty} e^{-ita'\tilde{\pi}_{21}} \cdot \phi(t)dt \quad (3.2)$$

The resulting expression is given

$$pdf(a'\tilde{\pi}_{21}) = (2\pi)^{-1/2} exp\left[\frac{-T}{2\sigma_2^2}\pi_{22}'\pi_{22}\right]$$

$$\cdot\ exp\left[\frac{T}{2\sigma_1^2(1-\rho^2)a'a}\left[a'\tilde{\pi}_{21} - a'\pi_{22}(\beta - \frac{\rho\sigma_1}{\sigma_2})\right]^2\right]$$

$$\cdot \sum_{k=0}^{\infty}\sum_{\ell=0}^{\infty} \frac{(\frac{K_2-1}{2})_\ell\,(\frac{K_2}{2})_k}{k!\,\ell!\,(\frac{K_2}{2})_{k+\ell}}(\frac{1}{2})^{k+\ell}$$

$$\cdot \sum_{\substack{k_1,k_2,k_3 \\ (k = k_1+k_2+k_3)}} \frac{k!}{k_1!k_2!k_3!} \sum_{\substack{\ell_1,\ell_2 \\ (\ell = \ell_1+\ell_2)}} \frac{\ell!}{\ell_1!\ell_2!}$$

$$\cdot \sum_{p=0}^{[k_1+\ell_2+(\frac{k_2+\ell_1}{2})]} \begin{bmatrix} 2k_1+k_2+2\ell_2+\ell_1 \\ 2p \end{bmatrix} (-1)^{k_1+\ell_2-p}$$

$$\cdot \left[a'\tilde{\pi}_{21} - a'\pi_{22}(\beta - \frac{\rho\sigma_1}{\sigma_2})\right]^{2k_1+k_2+2\ell_2+\ell_1-2p} 2^p(\tfrac{1}{2})_p$$

$$\cdot \left[\frac{\sigma_1^2}{T}(1-p^2)a'a\right]^{-(2k_1+k_2+2\ell_2+\ell_1+\frac{1}{2})+p}$$

$$\cdot \left[\frac{\sigma_1^2\rho^2}{T}\right]^{k_1} \left[\frac{\rho\sigma_1}{\sigma_2}\right]^{k_2} \left[\frac{T}{\sigma_2^2}\right]^{k_3} \left[\beta - \frac{\rho\sigma_1}{\sigma_2}\right]^{\ell_1} \left[\frac{\sigma_1^2}{T}(1-\rho^2)\right]^{\ell_2}$$

$$\cdot C_{k+\ell}^{k_1+\ell_2,k_2+\ell_1,k_3}\left[aa', (\pi_{22}a'+a'\pi_{22}),\pi_{22}\,\pi_{22}'\right] \qquad (3.3)$$

where $C_f^{f_1,f_2,f_3}(\cdot,\ \cdot,\ \cdot)$ with $f = f_1 + f_2 + f_3$ is the top order invariant polynomial with three matrix arguments as detailed in Chikuse [1980].

The second approach uses the fractional calculus results of Phillips [1984, 1987] and notes that

$$exp[ita'\mu(z_2) - \tfrac{1}{2}t^2a'\Sigma(z_2)a]$$
$$= exp[ita'\mu(\partial x) - \tfrac{1}{2}t^2a'\Sigma(\partial x)a]exp[x'z_2]\Big|_{x=0}$$

Consequently $\phi(t)$ is now given by

$$\phi(t) = exp[ita'\mu(\partial x) - \frac{1}{2}t^2 a'\Sigma(\partial x)a] \cdot exp[x'\bar{z}_2 + x'x\sigma_2^2/2]\Big|_{x=0} \tag{3.4}$$

and the pdf by

$$pdf(a'\tilde{\pi}_{21}) = (2\pi\zeta_x)^{-1/2} exp[-\frac{1}{2}(a'\tilde{\pi}_{21} - \eta_x)^2/\zeta_x] \cdot exp[x'\bar{z}_2 + \sigma_2^2 x'x/2]\Big|_{x=0} \tag{3.5}$$

where $\eta_x = a'\mu(\partial x)$

$$\zeta_x = a'\Sigma(\partial x)a.$$

The two expressions given by (3.3) and (3.5) are exact and in the latter case also very elegant. Unfortunately, they do not allow an easy analysis of the distribution. In the first case the problem is clearly the complexity of the expression involving the top order invariant polynomials of Chickuse [1980]. Analyzing this expression analytically or evaluating it numerically is indeed a challenge. In the second case the differential operator form while convenient for analytical manipulations is virtually impossible to evaluate numerically.

We now consider an alternative to the above approaches in which the distributional properties will be calculated numerically by evaluating the pdf and moments using Monte Carlo integration techniques.

The approach involves using Monte Carlo integration to integrate the conditional pdf given by (2.8) over z_2 thus isolating the marginal pdf of $a'\tilde{\pi}_{21}$. That is, the following integral is evaluated numerically:

$$pdf(a'\tilde{\pi}_{21}) = \int_{-\infty}^{\infty} pdf(a'\tilde{\pi}_{21} | z_2) pdf(z_2) dz_2.$$

In detail, the technique requires a two stage sampling scheme where the first stage generates a random vector z_2 from a normal distribution with mean $\bar{z}_2$ and variance σ_2^2. The vector z_2

specifies the mean, $a'\mu(z_2)$, and variance, $a'\Sigma(z_2)a$, of the conditional pdf of $a'\tilde{\pi}_{21}$ given z_2 and thus by sampling again from this distribution an observation from the unconditional pdf is easily generated. In essence, we average the conditional pdf over the distribution of z_2. The sample which results from repeated applications of this two stage approach may then be used to estimate the pdf, the cdf and the moments.

3.2 The Moments

Knight and Kinal [1989] also derived the moments of $a'\tilde{\pi}_{21}$ thus extending and generalizing the results of Nagar and Sahay [1978]. Using the pdf given earlier it is a straightforward process to solve the relevant integral,

$$E(a'\tilde{\pi}_{21})^m = \int (a'\tilde{\pi}_{21})^m \, pdf(a'\tilde{\pi}_{21}) \, d(a'\tilde{\pi}_{21})$$

and arrive at the following expression:

$$E(a'\tilde{\pi}_{21})^m = \sum_{j=0}^{[m/2]} \binom{m}{2j} (\eta_x)^{m-2j} (\zeta_x/2)^j \frac{(2j)!}{j!} \exp[x'z_2 + \sigma_2^2 x'x/2] \Big|_{x=0} \tag{3.6}$$

Alternatively, using the conditional $pdf(a'\tilde{\pi}_{21} | z_2)$ we have immediately

$$E(a'\tilde{\pi}_{21}) = E(a'\mu(z_2))$$

and

$$Var(a'\tilde{\pi}_{21}) = E(a'\Sigma(z_2)a) + Var(a'\mu(z_2)).$$

From Knight and Kinal [1989] we have for the two endogenous variable model

$$E(a'\tilde{\pi}_{21}) = a'\tilde{\pi}_{21} - \tfrac{1}{2}\pi_{22}(\beta - \alpha)e^{-\theta} f_{0,1} \tag{3.7}$$

where $\alpha = \dfrac{\rho\sigma_1}{\sigma_2}$ and $\theta = \dfrac{T\pi_{22}'\pi_{22}'}{2\sigma_2^2}$ and thus the estimator is unbiased if $\beta = \alpha$ and/or $\pi_{22} = 0$.

If $\rho = 0$ and $\beta = \alpha = 0$ then $\mu(z_2^{\cdot}) = 0$ and

$$Var(a'\tilde{\pi}_{21}) = E(a'\Sigma(z_2)a)$$
$$= \frac{e^{-\theta}\sigma_1^2(1-\rho^2)}{2\sigma_2^2}\left[(a'\tilde{\pi}_{22})^2 f_{1,2} + \frac{\sigma_2^2 a'a}{T} f_{0,1}\right] \quad (3.8)$$

where

$$f_{a,b} = \frac{\Gamma(\frac{K_2}{2} + a)}{\Gamma(\frac{K_2}{2} + b)}\ {}_1F_1(\frac{K_2}{2} + b;\ \theta).$$

To estimate these moments numerically we have the choice of either averaging the conditional moments or averaging the observations for $a'\tilde{\pi}_{21}$. The first method involves averaging $a'\mu(z_2)$ over all replications to find the mean and averaging both $a'\Sigma(z_2)a$ and $(a'\mu(z_2))^2$ to find the variance. The second method merely takes the N replications of $a'\tilde{\pi}_{21}$ and calculates the moments directly. It is the second approach which is followed in this study.

4. The Design of Experiments

Since the experiments consisted of a double sampling process the design must take this into consideration. In the first step the parameters which affect the distribution of the z_2's are: sample size, T; the vector of reduced form parameters π_{22} and the variance of reduced form errors, σ_2^2. For the second step we notice that T, π_{22} and σ_2^2 play a role both directly and indirectly. As well there are the additional parameters of p, σ_1^2 and β. These latter three parameters only affect the second step. There is one final parameter which although not entering into the pdf expressions directly does play a role. This parameter is the non–centrality parameter, θ, so important in the distribution of structural coefficient estimators. Its role in the distribution of the PRRF estimator will be examined in these experiments.

We conducted and will examine forty–two experiments in an effort to analyze the pdf of the PRRF estimator and its sensitivity to changes in the aforementioned parameters.

The reduced form equation considered was that related to an over–identified structural equation with two included endogenous variables and three excluded exogenous variables (i.e. $K_2 = 3$). All experiments except three set $\beta = 0.6$. In experiments 40, 41 and 42 β was set to zero. The forty–two experiments combined two vectors for π_{22}, three sample sizes, $T = 10, 20, 50$, two values both σ_1^2 and σ_2^2 and seven values of p. The two reduced form parameter sets for π_{22} were (.3216, .0402, .3081) and (.8329, .5247, .1760) for set 1 and 2 respectively. Table 1 gives the details on the other parameter values for all experiments.

Each experiment consisted of a two–step sampling scheme to generate the random sample from the unconditional pdf of $a'\tilde{\pi}_{21}$. In the first step the vector z_2 of length K_2 is generated from a normal distribution with mean $\sqrt{T}\ \pi_{22}$ and variance σ_2^2. This vector then specifies the mean and variance of the conditional pdf, i.e. $a'\Sigma(z_2)a$, respectively. A random number is now generated from the normal with mean $a'\mu(z_2)$ and variance $a'\Sigma(z_2)a$. The two–step process is replicated 10,000 times and the resulting 10,000 observations consist of a random sample from the pdf of $a'\tilde{\pi}_{21}$. For all experiments considered, a' was set to the vector (1,0,0), thus the process generated a sample from the marginal distribution of the first element in the vector $\tilde{\pi}_{21}$.

Using the 10,000 sample values the median, mean, variance, skewness and kurtosis coefficients were calculated. Using 512 points the distribution function (cdf) was calculated and a non–parametric estimator of the density (pdf) was derived using a normal kernel. The latter process was accomplished using the Fast Fourier Transform approach documented in Silverman [1986]. From the resulting cdf and pdf calculations, graphs were generated to highlight the shape characteristics of the distribution.

All calculations were performed on a Cyber 170/835 with 60 bit word effectively giving double precision.

5. Numerical Results

The discussion of the results will be undertaken in two parts. The first part will consider the moments and the second the distribution.

5.1 Moments

Dealing in the first instance with the mean and consequently the bias we have from the theoretical results of Section 3 that the bias is given by:

$$E(a'\tilde{\pi}_{21}) - a'\pi_{21} = -\pi_{22}(\beta-\alpha)e^{-\theta}f_{0,1}$$

and thus we can state that for $\pi_{22} > 0.0$ if $\alpha > \beta$ then the bias will be positive and when $\alpha < \beta$ the bias negative. We therefore would expect positive bias in experiments 3, 5, 6, 11, 12, 15, 20, 21, 24 and indeed that is exactly what we observe from Table 2.

We also know that if $\alpha = \beta$, theoretically, $a'\tilde{\pi}_{21}$ should be unbiased. In experiments 2, 14, 23, 32, 35, 40, 41, 42 the biases are quite small being consistent, numerically, with the bias being zero. Other small biases are recorded in experiments 9, 18 and 24. The finding in 9 and 18 can be readily explained by noting that the bias from formula (3.7) depends on both the value of θ and the difference $(\beta - \alpha)$. Now θ in 18 is five times larger than θ in 9. Yet $(\beta - \alpha)$ is the same viz., 0.034. As θ increases $e^{-\theta}f_{0,1}$ decreases in this case far more than π_{22} has increased from reduced form set 1 to 2. For experiment 24, while π_{22} is the same as experiment 18, $(\beta - \alpha)$ is larger and θ five times as large, thus accounting for the small bias.

All the numerical findings on the bias are consistent with a priori theoretical results. That is, for constant $(\beta - \alpha)$ and θ the differences in bias are due only to differences in π_{22} (e.g. compare 13 and 34). For the same $(\beta - \alpha)$ and π_{22} as θ increases the bias decreases (e.g. compare 1, 31 and 34; also 13 and 22). Also, for constant π_{22}, θ and β, the bias decreases as α increases (e.g. compare 7 and 4).

For variances we have similar results in that as σ_1^2 increases for fixed T, θ and ρ the variance of $a'\tilde{\pi}_{21}$ increases. This is to be expected as the variance in the second stage sample process is given by $\frac{\sigma_1^2(1-\rho^2)}{T} a'z_2(z_2',z_2)^{-1}z_2'a$ (e.g. compare 1 with 4 and 31 with 10). If both σ_1^2 and T increase with the ratio σ_1^2/T remaining constant then the variances are similar (e.g. compare 1 with 10 and 13 with 19). For fixed β, σ_1^2, ρ and π_{22} as T increases the variance decreases, a logical result. Also note that as ρ increases for fixed β, π_{22}, σ_1^2 and σ_2^2 the variance always increases.

For negative ρ and positive β, $(\beta - \alpha)$ cannot be zero and hence the estimator is always negatively biased. In this case the smallest bias is associated with small ρ in absolute terms and large T (see for example experiment 28).

From the pdf given in (3.5) we note immediately that the distribution is symmetric only when $k_2 = 0$ and $\ell_2 = 0$. This occurs when $\pi_{22} = 0$ or $\beta = \alpha$ and $\rho = 0$. Thus a priori the experiments 40, 41 and 42 should be symmetric. These experiments do in fact have the smallest skewness values and smallest biases.

5.2 Distribution

With forty–two experiments undertaken it is clearly not possible to display and examine individually the pdf and cdf for each experiment. Instead, in this section, we will concentrate on examining the effects on the distribution of varying one parameter while keeping the remaining ones constant. In this regard we will consider sets of three typical pdf or cdf graphs relevant to particular experiments which highlight the effects of the parameter change. The parameters of interest are sample size (T), correlation (ρ), and variances (σ_1^2 and σ_2^2). Set 1 examines the effects of changes in sample size. Set 2 the sensitivity to different degrees of correlation while Set 3 considers the effects of changes in σ_1^2 and σ_2^2. Set 4 examines the pdf in the only experiments in which the distribution is symmetric.

The pdfs in Set 1 relate to experiments 2, 32 and 35 and illustrate the shape in the unbiased case and how it is affected by increasing sample size. That is, as T increases from $T = 10$ for experiment 2 to $T = 50$ for experiment 35, the distributions shift to the right becoming less skewed and less peaked.

When $\alpha \neq \beta$ (the biased case) the effect of increasing T varies depending on whether $\alpha < \beta$ or $\alpha > \beta$. When $\alpha < \beta$ (i.e. say $\rho = 0.2$) a comparison of experiments 1, 31 and 34 reveals that as $T\uparrow$ the distributions shift to the right along with decreases in variances, skewness and kurtosis. These results are obtained from an examination of Table 2 and similar results are observed in all situations when ρ, σ_1^2 and σ_2^2 are fixed and T increases with $\alpha < \beta$. When $\alpha > \beta$ (i.e. say $\rho = 0.8$) we note that, from Table 2, as $T\uparrow$ the distributions now shift to the left with again the variance and kurtosis decreasing (see for example experiments 3, 33 and 36).

To see the effect of increasing ρ we may look at the cdfs in Set 2 for experiments 31, 32 and 33. Here the sample size is fixed at $T = 20$ and as $\rho\uparrow$ the distributions shift to the right. Similar results hold for other experiments where T, σ_1^2 and σ_2^2 are held constant and ρ varies. In particular as ρ increases from -0.8 to 0.8 (see experiments: 27, 26, 25, 37, 1, 2, 3) we note that the distributions shift to the right accompanied by decreases in the variance and kurtosis. The skewness, however, first increases up to $\rho = 0.2$ then decreases for $\rho = 0.6$ and 0.8 with the value at both ends (i.e. $\rho = \pm 0.8$) almost identical. The kurtosis for $\rho =$ 0.8 is about one fifth its value of $\rho = -0.8$.

The effects of changes in the variances σ_1^2 and σ_2^2 are illustrated in Set 3 which gives the cdfs for experiments 7, 10 and 31. In these situations $T = 20$ and $\rho = 0.2$. Experiment 31 can be considered the control with $\sigma_1^2 = \sigma_2^2 = 1.0$. Thus comparing experiment 31 with experiment 10 (where $\sigma_1^2 = 2.0$) we note the two distributions while having roughly the same median have different tail areas. The increase in σ_1^2 has lengthened both tails and consequently increased the variance.

The effects of increasing σ_2^2 from 1.0 to 2.0 are clear from a comparison of the cdfs for experiment 31 and 7 (σ_2^2 = 2.0). Here we note that an increase in σ_2^2 shifts the distribution to the left and increases the bias but leaves the variance virtually unchanged.

In the case where $\beta = \rho = 0.0$ we noted earlier that the distributions are symmetric and their pdfs are given in Set 4 for the three sample sizes of T = 10, 20, 50 (i.e. experiments 40, 41 and 42). Here the major effect of increase in sample size is the dramatic decrease in variance.

6. Conclusion

The analysis, in the previous sections, of the exact distribution of the PRRF estimator is of interest from two perspectives. Firstly, from a pedagogical point, it illustrates how easily the conditional distribution approach, used so effectively in analytical analysis, can be used to help in the numerical analysis of unconditional distributions. The associated two–step sampling process can be used in a variety of situations where the exact distribution is either unknown or numerically infeasible to calculate. It also helps with understanding the role played by each of the parameters of the distribution.

Secondly, this is the first attempt at estimating numerically the moments and pdf for this estimator. Given it is one of the few reduced form estimators whose moments exist and whose exact distribution is known it is clearly desirable to build on this knowledge with some numerical analysis.

Unfortunately, like Monte Carlo studies of econometric estimators, conclusions from the above analysis are seldom general. Thus what is now required are further studies of this estimator in a variety of situations in order to build a dossier on its performance and peculiarities. Further research along these lines in situations with more than two endogenous variables is currently underway and will be reported elsewhere.

TABLE 1

Exp #	R.F. Set	T	σ_1^2	σ_2^2	ρ	α	θ
1	1	10	1.0	1.0	0.2	0.200	1.0
2					0.6	0.600	
3					0.8	0.800	
4			2.0	1.0	0.2	0.283	1.0
5					0.6	0.848	
6					0.8	1.131	
7		20	1.0	2.0	0.2	0.141	1.0
8					0.6	0.424	
9					0.8	0.566	
10		20	2.0	1.0	0.2	0.283	2.0
11					0.6	0.848	
12					0.8	1.131	
13	2	10	1.0	1.0	0.2	0.200	5.0
14					0.6	0.600	
15					0.8	0.800	
16		20	1.0	2.0	0.2	0.141	
17					0.6	0.424	
18					0.8	0.566	
19		20	2.0	1.0	0.2	0.283	10.0
20					0.6	0.848	
21					0.8	1.131	
22		50	1.0	1.0	0.2	0.200	25.0

TABLE 1 (cont'd)

Exp #	R.F. Set	T	σ_1^2	σ_2^2	ρ	α	θ
23					0.6	0.600	
24					0.8	0.800	
25	1	10	1.0	1.0	–0.2	–0.200	1.0
26		10	1.0	1.0	–0.6	–0.600	
27					–0.8	–0.800	
28	2	50	1.0	1.0	–0.2	–0.200	25.0
29					–0.6	–0.600	
30					–0.8	–0.800	
31	1	20	1.0	1.0	0.2	0.200	2.0
32					0.6	0.600	
33					0.8	0.800	
34		50	1.0	1.0	0.2	0.200	5.0
35					0.6	0.600	
36					0.8	0.800	
37		10	1.0	1.0	0.0	0.0	1.0
38		20			0.0	0.0	2.0
39		50			0.0	0.0	5.0
40 } $\beta=0.0$		10	1.0	1.0	0.0		1.0
41 } $\beta=0.0$		20					2.0
42 } $\beta=0.0$		50					5.0

TABLE 2

Exp. #	True Value	Median	Mean	Bias	Rel. Bias	Variance	Skewness	Kurtosis
1	.1930	.0934	.1363	−.0567	.2936	.0502	.6572	1.0940
2		.1606	.1925	−.0005	.0026	.0606	.4487	.5164
3		.1965	.2200	.0271	.1402	.0690	.2323	.5015
4		.0993	.1525	−.0405	.2097	.0902	.5824	1.3377
5		.1802	.2293	.0363	.1883	.1091	.5489	1.0053
6		.2452	.2763	.0834	.4320	.1251	.2115	.6903
7		.0912	.1213	−.0716	.3713	.0284	.6816	.8102
8		.1453	.1683	−.0247	.1280	.0356	.4213	.2632
9		.1734	.1858	−.0071	.0370	.0408	.2298	.2074
10		.1250	.1580	−.0349	.1811	.0501	.5546	.9381
11		.1898	.2227	.0298	.1544	.0558	.5351	.5840
12		.2207	.2497	.0567	.2941	.0566	.4638	.5449
13	.4997	.4250	.4400	−.0598	.1196	.0767	.2928	.0244
14		.4783	.4957	−.0040	.0080	.0745	.3071	−.0039
15		.5204	.5338	.0341	.0682	.0739	.2784	−.1046
16		.4248	.4305	−.0692	.1385	.0428	.1493	−.2264
17		.4732	.4778	−.0219	.0439	.0443	.1578	−.0614
18		.4943	.4978	−.0020	.0039	.0451	.1290	−.0574
19		.4555	.4682	−.0316	.0632	.0703	.2371	.1458
20		.5101	.5191	.0194	.0387	.0692	.1933	.1448
21		.5317	.5405	.0408	.0816	.0695	.1943	−.0063
22		.4826	.4859	−.0138	.0277	.0159	.1243	−.0787

TABLE 2 (Cond't)

Exp. #	True Value	Median	Mean	Bias	Rel. Bias	Variance	Skewness	Kurtosis
23		.4946	.4985	–.0012	.0025	.0159	.1332	–.0261
24		.5044	.5062	.0064	.0129	.0156	.0982	.0318
25	.1930	.0407	.0740	–.1189	.6164	.0432	.4973	1.5833
26		.0079	.0200	–.1729	.8961	.0410	.3279	2.0986
27		–.0086	–.0151	–.2081	1.0785	.0419	.2327	2.3275
28	.4997	.4708	.4727	–.0271	.0542	.0159	.1127	.0463
29		.4576	.4607	–.0390	.0781	.0156	.1590	–.0180
30		.4533	.4549	–.0448	.0897	.0153	.0825	–.0406
31	.1930	.1241	.1486	–.0444	.2300	.0287	.6142	.6739
32		.1734	.1907	–.0023	.0119	.0307	.4753	.5083
33		.1991	.2149	.0220	.1138	.0332	.4330	.3068
34		.1619	.1717	–.0213	.1104	.0127	.4598	.2043
35		.1855	.1917	–.0012	.0064	.0130	.3704	.0685
36		.1949	.2021	.0092	.0476	.0132	.3685	–.0313
37		.0645	.1026	–.0903	.4681	.0451	.6210	1.4080
38		.1021	.1261	–.0668	.3463	.0264	.5651	.6913
39		.1485	.1588	–.0342	.1771	.0126	.4533	.2187
40	0.0	.0002	.0001	.0001		.0378	–.0131	1.7125
41		.0003	.0001	.0001		.0211	.0381	1.4725
42		–.0011	–.0027	–.0027		.0093	–.0442	.9485

SET 1

PDF for Experiment #2

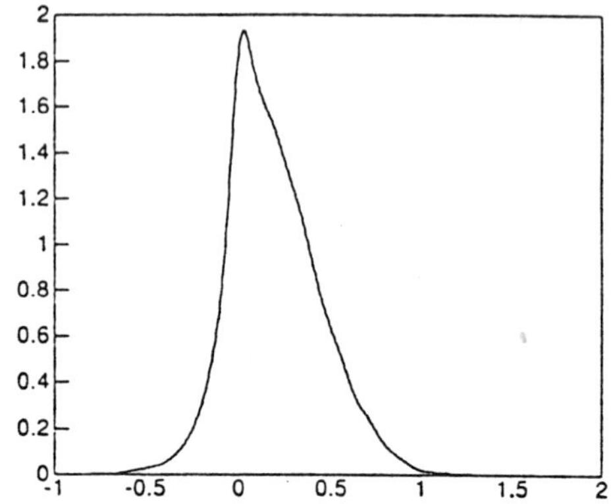

PDF for Experiment #32

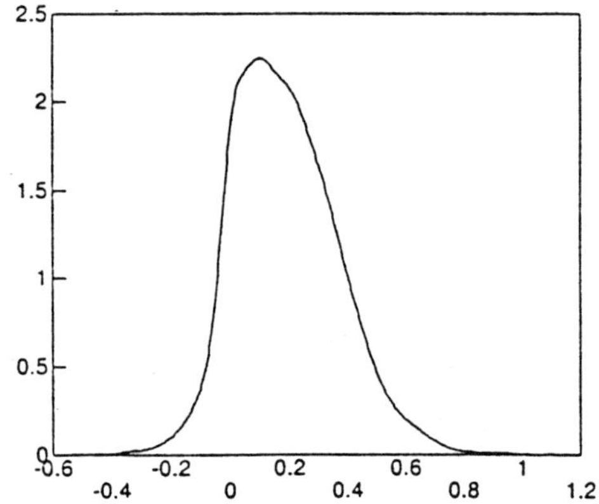

PDF for Experiment #35

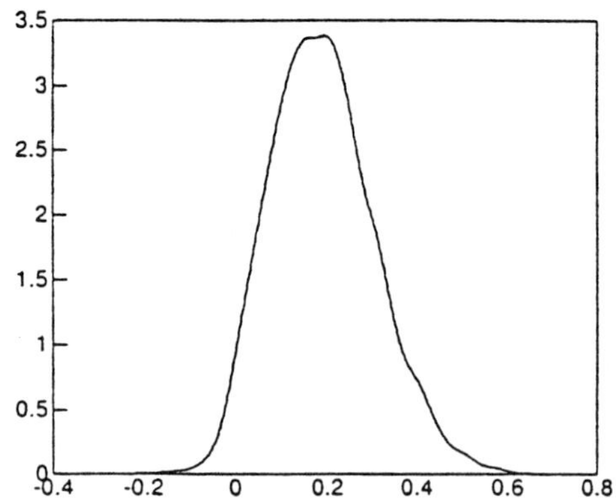

SET 2

CDF for Experiment #31

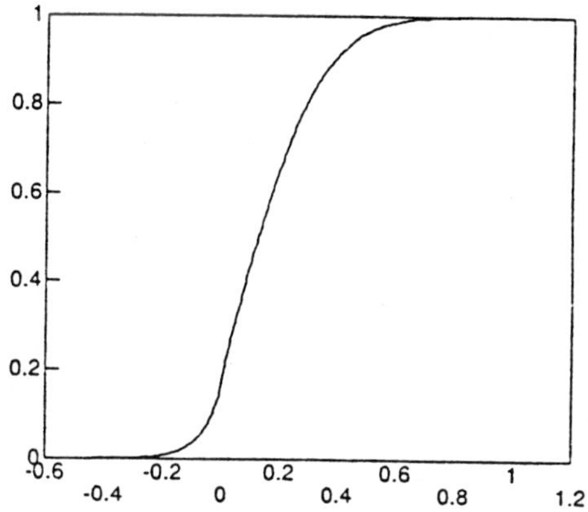

CDF for Experiment #32

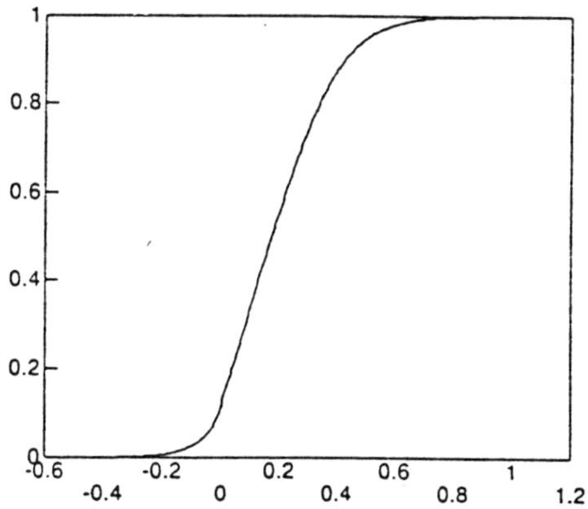

CDF for Experiment #33

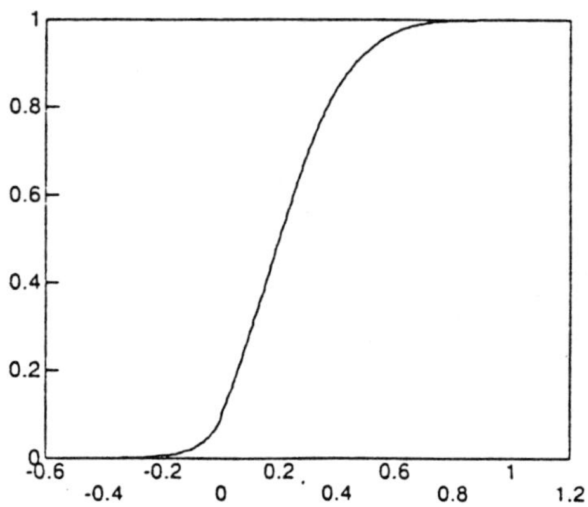

SET 3

PDF for Experiment #40

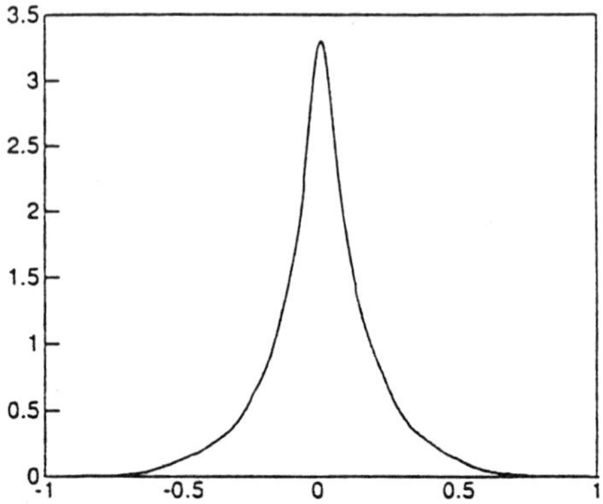

PDF for Experiment #41

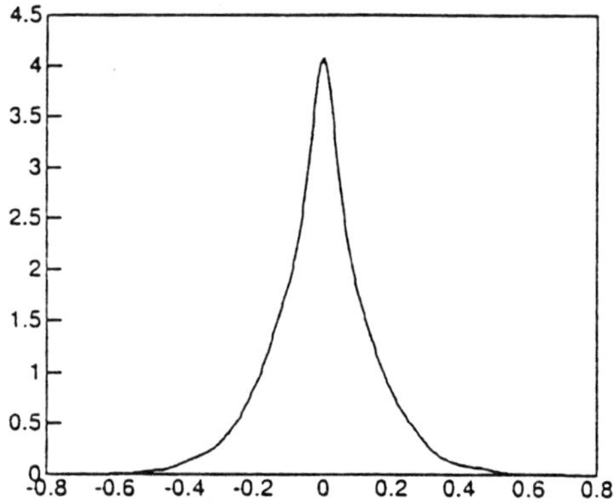

PDF for Experiment #42

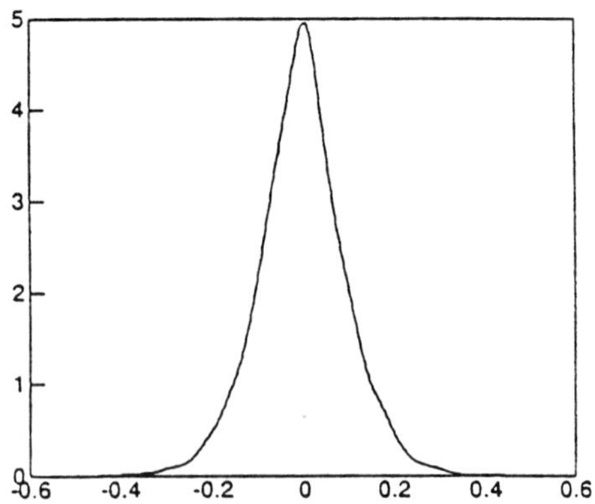

SET 4

CDF for Experiment #7

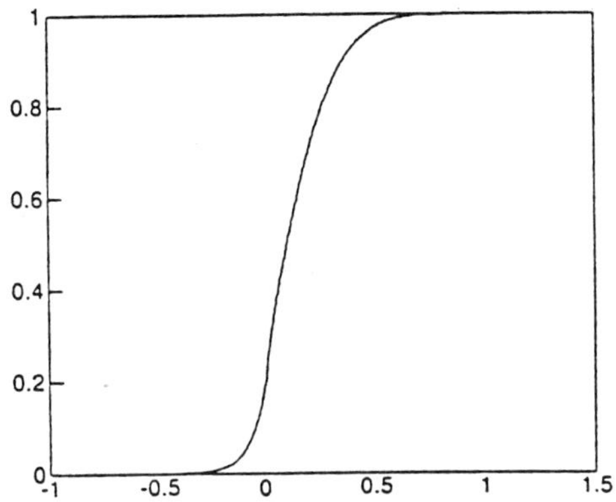

CDF for Experiment #31

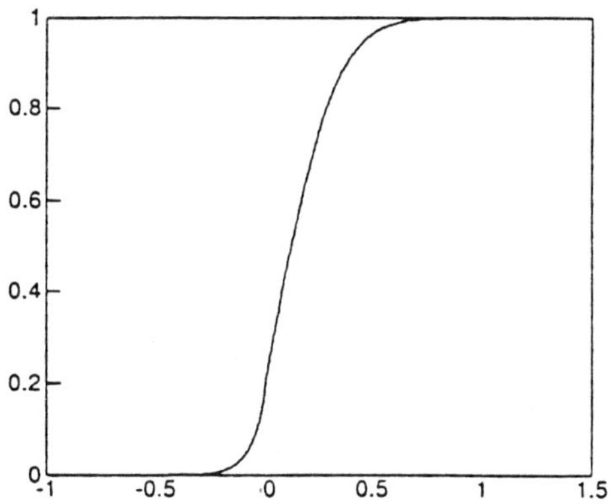

CDF for Experiment #10

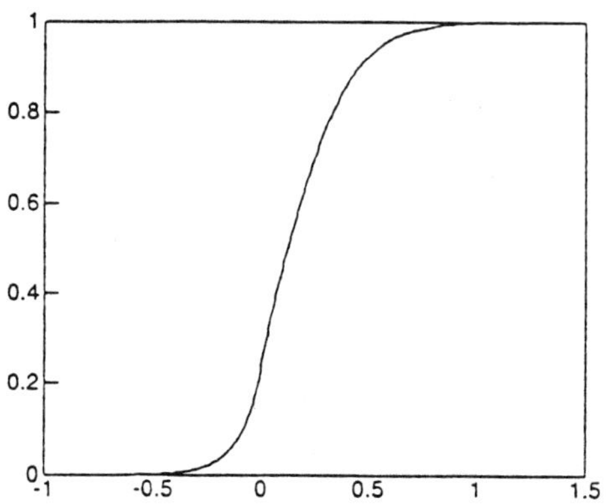

References

Chikuse, Y. [1980], Invariant Polynomials with Matrix Arguments and their Applications. In R. P. Gupta (ed.), *Multivariate Analysis*, pp. 53–68. Amsterdam: North–Holland.

Knight, J. L. [1977], On the Existence of Moments of the Partially Restricted Reduced–Form Estimators from a Simultaneous–Equations Model, *Journal of Econometrics*, 5, 315–321.

Knight, J. L. and T. W. Kinal [1989], Some Exact Distribution Results for the PRRF Estimator. Submitted for publication.

McCarthy, M. D. [1981], A Note on the Moments of Partially Restricted Reduced Forms, *Journal of Econometrics*, 17, 383–387.

Nagar, A. L. and S. N. Sahay [1978], The Bias and Mean Squared Error of Forecasts from Partially Restricted Reduced Form, *Journal of Econometrics*, 7, 227–243.

Phillips, P. C. B. [1984], The Exact Distribution of the Stein–Rule Estimator, *Journal of Econometrics*, 25, 123–131.

Phillips, P. C. B. [1987], Fractional Matrix Calculus and the Distribution of Multivariate Tests. In I. B. MacNeil and G. J. Umphrey (eds.), *Advances in Statistical Sciences: Time Series and Econometric Modelling*, Vol. 3, pp. 219–234. Dordrecht: R. Reidel.

Swamy, P. A. V. B. and J. S. Metha [1980], On the Existence of Moments of the Partially Restricted Reduced Form Coefficients, *Journal of Econometrics*, 14, 183–194.

Silverman, B. W. [1986], *Density Estimation for Statistics and Date Analysis*. New York: Chapman and Hall.

Developments in Double k–Class Estimators of Parameters in Structural Equations

V.K. Srivastava*

Lucknow University and University of Western Ontario

Abstract

For estimating the parameters in a structural equation of a simultaneous equations model, Nagar proposed the family of double *k*–class estimators characterized by two scalars. This article reviews briefly the results dealing with the properties of estimators. Specifically, the issues in finite sample properties are highlighted and an appraisal is presented.

1. Introduction

A quarter of a century has passed since Professor Nagar proposed a family of limited information estimators known as double *k*–class for the parameters in a structural equation of a simultaneous linear stochastic system. This family is characterized by two scalar quantities which when equal lead to the popular *k*–class estimators. The growth of literature dealing

---

*Some work on this paper was carried out during my visit to University of Western Ontario whose generous hospitality is gratefully acknowledged. I am also very thankful to A. Ullah for his comments and bringing to my attention some related references.

with the properties of various members of k–class has been enormous during the past three decades, so much so that it has overshadowed the double k–class; see, e.g., Agnihotri (1980), Anderson, Kunitomo and Morimune (1986), Basmann (1974), Mariano (1982), Phillips (1983) and Taylor (1983) for illuminating surveys. Consequently, the double k–class has received far less attention despite the fact that it offers comparatively more flexibility due to the presence of two choice scalars. Attributed to it is perhaps the failure to discover the double k–class estimators with unequal characterizing scalars having uniformly superior performance properties in comparison to those double k–class estimators with equal characterizing scalars, i.e., k–class estimators. This article reviews briefly the results related to double k–class estimators. Needless to mention that many results available for k–class estimations can be extended to double k–class estimators at the cost of little analytical complexity.

2. The Double k–Class Estimators

Let us consider a complete simultaneous linear stochastic system of G structural equations in G jointly dependent and L predetermined variables. Further, suppose that it is proposed to estimate the parameters of the following identifiable structural equation

$$
\begin{aligned}
y &= Y\beta + X_1\gamma + u \\
&= A\delta + u \quad A = (Y\ X_1),\ \delta = \begin{bmatrix}\beta \\ \gamma\end{bmatrix}
\end{aligned}
\tag{2.1}
$$

where is a $T{\times}1$ vector of T observations on the jointly dependent variable to be explained, Y and X_1 are $T{\times}g$ and $T{\times}\ell$ matrices of T observations on $g(< G)$ explanatory jointly dependent and $\ell\ (< L)$

explanatory predetermined variables respectively, β and γ are the column vectors associated with these variables and u is a $T\times 1$ vector of disturbances with mean vector 0 and variance covariance matrix $\sigma^2 I_T$, σ^2 being the unknown disturbance variance.

Assuming the existence of reduced form of the system, suppose that the reduced forms associated with the jointly dependent variables in (2.1) are given by

$$y = X\pi + v \tag{2.2}$$

$$Y = X\Pi + V \tag{2.3}$$

where $L\times 1$ vector π and $L\times g$ matrix Π denote the reduced form coefficients associated with explanatory variables, the $T\times 1$ vector v and $T\times g$ matrix V represent the reduced form disturbances and X is a $T\times L$ matrix of T observations on all the L predetermined variables in the system.

Without any loss of generality, we can assume that X_1 is formed by the first ℓ columns of X. If X_2 denotes the matrix formed by the remaining columns, we can write (2.2) and (2.3) as follows

$$y = X_1\pi_1 + X_2\pi_2 + v \tag{2.4}$$

$$Y = X_1\Pi_1 + X_2\Pi_2 + V \tag{2.5}$$

where X, π and Π are partitioned as

$$X = (X_1, X_2),\ \pi = \begin{bmatrix}\pi_1\\ \pi_2\end{bmatrix},\ \Pi = \begin{bmatrix}\Pi_1\\ \Pi_2\end{bmatrix} \tag{2.6}$$

It is assumed that the row vectors of the $Tx(g+1)$ matrix $(V \;\; v)$ are mutually uncorrelated and they are identically distributed with

$$E(V \;\; v) = 0$$

$$\frac{1}{T} E \begin{bmatrix} V' \\ v' \end{bmatrix} (V \;\; v) = \begin{bmatrix} \Omega_{11} & \omega'_{(1)} \\ \omega_{(1)} & \omega_{11} \end{bmatrix}. \tag{2.7}$$

It is easy to see that

$$\sigma^2 = \omega_{11} - 2\beta'\omega_{(1)} + \beta'\Omega_{11}\beta. \tag{2.8}$$

Nagar (1962) proposed the double k–class family of estimators for the coefficient vector δ defined by

$$\hat{\delta} = \left[A'(I_T - k\overline{P}_X)A\right]^{-1} A' \left[I_T - k_1 \overline{P}_X\right] y \tag{2.9}$$

where k and k_1 are scalars characterizing the estimator and $\overline{P}_X = I_T - X(X'X)^{-1}X'$.

Separating the double k–class estimators for β and γ, we get

$$\hat{\beta} = [Y'(\overline{P}_{X_1} - k\,\overline{P}_X)Y]^{-1} Y'(\overline{P}_{X_1} - k_1\overline{P}_X)y \tag{2.10}$$

$$\hat{\gamma} = (X_1'X_1)^{-1}X_1'(y - Y\hat{\beta}) \tag{2.11}$$

where $\overline{P}_{X_1} = I_T - X_1(X_1'X_1)^{-1}X_1'$.

If we substitute $k = (2-h)h$ and $k_1 = h$, we obtain the h–class estimators while if we set $k_1 = k$, we find the k–class estimators encompassing the popular limited information maximum likelihood, ordinary least squares and two stage least squares estimators. When $T = L$, the double k–class estimator collapses to ordinary least squares estimator in a trivial manner.

Stemming from (2.9), Nagar (1962) also presented an estimator for disturbance variance σ^2:

$$\hat{\sigma}^2 = \frac{1}{T}(y-A\hat{\delta})'(y-A\hat{\delta}). \tag{2.12}$$

3. Alternative Interpretations

The double k–class estimator can be regarded as an estimator arising from the application of ordinary least squares method to the following equation

$$y_* = Y_*\beta + X_1\gamma + \text{disturbance term} \tag{3.1}$$

which is essentially obtained by replacing y and Y in (2.1) by y_* and Y_* respectively where

$$\begin{aligned} y_* &= y + \left[\frac{1-k_1}{(1-k)^{\frac{1}{2}}} - 1\right]\tilde{v}\,;\ k < 1 \\ Y_* &= Y + \left[(1-k)^{\frac{1}{2}} - 1\right]\tilde{V} \end{aligned} \tag{3.2}$$

$\tilde{v} = \bar{P}_X y$ and $\tilde{V} = \bar{P}_X Y$ being the residual vector and residual matrix found by applying ordinary least squares to (2.2) and (2.3). This is very much in the spirit of two stage least squares estimator which can be construed as an estimator from the application of ordinary least squares method to an equation resulting from the replacement of Y in (2.1) by $(Y-\tilde{V})$.

Zellner (1986) considered a quadratic loss function

$$L = \left[X(\pi - \Pi\hat{\beta}) - X_1\hat{\gamma}\right]' \left[X(\pi - \Pi\hat{\beta}) - X_1\gamma\right] + p\left[y - X\Pi\hat{\beta} - X_1\hat{\gamma}\right]' \left[y - X\Pi\hat{\beta} - X_1\hat{\gamma}\right] \tag{3.3}$$

which is indeed a combination of two loss functions, the combination parameter p being a non–negative scalar. The first term on the right hand side of (3.3) arises from the failure of estimators to satisfy the relationship connecting the structural and reduced form coefficients while the second term reflects the lack of fit. Employing a Bayesian framework with diffuse prior disturbances for the reduced form coefficients and reduced form disturbance variance covariance matrix, Zellner (1986) obtained the optimal estimator by minimizing the posterior expected loss and found the resulting estimator to be of the form of double k–class estimator. Essentially the thus obtained extended minimum expected loss (EMELO) estimators form a subset of double k–class with

$$k = 1 - \frac{L}{(T-L-g-2)}$$

$$k_1 = 1 - \frac{L}{(1+p)(T-L-g-2)}, \quad (T-L-g-2) > 0 \tag{3.4}$$

If we write the two stage least squares estimator of δ as

$$d_{2SLS} = (A'P_X A)^{-1} A'P_X y \tag{3.5}$$

an identity connecting it with double k–class is given by

$$\hat{\delta} = d_{2SLS} + \left[A'(I_T - k\bar{P}_X)A\right]^{-1}\left[(1-k_1)A'\bar{P}_X y - (1-k)A'\bar{P}_X A d_{2SLS}\right] \tag{3.6}$$

where $P_X = X(X'X)^{-1}X'$; see Dhrymes (1969) and Srivastava and Tiwari (1977).

A similar relationship connecting ordinary least squares estimator with double k–class can be straightforwardly derived:

$$\hat{\delta} = d_{OLS} - \left[A'(I_T - k\bar{P}_X)A\right]^{-1}\left[k_1 A'\bar{P}_X y - kA'\bar{P}_X A d_{OLS}\right] \tag{3.7}$$

where

$$d_{OLS} = (A'A)^{-1}A'y. \tag{3.8}$$

If we multiply both the sides of (3.6) by k_1 and (3.7) by $(1-k_1)$, and then add the resulting equations, we find

$$\hat{\delta} = W_{2SLS}d_{2SLS} + W_{OLS}d_{OLS} \tag{3.9}$$

where

$$\begin{aligned} W_{2SLS} &= k_1 I_{g+\ell} - k_1(1-k)\left[A'(I_T - k\bar{P}_X)A\right]^{-1}A'\bar{P}_X A \\ W_{OLS} &= (1-k_1)I_{g+\ell} - k(1-k_1)\left[A'(I_T - k\bar{P}_X)A\right]^{-1}A'\bar{P}_X A. \end{aligned} \tag{3.10}$$

Thus the double k–class estimator can be interpreted as a matrix weighted combination of two stage least squares and ordinary least squares estimators. It becomes a convex combination in the sense

$$W_{2SLS} + W_{OLS} = I_{g+\ell}$$

if we choose

$$k_1 = -\frac{k}{(1-2k)}.$$

Further, if $k_1 = 1$ so that $W_{OLS} = 0$, the double k–class estimator assumes the form of a general shrinkage estimator arising from two stage least squares.

4. Asymptotic Properties

The double k–class estimators are consistent when characterizing scalars k and k_1 are functions of T, the number of observations, and satisfy the constraints

$$plim\ (k-1) = 0 = plim\ (k_1-1) \tag{4.1}$$

Further, if

$$plim\ T^{\frac{1}{2}}(k-1) = 0 = plim\ T^{\frac{1}{2}}(k_1-1) \tag{4.2}$$

the variance covariance matrix of the asymptotic distribution of $T^{\frac{1}{2}}(\hat{\delta} - \delta)$ will be the same as that of $T^{\frac{1}{2}}(d_{2SLS} - \delta)$.

When k and k_1 do not depend upon T, the conditions (4.1) and (4.2) are satisfied only for the choice $k = k_1 = 1$, i.e., two stage least squares estimator. Thus suppose that we choose k and k_1 such that they depend upon T and they satisfy the conditions (4.1). For instance, we may take

$$k = 1 + \sum_i \frac{a_i}{T^i}$$
$$k_1 = 1 + \sum_i \frac{a_{1i}}{T^i} \tag{4.3}$$

where a_i's and a_{1i}'s are free from T. Then all such double k–class estimators commonly share the asymptotic properties. They fail to reveal the differences in performances of estimators and do not therefore permit us to prefer one estimator over the other. This led Nagar (1962) to investigate the large sample asymptotic properties.

Before presenting the results, let us introduce the following notation

$$Z = (X\Pi \quad X_1), \quad Q = (Z'Z)^{-1}$$

$$q = \frac{1}{\sigma^2 T} E(A-Z)'u, \quad C = \frac{1}{\sigma^2 T} E(A-Z)'(A-Z) - qq', \tag{4.4}$$

$$r = L - (g+\ell).$$

It is assumed that the lagged endogenous variables are absent in the entire system and the scalars characterizing the double k–class estimator are given by

$$k = 1 + \frac{a}{T}, \quad k_1 = 1 + \frac{a_1}{T} \tag{4.5}$$

where a and a_1 are nonstochastic scalars independent of T. It is also assumed that the elements of matrix $(X'X)$ are of order $O(T)$.

For the double k–class estimators specified by (4.5), Nagar (1962) worked out the large sample asymptotic approximation for the bias vector to order $O(T^{-1})$:

$$\sigma^2\left[r - 1 - a_1 + (q'\delta)(a-a_1)\right]Qq + \sigma^2(a-a_1)QC\delta. \tag{4.6}$$

Further, if the disturbances are normally distributed, the large sample asymptotic approximation for the mean squared error matrix to order $O(T^{-2})$ is given by

$$\begin{aligned}&\sigma^2 Q + \sigma^4[(h_{11}q'Qq + h_{12}q'\delta\cdot q'Qq + hq'QC\delta + trQC)Q \\ &+ (h_{21}(q'\delta)^2 + h_{22}q'\delta + h_{23})Qqq'Q + h_3QCQ + h_4QC\delta\delta'CQ \\ &+ (h_{51}q'\delta + h_{52})Q(q\delta'C + C\delta q')Q]\end{aligned} \tag{4.7}$$

where the quantities h's depend upon a, a_1 and r; see Nagar (1962, Theorem 2).

Nagar (1962, Theorem 3) also evaluated the bias, to order $O(T^{-1})$, of the disturbance variance estimator (2.6).

Owing to the specification (4.5) for characterizing scalars, it may be noticed that the large sample asymptotic approximations for the bias vector and mean squared error matrix of double k–class estimators are not available when either or both of the scalars k and k_1 take the value 0 and λ, the scalars characterizing the ordinary least squares and limited information maximum likelihood estimators in k–class. Such cases are covered through small disturbance asymptotic approach. Employing it, Brown, Kadane and Ramage (1974) derived the small disturbance asymptotic approximations without placing any constraint such as (4.5) on k and k_1.

For nonstochastic scalars k and k_1, the small disturbance asymptotic approximation for the bias vector to order $O(\sigma^2)$ is given by

$$\sigma^2[T-g-\ell-1-(T-L)k_1 + (q'\delta)(k-k_1)(T-L)]Qq$$
$$+ \sigma^2(k-k_1)(T-L)QC\delta. \tag{4.8}$$

Further, if the disturbances are normally distributed, the small disturbance asymptotic approximation for the mean squared error matrix to order $0(\sigma^4)$ is

$$\sigma^2 Q + \sigma^4\Big[\Big[h^*_{11}q'Qq + h^*_{12}q'\delta\cdot q'Qq + h^*_{13}q'QC\delta + tr\; QC\Big]Q$$
$$+ \Big[h^*_{21}(q'\delta)^2 + h^*_{22}q'\delta + h^*_{23} + h^*_{24}\delta'C\delta\Big]Qqq'Q$$
$$+ \Big[h^*_{31}(q'\delta)^2 + h^*_{32}q'\delta + h^*_{33} + h^*_{34}\delta'C\delta\Big]QCQ$$
$$+ h^*_4 QC\delta\delta'CQ + \Big[h^*_{51}q'\delta + h^*_{52}\Big]Q(q\delta'C + C\delta q')Q\Big] \tag{4.9}$$

where h^*'s are functions of $(T-g-\ell)$, $(T-L)$, k and k_1; see Brown, Kadane and Ramage (1974, Theorem 3.2).

The large sample asymptotic approximations (4.6) and (4.7) can be straightforwardly recovered from (4.8) and (4.9) respectively by substituting (4.5) and retaining terms to the order of our approximation.

Brown, Kadane and Ramage (1974) also derived the small disturbance asymptotic approximations for the bias vector and mean squared error matrix when one of the characterizing scalars is stochastic, i.e., when $k = \lambda$ with nonstochastic k_1 and when $k_1 = \lambda$ with nonstochastic k. The resulting expressions as well as (4.8) and (4.9), and for that matter the large sample asymptotic approximation (4.6) and (4.7) too, are fairly intricate and no clear inference can be deduced regarding the relative performance of various members of double k–class. The search for simple optimal estimators such as those which are unbiased to the order of our approximation or those which optimize some criterion based on second order moments to the order of our approximation also turn out to be futile.

Now let us consider the asymptotic approximations for the density function of the double k–class estimators.

Specifying the structural equation (2.1) to contain merely one explanatory jointly dependent variable ($g=1$) and writing noncentrality parameter as

$$\theta = \frac{1}{2\Omega_{11}} \Pi_2' X_2' P_{X_1} X_2 \Pi_2 \tag{4.10}$$

Mariano (1973, Sec. 5) considered a normalized transform of $\hat{\beta}$ and obtained large noncentrality parameter approximation for its probability density function to order $O(\theta^{-1})$ when sample size T stays fixed. Under the same set–up accompanied with an additional assumption that $\left[\frac{\theta}{T} - plim \frac{\theta}{T}\right]$ is of order $O(T^{-1})$, Anderson and Sawa (1973, Sect. 10) envisaged a slightly different normalized transform of $\hat{\beta}$ and found the large sample asymptotic approximation for the density and distribution function to order $O(T^{-\frac{1}{2}})$. The results obtained by Mariano (1973) and Anderson and Sawa (1973) can be recovered from the small disturbance asymptotic approximation derived by Anderson, Kunitomo and Morimune (1986) for arbitrary number of explanatory endogenous variables ($g > 1$). In order to cover the case when both the scalars can be stochastic, they considered the double k–class estimator with

$$k = k^* + (\lambda - 1)m, \qquad k_1 = k_1^* + (\lambda - 1)m \tag{4.11}$$

where k^*, k_1^* and m are fixed scalars. If $m = 0$, we have fixed double k–class estimator. If $m \neq 0$, we get stochastic double k–class estimator. The small disturbance asymptotic approximation for the probability density function of $e = \frac{1}{\sigma}(\hat{\delta} - \delta)$ is given by

$$\left[1 + \sigma e_1 + \sigma^2 e_2\right] f(e) \tag{4.12}$$

to order $O(\sigma^2)$ where $f(e)$ denotes the probability density function of multivariate normal distribution with mean vector 0 and variance covariance matrix Q. The quantities e_1 and e_2 are of the following form

$$\begin{aligned} e_1 &= n_{11}\, q'e + n_{12}\delta' Ce - (q'e)(e'Q^{-1}e) \\ e_2 &= n_{20} + n_{21}(q'e)^2 + n_{22}(q'e)^2(e'Q^{-1}e) + n_{23}e'Q^{-1}e \\ &\quad + n_{24}(e'Q^{-1}e)^2 + n_{25}e'Ce + n_{26}(e'Ce)(e'Q^{-1}e) \\ &\quad + n_{27}(q'e)(\delta' Ce) + n_{28}(q'e)(\delta' Ce)(e'Q^{-1}e) + n_{29}(\delta' Ce)^2. \end{aligned}$$

where n_{ij}'s depend upon $(T-L)$, r, k^*, k_1^* and m besides parametric quantities $(q'\delta)$ and $(\delta' C\delta)$; see Anderson, Kunitomo and Morimune (1986, Theorem 7.1).

In view of (4.11) they postulated two double k–class estimators—one fixed double k–class estimator with

$$k = 1 + \frac{a}{T-L}, \qquad k_1 = 1 + \frac{a_1}{T-L}$$

and other stochastic double k–class estimator

$$k = 1 + \frac{a-r}{T-L}, \qquad k_1 = \lambda + \frac{a_1-r}{T-L}$$

where a and a_1 are scalars independent of T. Employing the criterion of mean squared error matrix to order $O(T^{-2})$, they demonstrated that the stochastic double k–class estimator is uniformly superior to the fixed double k–class estimator. This result remains true when the criterion of large sample asymptotic approximation for the concentration probability associated with any star–shaped set in $\mathbb{R}^{(g+\ell)}$ is used.

Tsurumi (1987) conducted a Monte Carlo experiment to examine the effect of the multicollinearity among exogenous variables and the correlation between explanatory jointly dependent variables and disturbances on the performance of several estimators like ordinary least squares, two stage least squares, limited information maximum likelihood, modified limited information maximum likelihood, minimum expected loss, conditional and unconditional limited information Bayesian and mode of the posterior probability density function besides the extended minimum expected loss (EMELO) estimator characterized by (3.4) with $p=3$ which is a member of double

k–class. An interesting finding emerging from the limited study is that EMELO estimator generally outperforms others and is certainly among the top three in all cases.

5. Exact Finite Sample Results

Assuming the scalars k and k_1 to be nonstochastic and

$$\omega_{11} = 1, \ \omega_{(1)} = 0, \ \Omega_{11} = I_{g+\ell}, \ X_1'X_2 = 0 \tag{5.1}$$

Srivastava, Agnihotri and Dwivedi (1980) compared the exact bias vector and mean squared error matrices of double k–class and k–class estimators (i.e., with $k=k_1$) under normality of disturbances and absence of lagged endogenous variables. It was observed that, according to exact mean squared error matrix criterion, the double k–class estimator is superior to k–class estimator when

$$(k_1-k)(2 - k - k_1) > 0 \tag{5.2}$$

which is satisfied if, given k, we choose k_1 between k and $(2-k)$. Since k should not exceed 1 for the existence of moments, the range of k widens more and more as $(-k)$ tends to be large. Interestingly, for $k=1$, the inequality (5.2) suggests that no member of double k–class will dominate the two stage least squares estimator.

When the specifications in (5.1) are violated, i.e., when X_1 and X_2 are not orthogonal and the variance covariance matrix of reduced form disturbances is not identity, the above results continue to hold true provided the variance covariance matrix of reduced form disturbances is known.

Restricting attention to the case of merely one explanatory jointly dependent variable in the structural equation (2.1) and assuming simply the orthogonality of X_1 and X_2, Dwivedi and Srivastava (1984) considered two distinct cases $k_1 = 1$ and $-1 < k_1 < 1$, and derived the exact expressions for the first two moments of β. Expressions for the case $-\infty < k_1 < -1$, it was pointed out, can be similarly obtained following Srivastava and Srivastava (1983).

The expressions brought out that the double k–class estimator is unbiased if we choose

$$k_1 = (k + \frac{\Omega_{11}}{\omega_{(1)}}\beta - 1)\alpha_k = k_u(\text{say}), \qquad \frac{\Omega_{11}}{\omega_{(1)}}\beta \neq 1 \tag{5.3}$$

where α_k has an intricate expression with terms containing double infinite series in powers of k and θ along with ratios of Gamma functions in $(L-1)$ and $(T-L)$; see Dwivedi and Srivastava (1984, p. 269).

For $(\Omega_{11}\beta/\omega_{(1)})$ equal to 1, we find the trivial case $k=k_1$ *of* unbiased double k–class estimator.

Next, the double k–class estimator has smaller mean squared error than the k–class estimator if we choose k_1 lying between k and $\bar{k}^*$ where $\bar{k}^*$, like α_k, has also an intricate form; see Dwivedi and Srivastava (1984, pp. 274–5).

Owing to the complex nature of the expression for k_u and $\bar{k}^*$, it is difficult to feel their magnitude and in fact even sign. Dwivedi and Srivastava (1984) therefore tabulated the values of

k_u and $\bar{k}^*$ for few selected of k and θ($k=0$, $\pm$ 0.2, $\pm$ 0.6, $\pm$ 1 and θ = 1,10,25,50,100) employing the framework of Sawa (1972) and Srivastava, Dwivedi, Belinsky and Tiwari (1980). Accordingly, setting

$$\beta = 1, \qquad \frac{\omega_{(1)}}{\Omega_{11}} = 0.4, \qquad \frac{\omega_{11}\Omega_{11} - \omega_{(1)}^2}{\Omega_{11}^2} = 1$$

three cases were considered:

(1) $L = 5$, $\ell = 2$, $T = 10,20,30,50$
(2) $L = 10$, $\ell = 3$, $T = 20,30,50$
(3) $L = 15$, $\ell = 5$, $T = 20,30,50$.

The analysis revealed that the majority of the values of k_u are found to be negative. They seem to become positive in the neighbourhood of $k=1$. Given k, the value of k_u shows an increasing trend for small θ and declining trend for large θ. Similarly, given r, k_u increases as T increases while, given T, it decreases as r increases. As k increases, k_u declines though k_u always turns out to be smaller than k over the range of investigation.

In the context of dominance of double k–class over k–class, the numerical value of $\bar{k}^*$ is found to be negative in most of the cases; it is positive only for $k=1$ and $\theta=1$. The relative growth in the magnitude of $\bar{k}^*$ as θ increases is seen to be rapid. As long as θ exceeds 10, the magnitude of $\bar{k}^*$ exhibits a declining tendency with the rise in T. Increasing trend is observed as r increases given T. The values of $\bar{k}^*$ are always found to be below the associated value of k.

Assuming $g = 1$, Lye (1987) examined the exact density and distribution functions of the double k–class estimators with fixed characterizing scalars and carried out a numerical evaluation for a few selected values of parameters, viz., $\beta = \pm 0.5, 2.0$; $(L-\ell) = 3$; $(T-L) = 10,30$; $\theta = 4.5, 21$. Two specific situations were considered—one in which k is set equal to 1 and k_1 is allowed to vary and the other in which k is permitted to vary but $k_1 = 1$. An implication of her analysis is that the shape of sampling distribution of double k–class estimators changes as the characterizing scalars k and k_1 vary but the change may not necessarily lead to larger probability of concentration. This is indeed interesting especially when probability of concentration is treated as a criterion for judging the performance of estimators. Lye (1987) also studied the effect of specification error which comprises incorrect exclusion of some exogenous variables from the structural equation under study but not from the model, and remarked that the specifiction error may increase the probability of concentration.

6. Generalizations

The double k–class of estimators has motivated the development of various families of full information estimators for the simultaneous estimation of the structural parameters in the system. For example, Roy and Srivastava (1966) proposed the generalized double k–class while Scharf (1976) formulated the double K–matrix–class estimators. Srivastava and Agnihotri (1979) proposed the double S–class estimators while developing a class of linear and consistent estimators.

References

Agnihotri, B.S. [1980], Some Properties of Double k–Class Estimators and Their Generalization in Simultaneous Equation Econometric Models, unpublished Ph.D. Thesis, Lucknow University, India.

Anderson, T.W. and T. Sawa [1973], Distributions of Estimates of Coefficients of a Single Equation in a Simultaneous System and Their Asymptotic Expansions, *Econometrica*, Vol. 41, 683–714.

Anderson, T.W., N. Kunitomo and K. Morimune [1986], Comparing Single Equation Estimators in a Simultaneous Equation, *Econometric Theory*, Vol. 2, 1–32.

Basmann, R.L. [1974], Exact Finite Sample Distribution for Some Econometric Estimators and Test Statistics—A Survey and Appraisal, Chapter 4 in *Frontiers in Quantitative Economics*, Vol. 2 (edited by M.D. Intriligator and D.A. Kendrick), North–Holland Publishing Company.

Brown, G.F., J.B. Kadane and J.G. Ramage [1974], The Asymptotic Bias and Mean Squared Error of Double k–Class Estimators when Disturbances are Small, *International Economic Review*, Vol. 15, 667–679.

Dhrymes, P.J. [1969] – An Identity Between Double k–Class and Two Stage Least Squares Estimators, *International Economic Review*, Vol. 10, 115–116.

Dwivedi, T.D. and V.K. Srivastava [1984] – Exact Finite Sample Properties of Double k–Class Estimators in Simultaneous Equations, *Journal of Econometrics*, Vol. 23, 263–283.

Lye, J.N. [1987], Further Exact Finite Sample Properties of Double k–Class Estimators in Simultaneous Equations," paper presented at the Econometric Society Australian Meeting, Christchurch, New Zealand.

Mariano, R.S. [1973], Approximations of the Distribution Functions of Theil's k–Class Estimators," *Econometrica*, Vol. 41, 715–21.

Mariano, R.S. [1982], Analytical Small–Sample Distribution Theory in Econometrics—The Simultaneous–Equations Case, *International Economic Review*, Vol. 3, 168–188.

Phillips, P.C.B. [1983], Exact Small Sample Theory in the Simultaneous Equations Model, Chapter 8 in *Handbook of Econometrics*, Vol. 1, (edited by Z. Griliches and M.D. Intriligator) North–Holland Publishing Company.

Roy, A.R. and V.K. Srivastava [1966], Generalized Double k–Class Estimators," *Journal of the Indian Statistical Association*, Vol. 4, 38–46.

Sawa, T. [1972], Finite–Sample Properties of the k–Class Estimators, *Econometrica*, Vol. 40, 653–680.

Scharf, W. [1976], K–Matrix–Class Estimators and the Full–Information Maximum–Likelihood Estimator as a Special Case, *Journal of Econometrics*, Vol. 4, 41–50.

Srivastava, V.K. and B.S. Agnihotri [1979], A Linear and Consistent Class of Econometric Estimators in Simultaneous Equations," *Journal of the Korean Statistical Society*, Vol. 8, 117–124.

Srivastava, V.K., B.S. Agnihotri and T.D. Dwivedi [1980], Dominance of Double k–Class Estimators in Simultaneous Equations, *Annals of the Institute of Statistical Mathematics*, Vol. 32, 387–392.

Srivastava, V.K., T.D. Dwivedi, M. Belinksy and R. Tiwari [1980], A Numerical Comparison of Exact, Large–Sample and Small–Disturbance Approximations of Properties of k–Class Estimators, *International Economic Review*, Vol. 21, 249–252.

Srivastava, V.K. and A.K. Srivastava [1983], A Note on Moments of k–Class Estimators for Negative k, *Journal of Econometrics*, Vol. 21, 257–260.

Srivastava, V.K. and R. Tiwari [1977], A Simple Derivation of the Identity Connecting Double k–Class and Two Stage Least Squares Estimators, *Sankhya*, Series C, Vol. 30, 1–2.

Taylor, W.E. [1983], On the Relevance of Finite Sample Distribution Theory, *Econometric Reviews*, Vol 2, 1–40.

Tsurumi, H. [1987], Comparing Bayesian and Non–Bayesian Limited Information Estimators, Working Paper, Rutgers University.

Zellner, A. [1986], Further Results on Bayesian Minimum Expected Loss (MELO) Estimates and Posterior Distributions for Structural Coefficients, *Advances in Econometrics*, Vol. 5, 171–182.

Finite Sample Econometrics: A Unified Approach

Aman Ullah*
Department of Economics
University of Western Ontario

Abstract

In the last six decades, a significant literature has developed on the finite sample econometrics. This includes approximate, analytical and simulation based research analysing the moments and distributions of various econometric estimators and test statistics. Many analytical results, however, are complicated and require the knowledge of various statistical methods.

In this paper we systematically develop unified methods for obtaining both the exact moments and the distributions of econometric estimators and test statistics. The results are derived for the normal case and extended for non–normal cases as well. A general result on the approximations is also given.

---

*The work on this paper was initiated in 1985 and it is partly an outcome of finite sample issues raised by A. Gregory in the context of generated regressors models. A preliminary version of this paper was presented at the Universities of New South Wales, Canterbury, Western Ontario, Windsor, Berkeley, Riverside, and Queen's, and I thank seminar participants at these places for useful suggestions. I am also thankful to R.A.L. Carter, Y. Fan, D.E.A. Giles, G. Judge, J. Kmenta, M. Smith, V.K. Srivastava and V. Zinde–Walsh for the comments and discussions on the subject matter of this paper. Any remaining errors are mine. The NSERC research grant and research facilities at the Stanford University are gratefully acknowledged.

1. Introduction

Fisher (1921, 1922, 1935), more than six decades ago, laid the foundation of modern finite sample theory. It was recognized by him then, and is well known now, that large sample inference procedures may give misleading results in practical situations where the sample size is usually small. It was in the forties and fifties that finite sample theory was brought into econometrics by the seminal work of Haavelmo (1947) and Anderson and Rubin (1949) on the confidence regions of structural coefficients, and that of Hurwicz (1950) on the least squares (LS) bias in an autoregressive model. The end of the fifties saw a major breakthrough through the pioneering work of Nagar (1959) on the asymptotic expansion, now known as Nagar's large–T approximations, of the moments of k–class estimators in simultaneous equations. This was followed by the important contributions of Basmann (1961), Kabe (1963, 1964) and Richardson (1968), among others, on the exact density of the two stage least squares estimator. A significant growth in the literature took place in the seventies and eighties through the dedicated work of Sargan and his students at the London School of Economics, Nagar and his students at the Delhi School of Economics, Basmann and his students at Texas A & M, and Anderson and his students at Stanford, among others. Here we do not review the past work for which there are excellent surveys by Basmann (1974), Anderson (1982), Mariano (1982), Phillips (1980, 1983) and Maasoumi (1989).

Despite these significant research developments, analytical finite sample econometrics has remained a bit controversial (See Taylor (1983)) and confined to a small number of econometricians. This becomes evident by noticing that the proportion of pages devoted to this topic, in elementary as well as advanced text books, is almost negligible. Usually a typical text book starts with analytical finite sample results (exact mean and variance, say, of the LS estimator) in the regression chapter and then continues using, instead, the asymptotic theory in the remaining chapters. Perhaps this may partly be the reason why finite sample econometrics is not covered even as a special topic in many graduate courses.

There are perhaps several reasons for such a state of affairs but I will list the ones which I think are the most important. First, the derivations of finite sample results, especially exact results, are often demanding and require knowledge of statistical distribution theory. Terms like Wishart distribution, zonal polynomials, manifolds, non–central distributions, have undoubtedly kept economists away from this area of research. In addition, the results are often complicated and lengthy. Second, results are mainly available for estimators in static simultaneous equations but not as much for other models such as heteroskedastic, dynamic regression, limited dependent variables, or rational expectations. Third, several different techniques have been developed to study the finite sample behaviour of a given estimator or test statistic. For example, at least six papers exist on the exact moments of two stage least squares and, similarly, several, papers on its exact density. Learning and mastering each and every technique is beyond the scope of most graduate students and researchers. No attempt is made in this paper to present these various techniques and interested readers are referred for detail references to Phillips (1983a, 1987), Mariano (1982) and Rothenberg (1984, 1988).

In this paper we attempt to provide a unified approach to finite sample study, which has the following features:

(i) a *single* technique for obtaining the exact and approximate moments of a large class of estimators and tests statistics is suggested; also a method for obtaining their exact distributions is given.

(ii) the technique is simple and straightforward. For example, for deriving the exact moments only the knowledge of getting derivatives of a function is needed.

(iii) most of the results can be derived in a few lines rather than several pages.

The basic technique for obtaining exact moments considered here is a significant generalization of and improvement on the procedures used in Ullah (1971, 1974) and Ullah and Nagar (1974). Essentially, the technique amounts to replacing the expectation of any real valued analytic function h(y) of $y \sim N(\mu, 1)$, by h(d), where the operator $d = \mu + \frac{\partial}{\delta\mu}$. To obtain exact density functions, the use of the Gurland (1948) – Imhof (1961) evaluation of the distribution function of the ratio of quadratic forms is proposed. This is useful because of a simple observation that a large class of econometric estimators can be written as a ratio of quadratic forms (Ullah (1987), Cribbett et al (1989), Lye (1987, 1988)). Finally, the nonparametric density estimation technique has been readvocated (Ullah and Singh (1985), Power and Ullah (1987)) for those problems not covered by the analytical techniques in this paper.

The plan of the paper is as follows. In Section 2 we present two lemmas to describe our approach to obtaining exact moments. Then, in Section 3, we give several special cases and econometric examples where this approach can be used. Section

4 describes the procedure for obtaining exact distributions along with econometric examples. The case of non–normal situations is considered in Section 5. In Section 6 we give a general result on the small–σ approximation of moments. Finally, in Section 7, multivariate extensions of the results in Section 2 are considered.

2. Exact Moments: Main Results

Let y be an n×1 vector which is distributed according to normal law with mean vector μ = Ey and positive definite variance covariance matrix Σ, i.e., y ~ N(μ,Σ). The density function of y can be written as

$$f(y) = (2\pi)^{-n/2} |\Sigma|^{-\frac{1}{2}} \exp\{-\tfrac{1}{2}(y-\mu)' \Sigma^{-1}(y-\mu)\}. \quad (2.1)$$

We assume that Σ is not related to μ. Then (2.1) gives

$$\frac{\partial}{\partial\mu} f(y) = \Sigma^{-1}(y-\mu)f(y). \quad (2.2)$$

Alternatively, (2.2) can be written as

$$yf(y) = \left[\mu + \Sigma\frac{\partial}{\partial\mu}\right] f(y) = df(y) \quad (2.3)$$

or

$$(y-d)f(y) = 0, \quad (2.4)$$

where d is the derivative operator

$$d = \mu + \Sigma\frac{\partial}{\partial\mu}. \quad (2.5)$$

The result in (2.3) or (2.4) can be generalized as

$$h(y)f(y) = h(d)f(y) \quad \text{or} \quad (h(y) - h(d))f(y) = 0 \tag{2.6}$$

where h(y) is any real valued analytic function of y. Here h(y) could be a scalar, a vector or a matrix function of y (see Section 7), and it is free form μ. The equality in (2.6) is obtained by using the Taylor series expansion of h(y) around d and then using (2.3) or (2.4). Note that (2.6) shows that if f(y) is a normal density, then, multiplying it by any function h(y) is identical to multiplying it by h(d) where d is the nonstochastic operator in (2.5). This basic property of the normal density helps us to obtain the following important expectations of the functions of y in a straightforward way.

Lemma 1. *If* $h_1(y)$ *and* $h_2(y)$ *are two real valued functions of the normal vector* y *in* (2.1), *and have finite expectations, then*

$$Eh_1(y)h_2(y) = h_1(d)Eh_2(y), \tag{2.7}$$

and if $h_2(y) = 1$ *then writing* $h_1(y) = h(y)$,

$$Eh(y) = h(d) \cdot 1 \tag{2.8}$$

where d *is as given in* (2.5).

Proof: Using (2.6), the result in (2.7) follows by noting that

$$
\begin{aligned}
Eh_1(y)h_2(y) &= Eh_1(y)f(y)f^{-1}(y)h_2(y) \\
&= Eh_1(d)f(y)f^{-1}(y)h_2(y) \\
&= Eh_1(d)h_2(y) \\
&= h_1(d)Eh_2(y). \qquad (2.9)
\end{aligned}
$$

where $f^{-1}(y) = 1/f(y)$ and $h_1(d)$ is nonstochastic. Further substituting $h_2(y) = 1$, (2.8) follows.

In deriving the moments of econometric estimators we often encounter h_2, which is an inverse function of y. More specifically we often find, $h_2(y) = w^{-r}$ where $w = y'Ny$ and N is any symmetric (often non–negative definite) matrix, and r is a nonnegative real number. For such an $h_2(y)$ we now present $Eh_2(y)$ in the following Lemma.

Lemma 2. If $w = y'\,N\,y$ is a real valued quadratic form in the normal vector y, and the rank of $N > 2r$ then

$$
Ew^{-r} = (\Gamma(r))^{-1}\int_o^\infty t^{r-1}|N_{ot}|^{-\frac{1}{2}}\exp\{-\tfrac{1}{2}\mu' N_{1t}\mu\}dt \qquad (2.10)
$$

where $|N_{ot}| = |I + 2t\,\Sigma N|$ and $N_{1t} = 2tNN_{ot}^{-1}$.

Proof: First we note from the gamma integral that

$$
w^{-r} = (\Gamma(r))^{-1}\int_0^\infty t^{r-1}\exp\{-tw\}dt. \qquad (2.11)
$$

Thus

$$Ew^{-r} = (\Gamma(r))^{-1} \int_0^\infty t^{r-1}\, E \exp\{-tw\}dt. \tag{2.12}$$

But $E \exp\{-tw\} = \int \exp\{-ty'Ny\}f(y)dy = |N_{ot}|^{-\frac{1}{2}} \exp\{-\frac{1}{2}\mu' N_{1t}\mu\}$, where f(y) is the normal density of y as given in (2.1). Substituting this in (2.12) the result in (2.10) follows.□

Notice that N_{ot} and N_{1t} in (2.10) are such that

$$|N_{ot}| = \prod_{j=1}^{n} (1+2t\lambda_j),\quad \mu' N_{1t}\mu = 2t\mu'\, \Sigma^{-1} PDP'\mu; \tag{2.13}$$

where $D = \Lambda(I + 2t\Lambda)^{-1}$, P is an orthogonal matrix such that $P'\Sigma NP = \Lambda$ and Λ is a diagonal matrix of eigenvalues $\lambda_1,\ldots,\lambda_n$ of ΣN. In the special case where ΣN is an idempotent matrix of rank p, $\lambda_1 = \ldots = \lambda_p = 1$ and $\lambda_{p+1} = \ldots = \lambda_n = 0$ so the result in (2.10), along with (2.13), can be written as an infinite series; see Ullah (1974, p. 147) and Bock et. al. (1984).

Remark 1. The result in lemma 1 provides a unified technique for obtaining exact moments of the various functions of the normal vector y. This technique essentially replaces the expectations of complicated functions with their derivatives, the latter being easily obtainable. Since in econometrics most of the estimators and test statistics can be written in terms of the function of a normal vector, lemma 1 provides a single method for obtaining their moments. We note, however, that for some econometric statistics lemma 1 is useful and for others lemma 1 along with lemma 2 is useful. Furthermore, the results in both the lemmas are simple and do not require any rigorous knowledge of statistical distribution theory.

Remark 2. Another interesting point is that lemma 1 provides a way to obtain expectations of the products of several functions in a simple recursive manner. For example, if $Eh_1(y)$ is known then $Eh_1(y)h_2(y) = h_2(d)Eh_1(y)$. Furthermore, once we have obtained $Eh_1(y)h_2(y)$, $Eh_3(y)h_1(y)h_2(y) = h_3(d)Eh_1(y)h_2(y)$. Similarly, if $Eh(y)$ is known then $Eh^2(y) = h(d)Eh(y)$. Also, the recurrence relationship among higher order moments of h(y) can be written as

$$Eh^r(y) = h(d)Eh^{r-1}(y) = h^{r-1}(d)Eh(y), \quad r \geq 1. \tag{2.14}$$

Remark 3. If $w = y'Ny$ is a positive definite quadratic form then a series representation of

$$Ew^{-r} = \int_0^\infty w^{-r} f(w)dw \tag{2.15}$$

can be obtained by using the f(w) given in Srivastava and Khatri (1979, Ch. 2), see also Phillips (1986) for f(w) in terms of invariant polynomials. Smith (1988) derives Ew^{-r} when N may even be positive semi–definite.

Remark 4. If $y \sim N(0,\Sigma)$ then the result (2.10) in lemma 2 reduces to

$$Ew^{-r} = (\Gamma(r))^{-1} \int_0^{\infty} t^{r-1} |N_{ot}|^{-\frac{1}{2}} dt. \tag{2.16}$$

Further if, ΣN is an idempotent matrix of rank p

$$Ew^{-r} = 2^{-r} \frac{\Gamma(\frac{1}{2}p - r)}{\Gamma(\frac{1}{2}p)}. \tag{2.17}$$

Remark 5. In the case of econometric estimators and test statistics the structures of μ, Σ and N are usually known. Thus using (2.13), the results in lemma 2 can easily be evaluated numerically. For computational simplicity one can use a variable transformation in (2.10) to get the range of integration between 0 and 1.

Remark 6. If N is a stochastic matrix but independent of y, then

$$Ew^{-r} = E_N E(w^{-r}|_N). \tag{2.18}$$

This can be obtained by taking the expectation of Ew^{-r} in lemma 2 with respect to the elements of N.

3. Special Cases

Here we show that the exact moments of various econometric estimators and test statistics can be obtained by using the technique in lemma 1. This technique is simple since it transforms the problem of obtaining complicated expectations to one of evaluation of derivatives. Thus, only the knowledge of simple calculus is required. Another important point is that the various results obtained below are based on the *single* technique of lemma 1. For illustrations we have considered some commonly used econometric statistics, results for which have been obtained earlier by alternative methods. We also, however, consider some new statistics and point out some others where the result of lemma 1, or lemma 1 along with lemma 2, can be applied.

3.1 Moments of Normal Vector

Let $h(y) = y \sim N(\mu,\Sigma)$. Then from lemma 1 the mean and variance of the normal vector y are

$$Ey = d \cdot 1 = \left[\mu + \Sigma\frac{\partial}{\partial\mu}\right] \cdot 1 = \mu \tag{3.1}$$

and

$$Eyy' = dd' \cdot 1 = \left[\mu + \Sigma\frac{\partial}{\partial\mu}\right]\mu' = \mu\mu' + \Sigma \tag{3.2}$$

which gives $V(y) = \Sigma$. The econometric applications of (3.1) and (3.2) are given below.

3.1.1 Econometric Examples

Consider the model

$$y = X\beta + u, \tag{3.3}$$

where y is an $n\times1$ vector, X is an $n\times k$ nonstochastic matrix, β is a $k\times1$ parameter vector and $u \sim N(0,\Sigma)$ is an $n\times1$ disturbance vector. Thus

$$y \sim N(\mu, \Sigma);\ \mu = X\beta. \tag{3.4}$$

The well known least squares and two–step generalized least squares estimators are respectively,

$$b = (X'X)^{-1}X'y \text{ and } \hat{\beta} = (X'\hat{\Sigma}^{-1}X)^{-1}X'\hat{\Sigma}^{-1}y, \tag{3.5}$$

where $\hat{\Sigma}$ is the estimator of Σ. In any given problem, say of heteroskedasticity or of serial correlation, one can observe that the well known estimators $\hat{\Sigma} = \Sigma(y)$ are random functions of the vector y. Thus, given X, $b = h(y)$ and $\hat{\beta} = h_1(y)$ are both functions of y and we can use lemma 1 to obtain their moments. Noting that $d \cdot 1 = \mu = X\beta$ and $dd' \cdot 1 = X\beta\beta'X' + \Sigma$ from (3.1), (3.2) and (3.4),

$$Eb = h(d) \cdot 1 = (X'X)^{-1}X'd \cdot 1 = \beta \tag{3.6}$$

and

$$\begin{aligned} Ebb' &= E[(X'X)^{-1}X'yy'X(X'X)^{-1}] = h(d)h'(d) \cdot 1 \\ &= (X'X)^{-1}X'(dd' \cdot 1)(X(X'X)^{-1} \\ &= (X'X)^{-1}X'(X\beta\beta'X' + \Sigma)X(X'X)^{-1} \\ &= \beta\beta' + (X'X)^{-1}X'\Sigma X(X'X)^{-1} \end{aligned} \tag{3.7}$$

which gives

$$V(b) = (X'X)^{-1}X'\Sigma X(X'X)^{-1}. \tag{3.8}$$

Similarly, since $\hat{\Sigma} = \Sigma(y)$,

$$\hat{\beta} = h_1(d)\cdot 1 = (X'\,\Sigma^{-1}(d)X)^{-1}X'\Sigma^{-1}(d)d\cdot 1 = \beta \quad (3.9)$$

and

$$\begin{aligned} E\hat{\beta}\hat{\beta}' &= h_1(d)h_1(d)'\cdot 1 \\ &=(X'\Sigma^{-1}(d)X)^{-1}X'\Sigma^{-1}(d) \\ &\quad (dd'\cdot 1)\Sigma^{-1}(d)X(X'\Sigma^{-1}(d)X)^{-1} \\ &= (X'\Sigma^{-1}(d)X)^{-1}X'\Sigma^{-1}(d) \\ &\quad (X\beta\beta'X'+\Sigma)\Sigma^{-1}(d)X(X'\Sigma^{-1}(d)X)^{-1} \\ &= \beta\beta' + H(d)\Sigma H'(d) \end{aligned} \quad (3.10)$$

which, using $H(d) = (X'\Sigma^{-1}(d)X)^{-1}X'\Sigma^{-1}(d)$, gives

$$V(\hat{\beta}) = H(d)\Sigma H'(d). \quad (3.11)$$

The unbiasedness result in (3.9) compares with that of Kakwani (1967). The result in (3.10) cannot be simplified without further research. In fact no exact expression is available for $V(\hat{\beta})$ in the literature. However, though not attempted here, (3.10) may be obtained for two–step estimators in, e.g., the AR(1) model (Magee et. al. (1987)), seemingly unrelated regressions model (Zellner (1962)), and the heteroskedastic models (Raj and Ullah (1981)).

3.2 Moments of Products of Quadratic Forms

Let $y'N_iy$ be a quadratic form in y, $y \sim N(\mu,I)$ and N_i is symmetric for i=1,...,m. Again, using lemma 1 the expectation of $h(y) = q_m = \prod_1^m y'N_iy$ is

$$Eq_m = E\prod_1^m y'N_iy = \prod_1^m (d'(N_id)\cdot 1 \quad (3.12)$$

where, because $\Sigma = I$, $d = \mu + \frac{\partial}{\partial\mu}$. For example, for m = 1,2, and 3, using (3.2) and $\Sigma = I$,

$$Ey'N_1y = (d'N_1d)\cdot 1 = trN_1(dd'\cdot 1) = \mu'N_1\mu + trN_1 \quad (3.13)$$

$$\begin{aligned} E(y'N_1y)(y'N_2y) &= (d'N_1d)(d'N_2d)\cdot 1 \\ &= (d'N_2d)E(y'N_1y) \\ &= \prod_{i=1}^{2} (\mu'N_i\mu) + 2\prod_{i=1}^{2} (\mu'N_iN_{3-i}\mu) \\ &+ \sum_{i=1}^{2} (\mu'N_i\mu)trN_{3-i} \\ &+ \prod_{i=1}^{2} trN_i + \sum_{i=1}^{2} tr\, N_iN_{3-i} \end{aligned} \quad (3.14)$$

$$\begin{aligned} E(y'N_1y)(y'N_2y)(y'N_3y) &= (d'N_1d)(d'N_2d)(d'N_3d)\cdot 1 \\ &= (d'N_3d)E(y'N_1y)(y'N_2y) \\ &= \prod_{i=1}^{3} (\mu'N_i\mu) + 4[(\mu'N_1\mu)(\mu'N_3N_2\mu) \\ &+ (\mu'N_2\mu)(\mu'N_1N_3\mu) \\ &+ (\mu'N_3\mu)(\mu'N_1N_2\mu)] \\ &+ 8\mu'(N_1N_3N_2+N_2N_3N_1+N_1N_2N_3)\mu \end{aligned}$$

$$+ 4 \prod_{i=1}^{3} (trN_i)a_{1i} + \sum_{i=1}^{3} (\mu' N_i \mu)a_{2i}$$
$$+ trN_1 trN_2 trN_3 +$$
$$+ 2\{(trN_1N_2)trN_3$$
$$+ (trN_1N_3)trN_2 + (trN_2N_3)trN_1\} + 8trN_1N_2N_3 \tag{3.15}$$

$$a_{11} = \mu' N_2N_3\mu + (\mu' N_2\mu)(\mu' N_3\mu),\ a_{12} = \mu' N_1N_3\mu + (\mu' N_1\mu)(\mu' N_3\mu) \tag{3.16}$$
$$a_{13} = \mu' N_1N_2\mu + (\mu' N_1\mu)(\mu' N_2\mu)$$
$$a_{21} = 3trN_2N_3,\ a_{22} = 3trN_1N_3,\ a_{23} = 3trN_1N_2.$$

The results for $m > 3$ can be similarly written by noting the recursive nature of (3.12), that is, for $m \geq 1$.

$$Eq_m = (d' N_m d)Eq_{m-1}. \tag{3.17}$$

We note that the above results can easily be written for the case of $y \sim (\mu, \Sigma)$ by writing $y' N_i y = y' \Sigma^{-\frac{1}{2}} \Sigma^{\frac{1}{2}} N_i \Sigma^{\frac{1}{2}} \Sigma^{-\frac{1}{2}} y = y^{*\prime} N_i^{*} y^{*}$ where $y^{*} = \Sigma^{-\frac{1}{2}} y \sim N(\mu^{*} = \Sigma^{-\frac{1}{2}}\mu, I)$ and $N_i^{*} = \Sigma^{\frac{1}{2}} N_i \Sigma^{\frac{1}{2}}$. Also N_i need not be symmetric since for nonsymmetric N_i we can always write $y' N_i y = y'(N_i + N_i')y/2$ where $(N_i + N_i')/2$ is symmetric.

In the special case where $N_i = N$, for $i=1,\dots,m$, we get results for $E(y' N y)^m$ from (3.12). Furthermore, if N is indempotent, the results (3.12) to (3.16) provide the moments of non–central χ^2 available in the statistics literature, see, e.g., Srivastava and Khatri (1979). In another special case of $y \sim N(0,I)$, that is $\mu = 0$, the results (3.12) to (3.15) reduce to those given in the literature, see e.g., Srivastava and Tiwari (1976).

3.2.1 An Econometric Example

Here we analyze the effect of misspecification on the moments of the residual variance estimator in a regression model. For this consider the model

$$y = X\beta + Z\delta + u \tag{3.18}$$

y, X, β and u are as in (3.3) with $\Sigma = I$ for simplicity, and Z is a $n \times L$ nonstochastic matrix of excluded variables. The investigator intead considers the model

$$y = X\beta + u$$

and uses the residual variance estimator

$$s^2 = \frac{\hat{u}'\hat{u}}{n-k} = \frac{y'My}{n-k}; \quad M = I - X(X'X)^{-1}X' \tag{3.19}$$

Since $y \sim N(\mu,I)$, $\mu = X\beta + Z\delta$, we get from (3.13) and (3.14)

$$\begin{aligned} Es^2 &= \frac{1}{n-k}[(X\beta + Z\delta)'M(X\beta + Z\delta) + (n-k)] \\ &= 1 + \frac{\theta}{n-k}, \quad \theta = \delta'Z'MZ\delta \end{aligned} \tag{3.20}$$

$$Es^4 = \left[\frac{1}{n-k}\right]^2 [\theta^2 + (n-k+2)(2\theta+n-k)] \qquad (3.21)$$

which gives

$$V(s^2) = \frac{2(\theta+n-k)}{(n-k)^2}. \qquad (3.22)$$

It is clear from (3.20) that s^2 is neither unbiased nor asymptotically unbiased under misspecification. This is true even if X and Z are orthogonal ($X'Z = 0$), in which case it is well known that the misspecification bias in the least squares estimator b vanishes, see also Kmenta (1986, pp. 444–45) on this point.

3.3 Moments of the Ratio of Quadratic Forms

In 3.1 and 3.2 we gave examples of the applications of lemma 1. Here we consider cases where lemma 1 along with lemma 2 is useful.

Consider a general form of the ratio of quadratic forms as

$$q^{m,r} = (y'N_1y)^m(y'Ny)^{-r} = (y'N_1y)^m w^{-r};\ r \geq 0,\ m \geq 0 \quad (3.23)$$

where $w = y'Ny$ and m is an integer. When $m = r$, $q^m = (y'N_1y/y'Ny)^m$, and when $m = r = 1$, q is the ratio of quadratic forms.

From lemma 1 (substituting $h_1(y) = (y'N_1y)^m$, $h_2(y) = (y'Ny)^{-r}$) the expectation of $q^{m,r}$ can be written as

$$Eq^{m,r} = (d'N_1d)^m Ew^{-r} \qquad (3.24)$$

where Ew^{-r} is as given in lemma 2. A recurrence relationship can be obtained for $m \geq 1$ as

$$
\begin{aligned}
Eq^{m,r} &= (d'N_1d)(d'N_1d)^{m-1}Ew^{-r} \\
&= (d'N_1d)Eq^{m-1,r}
\end{aligned}
\tag{3.25}
$$

Thus the expectation in (3.24) follows by simply taking the derivatives of Ew^{-r} given in lemma 2. As an illustration, we present below the expressions for m = 1,2. For simplicity we consider $y \sim N(\mu,I)$ so that $d = \mu + \partial/\partial\mu$. Using lemma 2,

$$
\begin{aligned}
Eq^{1,r} &= (d'N_1d)Ew^{-r} = \mathrm{tr}(N_1dd'Ew^{-r}) \\
&= (\Gamma(r))^{-1}\int_0^\infty t^{r-1}|N_{0t}|^{-\frac{1}{2}}(\mathrm{tr}N_1N_{0t}^{-1} + \mu'N_{2t}\mu) \\
&\cdot \exp\{-\tfrac{1}{2}\mu'N_{1t}\mu\}dt
\end{aligned}
\tag{3.26}
$$

and

$$
\begin{aligned}
Eq^{2,r} &= (d'N_1d)Eq^{1,r} \\
&= (\Gamma(r))^{-1}\int_0^\infty t^{r-1}|N_{0t}|^{-\frac{1}{2}}[(\mathrm{tr}N_1N_{0_t}^{-1} + \mu'N_{2t}\mu)^2 + \\
&+ 2\mathrm{tr}N_1N_{2t} + 4\mu'N_{ot}^{-1}N_1N_{2t}\mu]\exp\{-\tfrac{1}{2}\mu'N_{1t}\mu\}dt
\end{aligned}
\tag{3.27}
$$

where $N_{2t} = N_{ot}^{-1}N_1N_{ot}^{-1}$, and N_{ot}, N_{1t} are as given in lemma 2 with $\Sigma = I$. For r = 1,2 the results in (3.26) and (3.27) give the first and second moments, respectively, of the ratio of quadratic terms.

When N is an indempotent matrix we can get infinite series representations of (3.26) and (3.27) by using (2.13).

When $y \sim N(\mu, \Sigma)$, the results (3.26) – (3.27) are the same with μ, N_1 and N replaced by $\Sigma^{-\frac{1}{2}}\mu$, $\Sigma^{\frac{1}{2}}N_1 \Sigma^{\frac{1}{2}}$ and $\Sigma^{\frac{1}{2}} N \Sigma^{\frac{1}{2}}$ respectively. Smith (1988a) allows m and r to be real–valued, and provides the expression for $Eq^{m,r}$ in terms of invariant polynomials. He also gives the conditions for existence of $Eq^{m,r}$. Further, for integer m = r another alternative expression for $Eq^{m,m}$, along with the conditions for its existence, are given in Magnus (1986).

3.3.1 The Ratio of Bilinear to Quadratic Forms

A large number of econometric estimators are in terms of the ratio of bilinear to quadratic forms, and the moments of these are often of interest. Here we merely show that the moments of such ratios can be obtained from the moments of the ratio of quadratic forms given in 3.3.

Consider a general ratio of bilinear to quadratic form as

$$q_o^{m,r} = (y_2'M_1y_1)^m(y_2'My_2)^{-r}, \tag{3.28}$$

where y_2 and y_1 are n×1 vectors and M_1 and M_2 are n×n symmetric matrices. For m = r

$$q_0^{r,r} = \left[\frac{y_2'M_1y_1}{y_2'My_2}\right]^r . \tag{3.29}$$

Our problem is to obtain $E(q_0^{m,r})$. For this we first note that

$$y_2'M_1y_1 = y'N_1y \text{ and } y_2'My_2 = y'Ny \tag{3.30}$$

where

$$y = \begin{bmatrix} y_1 \\ y_2 \end{bmatrix}, N_1 = \frac{1}{2}\begin{bmatrix} 0 & M_1 \\ M_1 & 0 \end{bmatrix}, N = \begin{bmatrix} 0 & 0 \\ 0 & M \end{bmatrix}. \tag{3.31}$$

The important observation is that the bilinear form $y_2'M_1y_1$ can be written as a quadratic form. Thus, it immediately follows that

$$Eq_0^{m,r} = E(y'N_1y)^m(y'Ny)^{-r} = Eq^{m,r} \tag{3.32}$$

where $Eq^{m,r}$ is as given in 3.3 above with $y \sim N(\mu, \Sigma)$ being a $2n\times1$ vector and

$$\mu = \begin{bmatrix} \mu_1 \\ \mu_2 \end{bmatrix}, \Sigma = \begin{bmatrix} \Sigma_{11} & \Sigma_{12} \\ \Sigma_{21} & \Sigma_{22} \end{bmatrix}. \tag{3.33}$$

3.3.2 Econometric Examples

The number of econometric estimators and test statistics which can be written as the ratio of quadratic forms or the ratio of bilinear to quadratic forms are quite large. The consideration of each one of them is beyond the scope of this paper and we therefore present only some examples for illustrative purposes. No detailed study or expressions are presented but they can be obtained from 3.3 above.

a. R^2 in Regression Models

For the regression model $y = X\beta + u$ in (3.3), that is $y \sim N(X\beta, I)$, assuming that one of the regressors is constant we can write

$$R^2 = 1 - \frac{\hat{u}'\hat{u}}{(y-\bar{y})'(y-\bar{y})} = \frac{y'N_1y}{y'Ny} \tag{3.34}$$

where

$$N = I - \frac{ii'}{n}, \; N_1 = N - (I - X(X'X)^{-1}X'); \tag{3.35}$$

i is an n×1 vector of unit elements. Note that in (3.35) N is an idempotent matrix of rank n–k. The mth order moments of R^2, $E(R^2)^m$, can be obtained from 3.3 by substituting r for m. The results for a general Σ or $\Sigma = \sigma^2 I$ follow by the arguments in (3.3). For discussion on the moments of R^2, see Cramer (1987).

b. Durbin–Watson Statistic

For the regression model in (3.3) the Durbin–Watson statistic is

$$D = \frac{u'MAMu}{u'Mu} = \frac{y'MAMy}{y'My} = \frac{y'N_1y}{y'Ny} \tag{3.36}$$

where $y \sim N(X\beta, I)$, $N = M = I - X(X'X)^{-1}X'$ is idempotent, $N_1 = MAM$ and A is an n×n matrix of constants, see e.g. Theil (1971). The moments of D thus follow from (3.24). Note that $N\mu = MX\beta = 0$ here. The results for general Σ follow by arguments in (3.3).

c. <u>Test Statistics for Unit Roots</u>

Consider the model

$$y_0 = \alpha y_{-1} + u, \; u \sim N(0, I_{n-1}) \tag{3.37}$$

where $y_0 = [y_2, \ldots, y_n]'$ and $y_{-1} = [y_1, \ldots, y_{n-1}]'$. Further denote $y = [y_1, \ldots, y_n]'$ so that $y_0 = [0 \;\; I_{n-1}]y = D_1 y$ and $y_{-1} = [I_{n-1} \;\; 0]y = D_2 y$. Then the least squares estimator of α is

$$a = \frac{y_0' y_{-1}}{y_{-1}' y_{-1}} = \frac{y' D_1' D_2 y}{y' D_2' D_2 y} = \frac{y' N_1^* y}{y' N y} \tag{3.38}$$

where $N_1^* = D_1' D_2 + D_2' D_1)/2$ and $N = D_2' D_2$. The moments of a follow from (3.24). Also, see Sawa (1978).

Fuller (1976) considers the statistic for testing the hypothesis of a the unit root, $\alpha = 1$, as $t = n(a-1)$. The exact m^{th} order moments of this statistic, Et^m, can be written from (3.24) by noting that

$$t = n(a-1) = \frac{y' N_1 y}{y' N y}. \tag{3.39}$$

where $N_1 = n(N_1^* - N)$. Note that, assuming $y_0 = 0$ as in Fuller, $y \sim N(0, \Sigma)$ where $\Sigma = \Sigma(\alpha)$ is the well known matrix of AR(1) process.

d. <u>Forecasts in Dynamic Models</u>

For the model in (3.37) the forecast for the n+1 period is

$$\hat{y}_{n+1} = ay_n = a(\ell' y) \tag{3.40}$$

where $\ell = [0,...,0,1]'$ is an n×1 vector and $a = (y'Ny)^{-1}y'N_1^* y$ is as in (3.40). Thus by using $h_1(y) = (\ell' y)^m$, $h_2(y) = a^m$ in lemma 1, the mth moment of $\hat{y}_{n+1}$ is

$$E(\hat{y}_{n+1})^m = E(a^m(\ell' y)^m) = (\ell' d)^m Ea^m \tag{3.41}$$

where Ea^m follows from (3.24). For example for m = 1

$$E\hat{y}_{n+1} = [\ell'\mu + \ell'\Sigma\frac{\partial}{\partial\mu})Ea]_{\mu=0} = \left[\ell' \Sigma\frac{\partial}{\partial\mu} Ea\right]_{\mu=0} \tag{3.42}$$

Further details can easily be worked out.

e. <u>Double k–class Estimators in Structural Models</u>

We consider the moments of Nagar's (1962) Double k–class estimators of the structural parameter γ in the equation

$$y_1 = \gamma y_2 + X_1\beta_1 + u \tag{3.43}$$

where y_1 and y_2 are n×1 vectors of observations on the endogenous variables, X_1 is an n×k_1 nonstochastic matrix of exogenous variables, γ is a scalar parameter, β_1 is a k_1×1 parameter vector and u is an n×1 disturbance vector. We denote $X = [X_1, X_2]$ where X_2 is an n×k_2 matrix of exogenous variables appearing in the remaining, say G–1, equations of the model.

The Double k–class estimators of γ can now be written as

$$c = \frac{y_2' M_1 y_1}{y_2' M y_2} \tag{3.44}$$

where $M_1 = k_1(M_X - M_{X_1}) + (1-k_1)\bar{M}_{X_1}$ and $M = k_2(M_X - M_{X_1}) + (1-k_2)\bar{M}_{X_1}$; k_1 and k_2 are arbitrary nonstochastic constants and $\bar{M}_{X_1} = I - M_{X_1} = I - X_1(X_1'X_1)^{-1}X_1'$. The advantage of considering the estimator c is that the least squares ($k_1 = k_2 = 0$), the two stage least squares ($k_1 = k_2 = 1$), Theil's k–class ($k_1 = k_2 = k$), among others, are special cases of this estimator. In the past, various researchers have obtained the moments of these special cases separately and by using different techniques e.g., see Nagar and Ullah (1973), Takeuchi (1970), Sawa (1972), and Mehta and Swamy (1978). However the mth order moments of c can be obtained in a straightforward way by the simple observation made in (3.32), that is

$$Ec^m = E\left[\frac{y_2' M_1 y_1}{y_2' M y_2}\right]^m = E\left[\frac{y' N_1 y}{y' N y}\right] \tag{3.45}$$

where N_1 and N are as defined in (3.31) and $y = [y_1' \; y_2'] \sim N([\mu_1' \; \mu_2']', \Sigma)$ where $\mu_1 = X\pi_1$, $\mu_2 = X\pi_2$ (π_1 and π_2 are $K_1 \times 1$ and $K_2 \times 1$ reduced form parameter vectors) and

$$\Sigma = \begin{bmatrix} w_{11}I & w_{12}I \\ w_{21}I & w_{22}I \end{bmatrix}. \tag{3.46}$$

The last equality of (3.45) can be obtained from (3.24). For some interesting observations on the moments of c, see Dwivedi and Srivastava (1984).

f. Some Other Examples

The list of other estimators and test statistics for which the techniques of lemma 1 and lemma 2 can be used to obtain the moments is extensive. Here we mention just some of them, for example: the F statistic for testing general linear restrictions in the regression model (3.3); Stein–rule estimators of β in (3.3) [Vinod and Ullah (1981), Judge and Bock (1978)]; estimators of parameters and forecasts in dynamic regression models [Carter and Ullah (1979), Maasoumi and Ullah (1987), Hoque and Peters (1986)]; Macro models with expectations [Pagan (1984), Ullah (1987)]; residual variance and forecast estimators in simultaneous equations models [Brown et. al. (1985), Nagar and Sahay (1978)]; sample autocorrelations [DeGooijer (1980)]; estimators and test statistics in cointegrated and unit root models [Engle and Granger (1987), Banerjee et. al. (1986), Godfrey and Tremayne (1988)]. An area of potential application in economics is the evaluation of expected utility functions.

4. Exact Distributions

As in section 2, consider $y \sim N(\mu,\Sigma)$ and $h(y)$ as a real valued function of y. Then we can write the distribution function of $h(y)$ as

$$F(\xi) = P(h(y) \le \xi) = \int_{h(y) \le \xi} f(y)dy \tag{4.1}$$

where f(y) is as given in (2.1). Note however that (4.1) is true for any density f(y).

An alternative way to obtain the distribution function is to first obtain the characteristic function (c.f.) and then use the inversion formula. The c.f. of h(y) is

$$\begin{aligned} \Psi(t) &= E\exp\{ith(y)\} = \int_y \exp\{ith(y)\}f(y)dy \\ &= \exp\{ith(d)\} \end{aligned} \tag{4.2}$$

where the last equality follows by using lemma 1. Now, by inversion, the density function of h(y) at h(y) = ξ is

$$\varnothing(\xi) = \frac{1}{2\pi}\int_{-\infty}^{\infty} \exp\{-it\xi\}\Psi(t)dt \tag{4.3}$$

provided Ψ(t) is absolutely integrable. The distribution function can then be obtained by using (4.3). A direct way of obtaining the distribution function is given by Gil–Pelaez (1951).

Another representation of (4.1) is

$$F(\xi) = P(h(y) \le \xi) = E[I(h(y))] \tag{4.4}$$

where I( ) is the indicator function which takes the value 1 if $h(y) \le \xi$ and 0 otherwise.

It is clear that, unlike the expectation of h(y) in lemma 1, a simple expression for the distribution of a general h(y) may not be possible. However, as noted in 3.2 and 3.3, for a large class of econometric estimators and test statistics h(y) is a quadratic form, a ratio of quadratic form, or a ratio of bilinear to quadratic forms. Thus we turn to the distribution of such h(y) in section 4.1 and then consider a numerical solution of the distribution of a general h(y) in section 4.3.

4.1 Distribution of Ratios of Quadratic Forms and Ratios of Bilinear to Quadratic Forms

Let m = r = 1 in (3.23) and write the ratio of quadratic forms as

$$q = \frac{y'N_1y}{y'Ny} = h(y), \quad y \sim N(\mu,\Sigma). \tag{4.5}$$

Then

$$\begin{aligned} F(\xi) &= P[q \le \xi] = P[y'N_1y \le \xi y'Ny] \\ &= P[y'N_2y \le 0]; \quad N_2 = N_1 - \xi N \\ &= P[y'\Sigma^{-\frac{1}{2}}\Sigma^{\frac{1}{2}}N_2\Sigma^{\frac{1}{2}}\Sigma^{-\frac{1}{2}}y \le 0] \\ &= P[y^{*\prime} N_2^* y^* \le 0]; \quad N_2^* = \Sigma^{\frac{1}{2}}N_2\Sigma^{\frac{1}{2}}, \; y^* = \Sigma^{-\frac{1}{2}}y \\ &= P[y^{*\prime} PP'N_2^*PP'y^* \le 0] \\ &= P[z'\Lambda z \le 0] = P\left[\prod_{j=1}^{n} \lambda_j z_j^2 \le 0\right] \end{aligned} \tag{4.6}$$

where $z = P'y^* = P'\Sigma^{-\frac{1}{2}}y \sim N(\mu_z = P'\Sigma^{-\frac{1}{2}}\mu, I)$ and P is the orthogonal matrix (PP′ = I) of eigen vectors of N_2^* such that

$P'N_2^*P = \Lambda$; Λ is a diagonal matrix of eigen values $\lambda_1,...,\lambda_n$ of $N_2^* = \Sigma^{\frac{1}{2}} N_2 \Sigma^{\frac{1}{2}}$.

The second equality in (4.6) shows that the distribution of the ratio of quadratic forms reduces to the distribution of an indefinite quadratic form $y'N_2y$. The series representation of this is given in Gurland (1955), also see Taneja (1976). However the numerical evaluation of this is difficult. Imhof (1961) provided an integral representation of (4.6) which is based on the Gurland (1948) and the Gil–Pelaez (1951) numerical inversion formula, also see Davies (1973). Imhof's (1961) result is (using (4.6))

$$\begin{aligned} F(\xi) &= P(q \le \xi) = P(z'\Lambda z \le 0) \\ &= \frac{1}{2} - \frac{1}{\pi}\int_0^\infty t^{-1}\mathrm{Img}\{\Psi(t)\}dt \end{aligned} \tag{4.7}$$

where $\mathrm{Img}\{\varepsilon\}$ represents the imaginary part of ε and

$$\Psi(t) = \left[\prod_{j=1}^{n} (1-2i\lambda_j t)^{-\frac{n}{2}}\right] \exp\{i \prod_{j=1}^{n} \mu_{jz}^2 \lambda_j t(1-2i\lambda_j t)^{-1}\} \tag{4.8}$$

is the c.f. of $z'\Lambda z$; λ_j and μ_{jz} are as defined in (4.6). Programs for the numerical integration of (4.7) are described in Koerts and Abrahamse (1969) and Davies (1980). An advantage of the Davies program is that both the truncation and numerical integration errors are controlled with guaranteed accuracy. For the numerical implementation of these programs the eigen values and corresponding eigen vectors of the matrix $\Sigma^{\frac{1}{2}}(N_1-\xi N)\Sigma^{\frac{1}{2}}$ are needed. These can always be found numerically and in some cases, analytically. Palm and Sneek (1984) have suggested modifications which eliminate the need to compute eigenvalues. Evans and Savin (1984) have developed an algorithm which is efficient with regard to time taken in calculating the eigenvalues and eigenvectors. For more on numerical evaluations, see Lugannini and Rice (1984) and Farebrother (1984).

In general,

$$P(z'\Lambda z \le \xi_0) = \frac{1}{2} - \frac{1}{\pi}\int_0^\infty t^{-1}\mathrm{Img}\{\exp(-it\xi_0)\Psi(t)\}dt \quad (4.9)$$

where z and Λ are as in (4.7); see Imhof (1961, p. 422). The result in (4.9) can be used for evaluating distribution of quadratic form at ξ_0. For $\xi_0 = 0$ we have (4.7).

We note here that the distribution of q can also be obtained directly by the numerical inversion formula in Gurland (1948). This is

$$\begin{aligned} F(\xi) = P(q \le \xi) &= P\left(\left[\frac{y'N_1y}{y'Ny}\right] \le \xi\right) \\ &= \frac{1}{2} - \frac{1}{\pi}\int_0^\infty \mathrm{Img}\left[\frac{\Psi(t,-t\xi)}{t}\right]d\xi \end{aligned} \quad (4.10)$$

where $\Psi(u,v)$ is the joint c.f. of $y'N_1y$ and $y'Ny$.

Now consider the ratio of bilinear to quadratic forms

$$q_0 = \frac{y_2'M_1y_1}{y_2'My_2}$$

from (3.28) (m=r=1). It was shown in (3.30) that $(y_2'My_2)^{-1}(y_2'M_1y_1) = (y'Ny)^{-1}y'N_1y$ where y, N_1 and N are as given in (3.33). Thus the distribution of q_0 is the same as that of q in (4.6). That is

$$P\left[\frac{y_2'M_1y_1}{y_2'My_2} \le \xi_0\right] = P\left[\frac{y'N_1y}{y'Ny} \le \xi_0\right] \tag{4.11}$$

which follows from (4.6). This observation was made in Ullah (1987) in the context of a two step econometric estimator.

4.1.1 Econometric Examples

Here, we merely emphasize that the distribution of all estimators and test statistics in (3.2) and (3.3) (except forecasts in (3.40)) can easily be analyzed using one technique, that is the Imhof (1961) technique in (4.7) or (4.9). For example, the distribution of the residual variance in (3.19) can easily be evaluated using (4.9) even without knowing that it follows the noncentral χ^2 under misspecification. Similarly, the distribution of R^2 can be analyzed using (4.7) even under misspecification of type (3.18). The distribution of Durbin–Watson statistic in (3.36) has been already analyzed, see King (1987) for a survey.

Cribbett et al (1989) have analyzed the distribution of the two stage least squares estimator using the Imhof (1961) technique and found that their results compare with those of Anderson and Sawa (1973, 79) who have used the doubly non–central F algorithm. However, while Anderson and Sawa's procedure may not be easily extendable for the double k–class estimators in (3.44), Lye (1987) has shown that the Imhof technique is easily implementable even for these estimators. Lye

(1988) has also analyzed the distribution of several other econometric estimators using the Imhof technique.

Not much is known about the distribution of estimators and test statistics in dynamic models, although see Maekawa (1987) for the approximate distribution of forecasts in the autoregressive model (3.37). Extensive simulation studies include those of Nankervis and Savin (1985, 1987a) and Carter (1988). Monte Carlo analysis of the recently developed unit root tests and estimators in co–integrated models have appeared in the work of Peters and Veloce (1988), Godfrey and Tremayne (1988), and Hansen and Phillips (1988). We note that the exact distribution of some of these estimators and test statistics can be obtained using the techniques described in 4.1. For example, the unit root test in (3.39) is a ratio of quadratic forms and hence the Imhof technique can be applied, also see Evans and Savin (1981, 1984). Lye (1988) analyzes the distribution of least squares estimators in the dynamic regression model using the Imhof technique. Ellison (1988) and Fan (1988) have analyzed the distribution of estimators in co–integration models, and Giles (1988) in a pre–test problem.

4.3 Nonparametric Distribution Function of h(y)

In 4.1 it was indicated that, in general, obtaining an explicit analytical expression of the distribution function of any h(y) may be difficult. In such situations a useful alternative is to combine Monte Carlo with nonparametric density estimation techniques. This can be done as follows. Suppose we draw m samples of size n from $y \sim N(\mu = \mu_0, \Sigma = \Sigma_0)$. Then we get m values of h(y). Using these values, the Rosenblatt (1956) type kernel estimator of the density f(h(y)) at $h(y) = \xi$ is

$$\hat{f}(\xi) = \frac{1}{m\gamma} \sum_{i=1}^{m} K\left[\frac{h_i(y)-\xi}{\gamma}\right] \tag{4.12}$$

where $\gamma = \gamma_m \to 0$ as $m \to \infty$ is the window–width and K( ) is the kernel. The $\hat{f}(\xi)$ is a consistent estimator of $f(\xi)$. For the choices of kernel and γ, see Silverman (1985) and Ullah (1988) among others, and for Monte Carlo methodology, see Hendry (1984) and Davidson and Mackinnon (1988).

Since m can be chosen to be very large, $\hat{f}(\xi)$ will be a good approximation to the true density $f(\xi)$. This technique was proposed in Ullah and Singh (1985) and later used in Power and Ullah (1987) and Carter (1988) to analyze the distribution of the t–ratio in rational expectations and dynamic structural models, respectively. Racine (1988) analyzes the distribution of the t–ratio in an heteroskedastic model. The overall results are very encouraging. In future it would be more interesting to combine bootstrapping techniques of Efron (1975) with kernel density estimation. This will avoid the need for normality of y.

We should finally note that even the exact distributions in 4.1.1 are in fact approximate distributions in the sense that numerical integration is carried out which can be subject to approximation errors.

5. Non–Normal Errors

The results of Sections 3 and 4 can easily be extended to a class of non–normal distributions of y.

a. Mixtures of Normal

Consider the mixtures of normal

$$
\begin{aligned}
f(y) &= \int_0^{\infty} f(y|v)f(v)dv \\
&= E_v f(y|v) \qquad (5.1)
\end{aligned}
$$

where f(y|v) is a normal density with mean μ and variance vI, i.e. $y|_v \sim N(\mu,vI)$, and E_v represents the expectation with respect to a scalar random variable v with density f(v). For example, if f(v) is a gamma density then f(y) is a multivariate t density.

Under (5.1),

$$
\begin{aligned}
Eh(y) &= \int h(y)f(y)dy = \int h(y)E_v f(y|v) \\
&= E_v \int h(y)f(y|v)dy \\
&= E_v[E(h(y)|v)], \qquad (5.2)
\end{aligned}
$$

and similarly the density of h(y) is

$$
\begin{aligned}
f(h(y)) &= \int_v f(h(y)|v)f(v)dv \\
&= E_v f(h(y)|v). \qquad (5.3)
\end{aligned}
$$

The results in (5.2) and (5.3) indicate that the density and moments of h(y), under (5.1) can be obtained in two steps: (i) obtain the results under $y|_v \sim N(\mu,vI)$ as given in Sections 2 to 4. (ii) take expectation of these results with respect to v. Using these steps the results of Sections 2 to 4 can be extended for the case of mixtures of normal s.

As an illustration consider the least squares estimator

$$b = (X'X)^{-1}X'y = h(y)$$

as in (3.5). Here we consider f(y) to be multivariate –t density which is given by (5.1) with f(v) as a gamma density with m degrees of freedom. Then using (3.6) and (3.7) and (5.2)

$$\begin{aligned} Eb &= E_v[Eb|v] = E_v\beta = \beta \\ Ebb' &= E_v[Ebb'|v] = E_v[\beta\beta' + v(X'X)^{-1}] \\ &= \beta\beta' + m(X'X)^{-1} \end{aligned} \tag{5.4}$$

and $V(b) = m(X'X)^{-1}$.

b. Edgeworth Density

Suppose y is distributed with mean μ and variance I, that is $y \sim ?(\mu,I)$ or $y_i \sim ?(\mu_i,1)$. Then the Edgeworth density of y_i is

$$f(y_i) = \sum_{j=0}^{\infty} \left[\frac{c_j}{j!}\left[-\frac{d}{dy_i}\right]^j\right] f(y_i|\mu_i) \tag{5.5}$$

where $f(y_i|\mu_i)$ represents the normal density, i.e., $y_i\big|_{\mu_i} \sim N(\mu_i,1)$ and $c_0 = 1 = c_2 = 0$, $c_3 = \kappa_3$, $c_4 = \kappa_4$, $c_5 = \kappa_6$, $c_6 = \kappa_6 + 10\kappa_3^2$; κ's are cumulants. Davis (1976) gave an alternative convenient representation of (5.5) which is

$$f(y_i) = E_{w_i} f(y_i|\mu_i + w_i) \tag{5.6}$$

where w_i is a pseudo variate with mean and variance 0, and higher order cumulants the same as those of y_i no that $E_{w_i}(w_i^j) = c_j$.

Now, as in the case of mixtures of normal, the density and moments of h(y) under (5.5) or (5.6), can be obtained in two steps: (i) obtain the results under $y|_{\mu+w} \sim N(\mu+w,I)$ (ii) take expectation of these results with respect to w. That is

$$Eh(y) = E_w[E(h(y)\,|\,w)] \tag{5.7}$$

where, $E(h(y)\,|\,w)$ is the expectation of h(y) when $y|_{\mu+w} \sim N(\mu+w,I)$. Notice that in the mixtures of the normal case above the conditional normal density is affected by the variable v in the variance term whereas in the case (5.6) it is affected by the variable w in the mean. In both cases the final results are obtained by averaging over their respective pseudo variates.

As an illustration, again consider from (3.5)

$$b = (X'X)^{-1}X'y, \qquad y \sim ?(\mu = X\beta, I).$$

Then

$$\begin{aligned} Eb = E_w[E(b\,|\,w)] &= E_w\left[(X'X)^{-1}X'E(y\,|\,\mu+w)\right] \\ &= E_w[(X'X)^{-1}X'(\mu + w)] \\ &= \beta, \text{ because } E_w = 0 \end{aligned} \tag{5.8}$$

and

$$
\begin{aligned}
Ebb' &= E_w[Ebb' \mid w] \\
&= E_w[\beta\beta' + (X'X)^{-1} + Aww'A' \\
&\quad + \beta w'A + Aw\beta'] \\
&= \beta\beta' + (X'X)^{-1}
\end{aligned}
\tag{5.9}
$$

which is the same as in the normal case (3.7); note $Ew_i^2 = 0$ and $A = (X'X)^{-1}X'$.

The results for other cases in sections 2 to 4 can similarly be developed, e.g., see Knight (1985, 1986) for the two–stage least squares and forecast estimators, and Peters (1986) for dynamic models.

6. Approximations

Consider $y \sim N(\mu,\sigma^2 I)$. Then this can be written as

$$
y = \mu + \sigma\varepsilon, \qquad \varepsilon \sim N(0,I) \tag{6.1}
$$

Now we introduce

$$
\partial = \frac{\partial}{\partial\mu} \text{ and } \Delta = \frac{\partial^2}{\partial\mu\partial\mu'} \tag{6.2}
$$

as an n×1 vector and an n×n matrix respectively. Then we can present the following lemma.

Lemma 3. _If_ Eh(y) _is finite, then its small_ σ _expansion, up to_ $O(\sigma^4)$, _is,_

$$
Eh(y) = h(\mu) + \frac{\sigma^2}{2}\, tr(\Delta h(\mu) + \frac{\sigma^4}{4!}\,[tr\Delta)^2 + 2tr\Delta^2]h(\mu). \tag{6.3}
$$

Proof: Using the Taylor Series expansion about μ we can write, up to $O(\sigma^4)$,

$$h(y) = h(\mu) + \sigma(\varepsilon'\partial) + \frac{\sigma^2}{2}(\varepsilon'\Delta\varepsilon) + \frac{\sigma^3}{3!}(\varepsilon'\Delta\varepsilon)(\varepsilon'\partial)$$
$$+ \frac{\sigma^2}{4!}(\varepsilon'\Delta\varepsilon)^2]h(\mu). \tag{6.4}$$

Hence, taking expectations on both sides of (6.4) we get the result in Lemma 3.

Note that Lemma 3 is quite general and that it corresponds to both Lemmas 1 and 2 in the exact case. In fact, here $Ew^{-r} = E(y'Ny)^{-r}$, up to $O(\sigma^4)$, also follows from Lemma 3 by using $h(y) = (y'Ny)^{-r}$. The results for other estimators and test statistics in sections 2 and 3 can also be obtained by using (6.3). In this sense, the result in Lemma 3 provides a general treatment of Kadane's (1971) small–σ expansion.

In the non–normal case the results of Lemma 3 can easily be obtained by using the Davis technique in section 5. Alternatively, one can obtain Lemma 3 for the non–normal disturbances ε whose first four moments are finite, that is $E\varepsilon_i = 0$, $E\varepsilon_i^2 = \sigma^2$, $E\varepsilon_i^3 = \gamma_1$ and $E\varepsilon_i^4 = \gamma_2 + 3$, where γ_1 and γ_2 are Pearson's measures of skewness and kurtosis of the distribution. This can be done by using these four moments and taking expectations on both sides of (6.4). In a special case of $h(y) = (y'N_1y)^m(y'Ny)^{-r}$ the results are obtained in Ullah and Srivastava (1988) by an alternative method.

A general result for the density of h(y) can be obtained by using (6.4) and the inversion result in (4.3). This requires further work. For large–n approximations, see Phillips (1977).

7. Multivariate Case

Let Y be an n×p matrix whose n independent row vectors are distributed according to a p–dimensional normal law with means given by EY and variance–covariance matrix I_p. Then the density function of Y can be written as

$$f(Y) = (2\pi)^{-np/2} \exp\{-\tfrac{1}{2} \operatorname{tr}(Y - EY)(Y - EY)'\}. \quad (7.1)$$

Define the calculus operator as

$$D = EY + \frac{\partial}{\partial EY}. \quad (7.2)$$

Then, as in (2.3), we get Df(Y) = Y(f(Y)) or (D − Y)f(Y) = 0. Furthermore, if H(Y) is any real matrix valued analytic function of Y, then by using its Taylor Series expansion around D and noting that (D − Y)f(Y) = 0 we get

$$H(Y)f(\&) = H(D)f(Y). \quad (7.3)$$

This gives

$$\begin{aligned} EH(Y) &= H(D) \\ EH_1(Y)H_2(Y) &= H_1(D)EH_2(Y) \end{aligned} \quad (7.4)$$

provided the matrices H_1 and H_2 are conformable and $EH_2(Y)$ exists. For p = 1, (7.4) is Lemma 1 and (7.3) reduces to (2.6). The proof for (7.4) is exactly the same as in Lemma 1.

For p ≥ 1, the result corresponding to Lemma 2 can be

obtained for $W = Y'NY$. This is

$$\begin{aligned} EW^{-r} &= E(W^{-1}|W|)^r|W|^{-r} \\ &= E(\text{adj}\cdot W)^r|W|^r \\ &= EH(Y)|W|^{-r} \\ &= H(D)E|W|^{-r} \end{aligned} \tag{7.5}$$

where $H(Y) = (\text{adj}\cdot W)^r = (\text{adj}\cdot Y'NY)^r$, $H(D) = (\text{adj}\cdot D'ND)^r$ and use has been made of (7.3). Then $E|W|^{-r}$ can be obtained as

$$\begin{aligned} E|W|^{-r} &= E\left[\frac{1}{\Gamma(r)}\int_0^\infty e^{-|W|t}t^{r-1}\,dt\right] \\ &= \frac{1}{\Gamma(r)}\int_0^\infty E(e^{-|W|t})t^{r-1}dt \\ &= \frac{1}{\Gamma(r)}\int_0^\infty M(-t)t^{r-1}dt \end{aligned} \tag{7.6}$$

where $M(t)$ is the moment generating function of $|W|$. If N is an indempotent matrix of rank $m \leq n$ then W is a non–central Wishart matrix with m degrees of freedom. In this case a series representation of (7.6) is given in Constantine (1963, p. 1279).

Not much is known about the exact moments of the multivariate analogs of statistics in Sections 2 to 4, although see Hillier et. al. (1984) for the k–class estimators. However, though not given here, one can consider each statistic separately and study its moments by using (7.4), see, e.g., Wegge (1971) and Ullah (1988) for the moments of the least squares estimator in the regression model (3.3) with stochastic X independent of the error term u.

A large number of econometric estimators and test statistics, in the multivariate case, can be written as ratios of matrix quadratic forms. Thus it would be useful to extend Imhof's result in Section 4 for the multivariate case. This can be attempted by using Phillips (1985) and requires further work. Hillier (1985), among others, has studied the exact densities of instrumental variable estimators by an alternative method.

However their results and the results by the methods proposed here may not be written in simple form. Also, the calculations may involve multiple integrals. In view of these problems, the simple alternative would be to use the nonparametric approach suggested in (4.3), at least to analyze the marginal densities and their moments.

Finally, we merely indicate here that the extension of the exact results in (7.4) for the non–normal case can be done by following Section 5. Similarly, the small–σ approximate result in Lemma 3 can be extended for a general H(Y) where Y is non–normal, see e.g., recent papers by Ullah et. al. (1983), and Srivastava et. al. (1986) for the special cases of H(Y).

References

Anderson, T. W. (1982), "Some Recent Developments on the Distributions of Single–Equation Estimators," in *Advances in Econometrics*, Cambridge University Press.

________ and Rubin, H. (1949), "Estimation of the Parameters of a Single Equation in a Complete System of Stochastic Equation," *Annals of Mathematical Statistics* 20, 46–63.

________ and Sawa, T. (1973), "Distributions of Estimator of Coefficients of a Single Equation in a Simultaneous System and Their Asymptotic Expansions," *Econometrica* 41, 683–714.

________ and ________ (1979), "Evaluation of the Distribution Function of the Two–Stage Least Squares Estimate," *Econometrica* 47, 163–182.

Banerjee, A., J. J. Dolado, D. F. Hendry and G. W. Smith (1986), "Exploring Equilibrium Relationships in Economics Through Static Models: Some Monte Carlo Evidence," *Oxford Bulletin of Economics and Statistics* 48, 253–277.

Basmann, R. L. (1961), "Note on the Exact Finite Sample Frequence Functions of Generalized Classical Linear Estimators in Two Leading Overidentified Cases," *Journal of the American Statistical Association* 56, 619–636.

__________ (1974), Exact Finite Sample Distribution for Some Econometric Estimators and Test Statistics: A Survey and Appraisal, in *Frontiers of Quantitative Economics*, Vol. 2, North Holland.

Bock, M., G. G. Judge, and T. A. Yancey (1984), "A simple form for the inverse moments of non–central χ^2 and F random variables and for certain confluent hypergeometric functions," *Journal of Econometrics* 25, 217–234.

Brown, G. F., Ramage, J. G. and V. K. Srivastava (1985), "The R–class Estimators of Disturbance Variance in Simultaneous Equation Models," *Journal of Quantitative Economics* 2, 231–251.

Carter, R. A. L. (1988), "Nonparametric Monte Carlo Estimates of t–Ratio Distributions in Dynamic Simultaneous Linear Equations Models," manuscript, University of Western Ontario.

________ and A. Ullah (1979), "The Finite Sample Properties of OLS and IV Estimators in Special Rational Distributed Lag Models," *Sankhya*, Ser. D., 41, 1–18.

Constantine, A. G. (1963), "Some Noncentral Distribution Problems in Multivariate Analysis," *Annals of Mathematical Statistics* 34, 1270–1285.

Cramer, J. S. (1987), "Mean and Variance of R^2 in Small and Moderate Samples," *Journal of Econometrics*, 35, 253–266.

Cribbett, P., J. N. Lye and A. Ullah (1989), "Evaluation of the 2SLS Distribution Function by Imhof's Procedure," *Journal of Quantitative Economics* (forthcoming).

Davidson, R. and J. G. MacKinnon (1988), "Monte Carlo Experiments," manuscript, Queen's University.

Davies, R. B. (1973), "Numerical Inversion of a Characteristic Function," *Biometrika* 60, 415–417.

________ (1980), Seg. AS155, "The Distribution of a Linear Contribution of χ^2 Random Variables," *Applied Statistics* 29, 323–333.

Davis, A. N. (1976), "Statistical Distributions in Univariate and Multivariate Edgeworth Populations," *Biometrika*, 661–670.

DeGooijer, J. G. (1980), "Exact Moments of the Sample Autocorrelations from Series Generated by General ARIMA Processes of Order (p,d,q), d=0 or 1," *Journal of Econometrics* 14, 365–379.

Efron, B. (1979), "Bootstrap Methods: Another Look at the Jackknife," *Annals of Statistics* 7, 1–26.

Ellison, G. (1988), "Finite Sample Properties of a Co–integration Model," manuscript, Cambridge University.

Engle, R. F. and C. W. J. Granger (1987), "Co–integration and Error Correction: Representation, Estimation and Testing," *Econometrica* 55, 251–276.

Evans, G. B. A. and N. E. Savin (1981), "Testing Unit Roots: 1," *Econometrica* 49, 753–779.

Evans, G. B. A. and N. E. Savin (1984), "Testing for Unit Roots: 2," *Econometrica* 50, 1241–1289.

Farebrother, R. W. (1984), "A Remark of Algorithms AS106, AS153 and AS155: The Distribution of a Linear Combination of χ^2 Random Variables," *Applied Statistics* 33, 366–369.

Fan, Y. (1988), "The Finite Sample Properties of a Generalized Co–integration Model," manuscript, University of Western Ontario.

Fisher, R. A. (1921), "On the Probable Error of a Coefficient of Correlation Deduced From a Small Sample," *Metron* 1, 1–32.

________ (1922), "The Goodness of Fit of Regression Formulae and the Distribution of Regression Coefficients," *Journal of the Royal Statistical Society* 85, 597–612.

________ (1935), The Mathematical Distributions Used in the Common Tests of Significance, *Econometrica*, 3, 353–365.

Fuller, .(1976), *Introduction to Statistical Time Series*, New York: John Wiley.

Gil–Pelaez, J. (1951), "Note on the Inversion Theorem," *Biometrika* 38, 481–482.

Giles, D. E. A. (1988), "The Exact Distribution of a Simple Pre–Test Estimator," manuscript, University of Canterbury.

Godfrey, L. G. and A. R. Tremayne (1988), "On the Finite Sample Performance of Tests for Unit Roots," DP 88–03, University of Sydney.

Gurland, J. (1948), "Inversion Formulae for the Distribution of Ratios," *Annals of Mathematical Statistics*, 19, 228–237.

________ (1955), "Distribution of Definite and Indefinite Quadratic Forms," *Annals of Mathematical Statistics* 26, 112–127.

Haavelmo, T. (1947), "Methods of Measuring the Marginal Propensity to Consume," *Journal of the American Statistical Association* 42, 105–122.

Hansen, B. E. and P. C. B. Phillips (1988), "Estimation and Inference in Models of Cointegration: A Simulation Study," manuscript, Yale University.

Hendry, D. F. (1984), "Monte Carlo Experimentation in Econometrics," in *Handbook of Econometrics*, Vol. II, North–Holland.

Hillier, G., T. Kinal, and V. K. Srivastava (1984), "On the Moments of Ordinary Least Squares and Instrumental Variable Estimators in a General Structural Equation," *Econometrica* 52, 185–202.

________ (1985), "On the Joint and Marginal Densities of Instrumental Variable Estimators in a General Structural Equation," *Econometric Theory* 1, 53–72.

Hurwicz, L. (1950), "Least Squares Bias in Time Series," in T. C. Koopmans (ed.), *Statistical Inference in Dynamic Economic Models*, New York: Wiley.

Imhof, P. J. (1961), "Computing the Distribution of Quadratic Form in Normal Variables," *Biometrika* 48, 419–426.

Hoque, A. and T. Peters (1986), "Finite Sample Analysis of the ARMAX Models," *Sankhya* B, 48, 266–283.

Judge, G. and M. E. Bock (1978), *The Statistical Implications of Pre–Test and Stein–Rule Estimators in Econometrics*, North–Holland.

Kabe, D. G. (1963), "A Note on the Exact Distributions of the GCL Estimators in Two–Leading Overidentified Cases," *Journal of the American Statistical Association* 58, 535–537.

________ (1964), "On the Exact Distributions of the GCL Estimators in a Leading Three–Equation," *Journal of the American Statistical Association* 58, 881–894.

Kadane, J. (1971), "Comparison of k–Class Estimators When the Disturbances are Small," *Econometrica* 39, 723–737.

Kakwani, N. C. (1967), "The Unbiasedness of Zellner's Seemingly Unrelated Regression Equations Estimators," *Journal of the American Statistical Association.*

King, M. L. (1987), "Testing for Autocorrelation in Linear Regression Models: A Survey," in *Specification Analysis in the Linear Model*, Routledge and Kegan Paul.

Kmenta, J. (1986), *Elements of Econometrics*, New York: Wiley.

Knight, J. L. (1985), "The Moments of OLS and 2SLS When the Disturbances are Non–Normal," *Journal of Econometrics* 27, 39–60.

________ (1986), "Non–Normal Errors and the Distribution of OLS and 2SLS Structural Estimators," *Econometric Theory* 2, 75–102.

Koerts, J. and A. P. J. Abrahamse (1969), *On the Theory and Application of the General Linear Model*, Rotterdam University Press.

Lugannini, R. and S. O. Rice (1984), "Distribution of the Ratio of Quadratic Forms in Normal Variables—Numerical Methids, *SIAM Journal on Scientific and Statistical Computing* 5, 476–488.

Lye, J. N. (1987), "Some Further Results on the Distribution of Double k–Class Estimators," manuscript, University of Canterbury.

________ (1988), "On the Exact Distribution of a Ratio of Bilinear to Quadratic Form in Normal Variables with Econometric Applications," manuscript, University of Canterbury.

Maasoumi, E. (1989), *Contributions to Econometrics*, Vol. II, Cambridge University Press.

________ and A. Ullah (1987), "Specification Analysis in Special Rational Distributed Lag and Other Dynamic Models," *Journal of Quantitative Economics.*

Maekawa, K. (1987), "Finite Sample Properties of Several Predictors from an Autoregressive Model," *Econometric Theory* 3, 359–370.

Magnus, J. R. (1986), "The Exact Moments of a Ratio of Quadratic Forms in Normal Variable," *Annals d'Economie et de Statistique*, 4, 95–109.

Magee, L., A. Ullah, and V. K. Srivastava (1987), "Efficiency of Estimators in the Regression Model with First–Order Autoregressive Errors," in *Specification Analysis in the Linear Models*, Routledge and Kegan Paul.

Mariano, R. S. (1982), "Analytical Small–Sample Distribution Theory in Econometrics: The Simultaneous–Equations Case," *International Economic Review*, 503–533.

Mehta, J. S. and P. A. V. B. Swamy (1978), "The Existence of Moments of Some Simple Bayes Estimators of Coefficients in a Simultaneous Equations Model," *Journal of Econometrics* 7, 1–13.

Nagar, A. L. (1959), "The Bias and Moments Matrix of the General k–Class Estimators of the Parameters in Structural Equations," *Econometrica* 27, 575–595.

________ (1962), "Double k–Class Estimators of Parameters in Simultaneous Equations Models and Their small Sample Properties," *International Economic Review* 3, 168–188.

________ and S. N. Sahay (1978), "The Bias and Mean Squared Error of Forecasts From Partially Restricted Reduced Form," *Journal of Econometrics* 7, 227–243.

________ and A. Ullah (1973), "Note on Approximate Skewness and Kurtosis of the Two Stage Least Squares Estimator," *Indian Economic Review*, 70–80.

Nankervis, J. S. and N. E. Savin (1985), "Testing the Autoregressive Parameter with the t–Statistics," *Journal of Econometrics* 27, 143–162.

________ and ________ (1987), "Finite Sample Distributions of t and F Statistics in an AR(1) Model with an Exogenous Variable," *Econometric Theory* 3, 387–408.

Pagan, A. (1984), "Econometric Issues in the Analysis of Regressions with Generated Regressors," *International Economic Review* 25, 221–247.

Palm, F. C. and J. M. Sneek (1984), "Significance Tests and Spurious Correlation in Regression Models with Autocorrelated Errors," *Statistische Hefte* L5, 87–105.

Peters, T. (1986), *Least Squares in Dynamic Econometric Models*, Ph.D. Thesis, University of Western Ontario.

________ and W. Veloce (1988), "Robustness of Unit Root Tests in ARMA Models With Generalized ARCH Errors," manuscript, Brock University.

Phillips, P. C. B. (1977), "A General Theorem in the Theory of Asymptotic Expansions as Approximations to the Finite Sample Distributions of Econometric Estimators," *Econometrica* 65, 1517–1534.

________ (1980), "Finite Sample Theory and the Distributions of Alternative Estimators of the Marginal Propensity to Consume," *Review of Economic Studies*, Vol. 47, 183–224.

________ (1983a), "Exact Small Sample Theory in Simultaneous Equations Models," in *Handbook of Econometrics*, Vol. 1, Amsterdam: North–Holland.

________ (1983b), "ERA's: A New Approach to Small Sample Theory," *Econometrica* 51, 1505–1526.

________ (1985), "The Distribution of Matrix Quotients," *Journal of Multivariate Analysis* 16, 157–161.

________ (1986), The Exact Distribution of the Wald Statistic, *Econometrica*, 54, 881–895.

________ (1987), "Fractional Matrix Calculus and the Distribution of Multivariate Tests," in *Time Series and Econometric Modelling*, Boston: D. Reidell Press.

Power, S. and A. Ullah (1987), "Nonparametric Monte Carlo Density Estimation of Rational Expectations Estimators and Their t–Ratios," in *Advances in Econometrics*, JAI Press.

Racine, J. (1988), "Semi–Parametric Estimation in the Presence of Heteroskedasticity of Unknown Form," manuscript, University of Western Ontario.

Raj, B. and A. Ullah (1981), *Econometrics: A Random Coefficient Approach*, Croom Helm.

Richardson, D. H. (1968), "The Exact Distributions of a Structural Coefficient Estimator," *Journal of the American Statistical Association* 63, 1214–1226.

Rosenblatt, M. (1956), "Remarks on Some Nonparametric Estimates of a Density Function," *Annals of Mathematical Statistics* 27, 832–837.

Rothenberg, T. J. (1984), "Approximating the Distribution of Econometric Estimators and Test Statistics," in M. D. Intriligator and Z. Griliches (eds.), *Handbook of Econometrics*, Vol. 2, Amsterdam: North–Holland.

________ (1988), "Approximate Power Functions for Some Robust Tests of Regression Coefficients," *Econometrica*, 997–1019.

Sawa, T. (1972), "Finite Sample Properties of k–Class Estimators," *Econometrica* 40, 653–680.

________ (1978), "The Exact Moments of the Least Squares Estimator for the Autoregressive Model," *Journal of Econometrics* 8, 159–172.

Silverman, B. W. (1986), *Density Estimation for Statistics and Data Analysis*, New York: Chapman and Hall.

Smith, M. D. (1988) Convergent Series Expressions for Inverse Moments of Quadratic forms in Normal Variables, *The Australian Journal of Statistics* 30, 245–246.

________ (1988a), "On the Expectations of a Ratio of Forms in Normal Variables, DP #88–02, University of Sydney.

Srivastava, M. S. and C. G. Khatri (1979), *An Introduction to Multivariate Statistics*, New York: North–Holland.

Srivastava, V.K. and R. Tiwari (1976), "Evaluation of Expectation of Products of Stochastic Matrices," *Scandinavian Journal of Statistics* 3, 135–138.

________, J. L. Knight, and A. Agnihotri (1986), "Properties of k–Class Estimators in Simultaneous Equations Models with Not Necessarily Normal Disburbances," manuscript, University of Western Ontario.

Takeuchi, K. (1970), "Exact Sampling Moments of Ordinary Least Squares, Instrumental Variable and Two–Stage Least Squares Estimators, *International Economic Review* 11, 1–12.

Taneja, V. S. (1976), "Approximation to the Distribution of Indefinite Quadratic Forms in Noncentral Normal Variables," *Metron* 34, 255–268.

Taylor, W. E. (1983), "On the Relevance of Finite Sample Distribution Theory," *Econometric Reviews* 2, 1–39.

Ullah, A. (1971), *Statistical Estimation of Economic Relations in the Presence of Errors in Variables and In Equations*, Ph.D. Thesis, Delhi School of Economics.

________ (1974), "On the Sampling Distribution of Improved Estimators for Coefficients in Linear Regression," *Journal of Econometrics* 2, 143–150.

________ and A. Nagar (1974), "The Exact Mean of the Two State Least Squares Estimator of the Strutural Parameters in an Equation Having Three Endogenous Variables," *Econometrica* 42, 749–758.

________ and ________ (1987), "Unanticipated Macro Model Estimator," *Econometric Theory* 3, 163–167.

________ and ________ (1988), "On the Inverse Moments of Noncentral Wishart Matrix," manuscript, University of Western Ontario.

________ and R. S. Singh (1985), "The Estimation of Probability Density Functions and Its Applications in Econometrics," Technical Report 6, University of Western Ontario.

________, V. K. Srivastava and R. Chandra (1983), "Properties of Shrinkage Estimators in Linear Regression When Disturbances are Not Normal," *Journal of Econometrics* 21, 389–402.

Vinod, H. D. and A. Ullah (1981), *Recent Advances in Regression Methods*, Marcel Dekkar.

Wegge, L. (1971), "The Finite Sample Distribution of Least Squares Estimators with Stochastic Regressors," *Econometrica* 38, 241–251.

Zellner, A. (1962), "An Efficient Method of Estimating Seemingly Unrelated Regression and Test of Aggregation Bias," *Journal of the American Statistical Association.*

On Resampling Inference in Econometric Models

Jayasri Dutta

Barnard College, Columbia University

Abstract

This paper examines alternative applications of resampling methods to estimation and inference in econometric models. The major applications of resampling have been in the construction of sampling distributions. Here, we demonstrate that in models specified by moment condition, often referred to as generalised method of moments, resampling can be used to generate testable implications of these moment restrictions. We also use resampling techniques to correct for the bias of instrumental variables estimation. This estimates the leading term in the Nagar expansion for the bias of such an estimator. Monte Carlo experiments suggest that the correction can lead to sharp improvements in the bias of such estimators in small samples.

1 Introduction

Suppose we have a finite set of observations on some variables. *Resampling* refers , very generally, to a class of methods which use subsets of the original sample of observations. Suppose we observe $Z = [z_t; t = 1, \cdots, T)$. A resample is simply a subset of Z; and a resampling scheme is systematic method for generating such subsets. The simplest possible resampling scheme is a *partition*; this generates two, or more, mutually exclusive subsets of the original sample. The *jackknife* generates resamples by systematically deleting one observation at a time. Another resampling scheme, which has been used in time series observations is *recursive sampling*; this generates resamples by picking up one observation at a time, so that each resample contains the previous one . The *bootstrap* randomises the mechanism of generating resamples; each resample is random draw from the empirical frequency function of Z .

The traditional role of resampling was either as an aid to exploratory data analysis, or in testing for structural stability in parametric models. In data analysis, it is important to detect outliers . Once detected, their influence of such atypical observations on inference and prediction can be bounded. The natural method of detecting outlying observations in a body of data is to examine the data part by part, and check that it is indeed well-balnced relative to whatever prior notions of symmetry one may hold. Resampling thus provides a natural framework for measuring the effects of individual observations on estimation procedures. The jackknifing scheme has often been used to formally test for the presence of gross errors in the data (for example, Krasker *et. al.* (1983)) .

The use of sample partitioning schemes for tests of structural stability is probably more familiar in econometrics, from the work of Chow (1960) to test for constancy of the regression coefficients; and Goldfeld and Quandt (1969) for constancy of the error variance. Both types of techniques rely on an elementary resampling method. Under the maintained hypothesis that the data is homogenous, or identically distributed, the distribution of sample statistics is identical in subsamples of equal size. This allows for a formal test of this hypothesis to be based on the heterogeneity of subsample distributions. This idea was extended to recursive sampling by Brown, Durbin, and Evans (1975) ; the advantage of many , as opposed to one resample is that smoother schemes of parameter variation can be detected. This class of methods are natural to ordered data, and have been applied succesfully in time series analysis.

Perhaps the most exciting development in the use of resampling techniques comes from the work of Efron (summarised in Efron (1982)) . In several non-standard situations, the sampling distribution of test statistics is not available in closed form, at least in finite samples. As a result, the use of classical methods of approximating sampling distributions may force excessive reliance on limiting properties, or strict restrictions on the data generating distribution. A possible alternative is to simulate the distribution of the statistic based on the data itself. In a particular application, there is only one sample; however, this generates many possible sub-samples that we could have observed. The distribution of the statistic can be approximated by the empirical distributions generated by randomised resampling over the available set of observations:the " bootstrap". Under appropriate regularity conditions, this distribution estimates the true sampling distribution of the statistic, and the distributional properties of a variety of test statistics can be generated by sample replication alone, without putting too much faith in convergence to limit distributions.

Resampling has a potentially rich set of applications in estimation as well. This was evident from two papers by Wald ((1940),(1952)). The earlier paper , which is a classic in the estimation of errors in variables models, is concerned with finding a consistent estimation technique. Least squares is generally inconsistent , because of the correlation of the explanatory variables with the residuals. An instrumental variables estimator is consistent only if the instrument is uncorrelated with the residuals. The model is specified by the condition that the residuals have zero mean. Now, this condition is invariant to subsample choice, and hence to any resampling scheme. Obviously, if $Eu_t = 0$ hold for all t, then $E(\sum_t w_t u_t) = 0$ for any choice of weights. Thus, vectors of resampling weights provide precisely the instruments required. It is clear from this writing that as far as consistency is concerned, any resampling scheme suffices. In the bivariate model, we need only resample once; and Wald used the simplest weighting scheme, which is partitioning. The second paper, published in one of the Cowles Commission volumes, is concerned with inference in incomplete models, i.e. models which do not lead to unique reduced forms; the extreme form of such a model is one where all variables are endogenous, i.e. a multivariate errors in variables model. The method suggested there uses resampling to construct confidence intervals for the parameters , since simple hypotheses about the parameters generates testable restrictions on the reduced form. In both models, the problem is that there are insufficient restrictions to identify the parameters; however, the maintained hypothesis generates restrictions on every resample; taken together, these can be used to identify, and possibly estimate these parameters.

The first part of this paper builds on this notion. The most general approach to estimation and testing in econometric models relies on "specification by moment conditions . Thus, the econometric model consists of the restriction that a known function of the data and parameters , say $m(z_t, \theta)$ has expectation zero; if the restrictions are of the same dimension as the parameter θ , (i.e.the model is identified), they can be used to find method of moment estimators . In standard models, this yields classical estimators , such as least squares or instrumental variables. If the restrictions are of higher dimension (i.e. the model is overidentified), they can be simultaneously used for esstimation , and for testing, yielding the so-called generalised method of moments estimates and tests (e.g. Hansen(1982) and Newey(1987)) The approach of Wald fits in very naturally in this framework. Consider a model with K parameters, i.e. $\theta \in \mathbf{R}^K$; and identifying restrictions of the form $Em(z_t; \theta) = 0$, where m is also K-dimensional. Consider possible resamples , summarised as vectors $w_r = [\cdots, w_{rt}, \cdots]$, each normalised to sum to one. The fact that the specifying conditions are invariant to resampling implies that the restrictions $E \sum_t w_{rt} m(z_t; \theta) = 0$ are true. Hence, if one takes resampling into account, there are always overidentifying restrictions. While this may or may not be useful for estimation, these restrictions are testable. We demonstrate the nature of resampling specification tests which follow from this approach, and illustrate their properties in the linear regression model.

In the second part, we demonstrate the use of resampling methods to correct for the bias of instrumental variables estimates in an errors in variables model. In such models, this and other estimators are known to be consistent, but biased in finite samples. The exact bias of the estimator can be worked out in the Gaussian case. Apart from being tedious, these results are mostly unusable for bias correction because the bias as well as higher moments depend on unknown parameters, including parameters of the data generating process which are not specified by the restrictions defining the model. The Nagar expansion (Nagar(1959)) derives the bias of such an estimator; the leading terms of this bias continue to be functions of unknown parameters . We suggest techniques for estimating these parameters by the use of resampling techniques. Monte Carlo experiments for a small example suggest that the bias-corrected estimator can achieve substantial gains in small samples, where gains are measured in terms of the proportional bias. These results are quite exploratory in nature; however, the good numerical performance suggests that they may be worth more extensive study.

2 On Estimation with Resampling

We will consider a model as fully described by the parameter space and the moment conditions. For any set of observations, this specifies the estimation method. The approach of defining the model directly in terms of moment restrictions is a useful device . Apart from the economy of notation, it allows simultaneously for models estimated by maximum likelihood, minimum distance, and method of moments. For example, the linear regression m model can be specified as $y = x\beta + u; Eu|x = 0$ or by the moment condition $Ex'(y - x\beta) = 0$, which is implied by the model. Now, one may specify the estimator as the sample analog $\frac{1}{T}\sum_{t=1}^{T} x_t(y_t - x_t'b) = 0$. In this approach, the estimator and the parameters are defined dually, in terms of the sample and the population moments respectively. The work of Huber(1983) on M-estimation provides the natural framework for analysing such models .

2.1 Moment Restrictions

The set of observable variables in the model are $z \in Z \subseteq R^N$; the parameter space is finite, written as $\theta \in \Theta \subseteq R^K$. The moment conditions are written in terms of a function $m(z, \theta)$; with $m : Z \times \Theta \rightarrow R^K$. The moment restriction is $Em(z, \theta) = 0$.

To use this as a specifying condition, we have to define the probability distributions generating the data. We will assume that the data are independently , but possibly non-identically distributed.

Assumption 1 *The data generating process is defined by the sequence $F_t; t = 1, 2, \cdots$ For each t, F_t is a probability distribution on Z. The sequence of observations $z_t; t = 1, 2, \cdots$ are stochastically independent ; for any T, the probability distribution of $[z_1, \cdots, z_T]$ is written as $\prod_{t=1}^{T} F_t$.*

Assumption 2 *The moment function $m : Z \times \Theta \rightarrow R^K$ is continuous in θ for each $z \in Z$; and F_t-measurable for each $\theta \in \Theta$. The moment condition is $Em(z; \theta) = 0$.*

The moment conditions are in terms of the population moments of $m(z; \theta)$. The corresponding sample moments define the estimators ,i.e. the estimator $\hat{\theta}$ solves the equation

$$(T^{-1} \sum_{t=1}^{T} m(z_t, \theta) = 0.$$

To continue with the regression example, the moment restriction is $Ex'(y - x\beta) = 0$; and the estimator solves $X'(y - X\beta) = 0$, which yields, of course, the ordinary least squares estimate. In a model estimated by maximum likelihood, the moment conditions are just the score equations; let $L(Z; \theta) = \sum_{t=1}^{T} L(z_t, \theta)$ be the log-likelihood function. Write $m(z; \theta) = \partial L(z, \theta)/\partial\theta$; the restrictions are $Em(z, \theta) = 0$ –the score equation–, and the estimator is maximum likelihood. For estimators defined by the minimization of a distance function, the moment functions are just the first order conditions for a minimum. In many econometric applications, including linear and non-linear regression models as well as models with instrumental variables, the moment conditions can be written in the form $m(z, \theta) = z_1.g(z_2, \theta)$, i.e. an inner product of some of the variables with a parametric functions. These models are specified by orthogonality conditions.

The moment conditions define the parameters as characteristics of the data-. generating process, dually. If the data z_t are drawn i.i.from a distribution F, we can define, for each $\theta \in \Theta$, the function $m(F; \theta) = Em(z, \theta) = \int m(z; \theta)dF$; and θ solves $m(F; \theta) = 0$. In the linear regression problem, this is simply the definition $\beta = [V(x)]^{-1}cov(x, y)$. If the data is not identically distributed, there is nothing to ensure that the moments $m(F_t; \theta)$ and $m(F_{t'}; \theta)$ will coincide for all values of the parameters. We will assume that the equations $m(F_t; \theta) = 0$ have a unique common root. This will clearly be satisfied whenever the data are identically distributed, but does not require that this hold.

Assumption 3 *There exists $\theta_o \in \Theta$ such that for each t,*

$$m(F_t; \theta) = 0$$

if and only if $\theta = \theta_o$.

This assumptions defines θ_o as the true value of the parameter; since the sequence of data generating processes F_t are such that $m(F_t; \theta_o) = 0$, this restricts the possible heterogeneity of the data distributions; for example, in the linear regression model, the data distributions must maintain a constant variance-covariance ratio.

The next assumption ansures smoothness of $m(.; \theta)$ locally to the true value.

Assumption 4 *Let $U \in \Theta$ be any neighborhood containing θ_o. As U shrinks to θ_o ,*

$$E \sup_{\theta' \in U} |m(z; \theta') - m(z; \theta_o)| \to 0,$$

, for almost all z.

These assumptions ensure that the estimate $\hat{\theta}_T$ is strongly consistent for θ_o; and further, that $\sqrt{T}(\hat{\theta}_T - \theta_o)$ is asymptotically normal. We will state thes results without proof; these results are fairly standard, and can be shown to be true under somewhat weaker conditions (e.g. Huber(1983)).

Lemma 1 *If assumptions A.1-A.4 hold, $\hat{\theta}_t$ converges to θ_o almost surely as $T \to \infty$.*

In testing, the quantity of interest is the asymptotic variance -covariance matrix of the estimator $\hat{\theta}_T$, which we state below.

Lemma 2 *The asymptotic variance-covariance matrix of*

$$d_T = T^{-1/2}(\hat{\theta}_T - \theta_0)$$

is equal to $V(\theta_o) = A^{-1}BA'^{-1}$; *where*

$$A = \lim_{T\to\infty} \frac{1}{T} \sum_{t=1}^{T} Em'(z_t; \theta_o);$$

and

$$B = \lim_{t\to\infty} \frac{1}{T} \sum_{t=1}^{T} Em^2(z_t; \theta_o).$$

2.2 Resampling

Consider a sample $Z = [z_1, \ldots, z_T]$, of observations on z. A resample of this is any set $Z(R)$ each of whose elements are picked from Z. The simplest possible resamples are those which are proper subsets of Z; for example,

$$Z(R) = [z_1, \cdots, z_{T*}];$$

with $T* < T$. A resample can also contain more than one copy of a single observation,z_t;for example, consider

$$Z(R) = [z_1, z_1, z_2, \cdots, z_T].$$

A *resampling scheme* is a systematic method of generating resamples from a fixed set of observations; the individual resamples need not be mutually exclusive, or even exhaustive. A resampling scheme generates $Z(R_1), \cdots, Z(R_N)$, such that for each i, $Z(R_i)$ is a resample of Z. The *jackknife* is a resampling scheme which generates T resamples

$$Z(R_i) = [z_1, z_2, \cdots, z_{i-1}, z_{i+1}, \cdots, z_T].$$

The *bootstrap* generates $N \geq T$ resamples by randomly choosing elements z_t from Z.*Recursive Sampling* is a scheme which generates $N = T - R$ resamples such that

$$Z(R_i) = [z_{r+i}, \cdots, z_T].$$

Equivalently, a resampling scheme can be characterised by a weights matrix $W = ((w_{it}))$, where w_{it} is the weight of the t'th observation in the ith resample; clearly, $w_{it} \geq 0$. For the jackknife, the weights matrix is $W = ee' - I$, with e the unit vector; in bootstrapping, W is a (not necessarily square) matrix of random elements; each row is chosen from a uniform distribution on the simplex. The drawing of rows is independent. In recursive sampling, the matrix of weights is lower triangular, and all rows have equal elements adding upto one. We will use a slight generalization of the jackknife scheme, which we call the δ-jackknife; for any positive value of δ, the weights matrix is $W_\delta = ee' - (1-\delta)I$; thus, the t-th resample assigns weight δ to the t-th observation, and weight one to all other observations. Obviously,$\delta = 0$ yields the usual delete-one jackknife discussed above.

For any resampling scheme, we can generate the corresponding sequence of moment restrictions. Since these restrictions are used as estimating equations, this also allows a sequence of estimators to be defined correspondingly. Consider any row of W, written as w_i'. Define, correspondingly,

$$m_{Ti}(Z_T;\theta) = \sum_{t=1}^{T} w_{it} m(z_t, \theta)$$

as the resampled equation; and the estimate $\hat{\theta_{Tt}}$ is the solution to

$$m_{Tt}(Z;\theta) = 0$$

For example, in the linear regression model, the δ- jacknifed estimator β_i minimises

$$\sum_{t=1}^{T} u_t^2 + (\delta - 1)u_i^2.$$

The entire sequence of resampled estimates are

$$b(\delta) = [b_1(\delta), \ldots, b_T(\delta)].$$

Now define $m_{Tt}(Z_T, \hat{\theta_T})$, as the resampled moment restriction evaluated at the maximum likelihood estimate. With an assumption about the sequence of weights, we can state the limit properties of the resampled estimates and the resampled moment restrictions respectively.

Assumption 5 *The sequence of weights $w_{Tt}; t = 1, \ldots, T$ satisfy , for each T, the properties*

$$(1) \sum_{t=1}^{T} w_{Tt} = 1;$$

$$(2) \lim_{T \to \infty} \sum_{t=1}^{T} w_{Tt}^2 = 0.$$

There exists a positive sequence $\omega_t > 0, t = 1, \vdots,$ such that for each summable sequence y_t,

$$(3) \lim_{T \to \infty} \sum_{t=1}^{T} (T w_{Tt}^2 y_t) - \omega_t y_t) = 0$$

Note that the jackknife, the bootstrap, and the δ-jackknife all satisfy this assumption. Under this condition, and the ones previously utilised, we have the resampled being consistent; and the resampled moment restrictions are asymptotically normal.

Lemma 3 *Under the conditions of Lemma 1, the quantity*

$$\sum_{t=1}^{T} (\hat{\theta_{Tt}} - \theta_0)/T$$

converges to zero almost surely as $T \to \infty$.

Under the conditions ensuring the applicability of the central limit thorem to the estimate $\hat{\theta}_T$, the quantity $T^{1/2} m_{Tt}$ has an asymptotic normal distribution, with zero mean.

Lemma 4 *The asymptotic variance covariance matrix of*

$$d_{mT} = T^{1/2} m_{Tt}$$

is equal to

$$B(\omega) = lim_T \sum_{t=1}^{T} \omega_t E(m(z_t; \theta_0)^2).$$

Both lemmas are proved by taking the Taylor's expansion of individual elements $m(z_t;\theta_T)$ around $m(z_t;\theta)$. The uniform convergence conditions ensure that the second and higher order terms of the Taylor's expansion are bounded and converging to zero. It follows that $\hat{\theta_{Tt}} - \theta \doteq -(\sum w_{Tt}m(z_t;\theta)/\sum w_{Tt}m'(z_t;\theta)$. The consistency of resampled estimates immediately follows.

Next, note that

$$m_{Tt}(\theta_T) = m_{Tt}(\theta_0) + (\theta_T - \theta_0)m'_{Tt}(\theta_0)$$

for each Z; the variance of the second term is of order lower than $1/T$. Multiply through by $T^{1/2}$; taking limits of the variance of the first term yields the asymptotic variance result.

We propose two kinds of applications of resampling to inference in models defined by moment conditions. In the first place, they can be used to generate specification tests , even in models without overidentifying restrictions. The asymptotic normality of the resampled moment condition allows chi-square tests to be based on any weights sequence satisfying the mild conditions stated .The heuristic is quite simple. Suppose we have the moment restrictions $Em(z_t,\theta) = 0$, which are the specifying conditions of the problem. In generating estimators, we usually use only an implication of the full set of restrictions. Typically, with M-estimators, this is the sample-moment condition which is $\sum Em(z_t,\theta) = 0$. Clearly, the full set of conditions imply many more restrictions; in particular, that the expectation of any linear combination of the $m(z_t;\theta)$ is zero. Consider the particular linear combinations which are the resampled moment conditions $m_{Tt}(Z_T,\theta)$, corresponding to a scheme W. Under the maintained hypothesis, this has zero expectation for each i, and under additional regularity conditions, is asymptotically normal. Under the maintained hypothesis, the estimator $\hat{\theta}_T$ is consistent, and the the resampled moment restrictions, evaluated at this estimate, has the same distribution. A violation of this is therefore evidence against the maintained hypothesis that $Em(z_t;\theta_0)$ is equal to zero for all t, and a common root θ_0. In the linear regression model, we can set up an exact test procedure; because of the linearity of the moment conditions, the exact distribution can be derived in the Gaussian case. In the following section, we discuss the exact structure and interpretation of resampling specification tests in that model. As the results here indicate, the testing procedure is of much greater generality.

The alternative application is for situations where the estimator $\hat{\theta}$ is biased . The leading terms in the expansion of the bias of such an estimator can be shown to depend on the moments of $m(z_t, \theta)$ and functions of z_t. We consider a very simple case of instrumental variables estimation in the linear model, where the Nagar expansion for bias is applicable. The leading term in the bias of is estimated by resampling; we estimate the expectation of functions such as $f(z_t)m(z_t; \theta)$ by the sample moments of $f(z_t)m(z_t; \theta_t)$. The resampling method used is the Bootstrap . Monte Carlo experiments for a very simple case suggest that such a bias-correction can lead to substantial improvements in small samples.

3 Resampling Specification Tests in Linear Regression

In this Section, we construct a test procedure based on resampling in the linear regression model. This model, with errors normally distributed, has a structure simple enough to allow for exact testing, and one can find confidence intervals for finite samples. With non-linear models, or with other estimation methods other than linear least-squares, this fails, so that testing requires critical regions based on asymptotic distributions or approximations.

The model is the usual one, with standard notation. We write

$$y_t = x_t'\beta + u_t \tag{1}$$

where x_t is a vector of explanatory variables, assumed fixed and nonstochastic. The vector $u = [\ldots, u_t, \ldots]'$ is independently and identically distributed as normal, with zero mean and finite variance σ^2. The least squares estimator solves the minimization problem

$$\min_{\beta} Q(y, X, \beta) = \frac{1}{T} \sum_{t=1}^{T} (y_t - x_t'\beta)^2 \tag{2}$$

Consider any resample W, which picks observation t with weight w_t , normalised to set $\sum w_t$ equal to one. The reweighted criterion function Q_w can be written as

$$Q_w(y, X; \beta) = \sum_{t=1}^{T} w_t(y - x_t'\beta)^2, \tag{3}$$

and the corresponding minimisation problem yields a weighted least squares estimate

$$b_w = (\sum w_t x_t x_t')^{-1} (\sum w_t x_t y_t). \tag{4}$$

A resampling scheme is a set of resamples $(\ldots, W_i, \ldots)$, which corresponds to a sequence of minimisation problems , and hence, a sequence of weighted least squares estimates $(\ldots, b_i, \ldots)$. Put in this framework, the alternative schemes for resampling suggested in various parts of the literature can be understood simply as alternative ways of choosing the weights sequence W_i. The jackknife is a scheme which sets

$$W_i = (w, \ldots, 0, w, \ldots); w > 0 \tag{5}$$

By the normalisation rule, $w = \frac{1}{T-1}$. The bootstrap is generated by picking independent draws of a binary variable as $w*_{it}$; and normalise each row to set $w_{it} = \frac{w*_{it}}{\sum_t w*_{it}}$. Of course, these are not the only possible resampling schemes; for example, in nearest neighbour methods, it is usual to choose $w_{it} = w$ for $|t - i| < n$, and zero otherwise, n being the neighborhood size.

The jackknife has the attractive property of being square , that is, the number of resamples is the same as the number of observations, and symmetric, so that $w_{ii} = w_{tt}$ and $w_{it} = w_{ti}$. As demonstrated by Wu(1987), this allows for order preservation , which the bootstrap does not, so that the resulting inference is robust to ordered departures from the maintained hypothesis, such as monotone heteroskedasticity. We will use a smoothed version of the jackknife (the δ- jackknife), which continues to enjoy these properties. For $\delta \geq 0$, define the resampling scheme as

$$w_{tt} = \frac{\delta}{\delta + T - 1}; w_{it} = \frac{1}{\delta + T - 1}. \tag{6}$$

Clearly, for $\delta = 0$, we have the usual, or delete-one jackknife. For $\delta = 1$, each resample is simply a copy of the original sample. for values of δ greater than one, this scheme amounts to duplicating the t-th observation in order to generate the t-th resample.

The linearity of estimates in this models allows us to write the sequence of resampled estimates in closed form. Consider the t'th resample, defined by weights $\frac{1}{\delta+T-1}(1, \ldots, \delta, \ldots, 1)$. The least squares estimate , written as $b_t(\delta)$, is

$$b_t(\delta) = (X'X + (\delta - 1)x_t x_t')^{-1}(X'y + (\delta - 1)x_t y_t). \tag{7}$$

Expliciting for the term $(X'X + cx_t x_t')$ yields

$$\begin{aligned} b_t(\delta) &= b + (1-\delta)\frac{(X'X)^{-1}x_t x_t'}{1-(1-\delta)h_{tt}} b \\ &\quad - \frac{1-\delta}{1-(1-\delta)h_{tt}}(X'X)^{-1}x_t' y_t \end{aligned} \tag{8}$$

where $h_{tt} = x_t(X'X)^{-1}x_t'$, the diagonal elements of the hat matrix $H = X(X'X)^{-1}X'$. From this, it follows that

$$b_t(\delta) = \frac{\delta b + (1-\delta)(1-h_{tt})b_t(0)}{1-(1-\delta)h_{tt}} \tag{9}$$

where $b_t(0)$ is defined to be the t-th jackknifed estimate,and b is the least squares estimator applied to the full sample, as before. Further, the δ-residuals are

$$u_t(\delta) = y_t - x_t' b_t(\delta) = \frac{y - x_t' b}{1-(1-\delta)h_{tt}} \tag{10}$$

Writing $\hat{u} = (I - H)u = Mu$, the least squares residuals in usual notation, we have the vector of δ-residuals as

$$u(\delta) = \Delta \hat{u} = \Delta M u, \tag{11}$$

where Δ is the diagonal matrix with elements $[1-(1-\delta)h_{tt}]^{-1}$

It follows that the sum of squared δ-residuals is equal to

$S(\delta) = u'M\Delta^2 Mu = \hat{u}'\Delta^2\hat{u}$. Further, under the maintained hypothesis, the vector $u(\delta)$ has a singular normal distribution with zero mean and variance-covariance matrix equal to $\sigma^2\Delta M\Delta$. This can now be used to set up a specification test as a test of significance.

We will consider specification testing procedures based on the exact distribution of the quadratic form $q(V) = u'(\delta)Vu(\delta)$, normalised by the least squares variance. For each V, it is possible to define confidence intervals, and hence, critical regions of specified size. We will show that for alternative choices of V, we define the direction of the alternative tested for.

Define a class of test statistics as

$$t(V;\delta) = \frac{u'(\delta)Vu(\delta)}{\hat{u}'\hat{u}} = \frac{u'M\Delta V\Delta Mu}{u'Mu} \tag{12}$$

for positive semi-definite, symmetric matrices V. The test procedure rejects H_o for large values of $t(V;\delta)$. With normally distributed errors, this statistic has certain properties which allow for exact testing, as well as the interpretation of test results as providing evidence in alternative directions. The statistic, which is in the form of a ratio of quadratic forms in the vector normal variable u, is familiar from exact tests for covariance structure , employed, for example, in the work of Kadiyala(1969), Durbin and Watson(1971), Szroeter(1978) , as well as many others .

The first property, which follows from the structure of the test statistic, is that the statistic $t(V;\delta)$ is invariant to changes of the scale parameter σ^2. As a result, its critical value can be evaluated relative to the standard normal distribution; and perhaps more importantly, this critical region is unchanged under scale mixtures of the normal, which includes the Student's t -distribution.

The second, which is useful in evaluating the actual critical values, allows the statistic to be expressed in terms of a smaller dimensional normal vector. The matrix M is symmetric, idempotent, of rank $T - K$. This can be orthogonalised by a matrix R, of order $T \times (T - K)$ such that $RR' = M$, and $R'R = I$

Further, R can be chosen to simultaneously diagonalise the

matrix $\Delta V \Delta$. Then

$$t(V;\delta) = \frac{\hat{u}'\Delta V \Delta \hat{u}}{\hat{u}'\hat{u}} = \frac{u'RLR'u}{u'RR'u} \tag{13}$$

where L is a diagonal matrix of the eigenvalues of $R'\Delta V \Delta R$. By construction, $z = \frac{R'u}{\sigma}$ has a standard multivariate normal distribution of dimension $T-K$; hence,

$$t(V;\delta) = \frac{z'Lz}{z'z} \tag{14}$$

For any choice of V, we can find a critical value , c, for a preassigned size by evaluating the probability

$$P(\sum_{i=1}^{T-K} (l_i - c)z_i^2 > 0) = \alpha \tag{15}$$

from the standard normal distribution . Alternative evaluation methods have been discussed and applied; see, for example , Sargan and Bhargava(1983) for a full discussion.

The interesting question, of course, is the choice of the weights matrix V and its implication for testing. To proceed to this, we consider the following Lemma, first proved by Anderson(1948).

Lemma 5 *Let the maintained hypothesis be $y = X\beta + u$, and $u \sim N(0, \sigma^2 A)$, with $\sigma^2 > 0$, and A positive definite and symmetric. Write $A = (I - \theta B)^{-1}$. The locally most powerful test for the hypothesis $H_o : \theta = 0$, against $H_a : \theta > 0$, rejects for large values of $q(B) = \frac{\hat{u}'B\hat{u}}{\hat{u}'\hat{u}}$.*

This lemma has been useful in several applications, perhaps the most notable being the derivation of the Durbin-Watson test. In the linear regression model, a uniformly most powerful test for alternative covariance structures does not exist, except in the trivial situations where the OLS anf GLS coincide. The locally most powerful test maximises the slope of the power curve locally to the null hypothesis. This lemma can be used to derive tests for a particular covariance structure; alternatively, it can be used to derive the direction of the alternative for a particular test statistic of the form $q(B)$. In this case, the direction of the alternative is simply $\theta > 0$.

Notice that for each V, the test statistic $t(V;\delta)$ can be written in the form $q(B)$, by setting $B = \Delta V \Delta$, or equivalently, the covariance matrix of u under the θ- alternative as equal to $A = (I - \theta\Delta V\Delta)^{-1}$. Interestingly, this is the case whether we test directly for the size of the resampled objective function, or for the moment conditions.

Connsider first the test induced by $V = I$. This implies that the test statistic $t(I;\delta)$ is just $\frac{u'(\delta)u(\delta)}{\hat{u}'\hat{u}}$, the ratio of the lengths of the resampled to the ordinary residuals. This implies a natural alternative of

$$A_\theta = (I - \theta\Delta^2)^{-1} \tag{16}$$

which is a diagonal matrix with diagonal elements

$$a_{tt}(\theta) = \frac{(1-\delta h_{tt})^2}{(1-\delta h_{tt})^2 - \theta} \tag{17}$$

For values of δ in $[0,1)$, a_{tt} is increasing in h_{tt}. Thus, this specification test tests in the direction of variable-dependent heteroskedasticity. For example, if there is random variation in the fitted regression, so that

$$y_t = (x_t'\beta)(1 + e_t) + u_t, \tag{18}$$

with e_t independent of u_t, the variance of the composite error terms will depend on x_t. If the vector e is independent and identically distributed, the diagonal covariance matrix of the error term will have diagonal elements positively correlated with h_{tt}; in this sense, this test can be thought of as a finite sample version of the test for random coefficient variation suggested by Breusch and Pagan (1979). It is not an exactly corresponding version because the true covariance matrix depends on the parameter vector β under the alternative.

Another way of interpreting the results of this test comes from the role of the hat matrix in robust regression . Huber (1983) , as well as Krasker et. al. (1983) identify the quantities h_{tt} as measures of leverage ; in a badly balanced design, these quantities differ from their average value , K/T, significantly, and large values of h_{tt} are indicative of the fact that the particular observation has decisive influence. If, in addition, this observation is a true outlier – for example, has a large variance relative to the rest –the quality of the inference is questionable. Thus, this type of specification test is a check that high leverage points are not truly outlying.

An alternative specification test, which is more faithful to the moment restrictions approach, tests the defining condition of the model, which, in this case, is

$$Em(Z;\beta) = E(X'u) = EX'(y - X\beta) = 0 \tag{19}$$

Evaluating this restriction at the resampled residuals, we can write

$$EX'u(\delta) = 0 \tag{20}$$

Under the null hypothesis, the quantity $z(\delta) = X'u(\delta)$ is distributed as normal, with zero mean and variance covariance matrix

$$Ez(\delta)z'(\delta) = \sigma^2 X'\Delta M \Delta X \tag{21}$$

Accordingly, write the (chi-squared) test statistic as

$$t(V;\delta) = \frac{z'(\delta)Sz(\delta)}{\hat{u}'\hat{u}} \tag{22}$$

with $S = (X'\Delta M \Delta X)^{-1}$. Asymptotically, $T.t(V)$ is distributed as chi-squared with K degrees of freedom. In finite samples, the distribution is not chi-squared ; in the normal case, this is not a serious problem since the critical values can be evaluated for any exact sample, given the observations X; note that

$$V = \Delta X(X'\Delta M \Delta X)^{-1} X'\Delta \tag{23}$$

Since the natural family of alternatives are represented by the variance covariance matrices $(I - \theta V)^{-1}$, it follows that the moment test in fact tests for variable dependent covariance structure in the errors in finite samples. Notice that asymptotically, the chi-square test tests for the (resampled) orthogonality conditions $Ex_i'u_j = 0$.

4 Bias Correction with Resampling

In models which do not conform to the linear regression structure, we typically deal with estimators which are consistent but biased in finite samples. The finite sample moments of such estimators , even when they are available in closed form, usually involve unknown parameters; for example, to take a very simple case, suppose we are interested in estimating an errors in variables model by instrumental variables. The set of variables, including the instruments, are written as Z;, and the parameters to be estimated as θ. The estimator, call this $\hat{\theta}_T$ is a function of the observations Z_T, so that the moments of the estimator usually write as

$$\mu_T(r) = E(\hat{\theta})^r = g_r(\Omega_T, \theta) \tag{24}$$

where Ω_T are parameters of the joint distribution of the observations not restricted by the model itself; typically, for example, this includes cross moments of the instrument with the variables included in the relation. As a result, the possibility of correcting for bias, or variance, is limited by the extent to which we are willing to restrict the parameters of the data generating process.

If we are indeed able to estimate the parameters Ω_T, this yields a natural method of bias-correction . Consider a consistent estimate θ_1; the bias corrected estimate, call this θ_2, solves

$$\theta_1 = g_1(\Omega_T, \theta_2) \tag{25}$$

for g non-linear in θ, it is possible to set up an iteration routine with θ_1 as the initial value.

We will use an approximation for the first moment of an instrumental variables estimate, which liinearises the function g_1 ; this expansion is , of course, due to Nagar, and has been used in approximating the moments of alternative estimators and test statistics. The linearization allows the solution to be displayed in closed form. The essential problem remains the estimation of Ω parameters. We demonstrate a resampling method for a particularly simple case.

The model is written as follows.

$$y_{1t} = \gamma y_{2t} + x_t'\beta + u_t \tag{26}$$

where the residual u_t is independently and identically distributed with zero mean ; the variables x_t are nonstochastic. Further, y_{2t} is stochastic, and correlated with u_t ; and we can observe an instrumental variable z_t, such that

$$Ez_t u_t = 0 \tag{27}$$

The Instrumental Variables Estimate of γ is

$$\hat{\gamma} = \frac{z'My_1}{z'My_2} \tag{28}$$

where $M = I - X(X'X)^{-1}X'$, as usual. This estimator is biased in finite samples, since

$$E\hat{\gamma} = \gamma + E\frac{z'Mu}{z'My_2} \tag{29}$$

so that the bias of the estimator is the expectation of the ratio of quadratic forms. For notational convenience, we will define $s_{01} = z'My_1$ and $s_{02} = z'My_2$. The expectation of the instrumental variables estimator can be written as

$$E\hat{\gamma} = \gamma + E\frac{s_{01} - \gamma s_{02}}{s_{02}} \tag{30}$$

where $E(s_{01}) = \gamma E(s_{02})$, from the defining condition of the instrument. The Nagar expansion of moments follows from Taylor's expansion of the ratio of random variables n/d as

$$\frac{n}{d} = \frac{n}{1 + (d - Ed)/Ed} \doteq \frac{n}{Ed}(1 - \frac{d - Ed}{Ed}) \tag{31}$$

ignoring higher order terms in the expansion of the denominator. Taking expectations yields

$$E(\frac{n}{d}) \doteq \frac{En}{Ed} - \frac{cov(n,d)}{(Ed)^2} \tag{32}$$

Applying this to the variable $\hat{\gamma}$, and after mechanical substitutions, we have

$$E\hat{\gamma} \doteq -b_0(\Omega) + \gamma b_1(\Omega) \tag{33}$$

endequation where

$$b_0(\Omega) = \frac{cov(s_{01}s_{02})}{(Es_{02})^2} \tag{34}$$

$$b_1(\Omega) = \frac{Es_{02}^2}{(Es_{02})^2} \tag{35}$$

The bias corrected estimator is then defined as

$$\gamma_1 = \frac{\hat{\gamma} + b_0}{b_1} \tag{36}$$

whenever the b_i can be suitably estimated. The parameters Ω are moments of the random variables s_{0i}. For a given sample of size T, say, the quantity s_{0i} are in the form of sample sums, so that for each sample, there is only one observation. We will estimate this by bootstrap methods, as follows. Draw B bootsrap samples of size T from the set of observations $(y_{1t}, y_{2t}, z_t, x_t); t = 1, \ldots, T$ is chosen with equal probability. If the data is independently and identically distributed, we know that the computed bootstrap moments such as $\hat{s_{02}} = \frac{1}{B}\sum_{j=1}^{B} s_{02}^j$ is unbiased for the corresponding sample moments, where expectations are with respect to the randomization mechanism which generates the bootsrap (Efron (1982)). Once this is done, we have direct bootstrap estimates of b_i, and hence, a bias corrected instrumental variables estimator.

The unsatisfactory aspect of this analysis is precisely from the requirement that the data be independently and identically distributed. In order that this kind of method be more generally applicable, it is important that the techniques be reasonably robust to the possibility of the data generating process being either heterogenous, or dependent, or both. Unfortunately, the bootstrap technique is sensitive to both kinds of violations. With dependent data, the order of appearance is important, and cannot be maintained if the observations are replicated one at a time . Alternative methods, such as random subset sampling, may provide a more robust technique. With heterogeneity, the problem becomes further intractable, because the nuisance parameters Ω_T vary over different subsamples. As a result, the bias of the estimators are sample dependent, and cannot be replicated in resampling unless we impose more stringent structure on the data generating process.

4.1 A Numerical Example

The results of some Monte Carlo experiments with Bootstrap bias correction are reported in the Tables following. We consider a very simple example of instrumental variables estimation in a bivariate errors in variable model. The model is written as

$$y_{1t} = y_{2t}\gamma + u_t \tag{37}$$

such that y_{2t} is correlated with u_t; and an instrumental variable z_t is independent of u_t. All variables are independently and identically distributed. We generate (y_{1t}, y_{2t}, z_t) from a normal distribution with mean zero and variance-covariance matrix Σ. The elements of Σ are restricted so that

$$\sigma_{13} = \gamma\sigma_{23} \tag{38}$$

$$\sigma_{12} = (\gamma + \alpha)\sigma_{22} \tag{39}$$

We choose the variance terms σ_{ii} to be equal to unity. This leaves three free parameters in the variance covariance matrix:γ, α $\rho = \sigma_{23}$, the correlation of the instrumental variable with the regressor,y_2. For all replications, we fix the balue of γ at 0.5. In this case, α is constrained to be below 0.5 for the variance covariance matrix to be nonsingular, and ρ must be below 1. The variance of u is defined as $1 - \gamma^2 - 2\gamma\alpha$, which is declining in α. We evaluate the performance of the bias corrected estimator on a grid of values for α and for ρ, varying α from 0.1 to 0.4; and ρ from 0.1 to 0.8. The results are reported in Table I.

For the situation where $\alpha = 0$, the least squares estimator is known to be unbiased, since $cov(u, y_2) = 0$. We take this as a benchmark case, and evaluate the performance of the bias corrected estimator relative to the OLS, over a grid of values for ρ. This is reported in Table II.

Since the data is independently and identically distributed, this allows a major simplification of the bootstrap algorithm employed to reestimate the elements of Ω. We have to estimate the expectations and cross moments of quantities of the form

$Q = \frac{\sum q_t}{T}$. q_t is a function of the t'th observation alone. By ithe identical distribution property, we have that $EQ = Eq$; consider the normalised quantity $Q* = Q - EQ$. The cross moment of Q_i, Q_j can be written as

$$
\begin{aligned}
E(Q_i Q_j) &= E(Q *_i Q_j) + EQ_i EQ_j && (40)\\
&= T^{-1}(Eq *_i q_j) + Eq_i Eq_j && (41)
\end{aligned}
$$

To implement the bootsrap method, we replace the expectation operation E by the resampling analog $E*$; $E*$ is an expectation with respect to the (finite) distribution $P*$ which attaches probability $w*_t$ to the t-th observation. In any actual observation , the weights $w*_t$ are randomly generated , from a probability distribution with center T^{-1}. We generated these weights using a uniform random number generator, normalising these by the sum of the t numbers. The expectation of any quantity is evaluated as

$$E * (q) = \sum_{i=1}^{T} w *_i q_t \qquad (42)$$

The replications are for samples of size 50 for all experiments. The results appear very encouraging, especially for the situations where ρ is small, i.e. when the correlation between the instrument and the regressor is low. We evaluate relative bias , which is the absolute value of bias normalised by the parameter value. From the simulation results, the average value of the relative bias of the instrumental variables estimator is extremely high: it is usual to observe estimates which are 20 times the value of the parameter. In these situations, the first order bias correction is apparently highly effective, reducing the order of bias to values close to one. As ρ increases, the information carried by z and by y_2 are increasingly the same, so that the properties of the instrumental variable estimator begin to emulate those of least squares applied to the limiting regression model $y_1 = z\gamma + u$, which is of course, unbiased in finite samples. In these situations, uncorrected instrumental variables approaches unbiasedness, and the correction is pointless. Similarly, as α increases, the variance of the residual declines, and the bias of the estimators declines fairly fast. However, the correction factor improves bias in the situations where ir is most useful.

How good is such bias corrected estimator, relative to models where a linear unbiased estimate is in fact available? Clearly, this question cannot be answered in a standard errors in variables model, where the parameter cannot be estimated without finite sample bias. In order to make this comparison, we choose the situation where α is equal to zero, so that y_2 is independent of u_t. As can be expected, the bias of the corrected estimator is larger than that of OLS , which is unbiased. The relative bias factor is less than 0.5, and declines sharply as ρ increases, as we expect.

These replications are for a fixed value of the parameter γ, in order to facilitate comparisons. Simulations with varying values of γ exhibit very similar properties, and are not reported here. While these results are very encouraging, much remains to be done before resampling corrections can become an everyday technique for the econometrician's tool-box. The rather critical dependence of this, and other methods on the i.i.d nature of data is probably the major problem to be overcome. The assumption that the data are identically distributed, or at least that the Ω parameters are close to being stable, is important in even devising the bias correction method. On the other hand, independence can possibly be relaxed, at the cost of losing the computational simplicity of the bootstrap correction that we have employed. Another important issue is apparent from the simulation results. There are situations where the bias is too small to be corrected; in these situations, the bias correction factor may, and seems typically to, overcorrect.

References

[1] Anderson ,T.W. (1948) On the Theory of Testing Serial Correlation *Biometrika*, 58, 53-60.

[2] Breusch,T.S and Pagan, A (1979) A Simple Test for Heteroskedasticity and Random Coefficient Variation, *Econometrica* ,47, 1287-1294

[3] Brown,R.L., J.Durbin and J.M. Evans (1975) Techniques for Testing the Constancy of Regression Relations Over Time *Journal of the Royal Statistical Society. B*, 37, 149-192

[4] Chow, G (1960) Tests for Equality between Sets of Coefficients in Two Linear Regressions, *Econometrica*, 28, 591-605

[5] Durbin,J and G.S.Watson (1971) Testing for Serial Correlation in Least Squares Regression *Biometrika* ,58, 1-19

[6] Efron, Bradley (1982) *The Jackknife, the Bootsrap, and other Resampling Plans*, CBMS-NSF Monograph ,(38).

[7] Goldfeld ,S, and R Quandt (1965) Some Tests for Homoskedasticity *Journal of the American Statistical Association*, 60, 539-47

[8] Hansen, L (1982) Large Sample Properties of Generalized Method of Moment Estimators, *Econometrica*, 50, 1029-54

[9] Huber, P (1983) *Robust Statistics* ,New York, J.Wiley

[10] Kadiyala , K.R.(1970) Testing for the Independence of Regression Disturbances, *Econometrica* 38, 97-117

[11] Krasker , W.S., E. Kuh and R. Welsch, (1983) Estimation of Dirty Data and Flawed Models , in , *Z. Grilliches and M. Intrilligator, (ed.), Handbook of Econometrics, Vol I*, North-Holland

[12] Nagar , A.L (1959) The Bias and Moment Matrix of General k-class Estimators of the Parameters in Simultaneous Equations , *Econometrica*, 27, 575-90

[13] Newey ,W. K. (1985) Maximum Likelihood Specification and Conditional Moment Tests, *Econometrica*, 53, 1047-70

[14] Pagan, A and F.Vella (1988) Diagnostic Testing for Models Based on Individual Data : a Survey , mimeo , fothcoming *Applied Econometrics*

[15] Sargan,J.D and A.Bhargava (1983) Testing Residuals From the Least Squares Regression for Being Generated by the Gaussian Random Walk ,*Econometrica* 51,1, 153-174

[16] Szroeter ,Jerzy, (1978) A Class of Parametric Tests for Heteroskedasticity in Linear Econometric Models *Econometrica* 46, 6, 1311-1327

[17] Wald , A.(1940) The Fitting of Staight Lines when Both Variable are Subject to Error, *Annals of Mathematical Statistics* , 5, 40-46

[18] Wald , A. (1952) On the Estimation of Parameters in Incomplete Systems of Equations, in T.C.Koopmans,(ed.) *Statistical Inference in Dynamic Economic Models* , New York, J. Wiley

[19] White , H (1987) Specification Testing in Dynamic Models , in, T. Bewley, (ed.) *Advances in Econometrics, Vol I,* , Cambridge University Press

[20] Wu , C. F. J. (1987) Jackknife, Bootstrap, and other Resampling Plans in Regression Analysis (with Discussion) *Annals of Statistics* 14,4, 1261-1295

Table 1: Relative Bias and Bias Correction for IV Estimates

ρ	$\alpha =$	0.10	0.15	0.20	0.25	0.30	0.35	0.40
0.1	b1=	87.189	25.986	19.276	26.872	24.961	29.057	8.854
0.1	b2=	0.967	0.651	0.681	0.891	0.893	0.985	0.999
0.2	b1=	7.390	9.047	12.787	11.657	8.122	13.341	1.763
0.2	b2=	0.637	0.637	0.665	0.724	1.001	0.964	0.723
0.3	b1=	3.947	4.199	2.650	4.802	2.741	3.253	0.818
0.3	b2=	0.612	0.671	0.720	0.831	0.825	0.971	0.714
0.4	b1=	1.716	1.717	1.801	1.698	1.733	1.599	0.643
0.4	b2=	0.523	0.615	0.680	0.773	0.791	0.906	0.672
0.5	b1=	1.167	1.122	1.018	1.051	0.975	0.995	0.306
0.5	b2=	0.544	0.558	0.559	0.693	0.695	0.785	0.455
0.6	b1=	0.653	0.757	0.665	0.714	0.664	0.702	0.255
0.6	b2=	0.401	0.516	0.537	0.625	0.645	0.699	0.460
0.7	b1=	0.425	0.436	0.467	0.476	0.419	0.428	0.178
0.7	b2=	0.367	0.420	0.470	0.493	0.449	0.582	0.382
0.8	b1=	0.309	0.316	0.315	0.285	0.293	0.282	0.279
0.8	b2=	0.351	0.385	0.384	0.385	0.397	0.470	0.391

Notes

- $\gamma = 0.5$ for all replications
- relative bias $= |\frac{\hat{\gamma}-\gamma}{\gamma}|$
- 500 replications
- b1= relative bias of IV estimator; average of replications;
- b2= relative bias of corrected IV estimator; average of replications

Table 2: BIAS RELATIVE TO ORDINARY LEAST SQUARES

ρ		b2
0.00		0.4047
0.10		0.3786
0.20		0.3386
0.30		0.3191
0.40		0.3025
0.50		0.2929
0.60		0.2998
0.70		0.2589
0.80		0.2624
0.90		0.2283

b_0 = rel. bias of OLS= 0.1815; $\alpha = 0$; all replications.

Estimation and Testing of Regression Coefficients in Cobb-Douglas and Other Models

Michael D. McCarthy *
Department of Economics
Temple University

Abstract

The Cobb-Douglas production function often leads to situations in which the reduced form solutions for the inputs have elasticities of each input with respect to a given exogenous variable which are the same for all reduced form equations. This paper exploits this property to develop estimators that are in the spirit of full information maximum likehood (FIML) and to develop test statistics that are of the Student sort, provided that the reduced form errors have normal properties often used for analysis of this sort.

I. Introduction

The Cobb-Douglas production function has probably been one of the most popular production restrictions used by econometricians in modelling producer behavior. There are a number of reasons for this. First, the Cobb-Douglas captures to a first approximation (at least) some nonlinearities and substitution characteristics among production inputs hypothesized by economists. The observation that, in many production processes factor shares do not vary a great deal over long periods of time, adds to its appeal. So does its convenient log linear form. While the Cobb-Douglas function is certainly not applicable to all production processes, it is probably applicable to many. One purpose of this paper is to describe easy to compute estimation and powerful testing procedures for the coefficients of the solutions for factor inputs, when the Cobb-Douglas is

* Thanks to an anonymous referee for an excellent report.

the appropriate production constraint. The test statistics proposed will be shown to have "t" type finite sample distributions, assuming that the model errors are normal iid with zero means. The large sample properties of the proposed estimators are also of interest provided the model errors have zero means and are iid. While the estimation procedures outlined below will not quite match the efficiency of full information maximum likelihood (FIML) procedures, it is likely that they will be close. Moreover, the proposed estimators should provide good staring points for full blown FIML estimation.

Section II presents some useful distributional results derived from a special case of the multivariate regression model. This multivariate regression model - linear in the variables and parameters with m endogenous variables and n exogenous variables - is described, for example, in Malinvaud (1980). The special case is one in which the coefficients *for a given exogenous variable* are the same for all regression equations. In Section III it is shown with a few examples that Cobb-Douglas technologies often give rise to the special case described in Section II and it is suggested that there may be other applications. Section IV focuses on problems created by distributed lag responses.

II. A General Log-Linear Approach to Estimation and Testing

Suppose that we were faced with estimating the parameters of the following multivariate regression system :

$$\ln X_{ik} = \lambda_{0i} + \sum_{j=1}^{n} \lambda_j \ln Z_{jk} + u_{ik}; i = 1, 2, 3, ...m, \qquad (1)$$

where Z_{jk} represents the value of the jth exogenous variable at observation k; k = 1,2,...,N and X_{ik} represents the value of the *i*th dependent variable at k. Also u_{ik} represents a random error for the *i*th equation at k. Let U , of order $N \times m$, represent the matrix of errors for all equations and all observations with each row representing the complete system errors for a given observation. Suppose each of the rows of U are independent and distributed as N(0,Σ). Observe that λ_j appears as a coefficient in each equation in (1). Thus, ordinary least squares (OLS) permits the derivation of m distinct estimates of λ_j, say, $\hat{\lambda}^{j'} = [\hat{\lambda}_{1j}\hat{\lambda}_{2j}...\hat{\lambda}_{mj}]$. The vector, $\hat{\lambda}^j$, may be written:

$$\hat{\lambda}^j = \begin{pmatrix} 1 \\ 1 \\ \cdot \\ \cdot \\ \cdot \\ 1 \end{pmatrix} \lambda_j + \begin{pmatrix} \epsilon_{1j} \\ \epsilon_{2j} \\ \cdot \\ \cdot \\ \cdot \\ \epsilon_{mj} \end{pmatrix} = \ell\lambda_j + \epsilon_j, \qquad (2)$$

where $\ell' = [11...1]$ and $\epsilon_j' = [\epsilon_{1j}\epsilon_{2j}...\epsilon_{mj}]$. The formula for ϵ_j is developed and presented in connection with equations (4a) and (5a) below. Note that (2) may be viewed as a regression model with ℓ as the only exogenous variable. Given the assumptions outlined above $E[\epsilon_{sj}] = 0$, s = 1,2...m. However, $E[\epsilon_{sj} \cdot \epsilon_{ij}] \neq 0$ in general; i, s=1,2...m. Suppose that Cov $\epsilon_j = \Omega$ and that we have an unbiased estimator, $\hat{\Omega}$, of Ω that is independent of $\hat{\lambda}^j$ in (2) and hence of ϵ_j. An appealing estimator for λ_j would be

$$\tilde{\lambda}_j = [\ell'\hat{\Omega}^{-1}\ell]^{-1}\ell'\hat{\Omega}^{-1}\hat{\lambda}^j = \lambda_j + [\ell'\hat{\Omega}^{-1}\ell]^{-1}\ell'\hat{\Omega}^{-1}\epsilon_j \qquad (3)$$

and from the analysis in McCarthy(1987), it can be seen that $\tilde{\lambda}_j$ is in the spirit of full information maximum likelihood (FIML). It is shown below that an $\hat{\Omega}$, as described above, can be constructed such that, if $\lambda_j = 0$, the distribution of the test statistic,

$$t_j = [\ell'\hat{\Omega}^{-1}\ell]^{-1/2}\ell'\hat{\Omega}^{-1}\hat{\lambda}^j = [\ell'\hat{\Omega}^{-1}\ell]^{-1/2}\ell'\hat{\Omega}^{-1}\epsilon_j, \qquad (3.a)$$

is independent of Ω; i.e., the distribution of t_j does not depend on unknown parameters. The exact density function of a transformation of t_j is derived in Appendix A for the case when $\lambda_j = 0$. This transformed test statistic is distributed as Student's t.

Every equation in system (1) may be written (using all observations) as:

$X_i = Z\,\Lambda_i + u_i$, where

$X_i' = [\ln X_{i1}\ \ln X_{i2} \ldots \ln X_{iN}]$; $u_i' = [u_{i1}\ u_{i2} \ldots u_{iN}]$;

$$Z = \begin{pmatrix} 1 & \ln Z_{11} & . & . & .\ln Z_{n1} \\ 1 & \ln Z_{12} & . & . & .\ln Z_{n2} \\ 1 & \ln Z_{13} & . & . & .\ln Z_{n3} \\ . & . & . & . & . \\ . & . & . & . & . \\ . & . & . & . & . \\ 1 & \ln Z_{1N} & . & . & .\ln Z_{nN} \end{pmatrix} \text{ and}$$

$$\Lambda_i' = [\lambda_{0i}\lambda_1\lambda_2 \ldots \lambda_n].$$

There are m OLS estimates of , say , λ_1. These are

$$\hat{\lambda}_{i1} = (\hat{Z}_1'\hat{Z}_1)^{-1}\hat{Z}_1' X_i, i = 1, 2 \ldots m, \tag{4}$$

where $\hat{Z}_1 = [I - Z^1[Z^{1\prime}Z^1]^{-1}Z^{1\prime}]Z_1$, Z_1 represents the column of Z corresponding to the first exogenous variable (in this case the second column of Z) and Z^1 represents the matrix formed from Z by deleting Z_1 from its columns.

Observe that $\hat{\lambda}_{i1}$ may be written

$$\hat{\lambda}_{i1} = \lambda_1 + (\hat{Z}_1'\hat{Z}_1)^{-1}\hat{Z}_1' u_i, i = 1, 2, \ldots m. \tag{4a}$$

Also $\hat{\lambda}^1$, defined in connection with equation (2), may be written

$$\hat{\lambda}^1 = \begin{pmatrix} 1 \\ 1 \\ 1 \\ . \\ . \\ . \\ 1 \end{pmatrix} \lambda_1 + (\hat{Z}_1'\hat{Z}_1)^{-1}. \begin{pmatrix} \hat{Z}_1' u_1 \\ \hat{Z}_1' u_2 \\ . \\ . \\ . \\ . \\ \hat{Z}_1' u_m \end{pmatrix},$$

or more compactly

$$\hat{\lambda}^1 = \ell\lambda_1 + \epsilon_1, \tag{5}$$

where ℓ and ϵ_1 were introduced in (2) and $\epsilon_{i1} = (\hat{Z}_1'\hat{Z}_1)^{-1}\hat{Z}_1' u_i$, i = 1,2,...m. Also,

$$Cov\epsilon_1 = (\hat{Z}_1'\hat{Z}_1)^{-1} \cdot \begin{pmatrix} \sigma_{11} & \sigma_{12} & \cdot & \cdot & \cdot & \sigma_{1m} \\ \cdot & & & & & \\ \cdot & & & & & \\ \cdot & & & & & \\ \sigma_{m1} & \sigma_{m2} & \cdot & \cdot & \cdot & \sigma_{mm} \end{pmatrix} = \Omega,$$

if the regression equation errors have zero means, are iid and the σ_{ij} terms represent the covariances among the equation errors.

If Ω were known , an interesting estimator for λ_1 would be $\tilde{\lambda}_1 = (\ell'\Omega^{-1}\ell)^{-1}\ell'\Omega^{-1}\hat{\lambda}^1$. It is immediately clear that E $\tilde{\lambda}_1 = \lambda_1$. Also it is clear that this is an Aitken type estimator.

Since Ω is not known , we need an estimator of Ω with some desirable properties. We now introduce the following rule for estimating Ω : Replace the σ_{ij} terms in Ω by unbiased estimates of σ_{ij} computed using ordinary least squares ; i.e.,by

$$\hat{\sigma}_{ij} = \frac{1}{N-n-1} X_i'[I - Z[Z'Z]^{-1}Z']X_j.$$

Our estimator is then (Equation (3) repeated for λ_1):

$$\tilde{\lambda}_1 = [\ell'\hat{\Omega}^{-1}\ell]^{-1}\ell'\hat{\Omega}^{-1}\hat{\lambda}^1 = \lambda_1 + [\ell'\hat{\Omega}^{-1}\ell]^{-1}\ell'\hat{\Omega}^{-1}\epsilon_1 \qquad (3b)$$

It is well known , given (normal) zero mean, iid error assumptions and exogenous Z, that $\hat{\Omega}$ and ϵ_1 are independent and since $E\epsilon_1 = 0$, $E\tilde{\lambda}_1 = \lambda_1$. It also not difficult to show that $\tilde{\lambda}_1$ is asymptotically a more efficient estimator of λ_1 (conceivably much more efficient) than any unrestricted OLS estimator applied to a single equation in the system described by (1)[1]. In fact, it is more efficient than any estimator of λ_1 using the

[1] Note that we have implicitly assumed that N $\geq$ m+n+1, since we assumed that $\hat{\Omega}$ possessed an inverse (except on a set of zero measure). The requirement , N $\geq$ m+n+1 , is the same as Sargan's requirement (1975) that the number of observations must be greater than or equal to the number of variables in the system, if full information maximum likelihood (FIML) computations are to be done.

formula on the right hand side of (3) and a proper subset of OLS estimators of λ_1. A brief argument is given at the end of Appendix A.

From (2) , (3) and (3a) we have

$$\begin{aligned} t_1 &= [\ell'\hat{\Omega}^{-1}\ell]^{1/2}\lambda_1 &&+ [\ell'\hat{\Omega}^{-1}\ell]^{-1/2}\ell'\hat{\Omega}^{-1}\epsilon_1 \\ &= t_{11} &&+ t_{12}, \end{aligned}$$

which will yield an exact test of the hypothesis $H_0 : \lambda_1 = 0$ vs. $H_1 : \lambda_1 \neq 0$, given knowledge of the finite sample distribution of t_{12}. [When the sign of λ_1 is known *a priori*, the alternative hypothesis would be $H_1 : \lambda_1 > 0$ (or $\lambda_1 < 0$).] We first observe that $\mathrm{E}t_{12} = 0$, since $\hat{\Omega}$ is independent of ϵ_1 and $\mathrm{E}\epsilon_1 = 0$, and we now show that the distribution of t_{12} does not depend on unknown coefficients (or on the sample exogenous data).

Note that $\epsilon_1 \sim \mathrm{N}(0,\Omega)$ and is independent of (N-n-1)$\hat{\Omega}$ which is distributed as a central Wishart with means matrix Ω and degrees of freedom N-n-1. Let P' be such that $P'\Omega P = \mathrm{I}$. It follows that

$$t_{12} = [\ell^{*'}\Omega^{*-1}\ell^{*}]^{-1/2}[\ell^{*\prime}\Omega^{*-1}\epsilon_1^{*}],$$

where $\ell^* = P'\ell$; $\Omega^* = P'\hat{\Omega}P$, and $\epsilon_1^* = P'\epsilon_1$. Note that $\epsilon_1^* \sim N(0, I)$ and is independent of (N-n-1) Ω^* , which has a Wishart density with means matrix I and degrees of freedom (N-n-1). Next, let H be orthonormal and such that the product $H'\Omega^*H$ is defined. We may then write t_{12} as

$$t_{12} = [\tilde{\ell}'\tilde{\Omega}^{-1}\tilde{\ell}]^{-1/2}\tilde{\ell}'\tilde{\Omega}^{-1}\tilde{\epsilon}_1,$$

where $\tilde{\ell} = H'\ell^*; \tilde{\Omega} = H'\Omega^*H$ and $\tilde{\epsilon}_1 = H'\epsilon_1^*$.

Observe that $\tilde{\epsilon}_1 \sim \mathrm{N}(0,\mathrm{I})$ and is independent of (N-n-1) $\tilde{\Omega}$, which is distributed as a central Wishart with means matrix I and degrees of freedom (N-n-1). We are free to choose the first column of H as $H_1 = \| \ell'P \|^{-1} P'\ell$, where $\| \ell'P \|$ is the euclidian norm of $\ell^* = P'\ell$. In this case

$$\tilde{\ell}' = \ell'PH = [\| \ell' \ P \ \| 00..0].$$

Let $\tilde{\Omega}^{ij}$ represent the ijth element in $\tilde{\Omega}^{-1}$. It follows that

$$(\tilde{\ell}'\tilde{\Omega}^{-1}\tilde{\ell})^{-1/2} = \| \ell' P \|^{-1} (\tilde{\Omega}^{11})^{-1/2}$$

and

$$(\tilde{\ell}'\tilde{\Omega}^{-1}\tilde{\epsilon}_1) = \| \ell' P \| [\tilde{\Omega}^{11}\tilde{\Omega}^{12}\tilde{\Omega}^{13} ... \tilde{\Omega}^{1m}]\tilde{\epsilon}_1$$

and

$$t_{12} = (\tilde{\Omega}^{11})^{-1/2} [\tilde{\Omega}^{11}\tilde{\Omega}^{12}\tilde{\Omega}^{13} ... \tilde{\Omega}^{1m}]\tilde{\epsilon}_1 .$$

It is clear now that the density function for t_{12} cannot depend upon unknown parameters . It is shown in Appendix A that a transformation of t_{12} , say $\dot{t}_{12}$, is exactly distributed as a Student's t with degrees of freedom $(N - n_1 - n_2)$ where n_1 = n+1 is the number of reduced form exogenous variables and n_2 equals the number of reduced form equations.

The transformed test statistic is computed as :

$\dot{t}_{12} = [\frac{N-n_1-n_2+1}{N-n_1}]^{1/2} R$, where

R $= t_{12}/(1 + (N - n_1)^{-1}\alpha)^{1/2}$ and

$\alpha = \hat{\lambda}^{1\prime}\hat{\Omega}^{-1}\hat{\lambda}^1 - t_{12}^2 \geq 0.$

Note that the procedure described above yields both an *estimate* and *a test statistic*, which permits the use of one tailed tests, if the sign of λ_1 is known. The procedure cited in Anderson (1958) and Malinvaud (1980) yields only a test statistic for a null hypothesis, $H_0 : \lambda_1 = 0$ vs. $H_1 : \lambda_1 \neq 0$. See the discussion in IV.1.

The analysis in this and the following sections ignores the important fact that, in pooling cross section and/or time series data , it will be necessary to stratify the data set somewhat to assure that the models underlying each stratum are reasonably homogenous. In the case of cross sectional data sets the use of various "dummy" variables has been popular and in the case of time series models, smooth "time trend" dummies have been commonly employed. There are many ways that dummy variables can be introduced. The statistical analysis of this Section changes very little when such dummy variables are used. The intercept term in equation 1. will be augmented by the dummy variables and the "degrees of freedom "used in calculating $\hat{\Omega}$ will be reduced in an obvious manner.

III. Some Simple Cobb-Douglas Examples

In this section the observational subscripts and error terms used in Section II are suppressed.

Assume that a producer minimizes total cost = TC = $\sum_{j=1}^{n} P_j X_j$ subject to the production restriction:

$$q = B \prod_{j=1}^{n} X_j^{\alpha j},$$

where $\delta = \sum_{j=1}^{n} \alpha_j > 0$ and B and the α_j terms are positive constants. The terms X_j, P_j and q are respectively, the level of the jth input, the price of the jth input , taken as given and the level of output , also taken as given for the moment.

It is easily shown that the reduced form for X_1 is :

$$X_1 = C_1 [\prod_{j=2}^{n} (\frac{P_j}{P_1})^{\alpha_j^*}] \cdot q^{\frac{1}{\delta}}, \tag{6a}$$

where

$$C_1 = B^{\frac{-1}{\delta}} [\prod_{j=2}^{n} (\frac{\alpha_1}{\alpha_j})^{\alpha_j^*}]$$

and for i=2,3,...n=m

$$X_i = C_i (\frac{p_1}{p_i}) [\prod_{j=2}^{n} (\frac{P_j}{P_1})^{\alpha_j^*}] \cdot q^{\frac{1}{\delta}}, \tag{6b}$$

where

$$C_i = B^{\frac{-1}{\delta}} [\prod_{\substack{j=1 \\ j \neq i}}^{n} (\frac{\alpha_i}{\alpha_j})^{\alpha_j^*}]$$

and

$$\alpha_j^* = \frac{\alpha_j}{\delta}.$$

If the producer is a price taker in the factor markets, it is reasonable to assume that the $\frac{P_j}{P_1}$ terms are exogenous. In the particular case where $\delta = 1$, the system solution for X_i/q (i=1,2,...n=m) becomes

$$X_1/q = C_1[\prod_{j=2}^{n} (\frac{P_j}{P_1})^{\alpha_j}] \tag{7a}$$

and

$$X_i/q = C_i(\frac{p_1}{p_i})[\prod_{j=2}^{n} (\frac{P_j}{P_1})^{\alpha_j}] \tag{7b}$$

for i > 1. Notice that the elasticities in (6) and (7) are the same for a given exogenous variable in each of the regression equations. [In the case of (6b) and (7b) we would write the left hand side variable for estimation in log form as $\ln X_i - \ln(\frac{P_1}{P_i})$ or $\ln(X_i/q) - \ln(\frac{P_1}{P_i})$.]

Note that the regression system described in equation 1. need not be what an economist thinks of as a "reduced form" system, the latter being derived from a complete system of structural equations. Equation systems (6) and (7), for example, do not qualify as reduced forms unless q can really be assumed to be given. However, suppose that we introduce a demand curve which relates the relative price of output to the real income of the buyers, the relative prices of substitutes and compliments and to q. Also suppose that the demand curve is approximated satisfactorily by a log-log formulation. The complete system solution would involve choosing q such that price equals marginal cost in the pure competitive case or marginal revenue equals marginal cost in monopoly type cases or price equals average or marginal cost in natural monopoly cases. Assume that real income and the prices of substitutes and compliments are exogenous. Upon substituting the solution for q into equation systems (6) or (7) , we obtain (with a little algebra) a regression system like (1) , which in this case is also a reduced form. [2]

[2] Note that it is computationally feasible to estimate B and the α_j terms in (6) and (7) by applying ordinary least squares directly to the Cobb-Douglas production function. However, with output and the X_i terms endogenous , as they are in

Models like the Cobb-Douglas systems described above, though often popular, are highly specialized. They imply a structural represntation in which m-1 of the "structural" equations contain only one right hand side endogenous variable with a coefficient value of 1.0

The results reported in Section II are not necessarily limited to Cobb-Douglas cases. They could be relevant for regression systems where some or all of the exogenous variables enter each regression equation with the same elasticity. Exogenous real income, relative prices and real interest rates in household budget studies of the components of consumption may be examples.

IV. The Treatment of Distributed Lags [3]

The estimation and testing procedures described above should be appropriate for Cobb-Douglas and other applications to simple cross sectional data sets and for cross section-time series work , when the time series data are annual and separated in time with gaps of 5 to 10 years, as they often are with census type data. In the latter case distributed lag responses may not pose a serious problem. The statistical procedures outlined in Section II are, unfortunately, not generally appropriate for distributed lag analysis of pure time series data sets. The main complicating factor is that the lag response pattern of the different endogenous variables to a change in a given exogenous variable will be different. For example, the response of labor to an exogenous change could be of a geometric decay sort, while that of capital could be quadratic or cubic. Thus, the cross equation equality restrictions are lost. Still there are some useful things that can be done to analyze the system lag response properties. One can ask :

---

this paragraph, the estimators will be biased and inconsistent. They certainly will not be maximum likelihood estimators.

[3] The discussion in this section is possibly relevant only for cases where equation system (1) represents a reduced form.

1. What is the length of the system response to an exogenous change ?
2. What is the steady state elasticity of the endogenous variables with respect to an exogenous change ?

IV.1 Estimation of the Maximum Length of the Lagged Response of the Complete System to an Exogenous Shock

In this section we shall confine our attention to reduced form lag responses to exogenous changes which are finite in length and of the Almon PDL sort. In this case only the exogenous variables enter the structural form with lags of a finite length. [When distributed lags are encountered in the dependent variables of a structural system, the reduced form lags are commonly infinite in length and do not lend themselves to hypothesis statements about the response length of the system to exogenous changes in a straight foreward manner]. We now have the following proposition :

Proposition A

The length of the polynomial distributed lag for exogenous variable j is the same for each reduced form equation in the system.

The proposition is nothing more than a natural extension of the observation that (in absence of prior knowledge) every exogenous variable enters every reduced form equation. In the present case we are merely suggesting that, if exogenous variable j enters reduced form equation (1) with a lag of k periods, it probably enters all of the other reduced form equations with that lag. It is also true that the degree of the Almon PDL will be the same for any given exogenous variable in each reduced form equation, given the lag assumptions in this sections. See Appendix B. While this may be correct , the strength of the lag response to some exogenous variables could be weak for some endogenous variables well before the system maximum lag length is attained.

For exposition purposes only, assume that the lag operators are third degree polynomials. Proposition A means that exogenous variable Z_j enters the ith equation in the form

$$\ln X_{it} = \lambda_{0i} + \sum_{k=0}^{M_j} \lambda_{ijk} \ln Z_{jt-k}$$

+ distributed lags in the other exogenous variables

$$+u_{it}, \tag{8}$$

where t here represents a time index, k a lag length, M_j is the maximum lag length and $\lambda_{ijk} = \alpha_{0ij} + \alpha_{1ij}k + \alpha_{2ij}k^2 + \alpha_{3ij}k^3$. For the purposes of estimation and testing for the lag length, the dependent (left hand side) variable in the PDL equations analogous to those in Section III would be written as $\ln X_{it}$ for all i=1,2,...m. That is , we would not rewrite the left hand side variables as we did in (6b) and (7b) for estimation and testing purposes. We will use a similar set-up for estimation and testing of the steady state response. Let us suppress for the moment the i, j subscripts on λ_{ijk} , and on the "α" terms, as well as the i and j subscripts on the X , Z, u and M terms with the understanding that these subscripts will have to be assigned for estimation and testing purposes. Consider now the PDL formulation:

$$\ln X_t = \lambda_0 + \sum_{k=0}^{M} \lambda_k \ln Z_{t-k} \ldots\ldots + u_{it}, \tag{8a}$$

where $\lambda_k = \alpha_0 + \alpha_1 k + \alpha_2 k^2 + \alpha_3 k^3$. This implies that

$$\lambda_{-1} = \alpha_0 - \alpha_1 + \alpha_2 - \alpha_3 \tag{9a}$$

and

$$\lambda_{M+1} = \alpha_0 + (M+1)\alpha_1 + (M+1)^2\alpha_2 + (M+1)^3\alpha_3. \tag{9b}$$

Equations (9a) and (9b) may be solved to yield

$$\begin{pmatrix} \alpha_0 \\ \alpha_1 \end{pmatrix} = \eta_1^{-1} \begin{pmatrix} \lambda_{-1} \\ \lambda_{M+1} \end{pmatrix} - \eta_1^{-1}\eta_2 \begin{pmatrix} \alpha_2 \\ \alpha_3 \end{pmatrix}, \tag{9c}$$

where

$$\eta_1 = \begin{pmatrix} 1 & -1 \\ 1 & M+1 \end{pmatrix} \text{ and}$$

$$\eta_2 = \begin{pmatrix} 1 & -1 \\ (M+1)^2 & (M+1)^3 \end{pmatrix}.$$

Next λ_k may be written

$$\lambda_k = [1\ k] \begin{pmatrix} \alpha_0 \\ \alpha_1 \end{pmatrix} + [k^2 k^3] \begin{pmatrix} \alpha_2 \\ \alpha_3 \end{pmatrix}$$

and substituting from (9c) we have

$$\lambda_k = [1\ k] \left\{ \eta_1^{-1} \begin{pmatrix} \lambda_{-1} \\ \lambda_{M+1} \end{pmatrix} - \eta_1^{-1}\eta_2 \begin{pmatrix} \alpha_2 \\ \alpha_3 \end{pmatrix} \right\} + [k^2 k^3] \begin{pmatrix} \alpha_2 \\ \alpha_3 \end{pmatrix},$$

or

$$\lambda_k = [\beta_{1k}\beta_{2k}] \begin{pmatrix} \delta_1 \\ \delta_2 \end{pmatrix} + [\beta_{3k}\beta_{4k}] \begin{pmatrix} \delta_3 \\ \delta_4 \end{pmatrix}, \text{or}$$

$$\lambda_k = \beta_{1k}\delta_1 + \beta_{2k}\delta_2 + \beta_{3k}\delta_3 + \beta_{4k}\delta_4, \qquad (10)$$

where $[\beta_{1k}\beta_{2k}] = [1\ k]\eta_1^{-1}$; $[\beta_{3k}\beta_{4k}] = \{[k^2 k^3] - [1\ k]\eta_1^{-1}\eta_2\}$, and $[\delta_1\delta_2\delta_3\delta_4] = [\lambda_{-1}\lambda_{M+1}\alpha_2\alpha_3]$.

Upon substituting (10) into (8a) we see that

$$\ln X_t = \lambda_0 + \sum_{L=1}^{4} \lambda_L \sum_{k=0}^{M} \beta_{Lk} \ln Z_{t-k}$$

or

$$\ln X_t = \lambda_0 + \delta_1 Z_{1t}^* + \delta_2 Z_{2t}^* + \delta_3 Z_{3t}^* + \delta_4 Z_{4t}^* \ldots + u_t, \qquad (8b)$$

where

$$Z_{1t}^* = \textstyle\sum_{k=0}^{M} \beta_{1k} \ln Z_{t-k}, \; Z_{2t}^* = \sum_{k=0}^{M} \beta_{2k} \ln Z_{t-k}, \text{ etc.,}$$

or more compactly

$$x = Z^*\delta \ldots + u, \qquad (8c)$$

where $x' = [\ln X_N \ln X_{N-1} \ldots \ln X_1]$;

$$Z^* = \begin{pmatrix} 1 & Z_{1N}^* & Z_{2N}^* & \cdot & \cdot & .Z_{4N}^* \\ 1 & Z_{1N-1}^* & Z_{2N-1}^* & \cdot & \cdot & \cdot \\ \cdot & \cdot & \cdot & \cdot & \cdot & \cdot \\ \cdot & \cdot & \cdot & \cdot & \cdot & \cdot \\ \cdot & \cdot & \cdot & \cdot & \cdot & \cdot \\ 1 & Z_{11}^* & Z_{21}^* & \cdot & \cdot & .Z_{41}^* \end{pmatrix};$$

$\delta' = [\lambda_0 \delta_1 \delta_2 \delta_3 \delta_4]$ and
$u' = [u_N u_{N-1} ... u_1]$.

Note that for a given exogenous variable, in testing the hypotheses

H_0 : The longest lag affecting the reduced form system is M; vs.

H_1 : The longest lag response differs from M. We might wish to focus on the following competing hypotheses:

H_0^* : $\delta_2 = 0$ for all i (i=1,2,...m) vs.

H_1^* : $\delta_2 \neq 0$ for at least one i . [Note that $\delta_2 = 0$ for all i is a necessary condition for M to be the longest lag; it is not a sufficient condition. The power of the test procedure proposed below could be affected by this.]

There are m OLS estimators for δ_2 for the jth exogenous variable. We can form for that exogenous variable the vector ,

$$\hat{\delta}^2 = \begin{pmatrix} \hat{\delta}_{21} \\ \hat{\delta}_{22} \\ \cdot \\ \cdot \\ \cdot \\ \hat{\delta}_{2m} \end{pmatrix}$$

and an obvious test of the H_0^* vs. H_1^* hypotheses is provided by

$$F_2 = \frac{DF - m + 1}{m} \cdot [\frac{\hat{\delta}^{2\prime} \hat{\Omega}^{-1} \hat{\delta}^2}{DF}],$$

where $\hat{\Omega}$ is constructed in the same manner as described in Section II and DF represents the degrees of freedom involved in computing the OLS unbiased estimates of the σ_{ij} terms that enter $\hat{\Omega}$. Given the above assumptions, the analysis in Anderson(1958) shows that, if $\delta_2 = 0$, F_2 is distributed as a central F with respective numerator and denominator degrees of freedom m and (DF - m +1).

Note that Laitinen(1978) has used the Anderson statistic in testing for homogeneity in systems of demand equations. The problem addressed by Laitinen is formally the same as the problem treated in this Section, but the context is somewhat different.

The finite sample results developed above require that, for a given exogenous variable in the reduced form system, the length and degree of the Almon PDL be the same in all regression equations, when computing the components of F_2. However, the PDL length and degree can differ among exogenous variables. Also the intercept and any necessary dummy variables must be included in each regression equation. No restrictions are imposed on $\delta_1 = \lambda_{-1}$. The model in this case conforms to the standard regression model cited by Malinvaud(1980). Note that, if in one or more of the m equations, some *but not all* of the PDL's for a given exogenous variable are constrained to equal zero at $k = -1$ a problem arises. In such a case F_2 as described above will not be a drawing from a central F under the null hypothesis. Because different sets of exogenous variables are used in computing $\hat{\delta}^2$, the estimated covariance of $\hat{\delta}^2$ will not be a drawing from a central Wishart.

We remark that, if it is hypothesized that a subset of the δ_1 terms for a given exogenous variable are zero (a near term zero restriction), a test statistic similar to F_2 can be devised using only the estimates from equations in which it is hypothesized that $\delta_1 = 0$.

In closing it is noted that one could use statics like F_2 to test whether an elasticity in a model like (1) is zero or nonzero. However this would be essentially a two tailed test which does not take account of the equality of the elasticities across equations. One tailed tests are appropriate when the $\dot{t}_{12}$ test is used and the sign of the elasticity is known.

IV.2 Estimating and Testing The Steady State Response of the Endogenous Variables To an Exogenous Shock.

In this section the focus will be on the Cobb-Douglas case, but there may be other applications. In the case of cross sectional data sets of the sort described at the beginning of this section, distributed lag considerations may not be important in determining the variation in the system dependent variables. In the cases of monthly, quarterly and even annual data sets, this is not the case. The well known short run (cyclical) shifts in productivity, for example, point to interia in the adjustment process. This is particularly evident in monthly and quarterly data. We now have:

Proposition B:

Production functions are steady state concepts - not rigid restrictions in the short run.

In the case of (7a) and (7b), for example , the elasticity associated with $\frac{P_j}{P_1}$ is α_j for m-1 of the equations and α_{j+1} for one equation. [When log-log demand curves for q are introduced into systems like (6) and (7) *some* exogenous variables will actually have the same elasticity in all equations.] In view of Proposition B. it may not be unreasonable to impose restrictions of the sort just cited on the *steady state* elasticities of endogenous variables with respect to the exogenous variables.

In what follows we shall reintroduce the endogenous variable index (i) but continue to suppress the exogenous variable index (j) with the understanding that we are focusing on estimating and testing the total steady state response of the system to a given exogenous variable. Let λ represent the steady state elasticity for a given exogenous variable that enters, say, (7a) and (7b) We have m OLS estimates of λ, written as :

$$\hat{\lambda}_i = \beta_1\hat{\delta}_1^i + \beta_2\hat{\delta}_2^i + \beta_3\hat{\delta}_3^i + \beta_4\hat{\delta}_4^i = \sum_{k=0}^{M} \lambda_{ik}, \tag{11}$$

where $\beta_r = \sum_{k=0}^{M} \beta_{rk}$; r=1,2,...,4. and the $\hat{\delta}_r^i$ terms (i=1,2,..m) are the unrestricted OLS estimators of $\delta_1^i, \delta_2^i, etc.$ for the reduced form equations . The β_r terms are the sum over k=0 to M of the β_{rk} terms in equation (10) [In the case of the $(\frac{P_j}{P_1})$ terms appearing in equations like (7b), *one* of these elasticities would be computed as $\hat{\lambda}_i = \beta_1\hat{\delta}_1^i + \beta_2\hat{\delta}_2^i + \beta_3\hat{\delta}_3^i + \beta_4\hat{\delta}_4^i + 1.$] *We assume that the same set of complete system exogenous variables is used in computing the δ terms for all i.*

Equation (11) may be written more compactly as :

$$\hat{\lambda}_i = \beta'\hat{\delta}^i, \tag{11a}$$

where the definitions of β and $\hat{\delta}^i$ are obvious.

If the true steady state elasticities for a given exogenous variable have the regularity property (elasticity equal to λ for all m equations or equal to λ for m-1 equations and equal to $\lambda+1$ for one equation), then the m element vector, $\hat{\lambda}$, may be written

$$\hat{\lambda} = \begin{pmatrix} \hat{\lambda}_1 \\ \hat{\lambda}_2 \\ \cdot \\ \cdot \\ \cdot \\ \hat{\lambda}_m \end{pmatrix} = \ell\lambda + \epsilon, \tag{12}$$

where $\epsilon' = [\epsilon_1, \epsilon_2 ... \epsilon_m]$ is an error vector analogous to the error vector in 5. Given the assumptions of this paper $E\epsilon = 0$. If Cov $\epsilon = \Omega$ is known, then $\hat{\hat{\lambda}} = [\ell'\Omega^{-1}\ell]^{-1}\ell'\Omega^{-1}\hat{\lambda}$ has an obvious appeal as an Aitken estimator. An unbiased estimator , $\hat{\Omega}$, of Ω is available and can be shown to be independent of $\hat{\lambda}$. To construct $\hat{\Omega}$ we define :

$$x_i = Z^*\delta_i ... u_i, \tag{8c'}$$

where $(8c')$ has the same structure as (8c) in sub-section IV.1. except that the equation subscript i has been added; i = 1,2,...,m. Let $\hat{Z}$ represent the matrix of OLS calculated residuals of Z^* regressed on *all* other exogenous variables in the system, intercept and dummy variables variables included. That is, $\hat{Z} = [I - \tilde{Z}[\tilde{Z}'\tilde{Z}]^{-1}\tilde{Z}']Z^*$, where $\tilde{Z}$ is the matrix of all exogenous regressors in the system other than Z^*. An unbiased estimator of $\delta^{i'} = [\delta_1^i \ \delta_2^i \ \delta_3^i \ \delta_4^i]$ is :

$\hat{\delta}^i = [\hat{Z}'\hat{Z}]^{-1}\hat{Z}'x_i = \delta^i + [\hat{Z}'\hat{Z}]^{-1}\hat{Z}'u_i$. Note that Ω_{ij} is given by

$$\Omega_{ij} = E\epsilon_i\epsilon_j = \sigma_{ij}\beta'[\hat{Z}'\hat{Z}]^{-1}\beta \quad (i,j = 1,2,...m), \tag{13}$$

where $\epsilon_i = \beta'[\hat{Z}'\hat{Z}]^{-1}\hat{Z}'u_i$ and σ_{ij} represents the covariances among the reduced form equation errors. Construct $\hat{\Omega}$ by replacing the σ_{ij} terms in (13) by unrestricted OLS estimates, where the same set of complete system exogenous variables is used for each reduced form equation in computing $\hat{\sigma}_{ij}$ and $\hat{\lambda}$. The estimator of λ is then

$$\tilde{\lambda} = [\ell'\hat{\Omega}^{-1}\ell]^{-1}\ell'\hat{\Omega}^{-1}\hat{\lambda}. \tag{14}$$

It is easily shown that $E\tilde{\lambda} = \lambda$, and that $\tilde{t}_{12} = [\ell'\hat{\Omega}^{-1}\ell]^{-1/2}[\ell'\hat{\Omega}^{-1}\hat{\lambda}]$ has the same appealing usefulness in testing the hypothesis $H_0 : \lambda = 0$ vs. $H_1 : \lambda \neq 0$ (and perhaps strictly positive or negative). The distribution theory for such testing is completely developed in Appendix A. Note that the distribution theory that applies to $\tilde{t}_{12}$ is the same as that for t_{12} defined in Section II.

Appendix A

Derivation of the Exact Distribution of a Transformation of t_{12}

The derivation closely follows the procedure used in McCarthy (1987). Under the assumptions outlined in II, $\tilde{\epsilon}_1 \sim N(0, I)$ and is independent of (N-n-1)$\tilde{\Omega}$, which is distributed as a central Wishart with means matrix I [4]. The joint density function of $\tilde{\epsilon}_1$ and $\tilde{\Omega}$ may be written :

$$f(\tilde{\Omega}, \tilde{\epsilon}_1) = K_1 |\, \tilde{\Omega} \,|^{1/2(N-n_1-n_2-1)} e^{\frac{-(N-n_1)}{2} tr[\tilde{\Omega}+(N-n_1)^{-1}\tilde{\epsilon}_1\tilde{\epsilon}_1']}, \tag{A.1}$$

where N is the number of observations; n_1 = n+1 is the number of reduced form exogenous variables and n_2 equals the number of regression/reduced form equations. The intercept term, K_1 , can easily be inferred from the multivariate normal and Wishart densities found in any multivariate text and the Jacobian of the transformation $\tilde{\Omega} = (N - n_1)^{-1} Z_1$, where Z_1 is a drawing from a Wishart population with a means matrix

[4] See Section II ,the last three paragraphs, for the definitions of $\tilde{\Omega}$ and $\tilde{\epsilon}_1$.

of I. [Note that $Z_1 \sim W(n_2, N - n_1, I)$, using standard notation]. Let T be upper triangular and introduce the transformations, $\tilde{\Omega} = TT'$ and $F = T^{-1}\tilde{\epsilon}_1$ with respective Jacobians, $J_1 = 2^{n2} t_{11} t_{22}^2 \ldots t_{n_2 n_2}^{n_2}$ and $J_2 = \mid T \mid$. Equation (A.1) becomes

$$f = K_1 2^{n2} t_{11} t_{22}^2 \ldots t_{n_2 n_2}^{n_2} \mid TT' \mid^{1/2(N-n_1-n_2)}$$

$$\cdot e^{-(\frac{N-n1}{2}) trT'T[I+(N-n_1)^{-1}FF']}. \tag{A.2}$$

It is easy to verify that the first row of T^{-1} is $\tilde{\Omega}^{11-1/2}[\tilde{\Omega}^{11}\tilde{\Omega}^{12}\tilde{\Omega}^{13} \ldots \tilde{\Omega}^{1n_2}]$ defined in Section II. Considering the expression for t_{12} in the second to last paragraph of Section II, we see that the one-one element of F is t_{12}. Next, let W satisfy $WW' = [I + (N - n_1)^{-1} FF']$, where W is upper triangular and introduce the transformation Z = TW, holding W fixed. The Jacobian of the transformation is $J_3 = W_{11}^{-1} W_{22}^{-2} W_{33}^{-3} \ldots W_{n_2 n_2}^{-n_2}$. With these changes (A.2) becomes

$$f = K_1 2^{n_2} W_{11}^{-2} W_{22}^{-4} \ldots W_{n_2 n_2}^{-2n_2} \mid W'W \mid^{-1/2(N-n_1-n_2)}$$

$$\cdot Z_{11} Z_{22}^2 \ldots Z_{n_2 n_2}^{n_2} \mid Z'Z \mid^{1/2(N-n_1-n_2)}$$

$$\cdot e^{-(\frac{N-n1}{2}) trZ'Z}. \tag{A.3}$$

Upon integrating out the Z terms, (A.3) becomes :

$$f' = K_2 W_{11}^{-(N-n1-n2+2)} W_{22}^{-(N-n1-n2+4)} \ldots W_{n_2 n_2}^{-(N-n1+n2)}, \tag{A.4}$$

where K_2 is the new intercept resulting from the integration. Next use the fact that:

$$\prod_{i=j}^{n_2} W_{ii}^2 = 1 + (N - n_1)^{-1} \sum_{i=j}^{n_2} F_i^2, (j = 1, 2, \ldots n_2) \tag{A.5}$$

to conclude that

$$W_{11}^2 = (1 + (N - n_1)^{-1} \sum_{i=1}^{n_2} F_i^2)/(1 + (N - n_1)^{-1} \sum_{i=2}^{n_2} F_i^2) \tag{A.5.1}$$

$$W_{22}^2 = (1 + (N - n_1)^{-1} \sum_{i=2}^{n_2} F_i^2)/(1 + (N - n_1)^{-1} \sum_{i=3}^{n_2} F_i^2) \qquad (A.5.2)$$

$$\vdots$$

$$W_{n_2 n_2}^2 = \qquad (1 + (N - n_1)^{-1} F_{n_2}^2). \qquad (A.5.n_2)$$

These results are easily verified by equating the determinants and principal minors of $[WW']$ and $[I + (N - n_1)^{-1} FF']$. Upon substituting (A.5.i), i =1,2...n_2 into (A.4) we see that (A.4) may be written :

$$f' = K_2 H_1(F_2, F_3, ...F_{n_2})$$

$$.(1 + (N - n_1)^{-1} \sum_{i=1}^{n_2} F_i^2)^{-(N-n_1-n_2+2)/2} \quad , \qquad (A.6)$$

where $H_1(F_2, F_3, ...F_{n_2})$ is simply a function formed by collecting the terms in (A.4) involving $F_i (i = 2, 3, ...n_2)$. Equation (A.6) may be further rewritten as :

$$\begin{aligned} f' =& K_2 H_1(F_2, F_3, ...F_{n_2}) \\ &\cdot (1 + (N - n_1)^{-1} \sum_{i=2}^{n_2} F_i^2)^{-(N-n_1-n_2+2)/2} \qquad (A.6.1) \\ &\cdot (1 + (N - n_1)^{-1} R^2)^{-(N-n_1-n_2+2)/2} \quad , \end{aligned}$$

where

$$R = t_{12}/(1 + (N - n_1)^{-1} \sum_{i=2}^{n_2} F_i^2)^{1/2} \quad , \qquad (A.7)$$

since $F_1 = t_{12}$. Upon introducing the transformation (A.7) from R to F_1 holding the F_i fixed (i=2,....n_2) we have

$$f' = K_2 H_2(F_2, F_3, ...F_{n_2})(1 + (N - n_1)^{-1} R^2)^{-(N-n_1-n_2+2)/2}$$

and integrating out $F_i (i = 2, ...n_2)$, we have

$$f'' = K_3 (1 + (N - n_1)^{-1} R^2)^{-(N-n_1-n_2+2)/2}.$$

Introduce the transformation $\dot{t}_{12} = [\frac{(N-n_1-n_2+1)}{N-n_1}]^{1/2} R$ and we have (accounting for the Jacobian)

$$f'' = K_4 (1 + (N - n_1 - n_2 + 1)^{-1} \dot{t}_{12}^2)^{\frac{-(N-n_1-n_2+2)}{2}} \qquad (A.8)$$

and we see that $\dot{t}_{12}$ is exactly distributed as a student t with$N - n_1 - n_2$ degrees of freedom; it is an appropriate test statistic for the hypothesis stated in Section II; i.e., $H_0 : \lambda_1 = 0$ vs. $H_1 : \lambda_1 \neq 0$ (or $H_1 : \lambda_1$ is positive or negative, when reduced form signs are known *a priori*). Observe that, using the P and H transformations introduced in Section II , $\hat{\lambda}^{1\prime}\hat{\Omega}^{-1}\hat{\lambda}^1 = \epsilon_1'\hat{\Omega}^{-1}\epsilon_1 = \tilde{\epsilon}_1'\tilde{\Omega}^{-1}\tilde{\epsilon}_1 = F'F = F_1^2 + \sum_{i=2}^{n_2} F_i^2$ *under the null hypothesis* ($\lambda_1 = 0$). Under the null hypothesis, $F_1 = t_{12}$ and $\hat{\lambda}^{1\prime}\hat{\Omega}^{-1}\hat{\lambda}^1 = \sum_{i=1}^{n_2} F_i^2$ are computable and thus, $\sum_{i=2}^{n_2} F_i^2$ is computable from the sample data. Hence, R and $\dot{t}_{12}$ are computable from the sample data.

Note : we could also have derived the exact distribution of the (untransformed) t_{12} in a manner similar to that used in McCarthy(1987). The result would have been a confluent hyper-geometric function.

Some Limiting Distribution Considerations

The variance of the limiting distribution of $N^{1/2}(\tilde{\lambda}_1 - \lambda_1)$ is (See equation (3b)) :

A = $B(\ell'\Sigma^{-1}\ell)^{-1}$, where

B = $\lim_{N\to\infty}(\frac{\hat{Z}_1'\hat{Z}_1}{N})^{-1}$; $\Sigma = [\sigma_{ij}]$; $i, j = 1, 2, ...m$ and $\hat{Z}_1$ is defined in Section II.

Now, let $D'\Sigma D = \begin{pmatrix} \Sigma_{11} & 0 \\ 0 & I \end{pmatrix}$, where Σ_{11} is the partitioned matrix formed from the first , say n_3 , rows and columns of Σ , with $n_3 < n_2$ and D' is lower block triangular. Thus,the structure of D' is

$$D' = \begin{pmatrix} I & 0 \\ D_{21} & D_{22} \end{pmatrix}.$$

In this case

$$\Sigma^{-1} = D \begin{pmatrix} \Sigma_{11}^{-1} & 0 \\ 0 & I \end{pmatrix} D',$$

which implies that $\ell'\Sigma^{-1}\ell = \ell' D \begin{pmatrix} \Sigma_{11}^{-1} & 0 \\ 0 & I \end{pmatrix} D'\ell$. This in turn implies that $\ell'\Sigma^{-1}\ell$ may be written as $\ell'\Sigma^{-1}\ell = \ell_1'\Sigma_{11}^{-1}\ell_1 + C$ where C > 0 and $\ell_1{}'$ is a (lxn_3) vector of unit elements. An implication of this is that A must be less than the variance of the limiting distribution of any single OLS estimator of λ_1 *and* less than the limiting variance of any estimator of λ_1 formed by using the formula on the right hand side of 3. with fewer than m OLS estimators of λ_1.

Appendix B

The Degree of the Almon PDL Lags In the Reduced Form For a Given Exogenous Variable.

The general linear in the variables and parameters structural model may be written $AY_t = BX_t + U_t$ using the Cowles Foundation notation with "t " as a time index. The reduced form is

$$\begin{aligned} Y_t &= A^{-1}BX_t + A^{-1}U_t \\ &= A^{-1}B_1X_{1t} + A^{-1}B_2X_{2t} + ... + \eta_t, \end{aligned}$$

where $\eta_t = A^{-1}U_t$ and the B_i terms represent the ith column of B. Suppose that all lags enter through the exogenous variables in the Almon PDL way. In this case A is a matrix of constants and the elements of, say, B_1 are lag operator polynomials of the Almon sort. The elements of B_1 may be written as $B_1 = H_1Q_1$, where H_1 is a constant matrix and $Q_1' = [Q_{11}\ Q_{12} \ldots Q_{1\ MAX}]$. The elements of Q_1 are the usual Almon weighted sums of X_{1t} and its lagged values; also Q_{MAX} is the weighted sum that corresponds to the highest degree Almon polynomial in B_1. [Note that some of the elements in B_1 and the corresponding rows of H_1 may be zero.]

If the elements of A^{-1} have all nonzero entries, it is abvious that the reduced form coefficients, $A^{-1}B_1 = A^{-1}H_1Q_1$, are all Almon polynomials of degree MAX. This has to be the case since the MAX column of H_1 will have at least one non-zero entry. Upon collecting terms in X_{1t} and its lags we see that the degree of the polynomial describing the lag coefficients for exogenous variable X_1, will be the same for each reduced form equation, but the shape of the polynomials will differ. Note that in the Log-Log Cobb-Douglas case in the text, the dependent variable coefficient matrix may be written :

$$A = \begin{pmatrix} 1 & \delta_2 & \delta_3 & . & . & . & . & \delta_m \\ -1 & 1 & 0 & . & . & . & . & 0 \\ -1 & 0 & 1 & 0 & . & . & . & 0 \\ -1 & 0 & 0 & 1 & . & . & . & 0 \\ -1 & . & . & . & . & . & . & 1 \end{pmatrix},$$

where $\delta_j = \alpha_j/\alpha_1$ (j=2,3,...m = n) and the "α" terms are the Cobb-Douglas elasticities introduced in Section III. It is easy to show that A^{-1} is given by:

$$A^{-1} = \begin{pmatrix} \delta & 0 & 0 & . & 0 \\ \delta & 1 & 0 & . & 0 \\ \delta & 0 & 1 & . & 0 \\ . & . & . & . & 0 \\ \delta & 0 & 0 & . & 1 \end{pmatrix} \begin{pmatrix} 1 & -\delta_2 & -\delta_3 & . & . & -\delta_m \\ 0 & 1 & 0 & . & . & 0 \\ 0 & 0 & 1 & 0 & . & 0 \\ . & . & . & . & . & . \\ 0 & . & . & . & . & 1 \end{pmatrix},$$

where $\delta = 1/(1 + \sum_{j=2}^{M} \delta_i)$. Since the "$\alpha$" terms are strictly positive, A^{-1} is nonzero in all entries.

References

Anderson T.W. [1958], *An Introduction to Multivariate Statistical Analysis* (Wiley : New York),section 5.22 , pp. 105-107

Laitinen, Kenneth [1978], "Why Is Demand Homogeneity So Often Rejected",
Economics Letters, pp. 187-191.

Malinvaud,Edmund [1980], *Statistical Methods of Econometrics* (North Holland - Amsterdam. New York, Oxford), Third Ed. pp 195-200 and pp. 230-231.

McCarthy, Michael D. [1987], "Exact Finite Sample Test Statistics for Restricted Reduced Forms : A Generalization of Student's Result," IER , pp. 259-269.
Sargan , J.D.[1975], "Asymptotic Theory and Large Models, "IER, pp. 75-91.

TALES OF TESTING BAYESIANS*

by

Jacques H. Drèze

and

Michel Mouchart

Abstract

Are classical test statistics of any use to Bayesian statisticians and econometricians? If so, are these statistics put to the same use by Bayesians and classical statisticians? The modest aim of this paper is to illustrate, through elementary tales, why and how Bayesians may sometimes be led to use classical test statistics - either in their usual form or in some suitably modified form.The illustrations are chosen to bring out different facets of our answer to these two questions. The general message conveyed by our tales may be summarised in three simple points: (i) Bayesian statisticians should be open-minded as far as procedures are concerned: they may find sound practical uses for both classical test statistics and test statistics blending prior information with sample information. (ii) There are situations where Bayesian statisticians should compute classical test statistics and interpret them from a strict sampling-theory viewpoint. (iii) Yet one should not be misled by spurious similitudes: the guiding principle for selecting a statistical procedure should always be based upon the real decision problem at hand, and cannot be reduced to routine technical calculations.

* Paper prepared for the volume *Contributions to Economic Theory* edited by R.A.L. Carter, J. Dutta and A. Ullah. The authors are particularly grateful to E. de Regt , J. Duta and J.P. Florens for constructive criticisms on an earlier version of this paper and/or illuminating discussions on several of the isssues rised in this paper.

1. Testing Bayesians

Are classical test statistics of any use to Bayesian statisticians and econometricians? If so, are these statistics put to the same use by Bayesians and classical statisticians?

Some orthodox Bayesians have commented testily on classical testing procedures. Thus Raiffa and Schlaiffer (1961, p. vii) write: "... in most statistical practice,... decisions are actually made by treating the numbers .05 and .95 with the same supertitions awe that is usually reserved for the number 13". Yet we, like many other advocates of the Bayesian logic, have frequently looked at classical test statistics in the course of our statistical practice. (We even feel guilty for having failed to do so in instances of some significance.)

The modest aim of this paper is to illustrate, through elementary tales, why and how Bayesians may sometimes be led to use classical test statistics - either in their usual form or in some suitably modified form.The illustrations are chosen to bring out different facets of our answer to these two questions. Indeed, Bayesians may be led to use test statistics in a variety of ways, ranging from pure Bayesian decision-making to pure classical testing. Our answer, for which no particular claim to novelty is made, has a straight forward logical basis, that will be presented at the outset and illustrated in our first tale. Putting that logical answer to work often involves additional subtelties, compromises or ambiguities which the additional tales aim to bring out. This paper does not deal at all with classical approaches to testing, nor does it deal with the actual practice of classical testing in general. Thus it contains neither criticisms nor defense of classical tests.[1]

Many statistical decision problems are "two-actions" problems in which the set of available acts A has only two elements: $A = \{a_0, a_1\}$. If the choice of an act is to take place after making an observation $x \in X$, any decision rule $d : X \rightarrow \{a_0, a_1\}$ is equivalently specified by a partition of the

[1] On that topic, see for instance Berger and Delampady (1987).

observation space: $X = X_0 \cup X_1$ (with $X_0 \cap X_1 = \emptyset$); choose a_0 if $x \in X_0 \equiv d^{-1}(a_0)$ and choose a_1 if $x \in X_1 \equiv d^{-1}(a_1)$. Thus, any solution to the decision problem takes the simple form of defining the "region" X_0 in the observation space X for which a_0 is the best action.

When that "region" corresponds, possibly after a suitable transformation, to the acceptance region of a hypothetical classical test, then it may prove convenient or perhaps instructive for the Bayesian statistician to formulate his or her decision rule in terms of a classical test statistic. Our first two tales illustrate that property, and bring out successively two points. First, when the relevant decision problem is fully specified, with its own loss strucure, the decision rule (the region X_0 in sample space for which a_0 is optimal) beomes endogenous - as illustrated in our first tale. Only by a rare chance will the magic numbers .05 or .95 play a role. Actual decision making requires a more flexible mental attitude. Of course classical statisticians would agree with us that decision rules must be chosen with due regard for the specific consequences of the actions to which these rules may lead. We are not taking issue here with intelligent use of classical procedures; rather, we are interested in their legitimate use by Bayesians.

Our second tale also involves an endogenously defined decision rule, but with an additional feature: altough implementation of the decision rule amounts to"performing a classical test of the null hypothesis H_0", actually no "testing" is at stake, since it is known with probability 1 that H_0 is true. The tale thus brings out forcefully the simple point that reliance on the technical apparatus of classical testing may be justified for reasons entirely unrelated to the logic of classical testing.

The third tale describes a situation where, we feel, Bayesian statisticians do use test statistics in the same way as classical statisticians do, on grounds of expediency and cost savings. Such practice is eminently sensible and in full agreement with the logic of decision theory, particularly when the statistician is willing to let the data influence to some extent the specification of the sampling model.

Finally our fourth tale describes a situation where some form of testing seems to be called for as part of the reporting and/or decision process. The use of a classical test statistic may again be chosen by a Bayesian statistician as an expedient short cut. We show that the Bayesian approach suggests alternative procedures, thereby providing the additional flexibility required to cope with different real situations. This is an area where further work would be welcome.

Thus the four tales bring out situations with a wide range of approaches regarding the use by Bayesians of test statistics: from a purely formal analogy with a totally different logic (tales 1 and 2) to an essentially classical use (tale 3); from a strictly classical test statistic (tale 3) to statistics blending sampling and Bayesian ingredients (tales 1 and 4).

These four tales are presented in Section 2 while the main messages carried by these four tales are summarised in Section 3. Some formulae used in the second tale are collected in an appendix.

2. Four Tales

First Tale

The presidential election of Borduria is due to take place in a few weeks. Voting is not compulsory. The incumbent President is running for reelection. She knows from experience that she can win the election handsomely if she contracts with a taxicab company to take to the polls (at her expense) every member of her party aged 65 or more - a large group among which electoral participation is otherwise known to be very small. The cost of that contract is a flat C zlotys. The president would be prepared to incur an expense of E Zlotys ($E > 2C$) to avoid loosing the election. She feels very uncertain about the outcome of the vote. Fortunately, a sophisticated survey sample organisation is about to publish the result of a survey among 2500 voters. The President has decided to use that survey as her single source of information and to contract with the taxicab company if and only if the posterior probability that she receives less than 50% of the vote, in the absence of the contract, is superior to $\frac{C}{E}$. Indeed, writing π for the percentage of the vote going to her in the absence of the contract, the relevant loss table is

	$\pi \leq .50$	$\pi > .50$
a_0 contract for taxicabs	0	C
a_1 do not contract	$E - C$	0

It is thus seen that a_0 is better than a_1 if and only if

$$C\ P[\pi > .50] \leq (E - C)\ P\ [\pi \leq .50] \quad \text{i.e.} \quad P\ [\pi \leq .50] \geq \frac{C}{E}.$$

Using a uniform prior density for π over $[0, 1]$, and denoting the sample proportion of favourable votes by x, it is immediate that $(\pi \mid x)$ is approximately distributed as $N(x,\ .0001)$. The posterior probability that π is lower than .50 is readily computed from that distribution. It will be inferior to $\frac{C}{E}$ if and only if the null hypothesis $H_0 : \pi \leq .50$ is rejected at the level $\frac{C}{E}$ in a classical test based on the same sample evidence (with the alternative hypothesis $H_1 : \pi > .50$). This is so because X_0 the region of the sample space where a_0 is optimal, or the "acceptance" region of H_0, may be approximately described as follows:

$$X_0 = \left\{ x \mid P[\pi \leq .50 \mid x] \geq \frac{C}{E} \right\}$$
$$= \left\{ x \mid \Phi\left(\frac{.50 - x}{.01}\right) \geq \frac{C}{E} \right\} = \{x \mid x \leq .50 - .01 z_c\}$$

where Φ is the standardised normal distribution function, and $z_c < 0$ is defined by $\Phi(z_c) = \frac{C}{E}$, where $\frac{C}{E} < \frac{1}{2}$.

Second Tale

The population of Syldavia consists of 50% men and 50% women. An investigator is interested in the average amount of money spent (per year) by Syldavians in movie attendance, $\bar{\mu}$. It is known from previous studies that the variance of amounts spent is the same for men and women and equal to σ^2, a known number. Mean spending is expected to differ as between men and women, the respective means being $\bar{\mu}_1$ and $\bar{\mu}_2$ respectively. A pilot study has led to the (posterior) distribution $(\mu_1, \mu_2) \sim N(\mu_1, \mu_2 \mid m_1, m_2, I)$, a normal distribution with covariance matrix I (identity).

The investigator sees a report from a new sample survey, covering n randomly drawn Syldavians of which pn were men and $(1-p)n$ were women, and for which mean spending (per year) on movie attendance was $\bar{x}$. Noting that $p \neq \frac{1}{2}$, the investigator asks the agency responsible for the survey whether they could communicate to her separately the mean spending of men (say $\bar{x}_1$) and that of women ($\bar{x}_2$).(By definition, $\bar{x} = p\bar{x}_1 + (1-p)\bar{x}_2$.) She is told that a charge of 1000 zlotys would be required to recompute the partial means from the original documents.

The decision problem faced by the investigator calls for deciding first whether or not to buy the additional information contained in the separate means $(\bar{x}_1, \bar{x}_2)$. Next, the investigator will submit an estimate c of $\bar{\mu}$, based on whatever information she has. This is a standard statistical decision problem, as encountered for instance in experimental design.

To formalise the problem, let $a = (b, c) \in \{0, 1\} \times I\!R$. The binary variable b corresponds to the decision whether or not to buy the additional information - say with $b = 0$ corresponding to "not buying" and $b = 1$ corresponding to "buying". The continuous variable c is the best "conjecture" about $\bar{\mu}$. Let then the loss function of the investigator be $L(a, \bar{\mu}) = \alpha b + (c - \bar{\mu})^2$, where α measures the cost of the additional information (1000 zlotys) in terms of the cost of the squared estimation error $(c - \bar{\mu})^2$. Under $b = 0$, the available information is summarised by $(p, \bar{x})$; under $b = 1$, it will be $(p, \bar{x}_1, \bar{x}_2)$. The corresponding risk functions (expected losses) are:

$$r_0^*(p, \bar{x}) = \min_c \ E[(c - \bar{\mu}^2) \mid p, \bar{x}] = V(\bar{\mu} \mid p, \bar{x}) \qquad (1)$$

$$\begin{aligned} r_1^*(p, \bar{x}) &= \alpha + E\{\min_c \ E\ [(c - \bar{\mu})^2 \mid p, \bar{x}_1, \bar{x}_2] \mid p, \bar{x}]\} \\ &= \alpha + E\ [V(\bar{\mu} \mid p, \bar{x}_1, \bar{x}_2) \mid p, \bar{x}] \end{aligned} \qquad (2)$$

where V is also the conditional variance of $\bar{\mu}$ given the available information. In (2) we must take the expectation of that conditional variance with respect to the as yet unknown separate means; that expectation is computed from the distribution of (μ_1, μ_2), conditionally on the information $(p, \bar{x})$. The difference

$$V(\bar{\mu} \mid p, \bar{x}) - E\ [V(\bar{\mu} \mid p, \bar{x}_1, \bar{x}_2) \mid p, \bar{x}] \geq 0 \qquad (3)$$

is a measure of the "expected value of additional information" $EVAI(p, \bar{x})$, a familiar concept. The investigator will choose $b = 1$ (buy the additional information) if and only if $EVAI(p, \bar{x}) > \alpha$. A routine calculation, performed in appendix, shows that

$$\begin{aligned} &EVAI(p, \bar{x}) \\ &= V(\bar{\mu} \mid p, \bar{x}) - E\ [V(\bar{\mu} \mid p, \bar{x}_1, \bar{x}_2) \mid p, \bar{x}] \\ &= \frac{2h^3 p(1-p)(\frac{1}{2} - p)^2}{(2+h)^3 + 2h(2+h)(1-2p)^2 - h^3(1-2p)^4} \geq 0, \end{aligned} \qquad (4)$$

where $h = \frac{n}{\sigma^2}$ measures the known precision of $\bar{x}$. (Similarly, hp is the precision of $\bar{x}_1$). It is readily verified that $EVAI(p, \bar{x})$ is an increasing function of h. For sufficiently high (respectively low) values of $\frac{h}{\alpha}$ (interpreted as the "precision to cost ratio" of the additional information), there exist values of p for which $EVAI(p, \bar{x}) > \alpha$ (respectively $< \alpha$).

It is interesting to note from (4) that in this problem, the $EVAI$, which in principle depends upon the sufficient statistic $(p, \bar{x})$ of the pooled sample, depends only upon p. This is so because the posterior variance of a mean is independent of the sample mean in the normal process (with natural-conjugate prior). Furthermore we note that $EVAI(p, \bar{x}) = EVAI(p) = 0$ for $p \in \{0, \frac{1}{2}, 1\}$. When $p = 0$ or $p = 1$, the sample mean is already a "separate" mean ($\bar{x}_2$ or $\bar{x}_1$ respectively), and no additional information is in store. When $p = \frac{1}{2}$, the additional information is worthless, because the variances of the separate means are the same.

The "acceptance region" for the decision $b = 0$, i.e. the set of values of p for which $EVAI \leq \alpha$, will thus consist of 3 intervals, typically non-empty and disjoint, containing respectively the values $0, \frac{1}{2}$ and 1. By way of illustration, let $h = 400$ and $\alpha = .025$. Then, $EVAI(p, \bar{x}) \leq \alpha$ for all p in the union of the three intervals $[0,\ 0.00015], [0.385,\ 0.615]$ and $[0.99985,\ 1]$. The two extreme intervals are negligible. With $h^{-1} = \frac{\sigma^2}{n} = \frac{1}{400} = (0.05)^2$, the middle interval, namely 0.5 ± 0.115 or $0.5 \pm 2.3\ (\frac{\sigma}{\sqrt{n}})$, is also the acceptance region for a 2% test of the hypothesis that the population mean is equal to $\frac{1}{2}$.

We have thus exhibited a simple two-action decision problem, the solution of which involves a partition of the sample space (here the space of the ancillary statistic p) in two regions, which may be called respectively "acceptance" region and "rejection" region. In our example, they take the same form as the classical acceptance and rejection regions for the null hypothesis that the percentage of men in the population is equal to $\frac{1}{2}$. But the regions themselves are defined endogenously; and the decision problem (whether or not to buy the additional information) is totally unrelated to the notion of testing a hypothesis about the population. Indeed, the percentage of men in the population is *known* ($\frac{1}{2}$) and not subject to test. Although the *solution* of the decision problem could be described in terms of a classical test statistic, the logic is entirely different.

It was noted by J. Dutta that this second tale, being centered on costly signal extraction, should be of interest to rational expectations specialists. The idea that costly data analysis is more naturally triggered by surprise than by lack of it is probably not fully general, but highly plausible in many contexts. It is interesting to note that it would be associated with rational decisions about costly signal extraction.

Third Tale

The standard regression model proceeds from the assumption that residuals are identically *independently* distributed. In economic time series contexts, there are many reasons to question the validity of the independence assumption - ranging from adjustment lags in behavior to arbitrariness of the measurement period. (Why would a particular influence on the dependent variable always exert itself within a single measurement period?) A more general specification, like first-order autocorrelation of residuals, is often more convincing. Working with the more general specification is, however, computationally more demanding. In the Bayesian framework, the posterior marginal density for the regression coefficients is, at best, approximated by a $2-1$ poly-t density, instead of taking the simple Student form (see Drèze 1977, Section 4.4 or Zellner 1971, Section 4.1).

Econometricians are thus often faced with the decision whether or not to incur the additional cost of using the more general framework, a situation not unlike that considered in our second tale. How do they approach that decision problem?

A formal treatment is conceivable. Given, say, a prior density on the autocorrelation parameter ρ, one could attempt to evaluate the expected value of additional information associated with the use of the more general model, which could then be compared with the additional cost of using that model. But such an approach is self-defeating ... because the computational cost of the formal analysis would itself exceed the computational cost of using the more general model outright! Spending \$ 10 in the hope of at best saving \$ 5 is a clear violation of the Sure Thing Principle ... Better excercise subjective judgment to decide whether you should start with the simpler formulation, while remaining prepared to adopt the more general one upon examination of your results; or whether you should start outright with the more general formulation. Because the simpler model is so economical computationally, judgement often suggests using it as a starting point in a sequential strategy. A diagnostic test for autocorrelation based on the estimated residuals does belong in a sequential strategy, however. Visual inspection of the plot of residuals is a sound diagnostic procedure. Because that procedure is still costly, time-consuming and ill-suited for reporting purposes, most classical softwares include a Durbin-Watson statistic in their standard output. That Bayesian softwares do not provide systematically a similar signal is rightly perceived as a drawback. Indeed, a Bayesian econometrician may well find it useful to compute a Durbin-Watson statistic as part of a sequential strategy for model specification. We would thus suggest incorporating the computation and reporting of such a statistic in standard Bayesian softwares and practice - while insisting that visual inspection of the residuals be the next step, either towards final acceptance of the simple i.i.d. model, or towards analysis of a more general specification.

Some interesting side-questions arise. When analysing a regression model with prior information on the coefficients, should the econometrician look at the autocorrelation of the OLS residuals, or of the expected residuals associated with the use of prior information? In principle, he should look at the latter - but computational costs may again suggest looking instead at the former. Should theoretical Bayesian econometricians continue to develop their own diagnostic test, possibly incorporating prior information on the autocorrelation parameter? Yes ... especially in a world where the (academic) cost of producing new theoretical results is negative! Should the ultimate decision to use or not to use the more general model with autocorrelation be based on conclusions about the autocorrelation parameter, as in a significance test; or should it be based on an assessment of the impact of that decision on inference about the parameters of interest (for instance, the regression coefficients), as in a specification test à la Hausman (1978)? We defer that question to our final tale...

Fourth Tale

A pharmacist suspecting that she might have inadvertently substituted one drug for another in filling a prescription feels duty bound to throw away her preparation and start afresh. A statistician suspecting that she might have inadvertently substituted one statistical series for another in analysing a data set feels duty bound to replicate her analysis with the proper series before publication. If that were not possible, she would use every means at her disposal to detect evidence about (to test for) the substitution. She would then either forego publication, or inform readers about the potential substitution and about the results of her tests. By the same token, a statistician suspecting that her model might fail to be identified should use every possible means of detection and report her findings faithfully.

And yet, it has been claimed that identification is not an issue in a Bayesian framework. "Whenever the prior density function is well defined, and the likelihood is dominated, the posterior density will be well defined as well, whether the model is identified or not. This is the rationale for the remark by Lindley (1971, p. 46): 'In passing it might be noted that identifiability causes no real difficulty in the Bayesian approach' " (quoted form Drèze 1975, p. 167).Does that remark dispense statisticians from attempting to detect a potential lack of identification, and reporting their findings?

That issue has been raised by Maddala (1976), in a comment about some results reported by Drèze (1972, 1976) in a Bayesian Limited Information Analysis of a simultaneous equations model. The essential features of the underlying problem, and of the general question under discussion, are present in the simpler context of estimating the ratio of two normal means.

Specifically, consider a sampling process generating $x = (y, z) \in R^2$:

$$\left(\begin{matrix} y \\ z \end{matrix} \mid \theta, \Sigma \right) \sim N\left(\left(\begin{matrix} \mu \\ \mu\alpha \end{matrix} \right), \Sigma \right) \tag{5}$$

where $\theta = (\mu, \alpha)$ and Σ is a known 2×2 PDS matrix.

Thus,

$$p(y, z \mid \mu, \alpha, \Sigma)$$
$$= (2\pi)^{-1} \mid \Sigma \mid^{-\frac{1}{2}} \exp - \frac{1}{2}(y - \mu, z - \alpha\mu)\Sigma^{-1} \begin{pmatrix} y - \mu \\ z - \alpha\mu \end{pmatrix} . \tag{6}$$

This model is identified for $\theta \in \Theta_0 = (R \setminus \{0\}) \times R$, but it is not identified at $\mu = 0$, hence also not for $\theta \in \Theta = R^2$. Conditionally on $\mu = 0$, the observations are not informative about α (the likelihood is constant with respect to α), so that the prior distribution for α is not revised by the observations. Note that (5) is also the reduced form of the system of two structural equations $y - \mu\iota = u_1$, $z - \alpha y = u_2$ for which $\mu \neq 0$ is the rank condition for identification of the second equation.

If μ is the parameter of interest, the identification issue is irrelevant; the posterior marginal distribution of μ is well defined and can be evaluated for y and z equal to, or close to, zero.

On the other hand, if α is the parameter of interest, it is important to realize that the observations are not informative about α when $\mu = 0$. Should the statistician suspect that μ

could well be equal to zero, he or she might prefer to disregard the sample information altogether, and proceed on the basis of prior information alone.

One might hope that the posterior marginal distribution on α would be very close to the prior distribution when the data strongly suggest that μ is close to zero. Unfortunately, matters are not so simple, as can be verified on a special case of our simple model. An appropriate testing process is needed, should one wish to assess the danger of lack of identification.

The special case consists in imposing (for the sake of illustration) that $\alpha \in \{0,1\}$, with prior probabilities $Pr(\alpha = 0) = p_0$, independently of μ i.e. $p(\alpha) = (1-p_0)^\alpha \, p_0^{1-\alpha}$. One can solve explicitly for the posterior marginal probabilities $p(\alpha \mid y, z)$ as follows. For the sake of simplicity, let the covariance matrix Σ be known, with $\sigma_{11} = 1, \sigma_{22} = \sigma^2, \sigma_{12} = 0$; and let the prior distribution on μ be $N(0, v)$. Then:

$$
\begin{aligned}
&p(\alpha, \mu \mid y, z) \\
&\propto (1-p_0)^\alpha p_0^{1-\alpha} \exp -\frac{1}{2}\left\{\frac{\mu^2}{v} + (\mu - y)^2 + \frac{(\mu\alpha - z)^2}{\sigma^2}\right\} \\
&\propto (1-p_0)^\alpha p_0^{1-\alpha} \exp -\frac{1}{2}\left(\frac{1}{v} + 1 + \frac{\alpha^2}{\sigma^2}\right)\left(\mu - \frac{y + \frac{\alpha z}{\sigma^2}}{\frac{1}{v} + 1 + \frac{\alpha^2}{\sigma^2}}\right)^2 \\
&\qquad \exp -\frac{1}{2}\left[y^2 + \frac{z^2}{\sigma^2} - \frac{(y + \frac{\alpha z}{\sigma^2})^2}{\frac{1}{v} + 1 + \frac{\alpha^2}{\sigma^2}}\right]
\end{aligned}
\tag{7}
$$

Therefore:

$$
(\mu \mid \alpha, y, z) \sim N\left(\frac{y + \frac{\alpha z}{\sigma^2}}{\frac{1}{v} + 1 + \frac{\alpha^2}{\sigma^2}}, \frac{1}{\frac{1}{v} + 1 + \frac{\alpha^2}{\sigma^2}}\right); \tag{8}
$$

$$
\begin{aligned}
&p(\alpha \mid y, z) \\
&\propto (1-p_0)^\alpha \, p_0^{1-\alpha} \left(\frac{1}{v} + 1 + \frac{\alpha^2}{\sigma^2}\right)^{-\frac{1}{2}} \exp \frac{1}{2} \frac{(y + \frac{\alpha z}{\sigma^2})^2}{\frac{1}{v} + 1 + \frac{\alpha^2}{\sigma^2}};
\end{aligned}
\tag{9}
$$

$$\frac{P(\alpha = 0 \mid y, z)}{P(\alpha = 1 \mid (y, z)}$$

$$= \frac{p_0}{1 - p_0} \frac{(\frac{1}{v} + 1 + \frac{1}{\sigma^2})^{\frac{1}{2}}}{(\frac{1}{v} + 1)^{\frac{1}{2}}} \exp \frac{1}{2} \left\{ \frac{y^2}{\frac{1}{v} + 1} - \frac{(y + \frac{z}{\sigma^2})^2}{\frac{1}{v} + 1 + \frac{1}{\sigma^2}} \right\}. \tag{10}$$

It is easy to pick values of v, σ^2, y and z such that

(i) $\dfrac{P(\alpha = 0 \mid y, z)}{P(\alpha = 1 \mid y, z)}$ is very far from $\dfrac{p_0}{1 - p_0}$

whereas $\mu = 0$ would not be rejected in any reasonable test;

(ii) $\dfrac{P(\alpha = 0 \mid y, z)}{P(\alpha = 1 \mid y, z)} = \dfrac{p_0}{1 - p_0}$

whereas $\mu = 0$ would be rejected in any reasonable test.

To establish (i), take $y = z = 0$; then

$$\frac{P(\alpha = 0 \mid y, z)}{P(\alpha = 1 \mid y; z)} = \frac{p_0}{1 - p_0} \left(1 + \frac{1}{\sigma^2(\frac{1}{v} + 1)}\right)^{\frac{1}{2}} \tag{11}$$

which can take any value between $\frac{p_0}{1-p_0}$ and $+\infty$, by letting σ^2 range from $+\infty$ to 0 for any fixed value of v. With $y = z = 0$ or, from (8), with $E(\mu \mid \alpha, \bar{y}, \bar{z}) = 0$, the hypothesis "$\mu = 0$" is hard to reject...

To establish (ii), we must find values of the parameters such that $\mu = 0$ be rejected and

$$\left(1 + \frac{1}{\sigma^2(\frac{1}{v} + 1)}\right)^{\frac{1}{2}} \exp \frac{y^2}{2(\frac{1}{v} + 1)} \left[1 - \frac{(1 + \frac{z}{y\sigma^2})^2}{1 + \frac{1}{\sigma^2(\frac{1}{v}+1)}}\right] = 1. \tag{12}$$

Rewrite (12) as $(1 + x)^{\frac{1}{2}}$ $\exp k^2[1 - \frac{\zeta^2}{1+x}] = 1$ and define $\gamma := ln(1 + x) > 0$. A solution to (12) is then given by $\zeta^2 = (1 + \frac{\gamma}{2k^2})e^{\gamma} > 1$ and can be constructed with arbitrary large

k through appropriate choice of the remaining parameters. Intuitively, it makes sense that we could observe $y \gg 0$ and $z \sim \frac{y}{2}$ equally likely under $\alpha = 0$ and $\alpha = 1$.[2] Note also that the left hand side of (12) tends to one as σ^2 tends to infinity, identically in y, z and v. That is, when the variance of z is very large, the observations are uninformative about α, no matter what information they convey about μ.[3]

Thus, case (ii) brings out the natural possibility that the posterior probabilities for α be very close to the prior probabilities, for reasons unrelated to identifiability. One could thus never infer conclusively the lack of identifiability from properties of the posterior distribution. The only legitimate conclusion to be drawn when $p(\alpha \mid y, z)$ is equal to or close to $p(\alpha)$ is that identifiability is not an issue - because opinions about α are not affected by the observations, whatever the reason may be.

Conversely, when $p(\alpha \mid x, y)$ is far from $p(\alpha)$, could one conclude that α is identified in the observations? Case (i) brings out the possibility that the posterior probabilities for

---

[2] By way of illustration, consider the simplified problem where

$$(x \mid \alpha) \sim N(\alpha, \sigma^2), \alpha \in \{0, 1\}$$

with $p(\alpha) = (1 - p_0)^\alpha p_0^{1-\alpha}$ and σ^2 known; we find:

$$P(\alpha = 0 \mid x) = \frac{p_0 \cdot f_{N(0,\sigma^2)}(x)}{p_0 f_{N(0,\sigma^2)}(x) + (1 - p_0) f_{N(0,\sigma^2)}(1 - x)]}$$

$$= \frac{p_0}{p_0 + (1 - p_0)\exp \ - \frac{(1-2x)}{2\sigma^2}} = p_0 \leftrightarrow x = \frac{1}{2}.$$

That illustration is readily extended to the more general case in the text, but the solution of (12) for $z \sim \frac{y}{z}$ is no longer transparent.

[3] Of course, a very large variance for z is another form of poor identification of α.

α be *numerically* very different from the prior probabilities, even though all the evidence points to a most likely value for μ equal to zero.[4]

A Bayesian procedure to compare the prior and posterior distributions of α has recently been proposed by Florens and Mouchart (1989), and could be used here. Let d denote a distance, or divergence, between $p(\alpha) = p(\alpha \mid x, \mu = 0)$ and $p(\alpha \mid x)$. Clearly, $d(p(\alpha), p(\alpha \mid x))$ is a function of the observations x - say $t(x)$. In principle, one could always construct (or simulate) the predictive density of $t(x)$ and evaluate the probability of values in excess of the observed one.[5] Of course, the conclusion that $d(p(\alpha), p(\alpha \mid x))$ is small enough to be imputed to sampling errors does not necessarily mean that μ is close to zero. It only means that the hypothesis "the data are not informative about α" could not be rejected.

---

[4]For the purpose of detecting a possible lack of identification, the numerical posterior probabilities for α should be considered in relation to their predictive (or sampling) distribution, in order to ascertain whether they are *significantly* different from the prior probabilities.

[5]In our example, a natural distance function would be

$$\begin{aligned} d &= 2\{\log \frac{P(\alpha = 0 \mid y, z)}{P(\alpha = 1 \mid y, z)} - \log \frac{p_0}{1 - p_0}\} \\ &= \frac{y^2}{\frac{1}{v} + 1} - \frac{(y + \frac{z}{\sigma^2})^2}{\frac{1}{v} + 1 + \frac{1}{\sigma^2}} + \log \frac{\frac{1}{v} + 1 + \frac{1}{\sigma^2}}{\frac{1}{v} + 1} \end{aligned} \qquad (13).$$

The predictive distribution of that expression can be computed from the predictive distribution of y and z whicn is a mixture of two bivariate normal distributions, namely:

$$p(y, z) \propto \Sigma_{\alpha=0}^{1}\, p(\alpha) \exp - \frac{1}{2} [y^2 + \frac{z^2}{\sigma^2} - \frac{(y + \frac{\alpha z}{\sigma^2})^2}{\frac{1}{v} + 1 + \frac{\alpha^2}{\sigma^2}}] \quad (14).$$

The distribution of d itself must however be treated numerically, which presents no difficulty in this case.

3. Bayseian Testing

The message of the last tale is the following: although a test of the identification condition is not stricIty needed to use the posterior distribution of α for decision purposes, still such a test is needed to decide whether or not that posterior distribution should embody the (possibly irrelevant) sample information, and the outcome of such a test belongs naturally in a report about the inference process.

This message is not different is spirit from that of our previous tale about independence of disturbances. The analogy would stand out more strongly if we added that a formal testing procedure of the kind just outlined may be computationally demanding, in which case a classical identification test might be the more practical alternative. But one would expect computational demands to play a less decisive role in this case than in our third tale - so that further research on appropriate test procedures is all the more justified.

We have also illustrated a useful point about significance tests versus specification tests. A test of the hypothesis "$\mu = 0$" would naturally take the form of a significance test. The main difference between a Bayesian approach and a classical approach will lie in the fact that prior information on μ is naturally part of the Bayesian, but not of the classical, procedure. One could also test the extent to which the hypothesis "$\mu = 0$" affects the inference about α. We have suggested doing this in terms of the distance $d(p(\alpha \mid x), p(\alpha \mid x, \mu = 0) = d(p(\alpha \mid x), p(\alpha))$. (We note in passing that such a specification test is less natural in a classical approach, since α is not estimable when $\mu = 0$.) We have also noted that the specification test is by no means equivalent to a significance test. The point to be noted is that each test serves its own purpose, and provides information about a different issue. Whether or not $\mu = 0$ is a question addressed to the significance test. The specification test reveals whether the identifiability condition "$\mu \neq 0$" makes a difference for the posterior distribution of α.

These are clearly distinct issues. The answer to the question raised at the end of Section 2 is, accordingly, that the choice of a test is a matter of motivations.

Our last tale is meant to illustrate a more general point, namely that tests of model specification have a place in Bayesian decision procedures, whenever model adequacy is open to doubt - whether on grounds of identification or on any other grounds. Further research by Bayesian statisticians and econometricians is called for to develop efficient procedures, making proper use of all the avaible information.

The general message conveyed by our tales may be summarised in three simple points.

(i) Bayesian statisticians should be open-minded as far as procedures are concerned: they may find sound practical uses for both classical test statistics and test statistics blending prior information with sample information.

(ii) There are situations where Bayesian statisticians should compute classical test statistics and interpret them from a strict sampling-theory viewpoint.

(iii) Yet one should not be misled by spurious similitudes: the guiding principle for selecting a statistical procedure should always be based upon the real decision problem at hand, and cannot be reduced to routine technical calculations.

Appendix

To establish (4), we first evaluate (1) and (2).

Given the ancillary character of p, the posterior distribution $f(\mu \mid p, \bar{x})$ is obtained by multiplying the prior distribution $f(\mu) \sim N(\mu \mid m, I)$ by the p-conditional sampling distribution $f(\bar{x} \mid p, \mu)$.

Defining $h = \frac{n}{\sigma^2}$ and $\iota_p' = (p, 1-p)$, we note that

$$\begin{aligned} f(\bar{x} \mid p, \mu) &\sim N(\bar{x} \mid p\mu_1 + (1-p)\mu_2, h^{-1}) \\ &\propto \exp -\frac{h}{2}(\mu_1 - \bar{x}, \mu_2 - \bar{x})\iota_p\iota_p'(\mu_1 - \bar{x}, \mu_2 - \bar{x})' \end{aligned}$$

so that

$$\begin{aligned} &f(\mu \mid p, \bar{x}) \\ &\propto \exp -\frac{1}{2}(\mu - m)'(\mu - m) \exp -\frac{h}{2}(\mu - \iota\bar{x})'\iota_p\ \iota_p'(\mu - \iota\bar{x}) \\ &\propto \exp -\frac{1}{2}(\mu - m^*)'[I + h\ \iota_p\ \iota_p'](\mu - m^*), \end{aligned}$$

where $m^* = [I + h\ \iota_p\ \iota_p']^{-1}(m + h\ \iota_p\bar{x})$.

Thus,

$$\begin{aligned} f(\mu \mid p, \bar{x}) &\sim N(\mu \mid m^*, [I + h\ \iota_p\iota_p']^{-1}) \\ &\sim N\left(\mu \mid m^*, I - \frac{h\ \iota_p\iota_p'}{1 + h\iota_p'\iota_p}\right) \end{aligned}$$

and

$$V(\bar{\mu} \mid p, \bar{x}) = V(\frac{1}{2}\mu_1 + \frac{1}{2}\mu_2 \mid p, \bar{x})$$

$$= \left(\frac{1}{2}\iota\right)' \left(I - \frac{h \ \iota_p \iota_p'}{1 + h\iota_p' \iota_p}\right) \left(\frac{1}{2}\iota\right)$$

$$= \frac{1}{4} \left(2 - \frac{h}{1 + \frac{h}{2}[1 + (1 - 2p)^2]}\right)$$

$$= \frac{1}{4} \frac{2 + h(1 - 2p)^2}{1 + \frac{h}{2}[1 + (1 - 2p)^2]}$$

since $\iota' \iota_p = 1$ and $\iota_p' \iota_p = \frac{1}{2}[1 + (1 - 2p)^2]$

On the other hand, the p-conditional sampling distribution of $(\bar{x}_1, \bar{x}_2)$ is normal with expectation (μ_1, μ_2) and covariance matrix

$$\begin{bmatrix} \frac{\sigma^2}{np} & 0 \\ 0 & \frac{\sigma^2}{n(1-p)} \end{bmatrix} = \begin{bmatrix} hp & 0 \\ 0 & h(1-p) \end{bmatrix}^{-1}.$$

Acordingly, the posterior distribution of μ given $(p, \bar{x}_1, \bar{x}_2)$ is normal with covariance matrix

$$\begin{bmatrix} 1 + hp & 0 \\ 0 & 1 + h(1-p) \end{bmatrix}^{-1},$$

independent of $(\bar{x}_1, \bar{x}_2)$, so that

$$\begin{aligned}
&E[V(\bar{\mu} \mid p, \bar{x}_1, \bar{x}_2) \mid p, \bar{x}] \\
&= (\frac{1}{2}\iota)' \begin{bmatrix} 1 + hp & 0 \\ 0 & 1 + h(1-p) \end{bmatrix}^{-1} (\frac{1}{2}\iota) \\
&= \frac{1}{4}[(1 + hp)^{-1} + \{1 + h(1-p)\}^{-1}] \\
&= \frac{1}{4}(2 + h)[1 + h + h^2 p(1-p)]^{-1} \\
&= \frac{1}{4}(2 + h)[(1 + \frac{h}{2})^2 - \frac{h^2}{4}(1 - 2p)^2]^{-1} \\
&= (2 + h)[(2 + h)^2 - h^2(1 - 2p)^2]^{-1}
\end{aligned}$$

since $p(1-p) = \frac{1}{4}[1 - (1 - 2p)^2]$.

Formula (4) then follows from the routine calculation

$$\begin{aligned}
&V(\bar{\mu} \mid p, \bar{x}) - E[V(\bar{\mu} \mid p, \bar{x}_1, \bar{x}_2) \mid p, \bar{x}] \\
&= \frac{1}{4}\left[\frac{4 + 2h(1-2p)^2}{2 + h + h(1-2p)^2} - \frac{4(2+h)}{(2+h)^2 - h^2(1-2p)^2}\right] \\
&= \frac{1}{4}\frac{8h^3 p(1-p)(1-2p)^2}{(2+h)^3 + 2h(2+h)(1-2p)^2 - h^3(1-2p)^4} \geq 0.
\end{aligned}$$

References

Berger, J.O. and M. Delampady (1987), "Testing Precise Hypotheses (with discussion)", *Statistical Science,* 2, 3, 317-352.

Drèze, J.H. (1972), "Econometrics and Decision Theory", *Econometrica* 40, 1-17; Chap. 20 in *Essays on Economic Decisions under Uncertainty*, Cambridge, Cambridge University Press.

Drèze, J.H. (1975), "Bayesian Theory of Identification in Simultaneous Equations Models", pp. 159-174 in *Studies in Bayesian Econometrics and Statistics*, Eds: S.E. Fienberg and A. Zellner, North-Holland.

Drèze, J.H. (1976), "Bayesian Limited Information Analysis of the Simultaneous Equations Model", *Econometrica* , 44, 5, 1045-1075.

Drèze, J.H. (1977), "Bayesian Regression Analysis Using Poly-t Densities", pp. 153-184 in *New Developments in the Applications of Bayesian Methods*, Eds: A. Aykaç and C. Brumat, North-Holland.

Florens, J.-P. and M. Mouchart (1989), "Bayesian Specification Tests" in *Contributions to Operations Research and Economics*, Eds: B. Cornet and H. Tulkens, Proceedings of the CORE XXth Anniversary Symposium, Cambridge, MIT Press.

Hausman, J.A. (1978), "Specification Tests in Econometrics", *Econometrica*, 46, 1251-1271.

Lindley, D.V. (1971), "Bayesian Statistics: A Review", Philadelphia, *SIAM.*

Maddala, G.S. (1976), "Weak Priors and Sharp Posteriors in Simultaneous Equation Models", *Econometrica*, 44, 2, 345-351.

Raiffa, H. and R. Schlaifer (1961), *Applied Statistical Decision Theory*, Cambridge, MIT Press.

Zellner, A. (1971), *An Introduction to Bayesian Inference in Econometrics*, New York, Wiley.